TROPE

ABOVE & ACROSS

LONDON

PHOTOGRAPHS BY

BEN MOORE

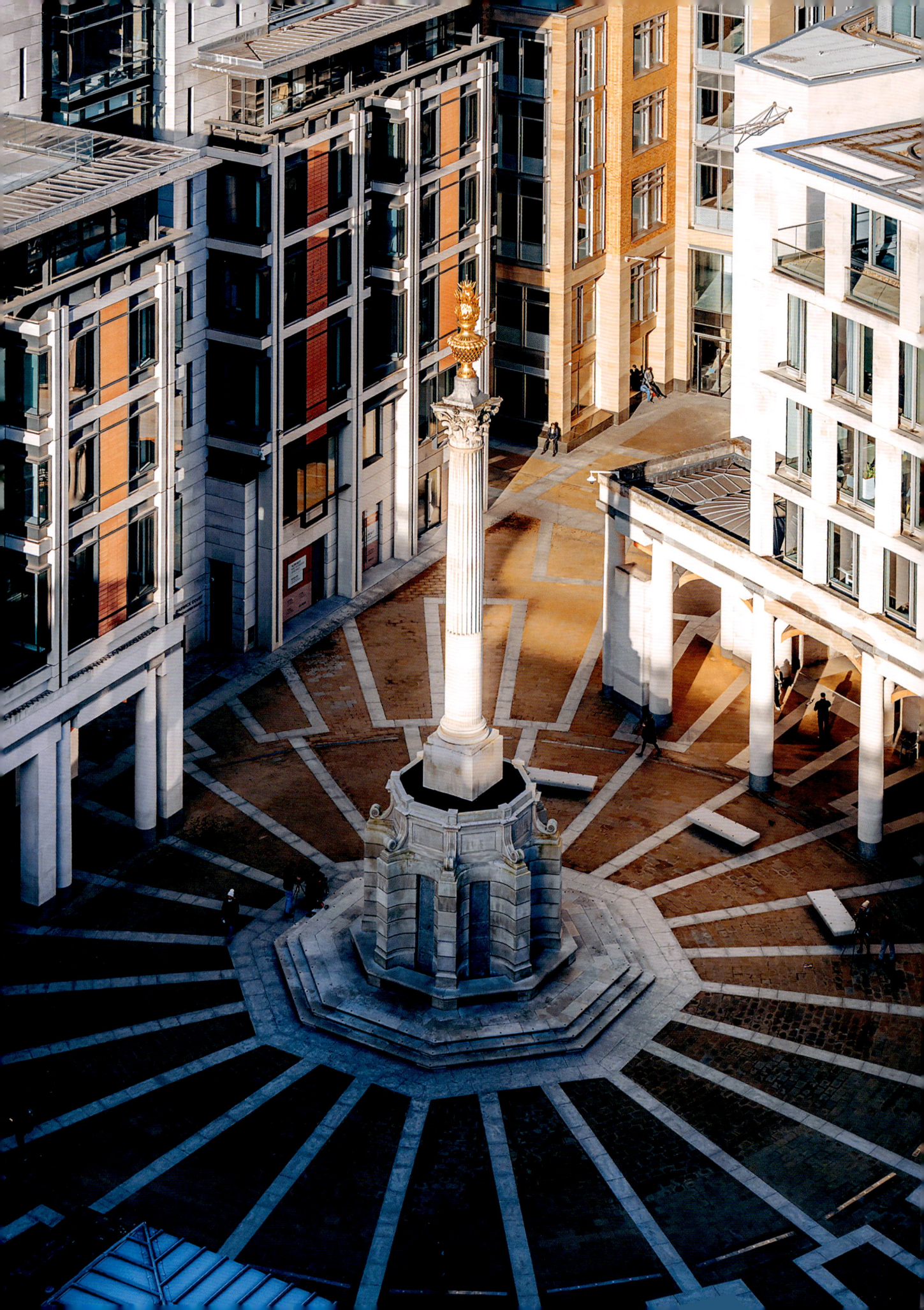

"London is a city that is both ancient and modern, where the past is always part of the present."
—*Sir David Cannadine, British Author and Historian*

Above & Across London is a curated collection of 172 aerial photographs of London taken by photographer Ben Moore.

A global hub known for its iconic landmarks, rich history, and vibrant culture, London has also become one of the world's most important centers of design. Its creativity and innovation play out everywhere—in museums, government buildings, markets, and even Tube stations. A quick look upward at London's skyline is to be reminded of the capital city's architectural genius.

London is a city rooted in history, yet constantly moving forward. From the majesty and grandeur of St Paul's Cathedral and Tower Bridge to the modern architectural marvels of the Gherkin and The Shard, London is a mecca for photographers and one of the most photogenic cities in the world. The photographs in this collection, taken from helicopters, from observation decks and atop buildings, and with the use of drones, capture the juxtaposition of time—presenting London from a new perspective.

Let *Above & Across London* transport you and experience the breathtaking beauty of London— from above & across.

Michelle Fitzgerald
Editor

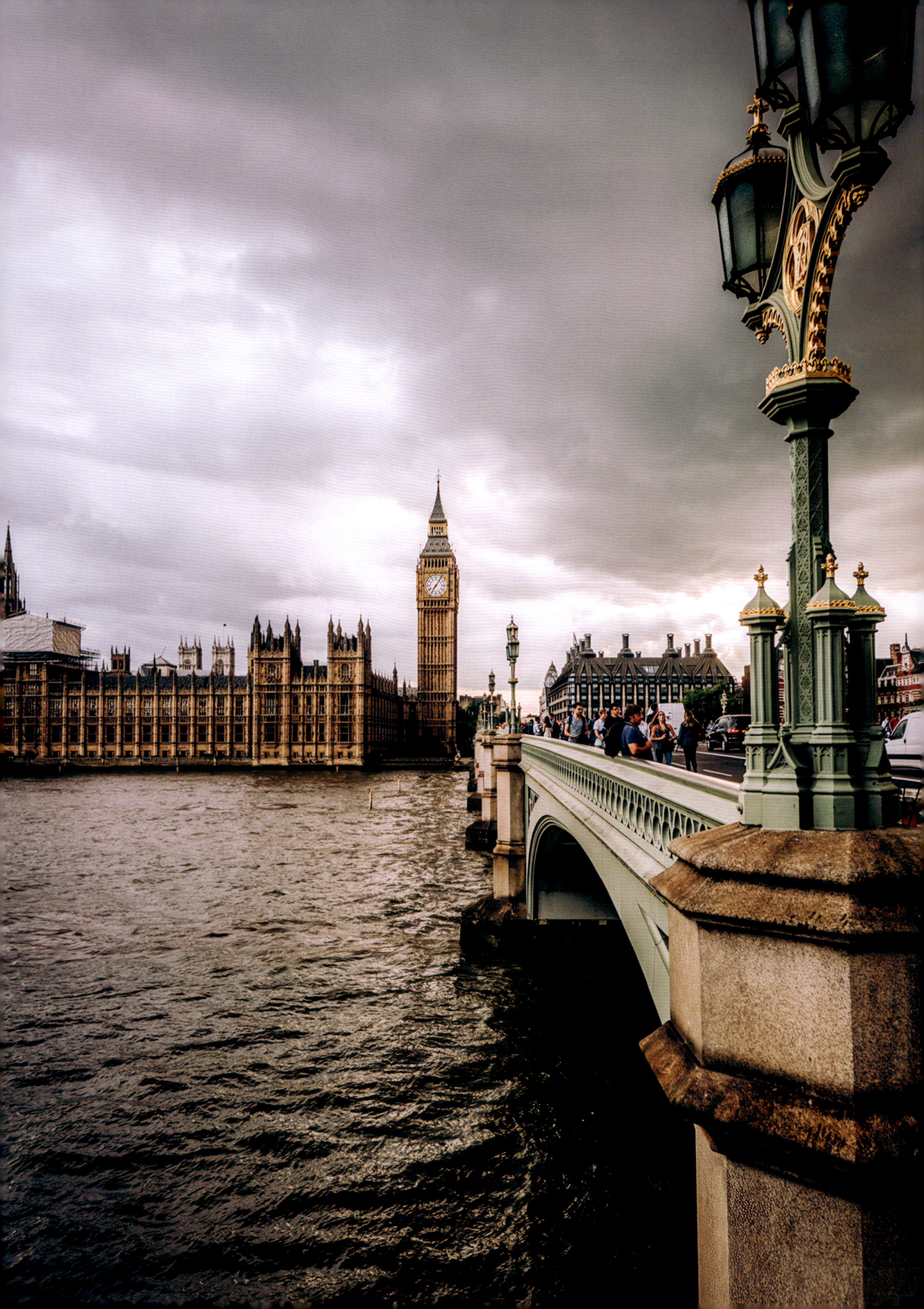

"When a man is tired of London, he is tired of life; for there is in London all that life can afford."
—*Samuel Johnson, English Writer, Poet, and Playwright*

London is a city that lives in layers. I know this because I am a Londoner, and I love this city.

At its heart lie the ancient stones of Londinium, a Roman outpost founded nearly two thousand years ago on the northern bank of the River Thames. That same river—broad, tidal, and unhurried—still winds through the city like a spine, shaping the landscape and feeding its growth. It carried trade and empire, ideas and revolutions, immigrants and monarchs. It carried London itself into the modern age. As Joseph Conrad once wrote, the Thames is "the silent highway bearing the burden of men's dreams."

From those early foundations, London has expanded outward across the centuries, absorbing surrounding villages and meadows into its orbit. It is a city built not in one grand plan but in countless improvisations—organic, chaotic, resilient. Over time, it became what Samuel Johnson called "*a nation, not a city.*" From cobbled lanes to soaring towers, from Tudor timbers to steel and glass, every street tells a story. This book of photographs captures the extraordinary variety of those stories—of a city always becoming.

Modern London is a skyline of contrasts: The Shard rises like a fragment of ice above the South Bank, a monument to ambition and architectural daring. The Tate Modern stands nearby, its once-sooty power station skin now reimagined as a temple of art. Further west, Battersea Power Station—once a symbol of industrial might—has been reborn as a gleaming complex of shops, restaurants, and homes. Even the Post Office Tower, once the city's most futuristic silhouette, is now being transformed into a luxury hotel, yet another chapter in its evolving life. In London, buildings don't just endure—they adapt.

Yet this city is not merely a monument to steel, stone, and reinvention. It is also one of the greenest capitals on earth. With over eight million trees spread across its parks, squares, gardens, and streets, the United Nations officially classifies London as a forest. From the wild grass of Hampstead Heath to the meticulously kept lawns of Regent's Park, green space is not just a luxury—it is a birthright. Nature and urbanity live side by side here in a delicate, deeply rooted balance.

London also carries its scars with quiet dignity. The Blitz of World War II left vast swathes of the city in ruin, and yet out of that devastation came innovation. New estates, bold public buildings, and a resilient civic spirit emerged. As Winston Churchill declared during the war, "London can take it." And take it, she did—surviving not just the bombs, but the challenges of austerity, immigration, reconstruction, and reinvention.

This endurance, this openness to change, is part of why London has always drawn outsiders. It is a magnet for dreamers, dissenters, creators, and exiles. Karl Marx wrote *Das Kapital* in Soho. Mozart composed symphonies here as a child. From Joseph Conrad to Zadie Smith, from Malala Yousafzai to Freddie Mercury, the city has provided a home for talents from every continent, each of them reshaping it in turn. London listens, absorbs, and transforms.

In the pages ahead, you'll find a portrait of a city in motion. 172 aerial photographs of London taken by photographer Ben Moore. A city where history is never quite buried and the future never far off. From forgotten alleyways to shimmering new towers, from centuries-old bridges to futuristic station canopies, these images show a place that is both museum and laboratory, archive and engine.

As Virginia Woolf once wrote, London is "a city of shifting glimpses, of sudden disappearances, of inexplicable presences." And this book, like the city itself, is full of those glimpses — moments frozen in time, layered with meaning.

This is not just a city you visit. London is a city you experience, inhabit, and carry with you. A city that remembers everything and yet is never finished. This book will inspire you to immerse yourself in the great city that is London.

Vivien Godfrey
Chairman & CEO,
Edward Stanford Group Limited

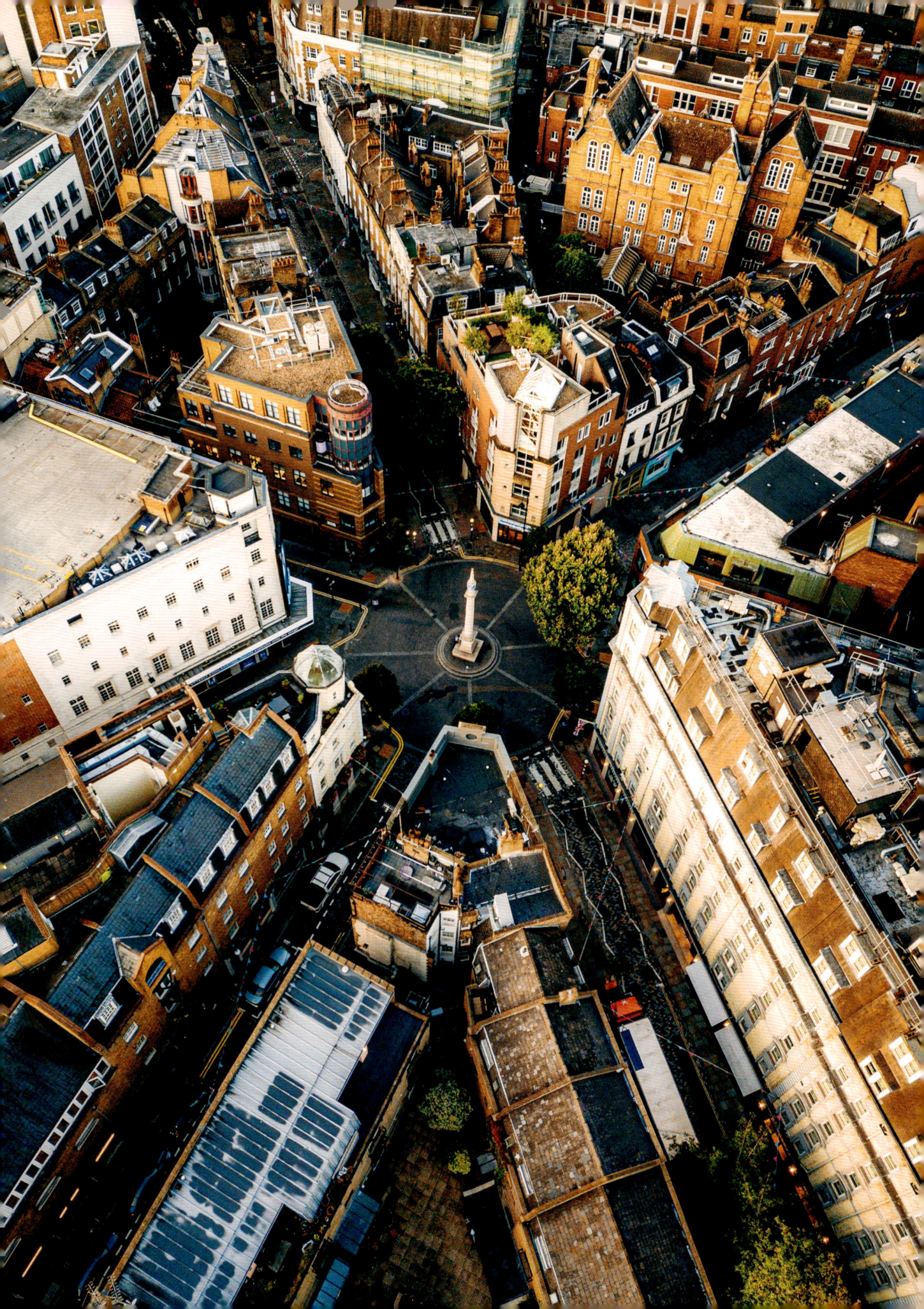

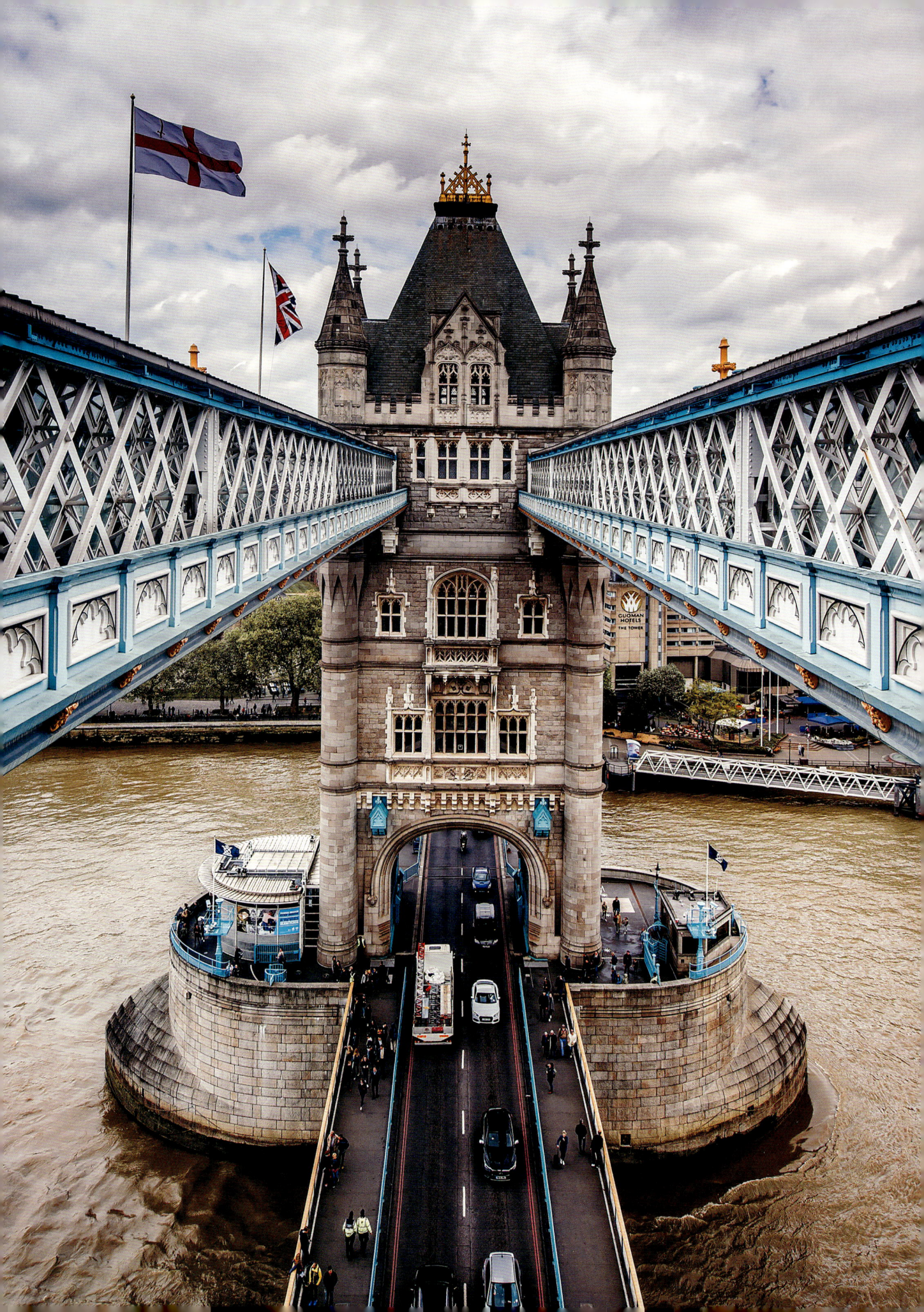

The River Thames ♦ 215 miles end to end, England's longest river famously snakes right through the heart of central London. Once the backbone of the capital and a major trade route, the River Thames holds much of London's history in its tidal and non-tidal currents. ♦ 21 tributaries, largely unknown to most city dwellers, feed somewhat secretly into the capital's main line. Starting as early as the 1460s, the waterways were seen as filthy and inconvenient and were paved over to make way for London's mass expansion. Today, nearly two-thirds of the River Thames's branches in Greater London are covered, however they are still flowing—spotted by knowing eyes as they course discreetly through culverts and under grating. ♦ A 180-mile footpath jogs alongside the majority of the river, traveling from lush meadows and rural villages to the center of the city and right past some of London's most famous icons. One of the river's most recent additions, a 135-meter tall, cantilevered wheel of steel and glass known as the London Eye was launched in 2000 as a temporary structure, but its near-universal popularity earned it a permanent place on the banks of the River Thames. ♦ Designed by Horace Jones and completed in 1894, Tower Bridge was the answer to London's growing traffic problem—serving as a much-needed conduit to the east side of the city while still allowing tall ships to come into port up to 30 times a day. Tower Bridge's genius lays in its hydraulic lighting mechanism, hidden in the two neo-Gothic towers, that could lift both 1,000-ton bascules, drawbridge-style, in minutes. 80 people were needed to maintain the engines and keep the bridge working until the system switched from steam power to electricity in 1974. ♦ Two high-level walkways stretch between the pinnacle towers, 42 meters above the River Thames. In 2014, glass panels were installed in the walkways—giving visitors not only a full panorama of the city from above, but a breathtaking and unrivalled view of the River Thames below.

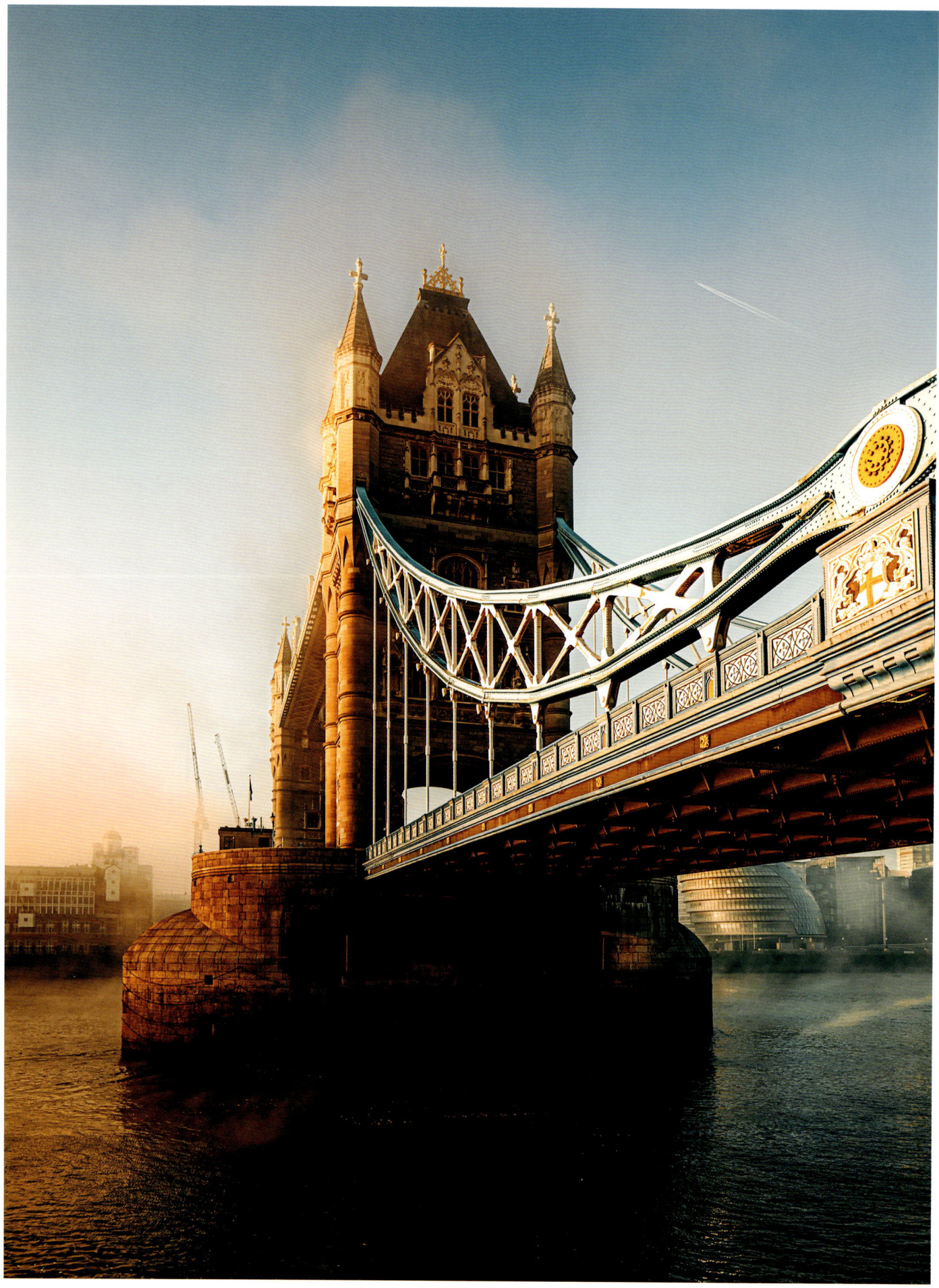

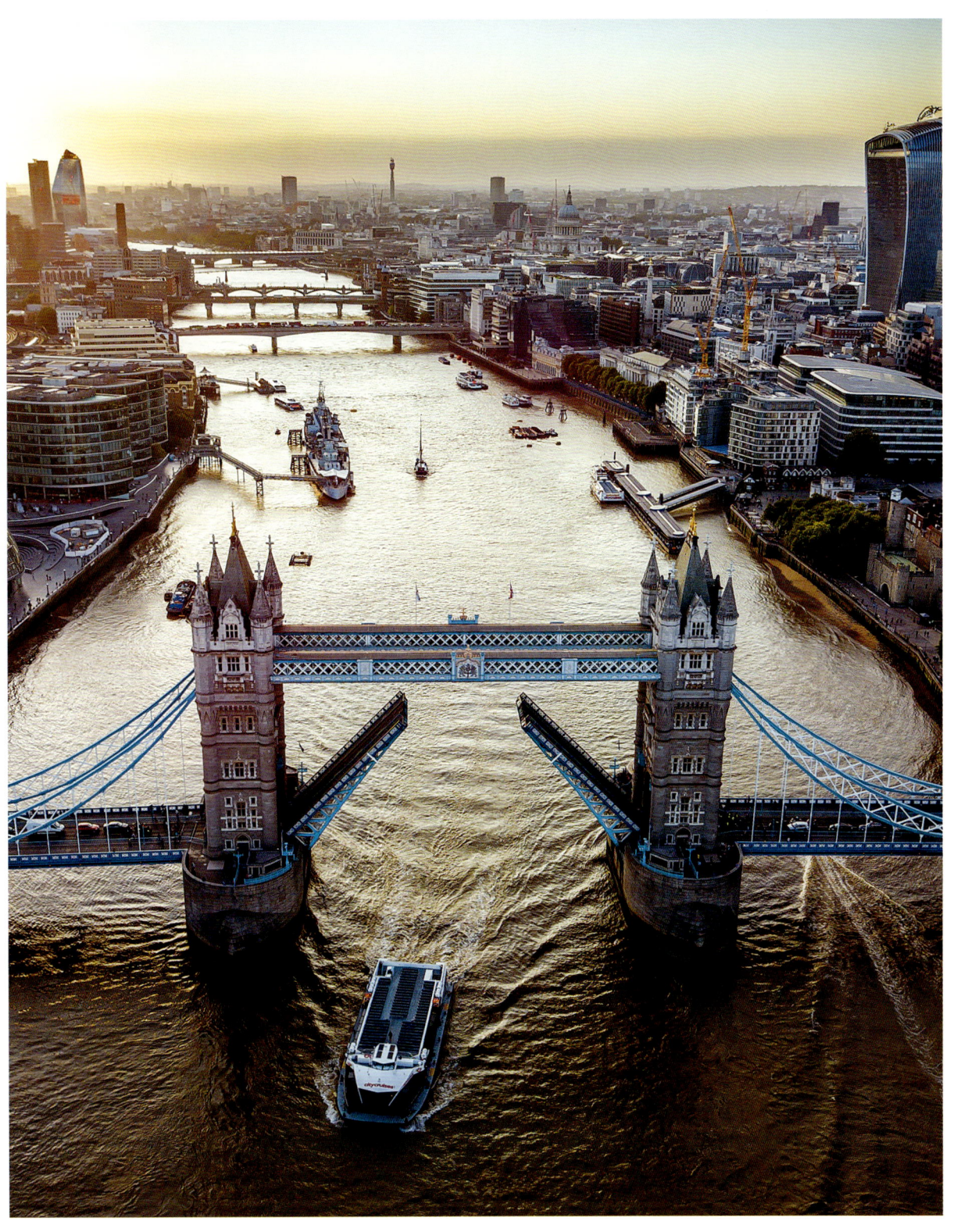

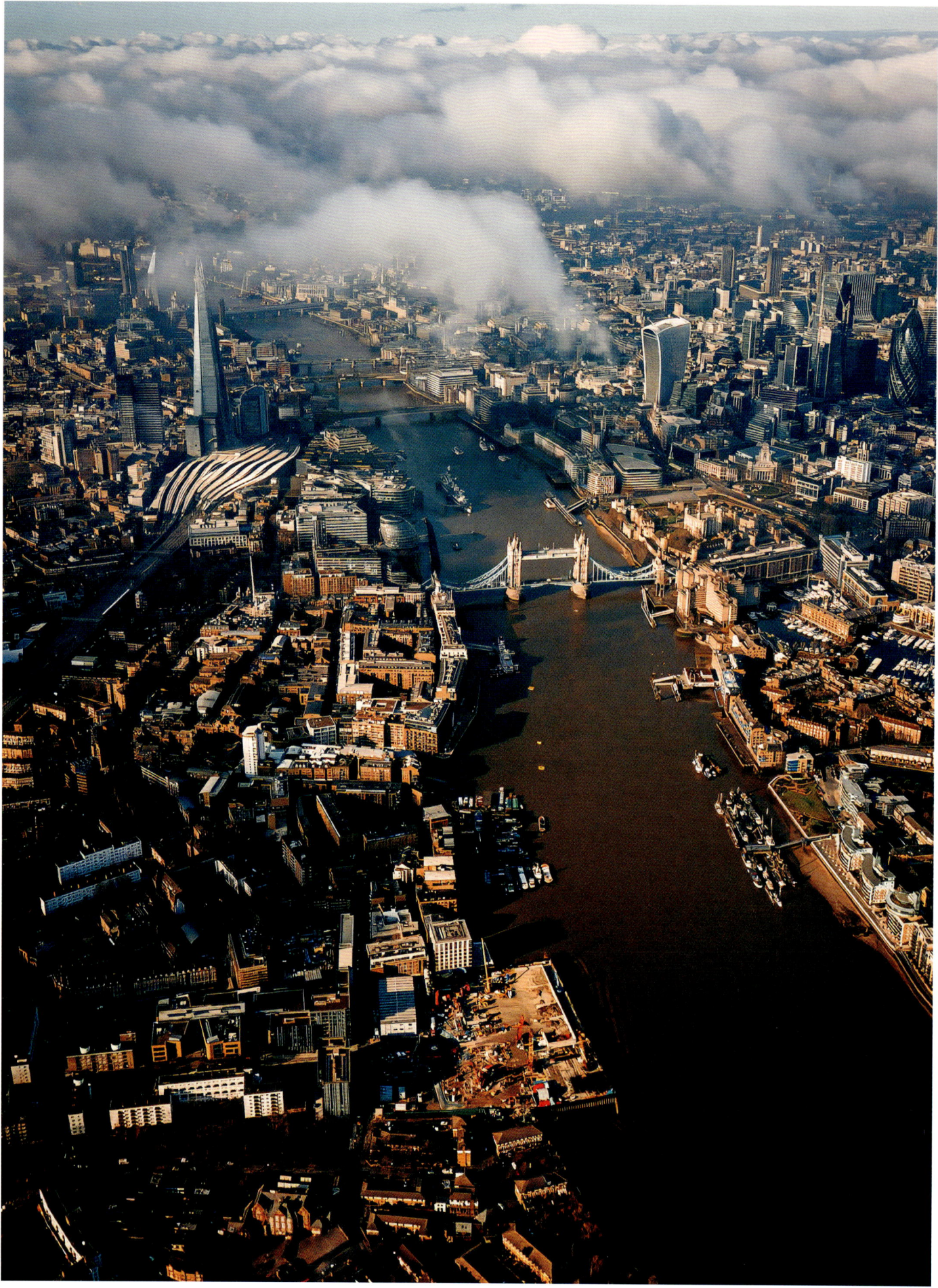

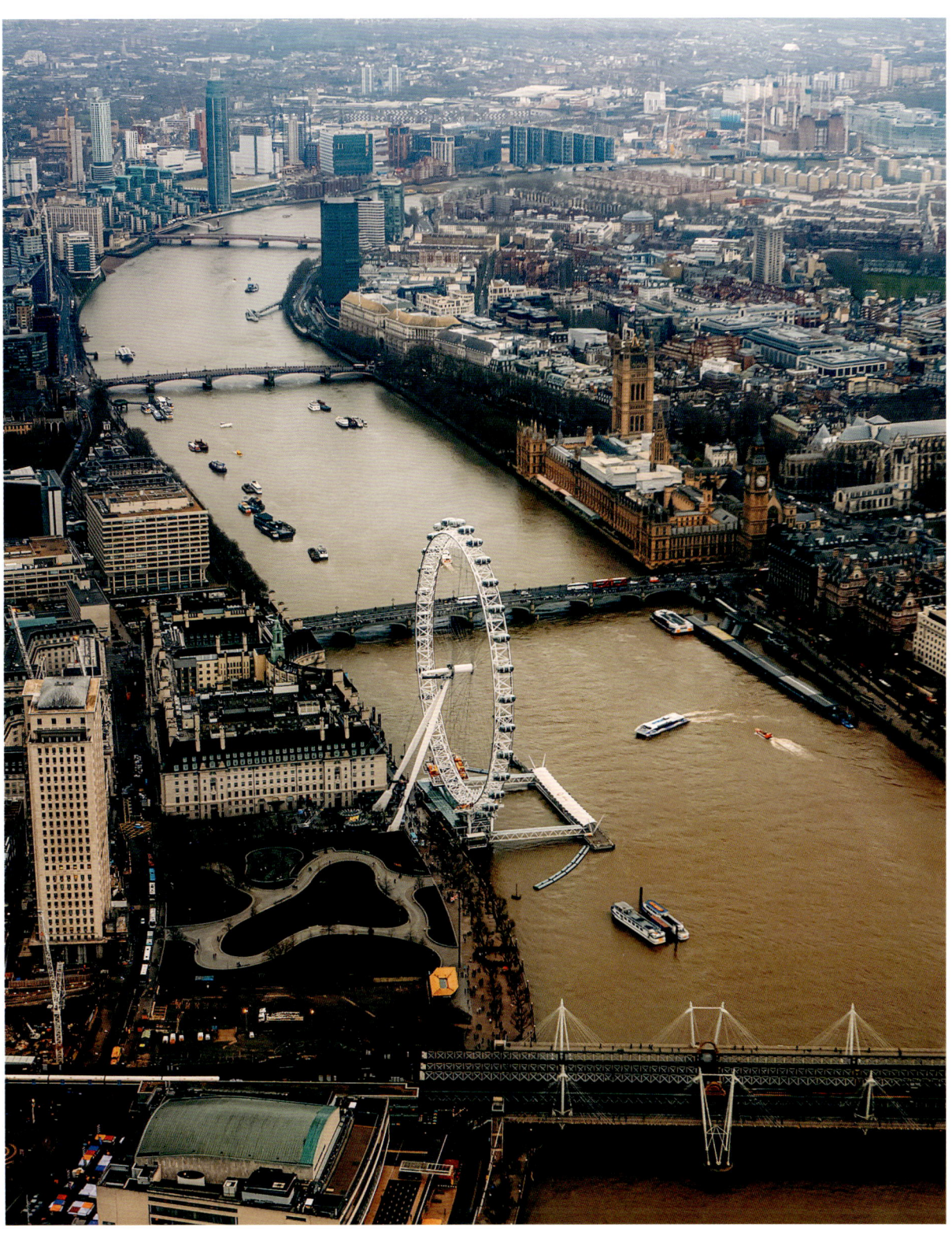

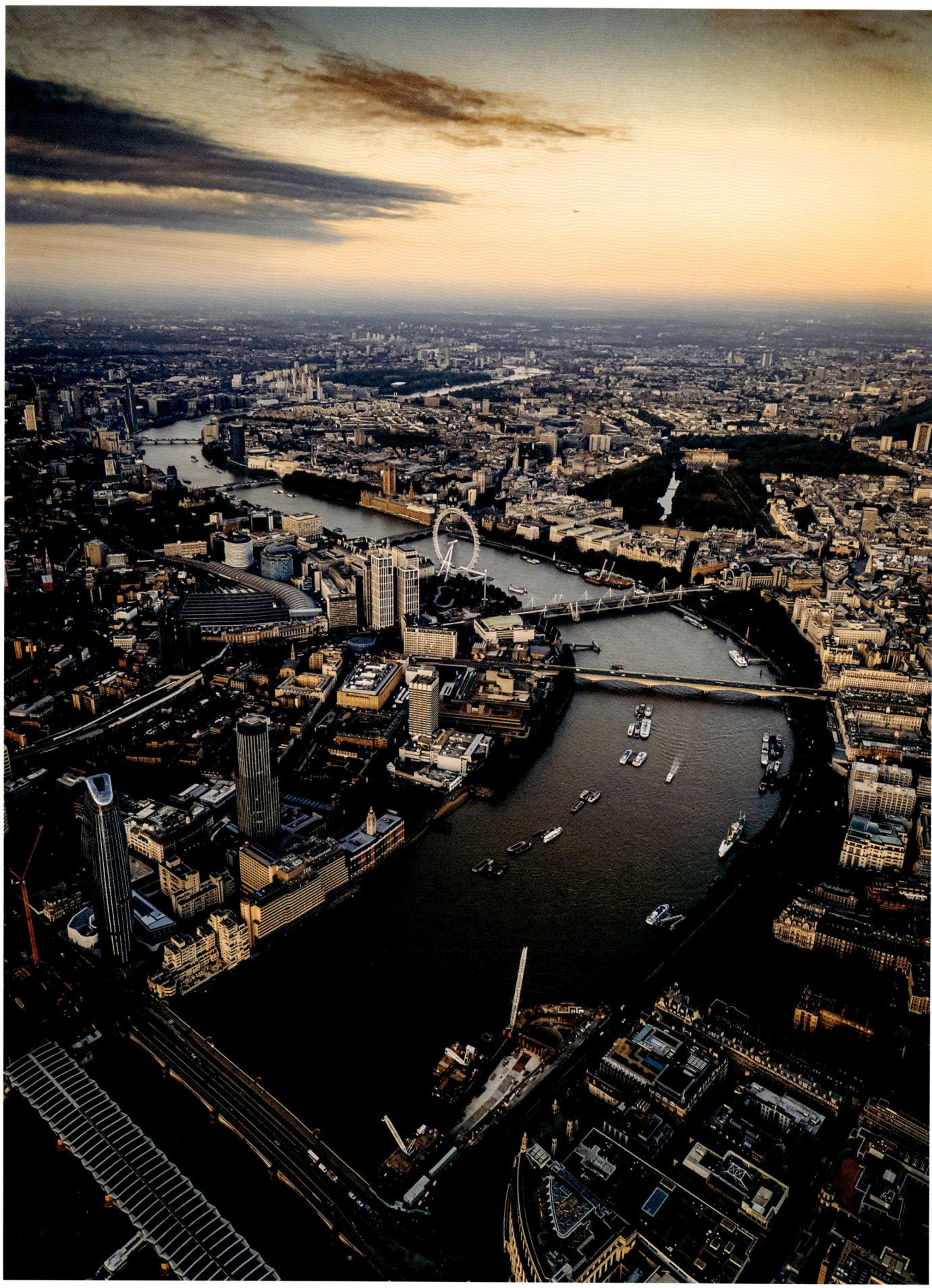

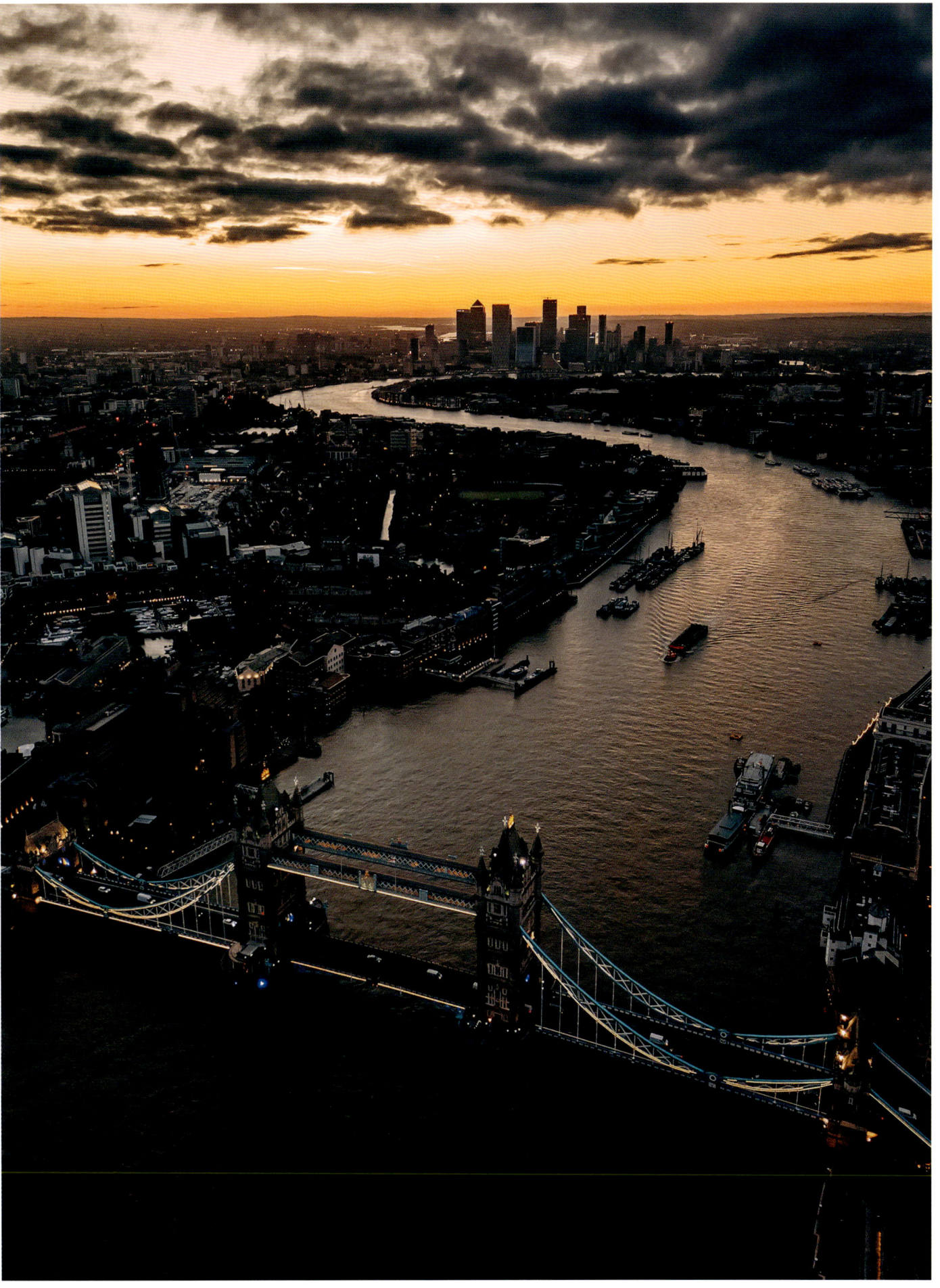

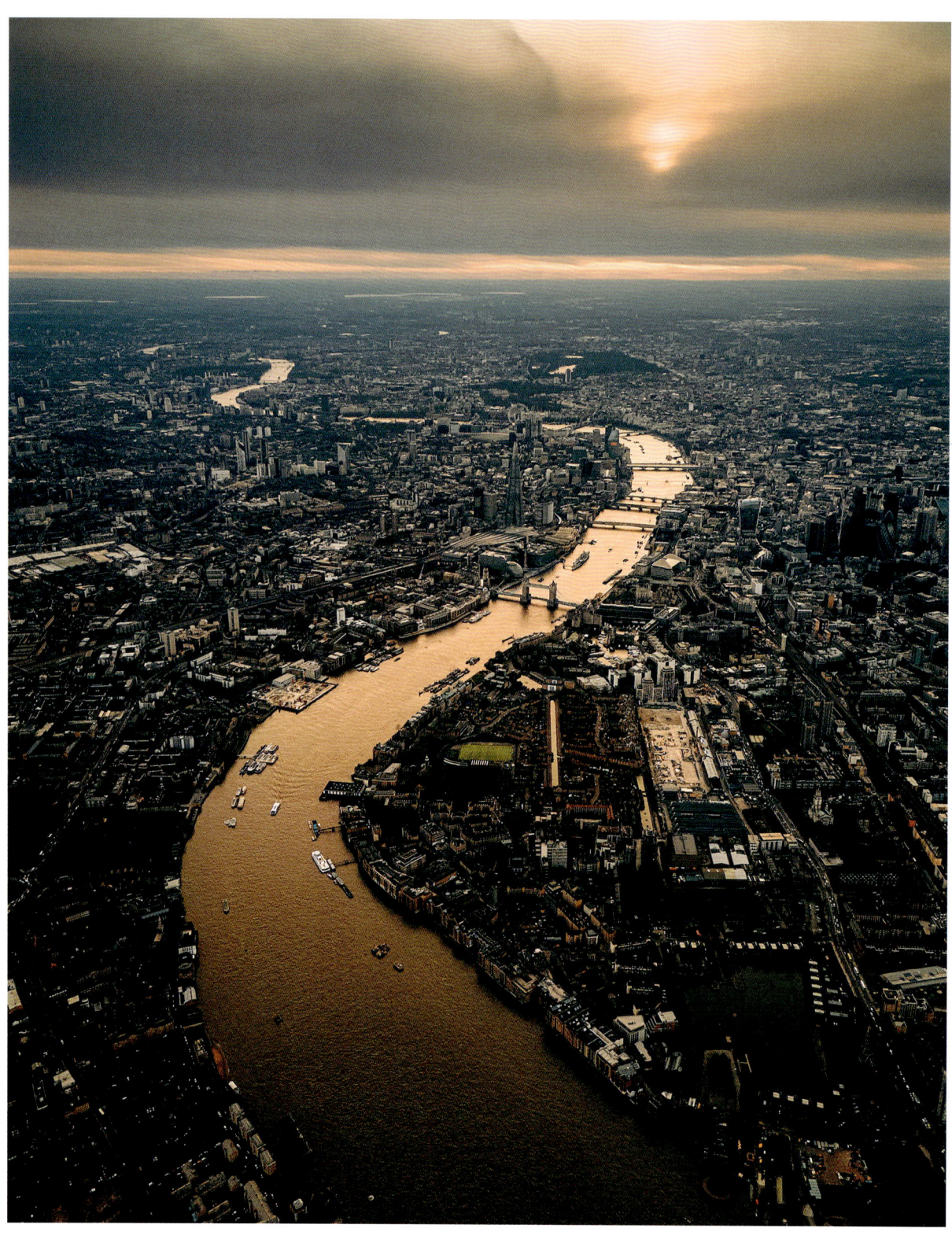

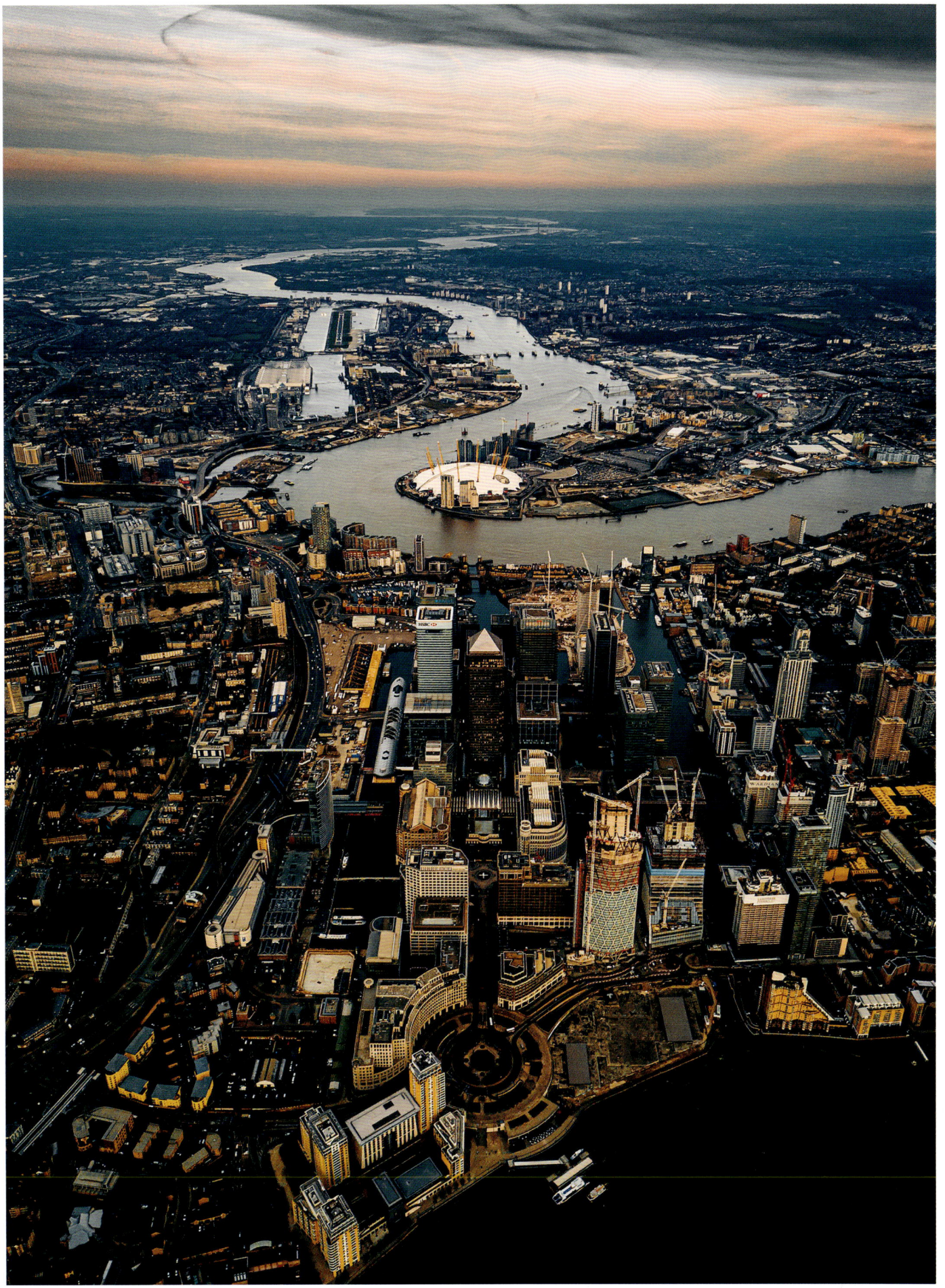

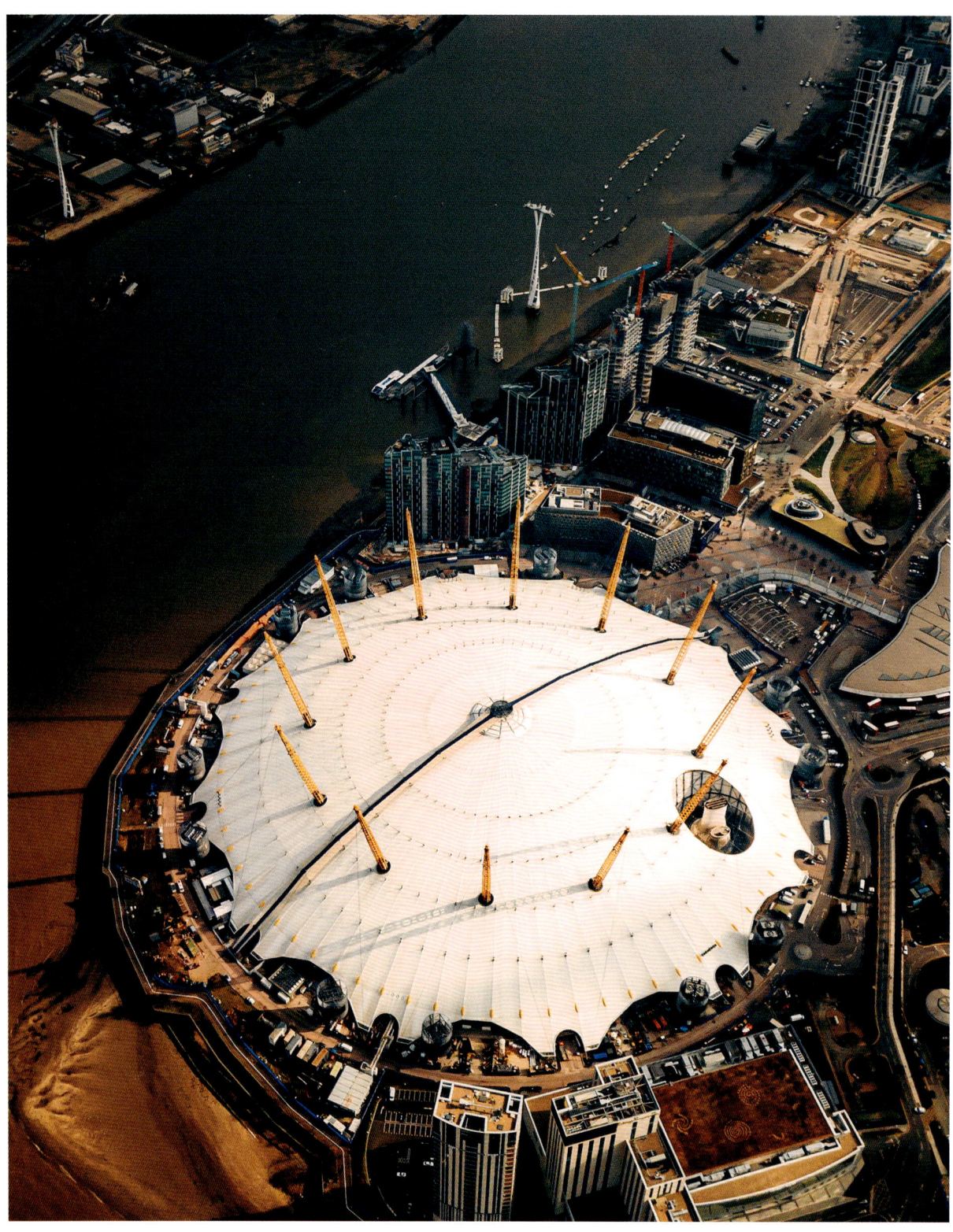

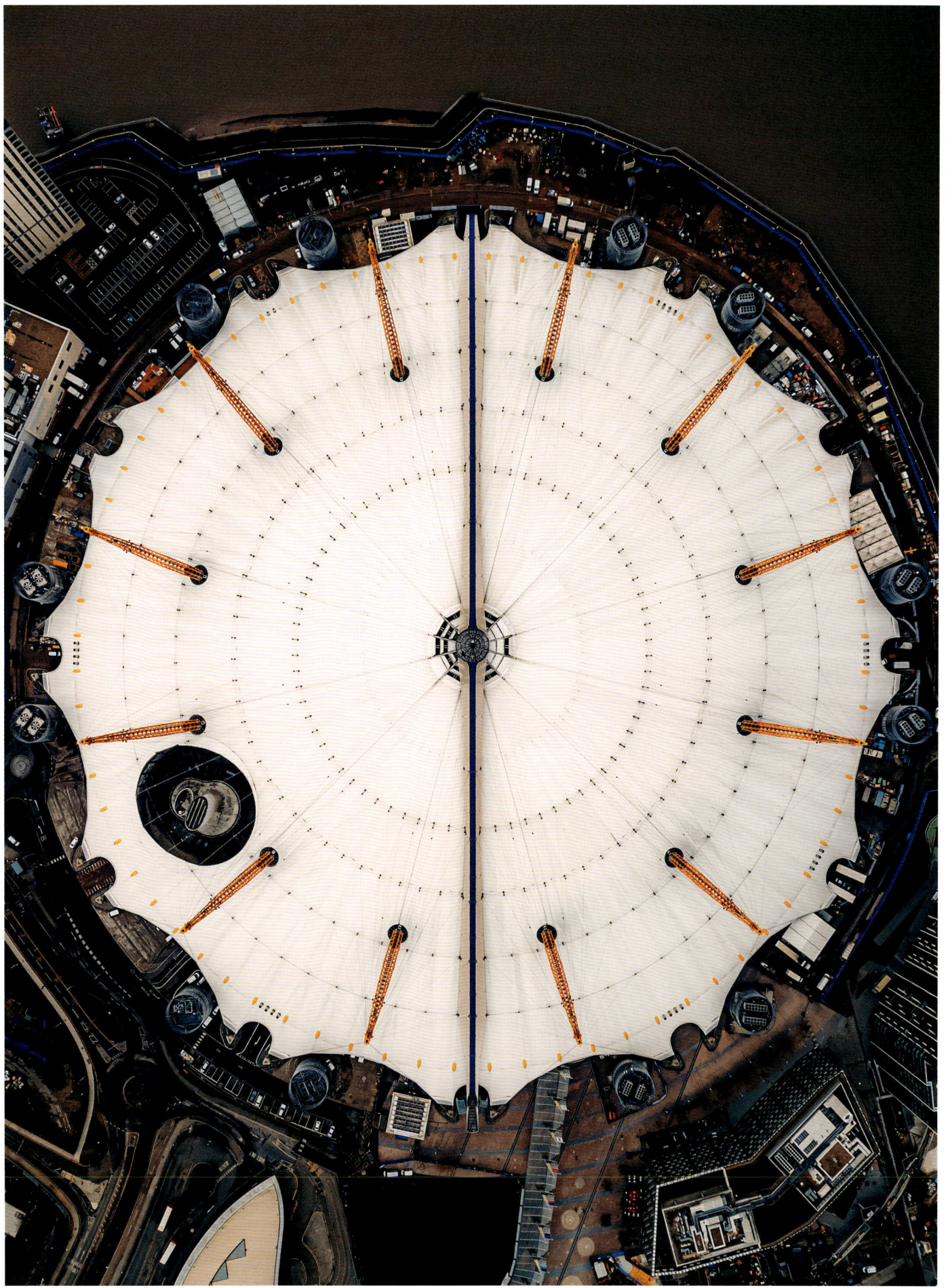

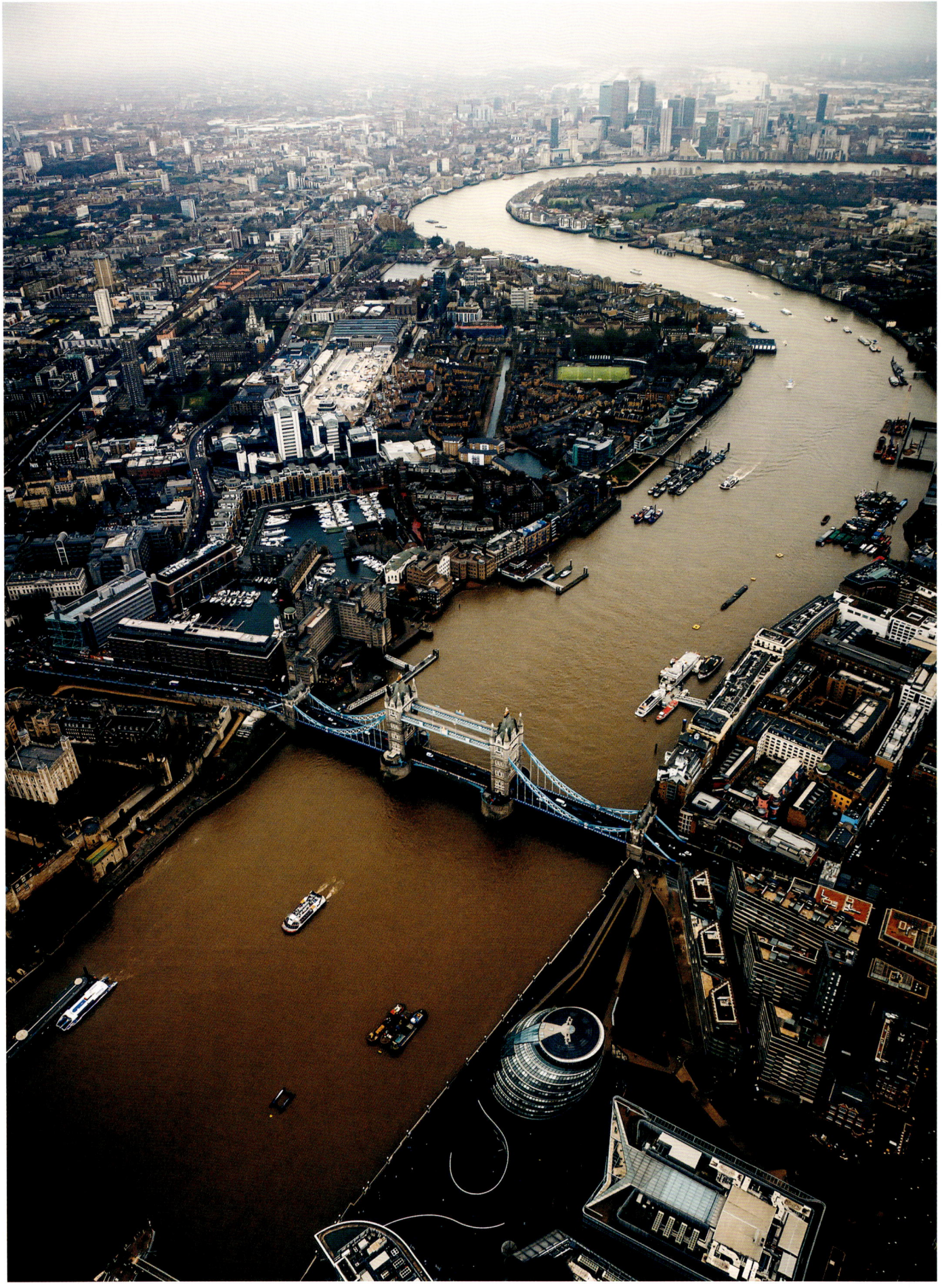

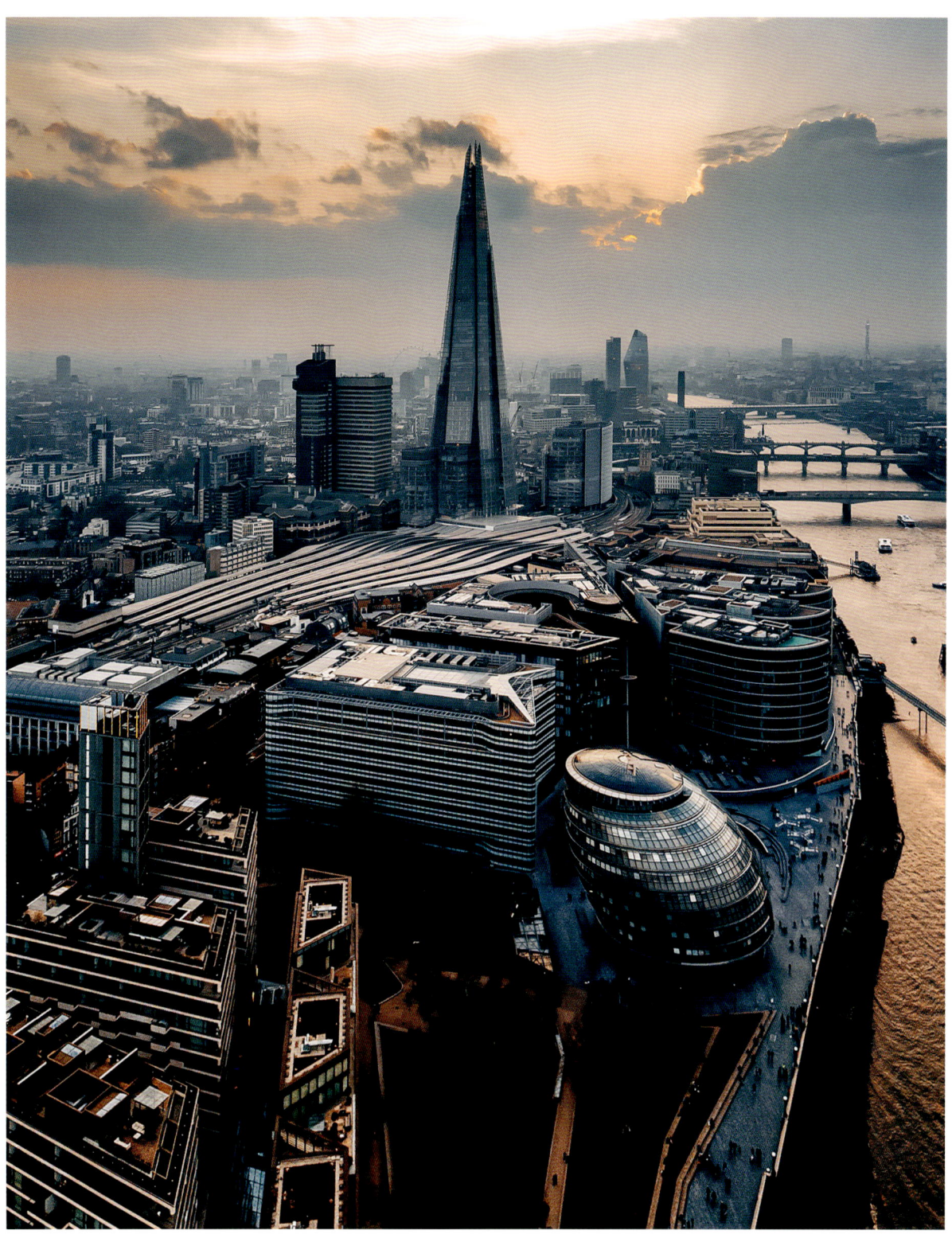

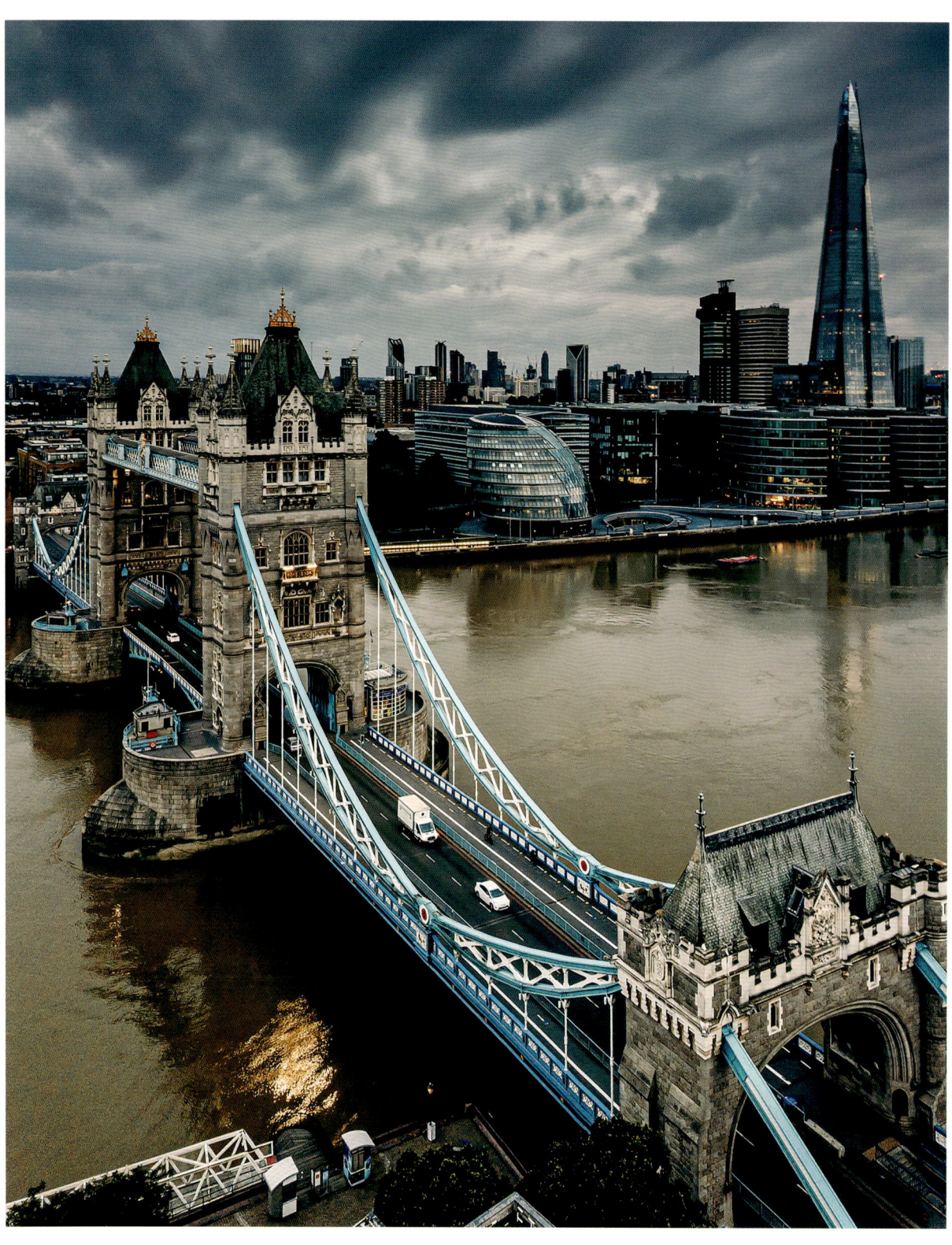

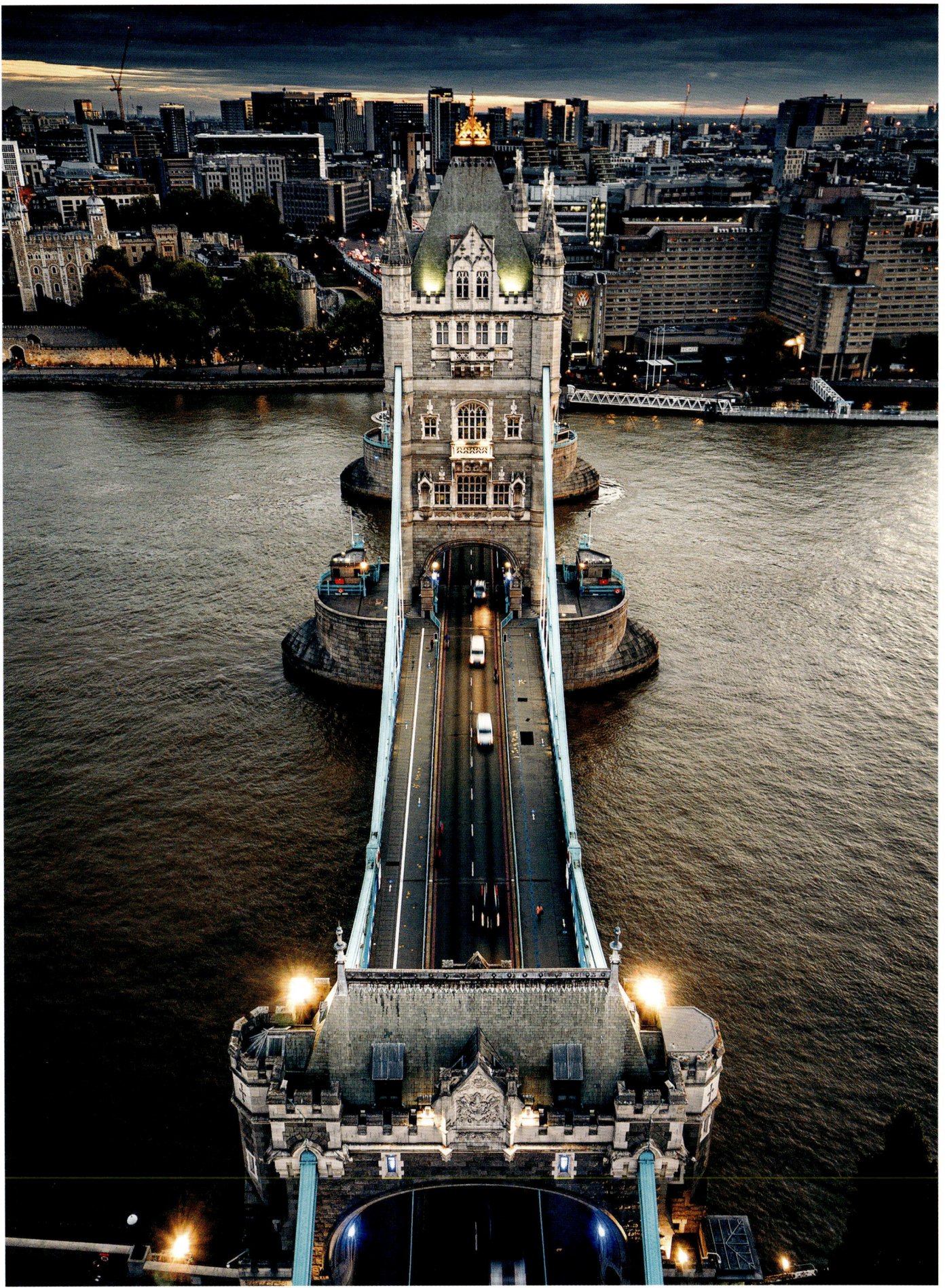

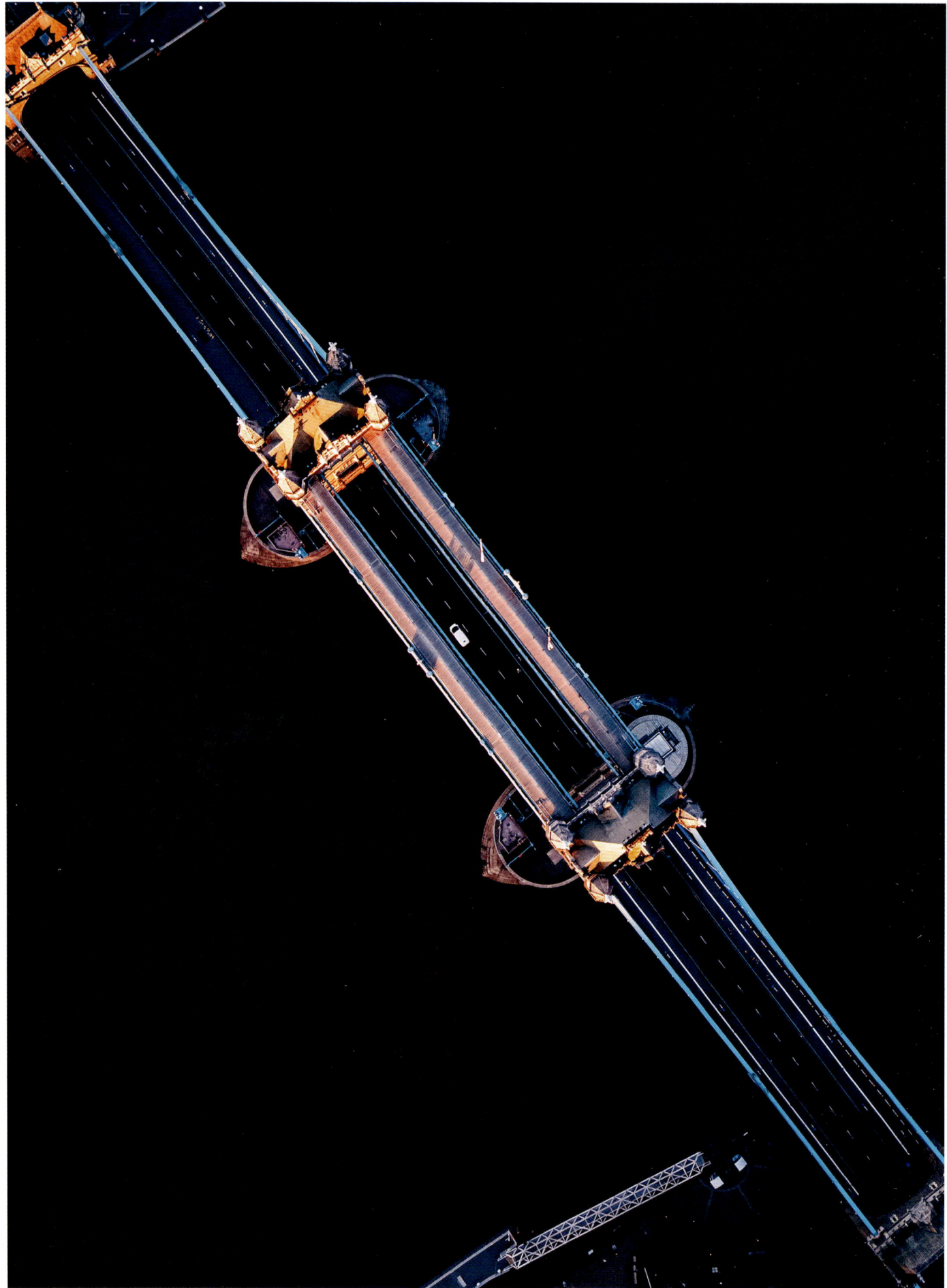

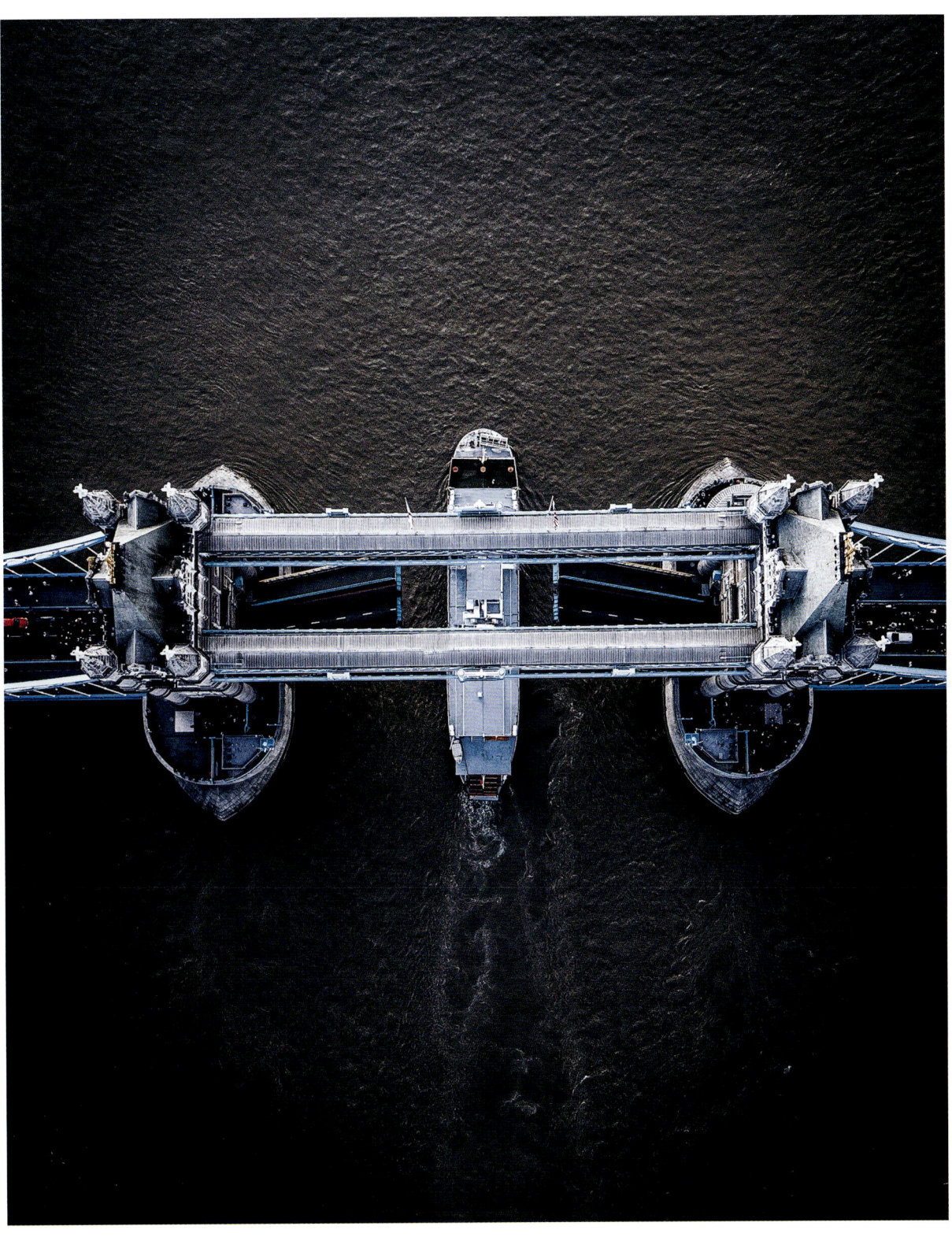

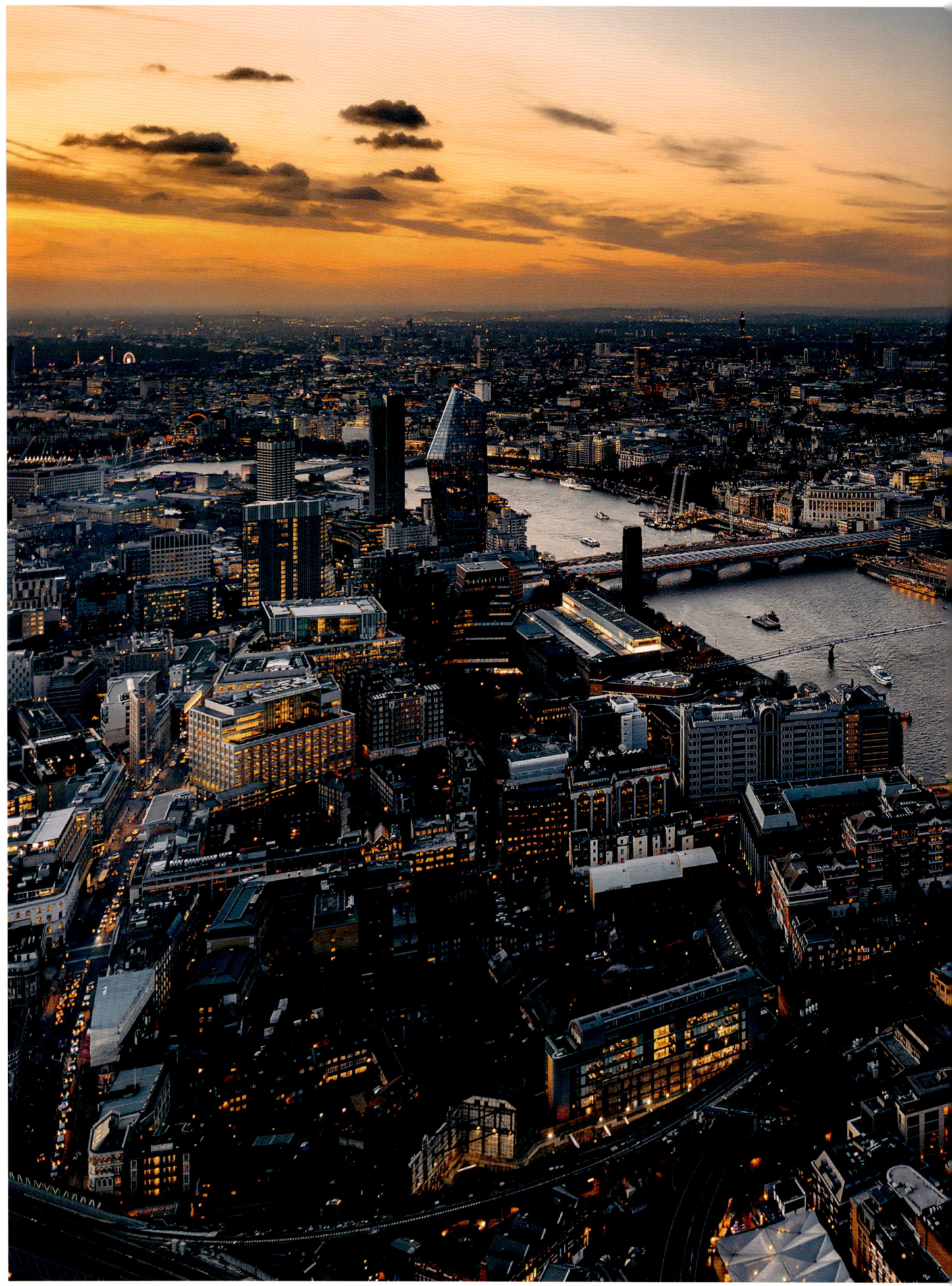

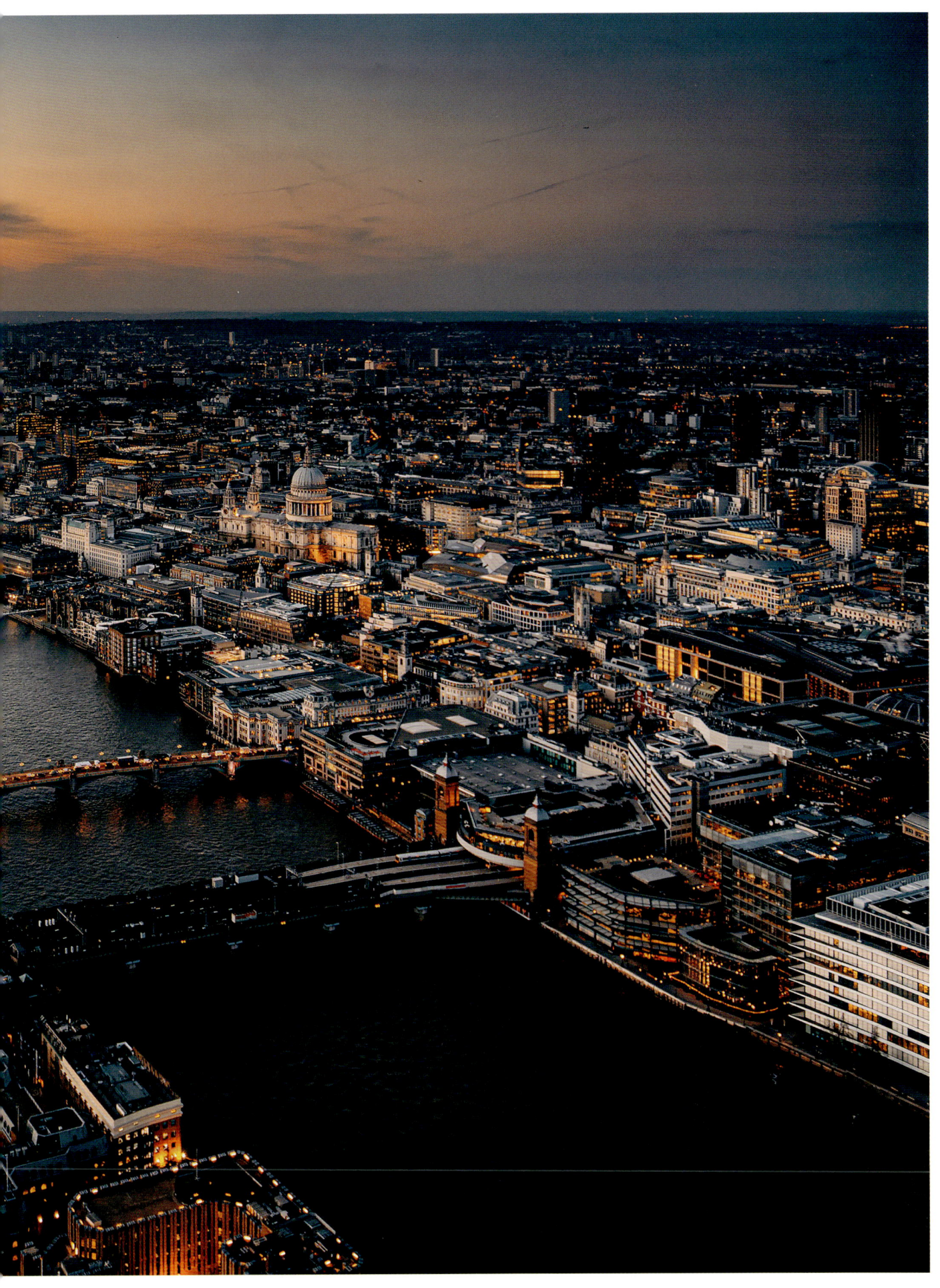

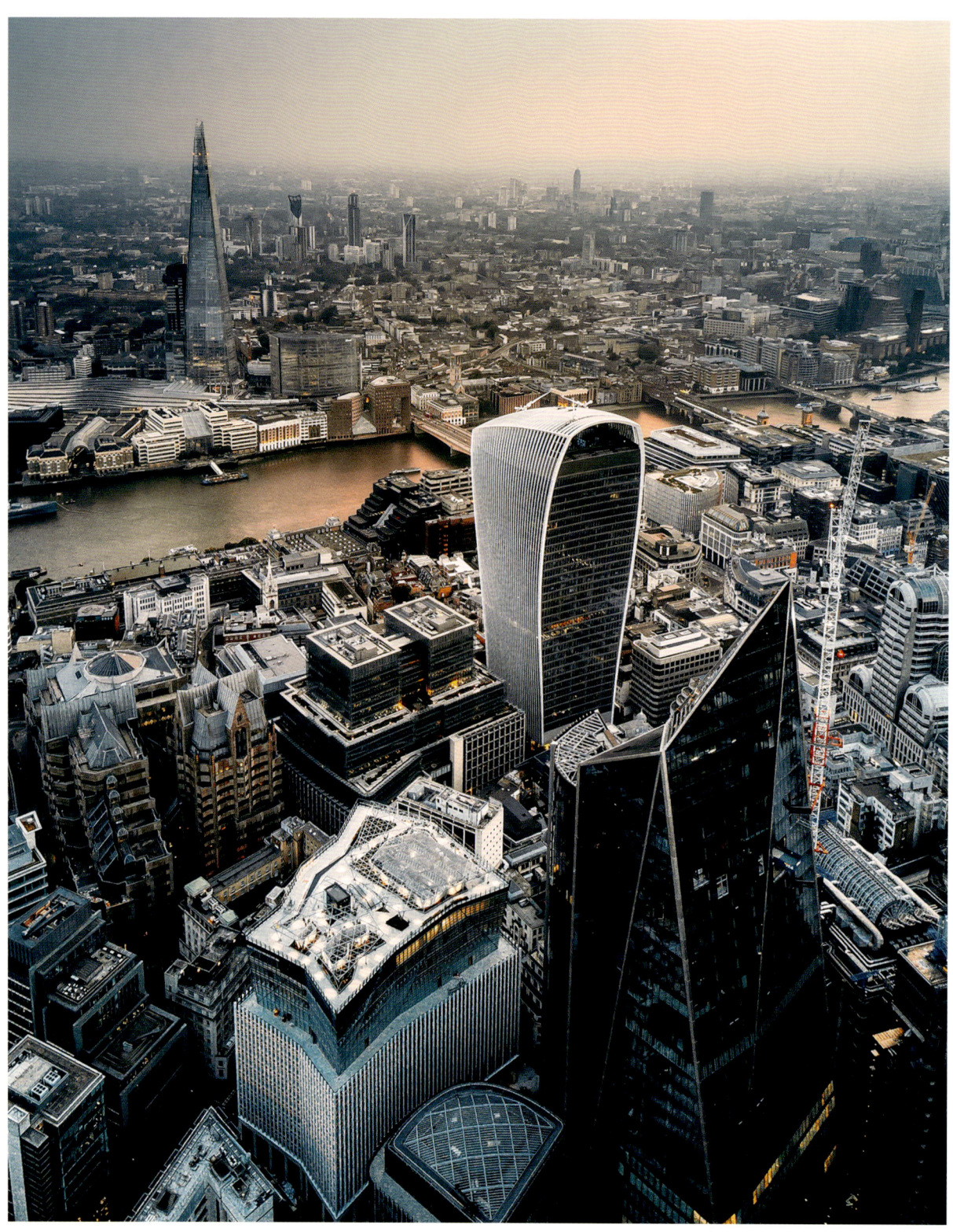

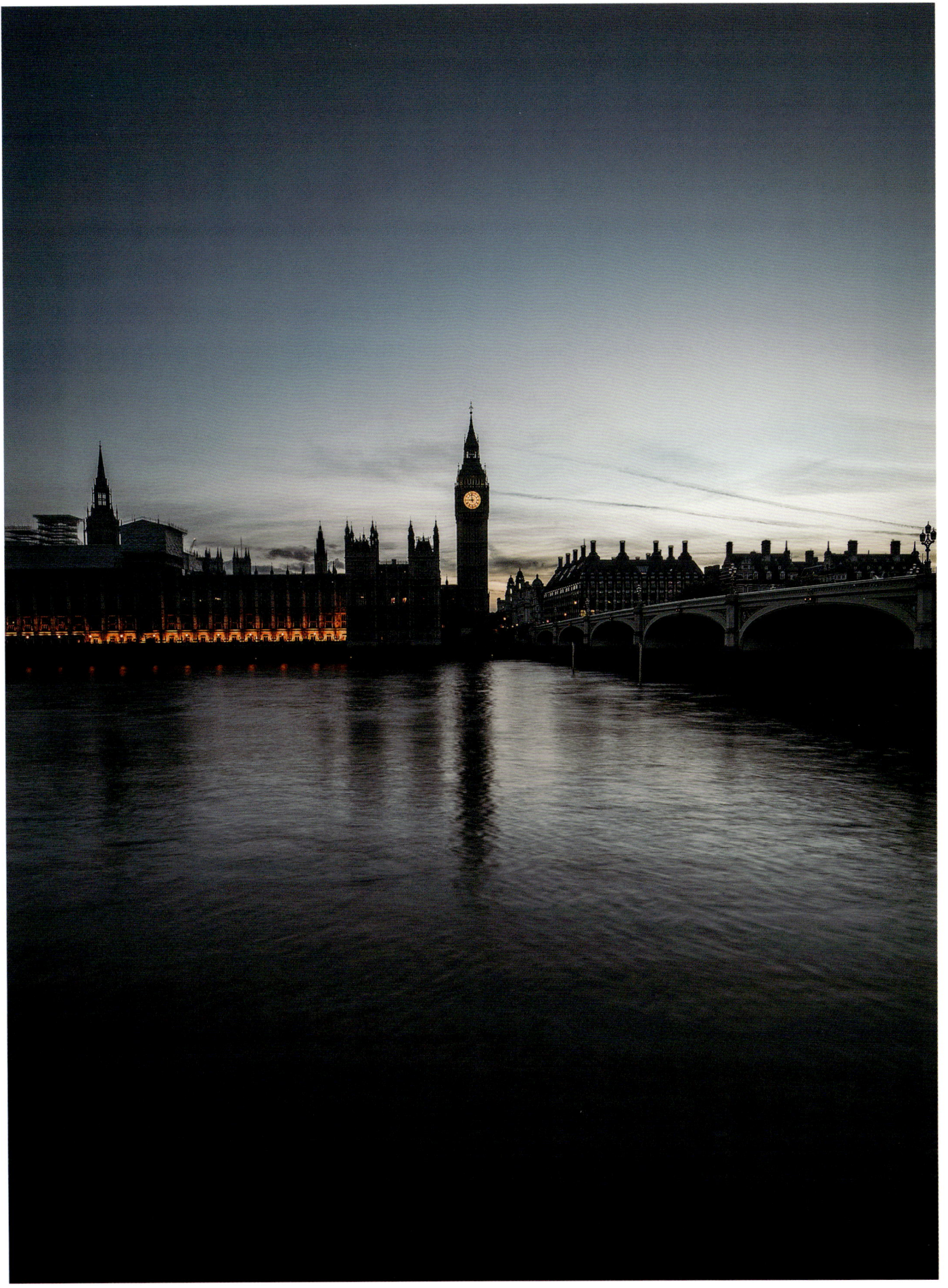

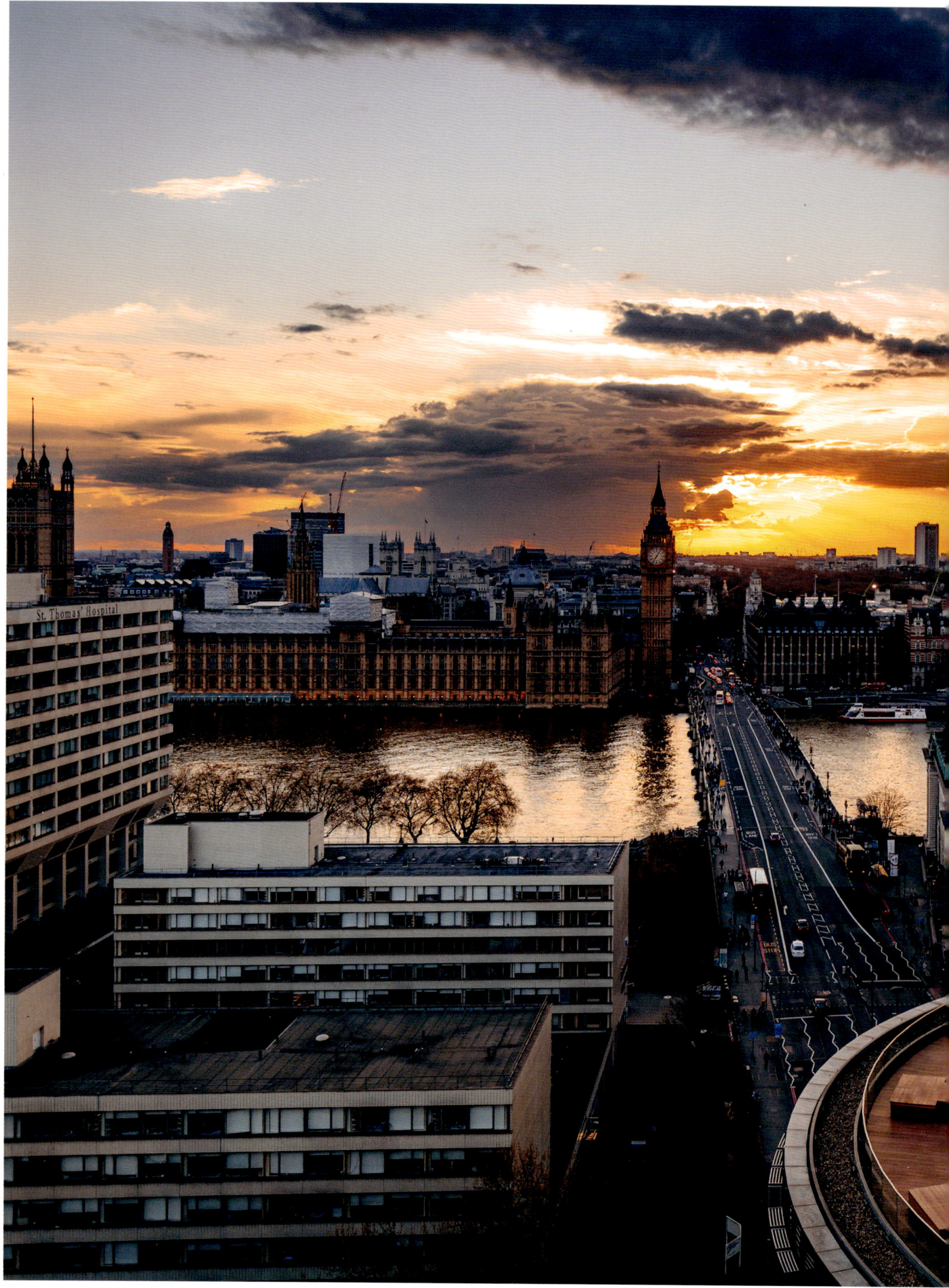

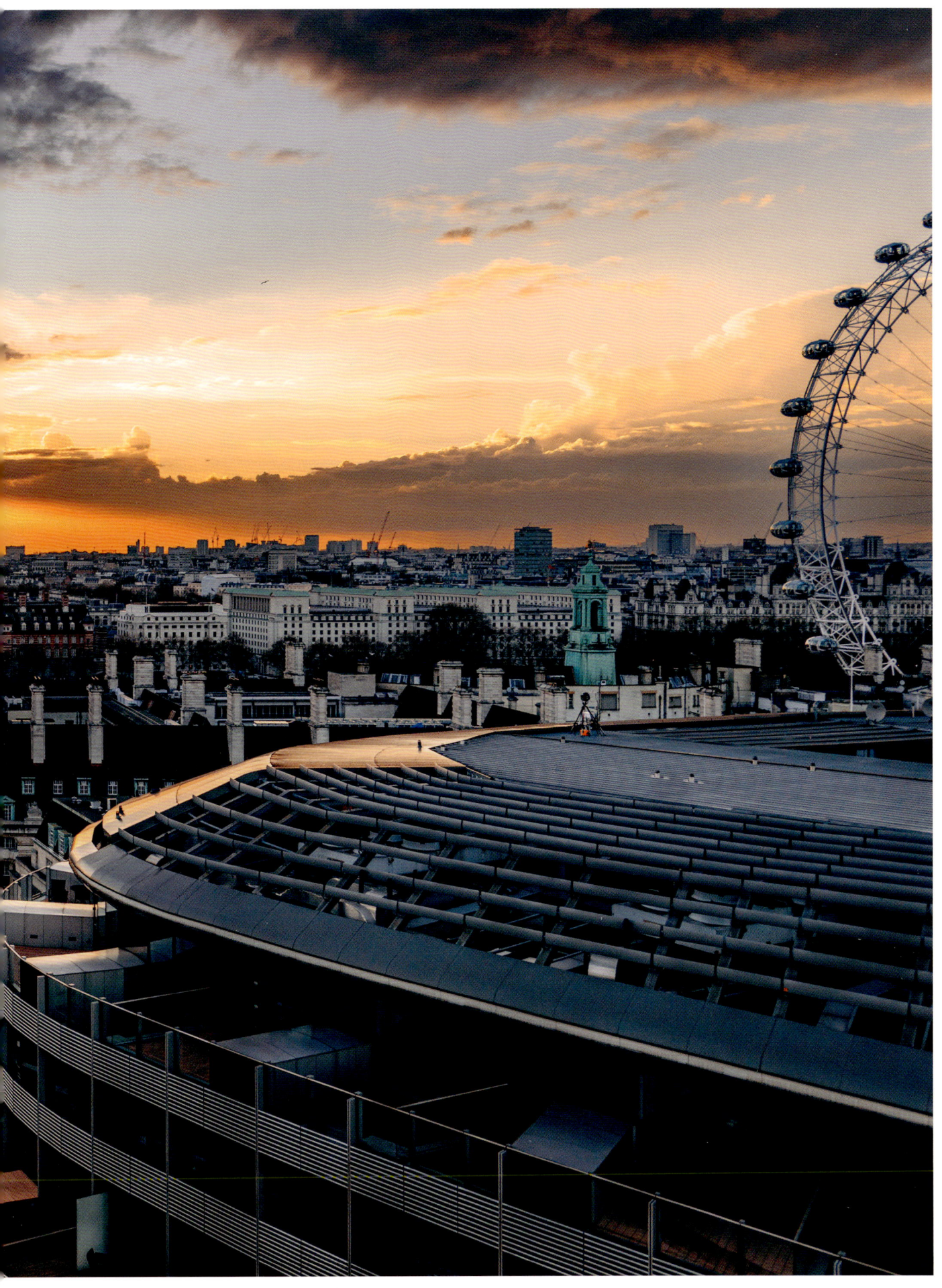

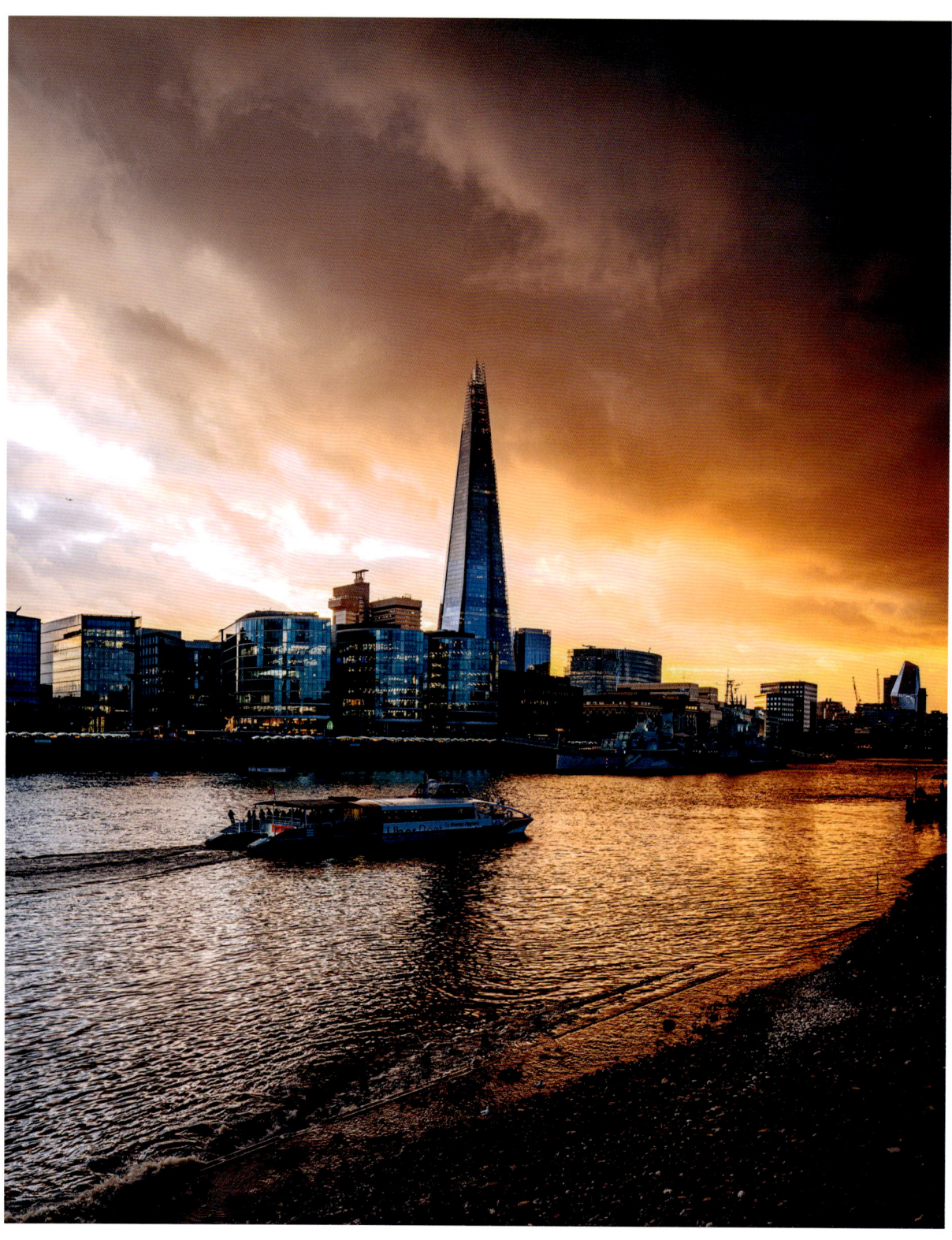

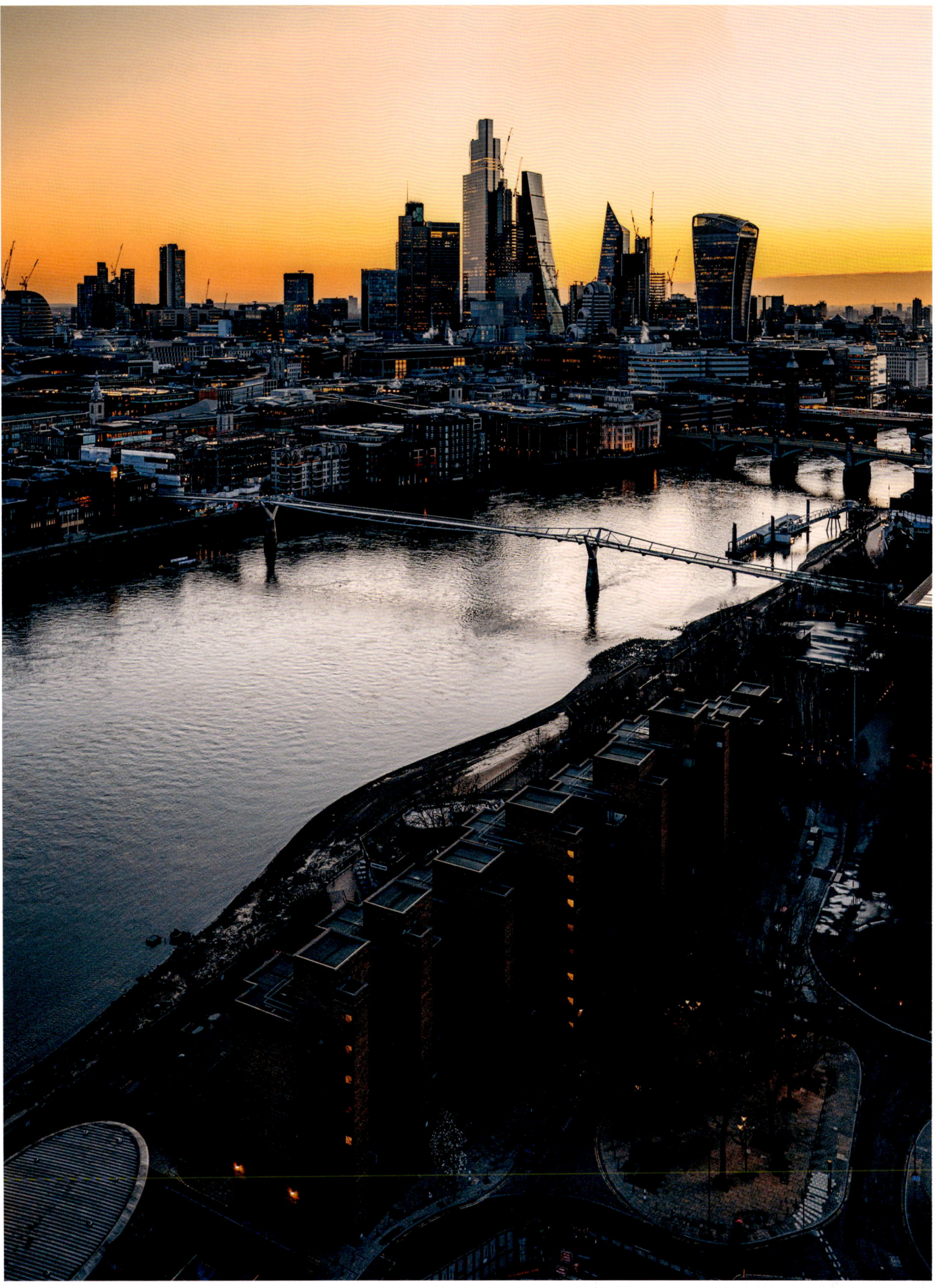

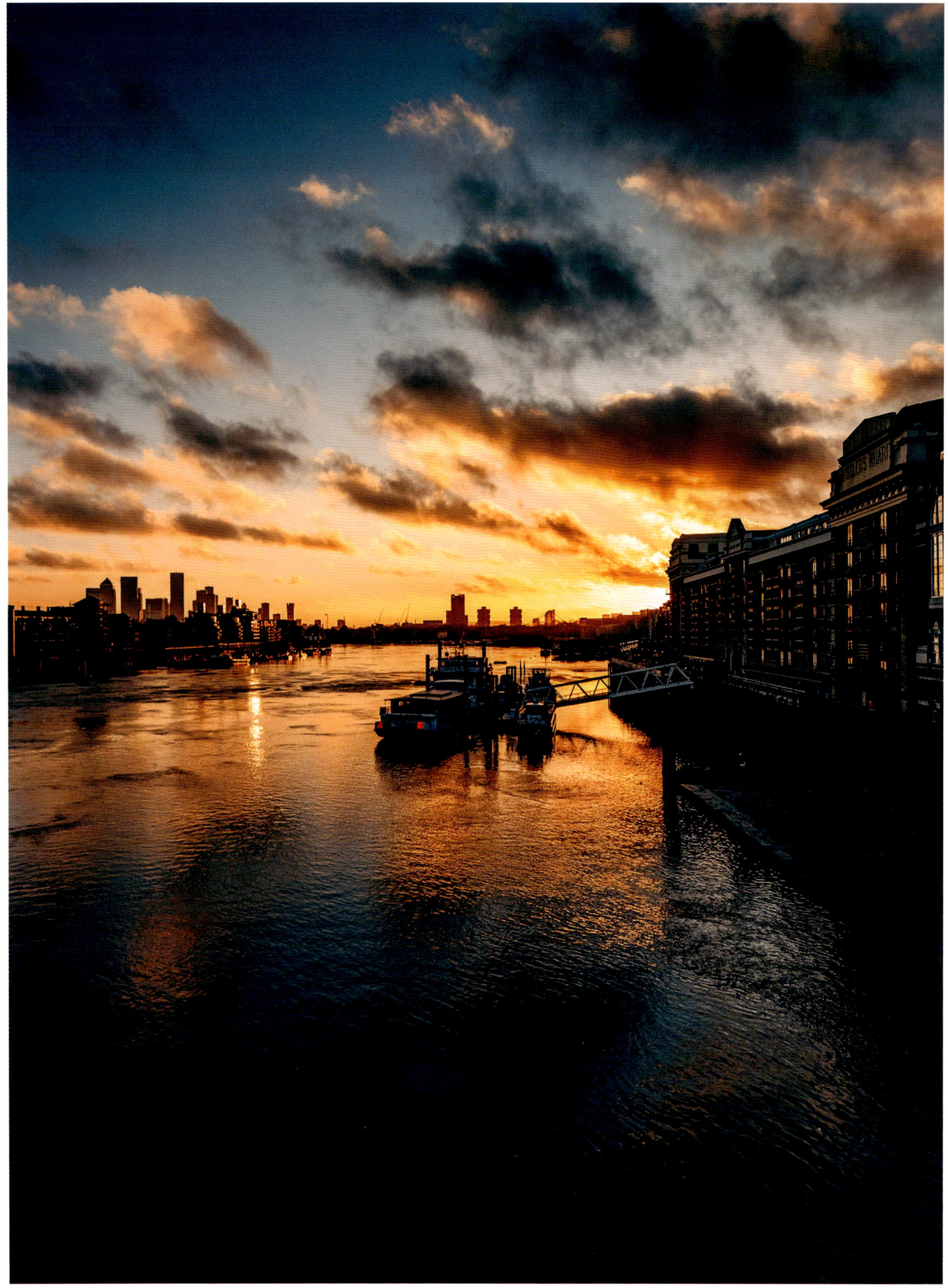

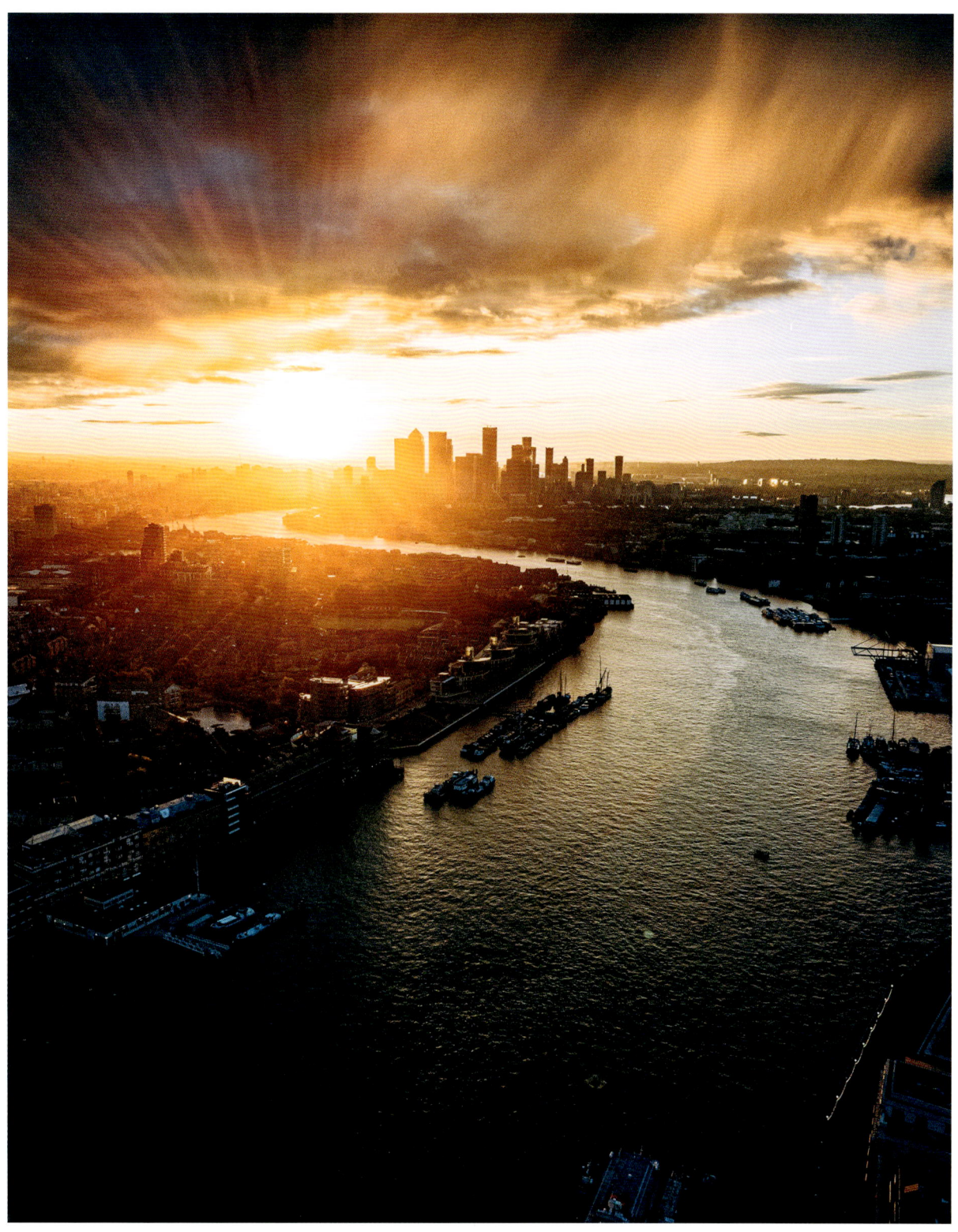

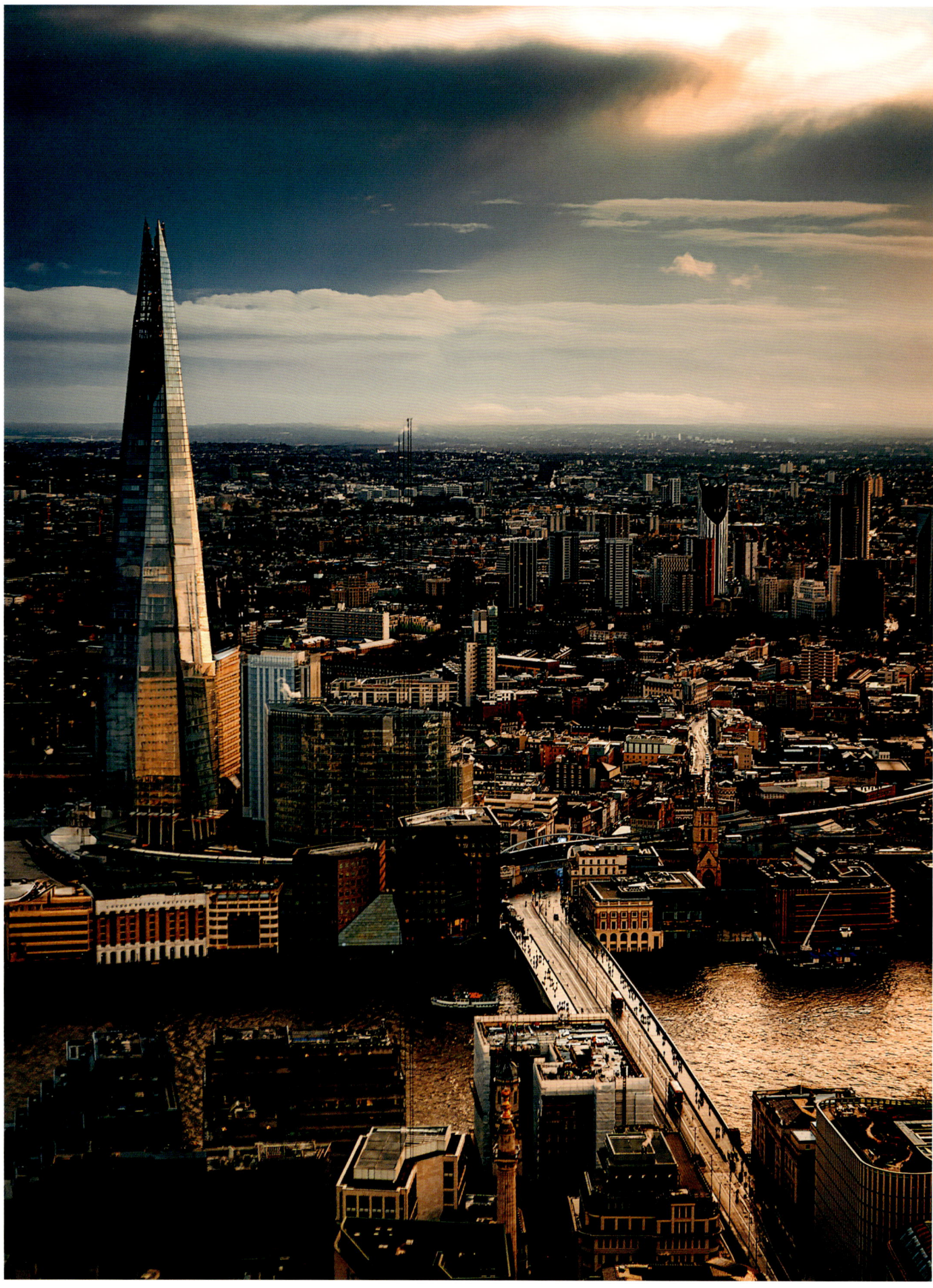

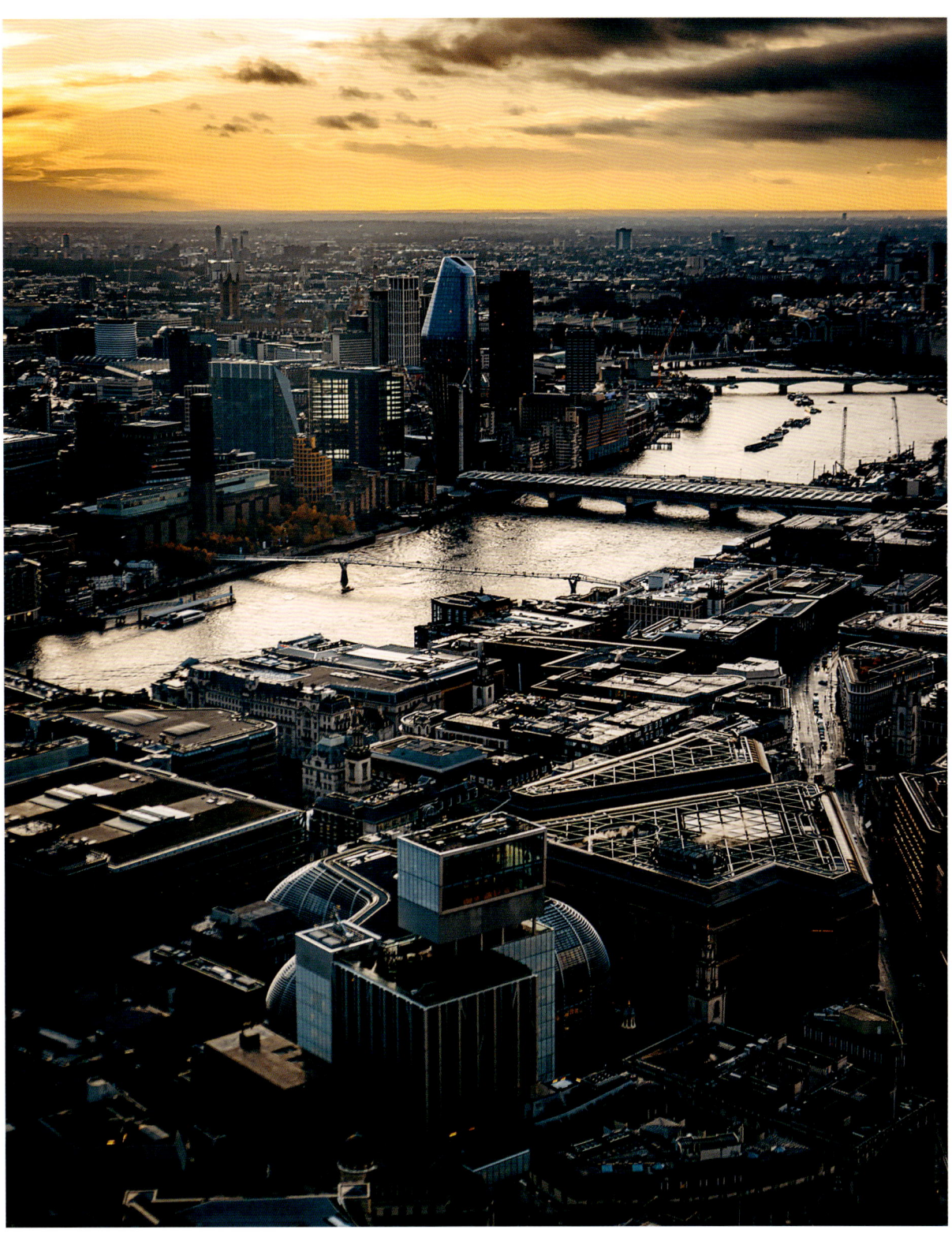

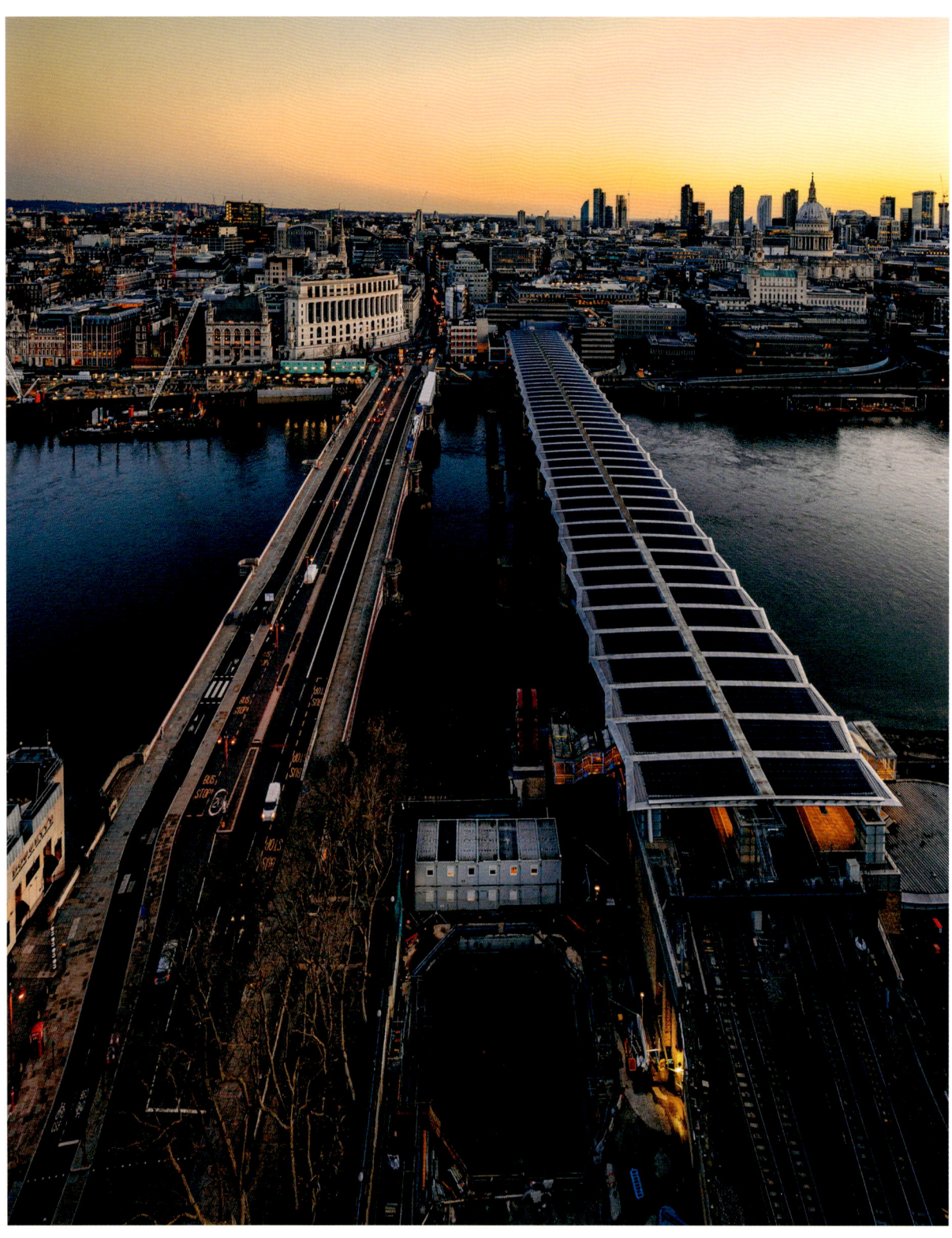

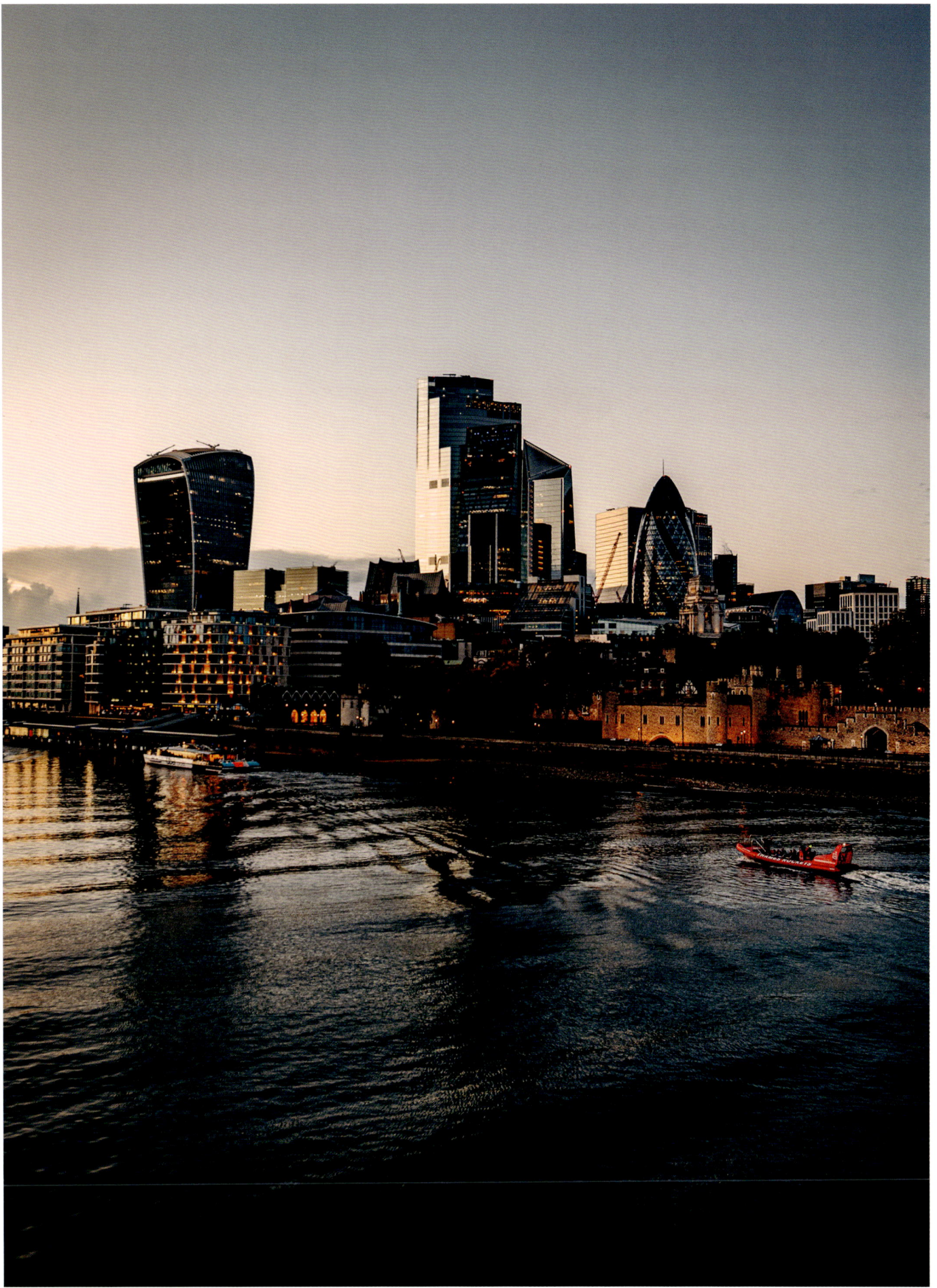

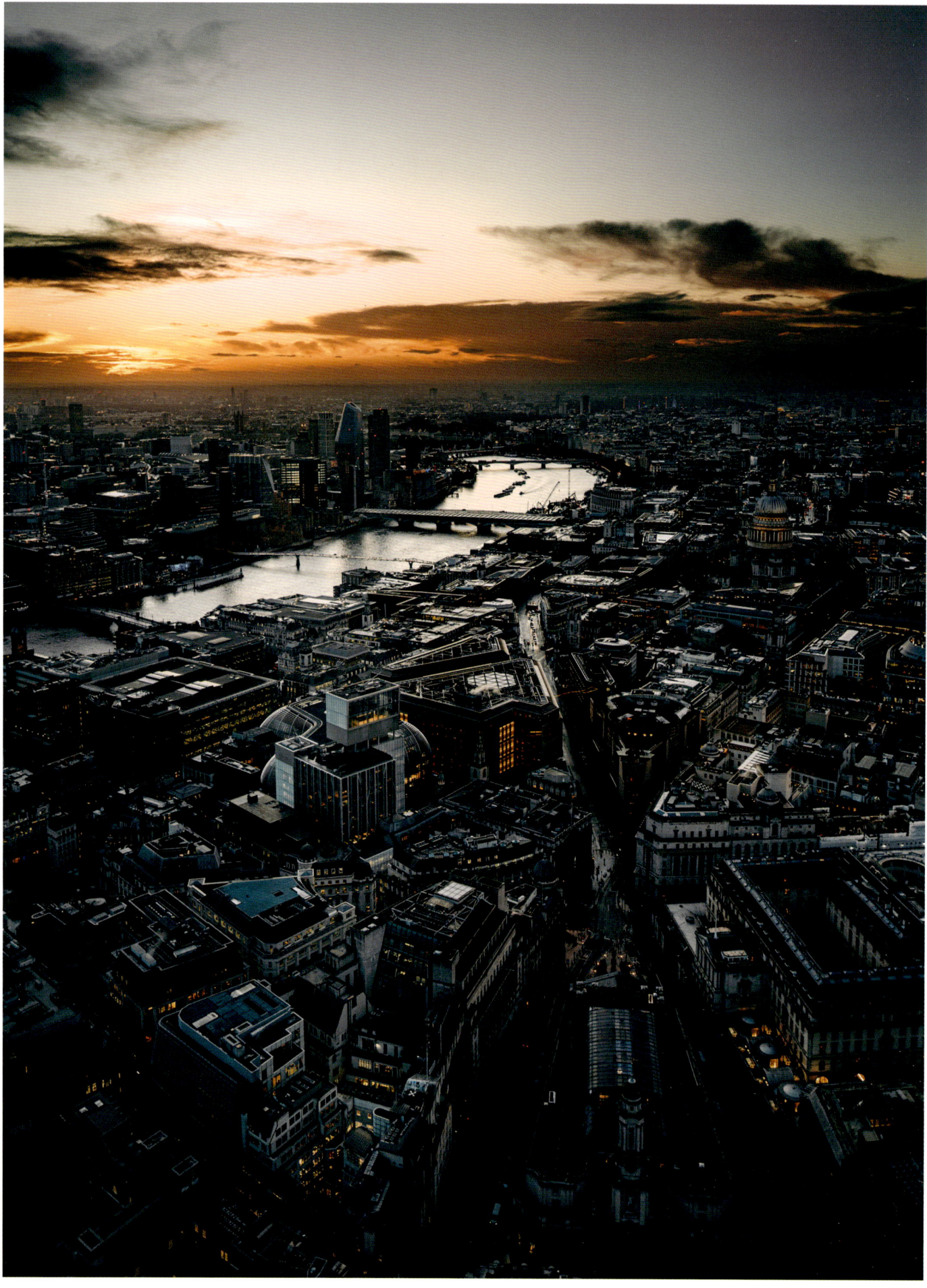

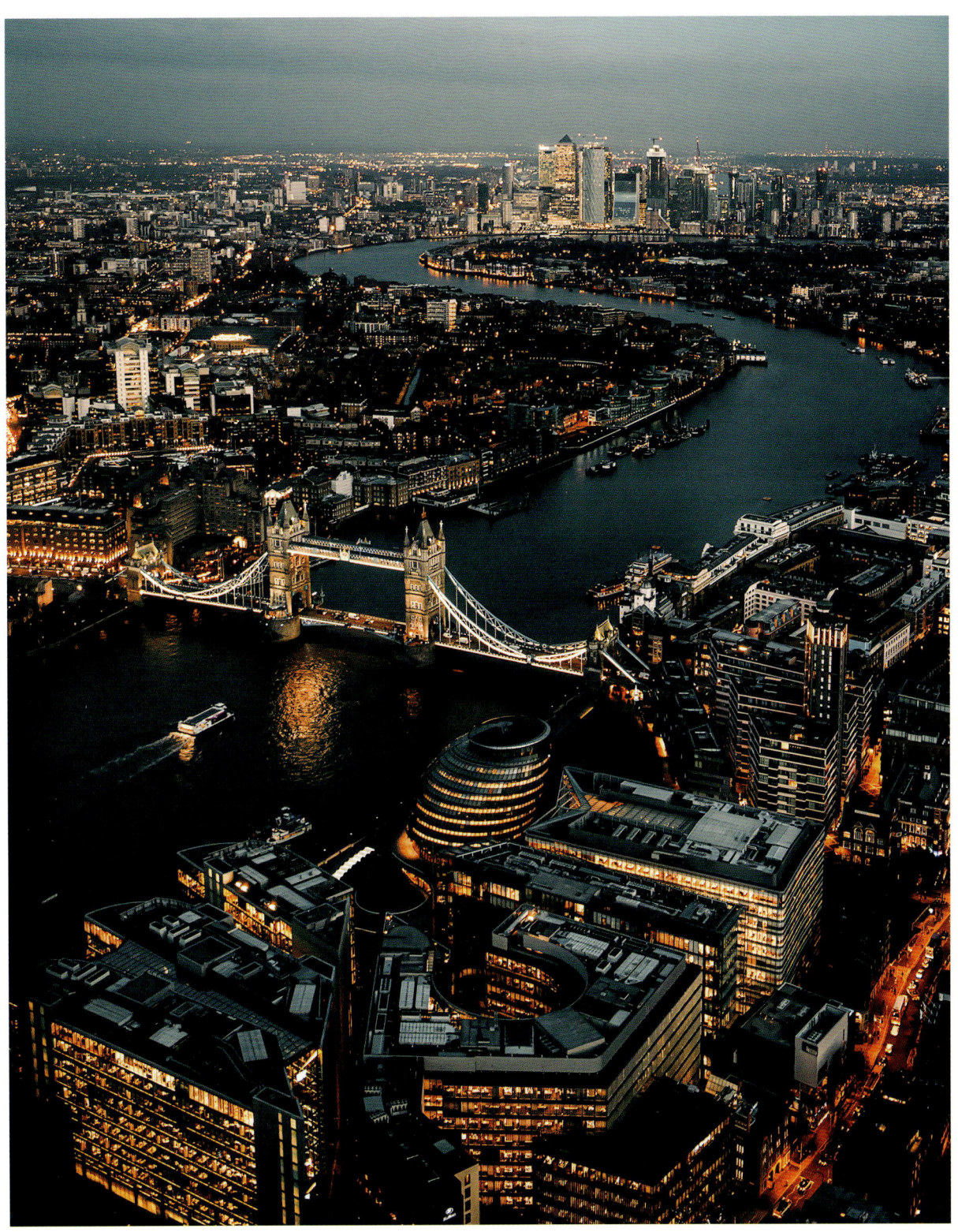

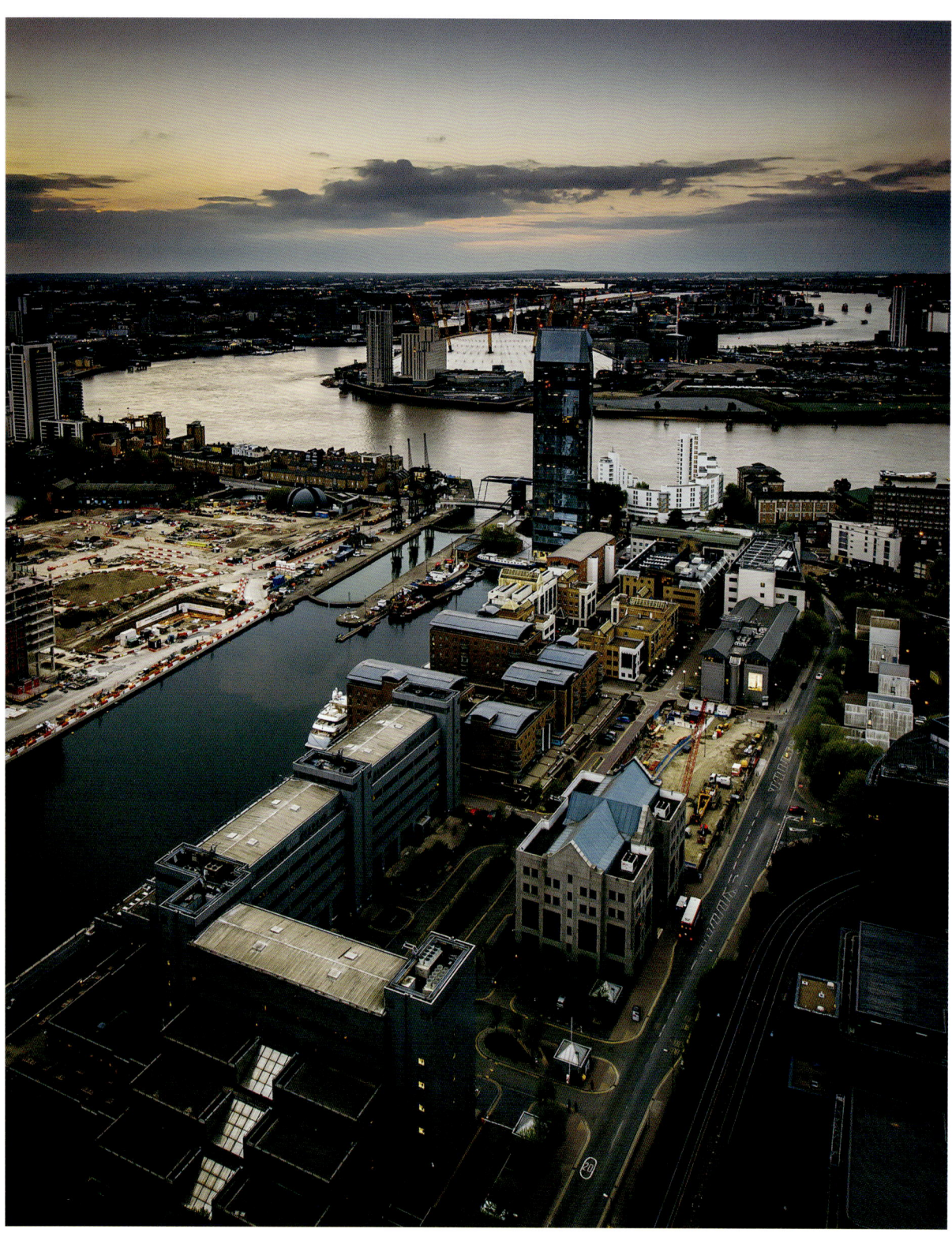

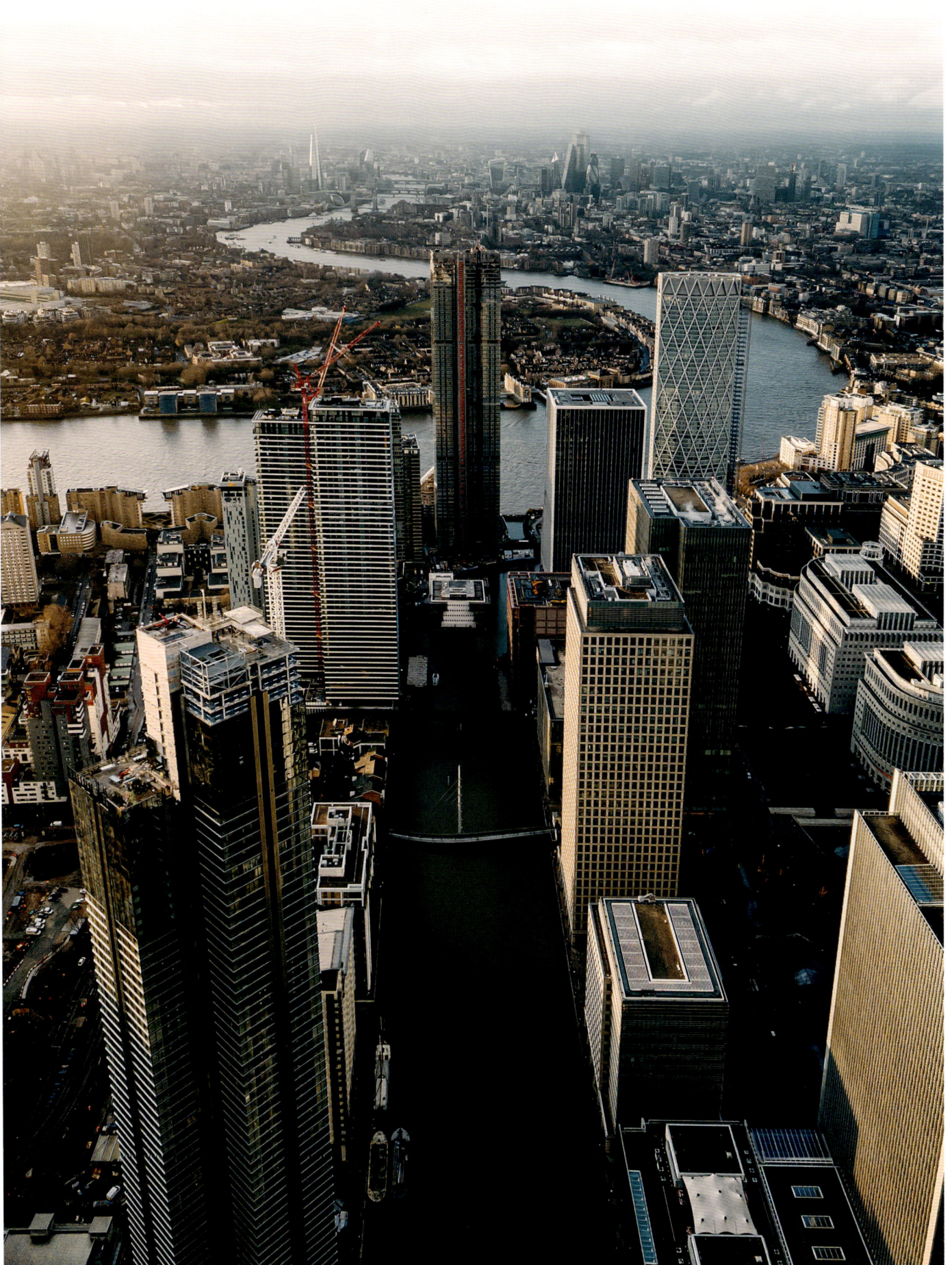

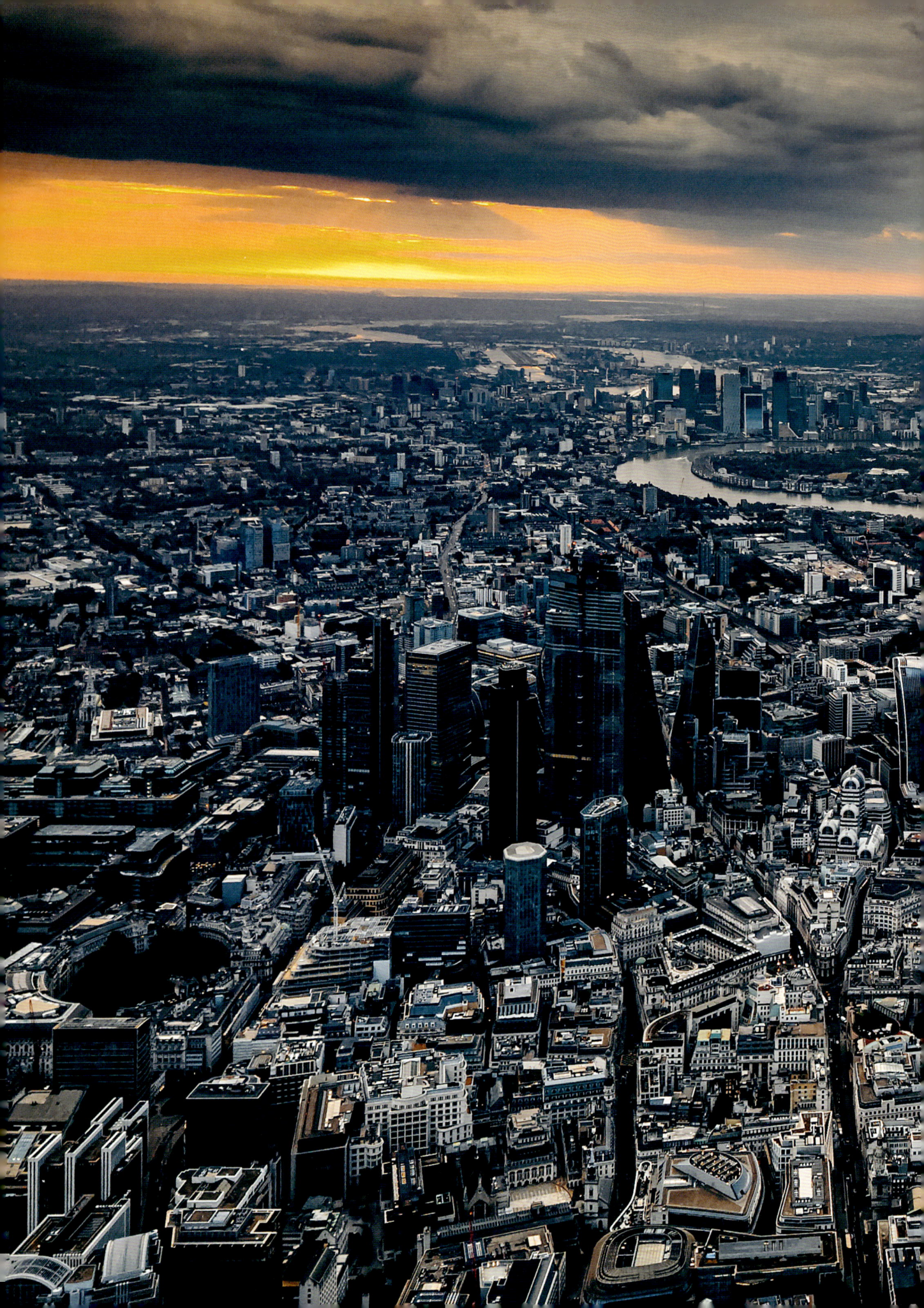

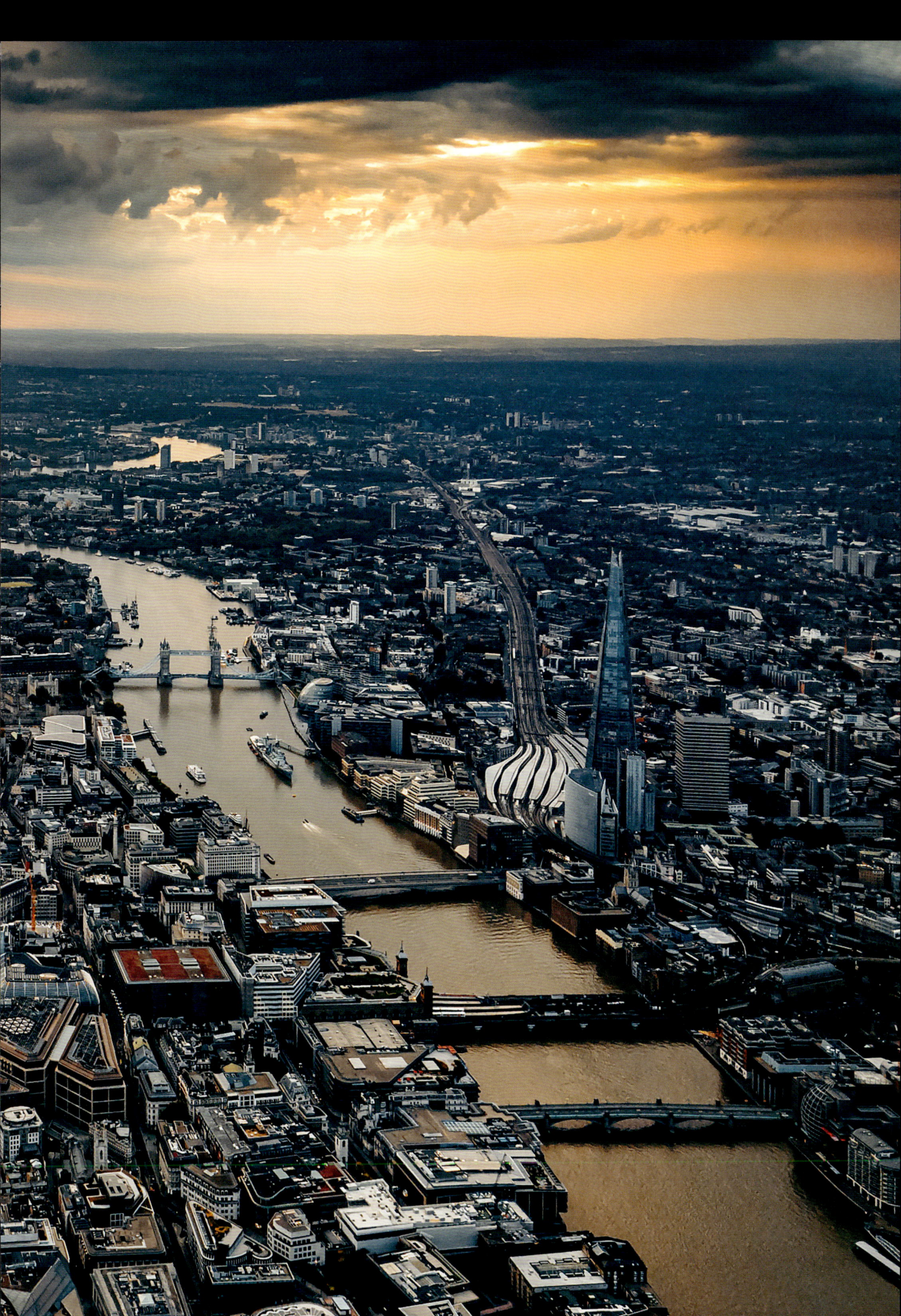

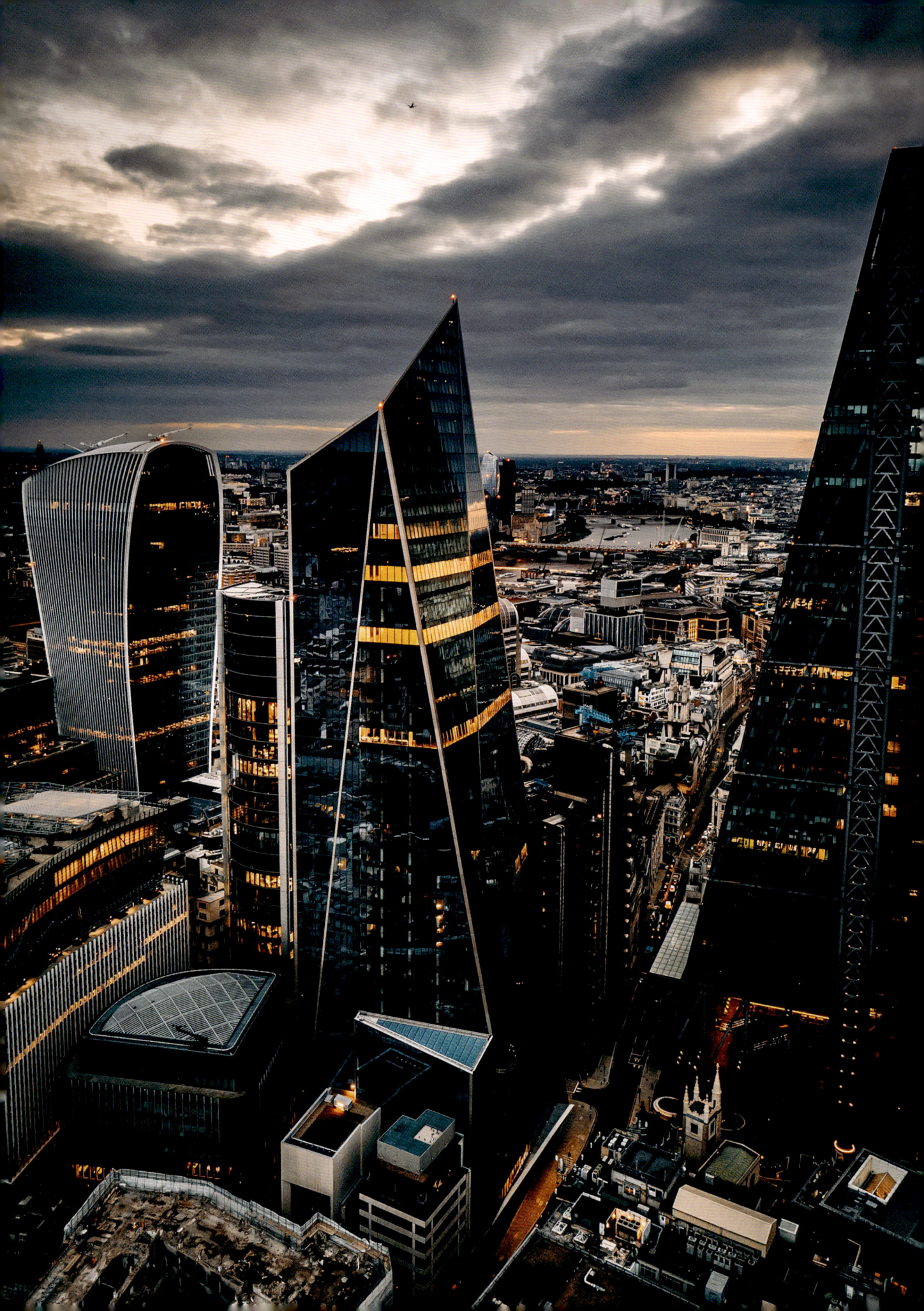

The Traditional Meets the Modern ♦ London is an amalgamation of history and progress. With centuries-old buildings standing next to modern architectural marvels, London's layout creates a rich and beautiful tension that demands acknowledgment of the city's past and respect for its incessant forward movement. ♦ With 21st-century skyscrapers rising up around it, St Paul's Cathedral stands as a symbol of London's resilience and renewal. Built on the highest point in the City—the original heart of London and today's bustling financial district—the present cathedral is at least the fourth of its name to stand in that very spot. The first two were destroyed by the elements, and the third was destroyed by the Great Fire of London in 1666. Architect Sir Christopher Wren set to work soon after, building the now iconic English Baroque masterpiece with its triumphant 365-foot dome. ♦ Standing 41 stories tall at 30 St Mary Axe, the Gherkin is one of the most instantly recognizable towers in the London skyline and, quite possibly, the world. Designed by architect Norman Foster and completed in 2003, the iconic building architecturally, technically, socially and spatially defies the norm. Its curvaceous form is a response to the constraints of the site, widening in profile as it rises from the ground and then tapering to its peak —maximizing square footage while appearing more slender than a rectangular tower of equal size. ♦ A 95-story glass pyramid that disappears into the sky, The Shard was a polarizing addition to the London skyline in 2012. Designed by master Italian architect Renzo Piano, who historically viewed high rises as "arrogant and aggressive," The Shard was intentionally built to be different—light, airy, and elegant. 11,000 extra white glass panels line the exterior, creating a façade that changes with the weather and the seasons. Conceived as a "vertical city," The Shard was built to reflect the skyline, not disturb it. The building's tall, tapered structure allows for epic photography. Floors 68, 69, and 72 hold the highest viewing areas in all of the UK, boasting 360-degree sights and 40 miles of visibility on a clear day.

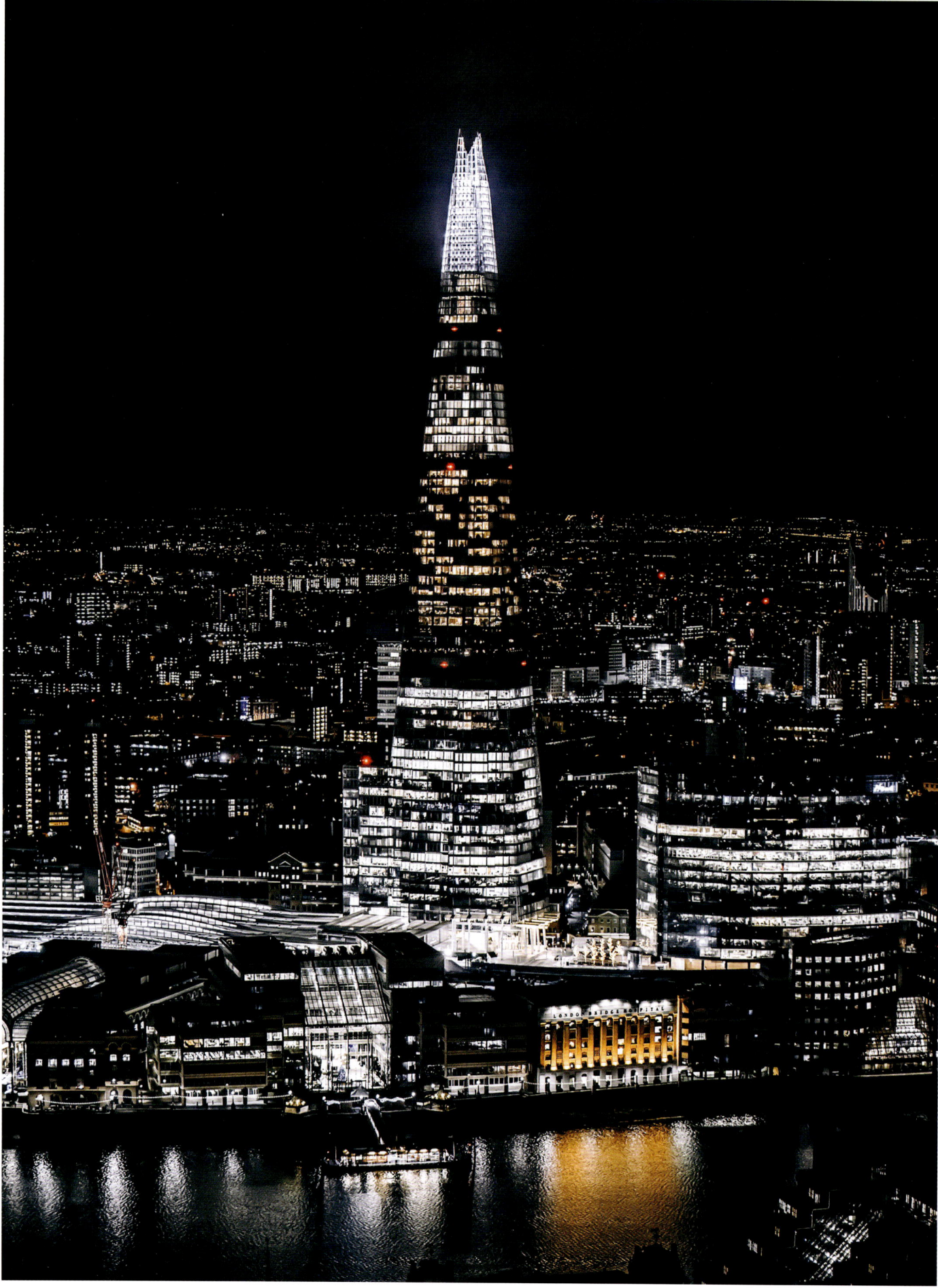

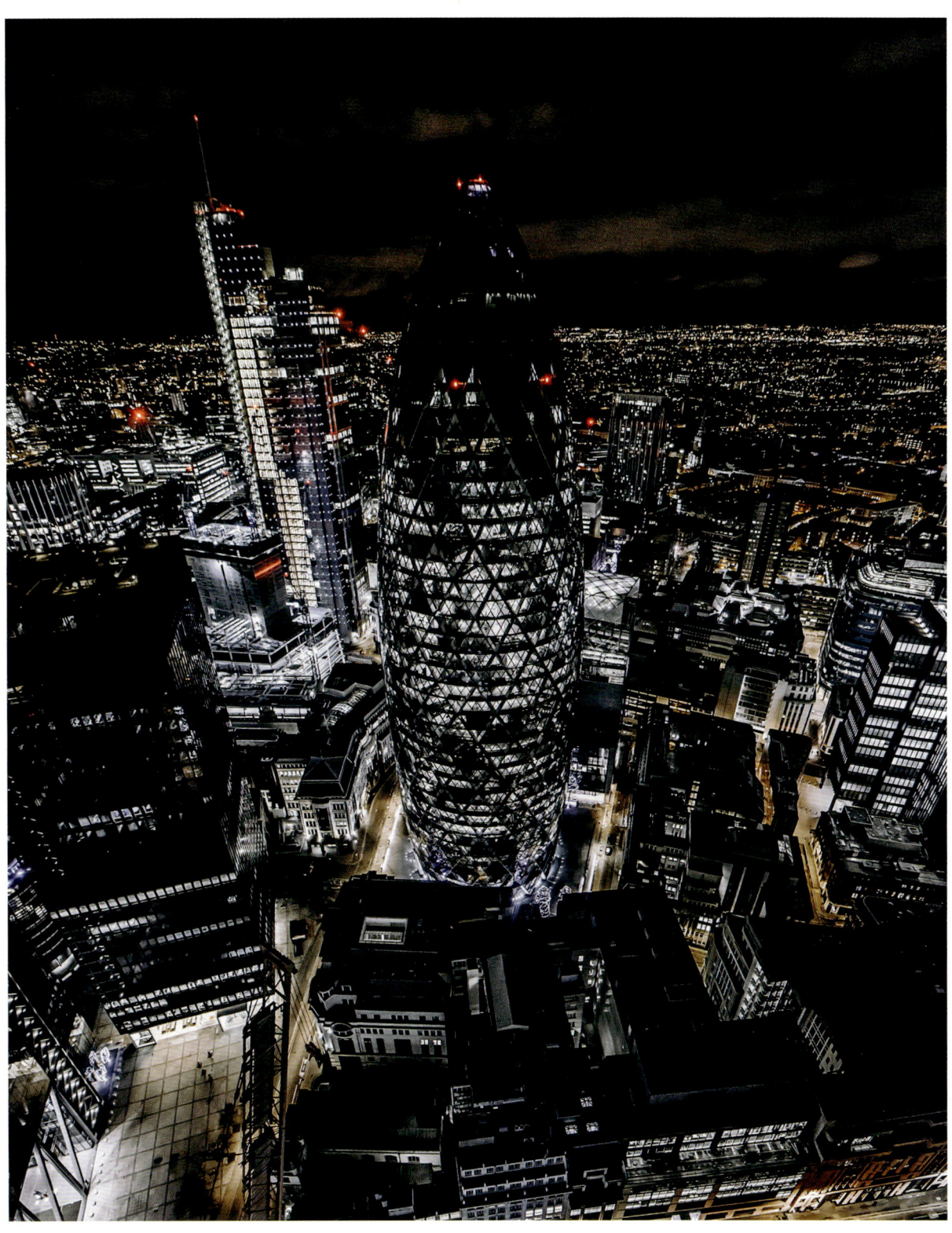

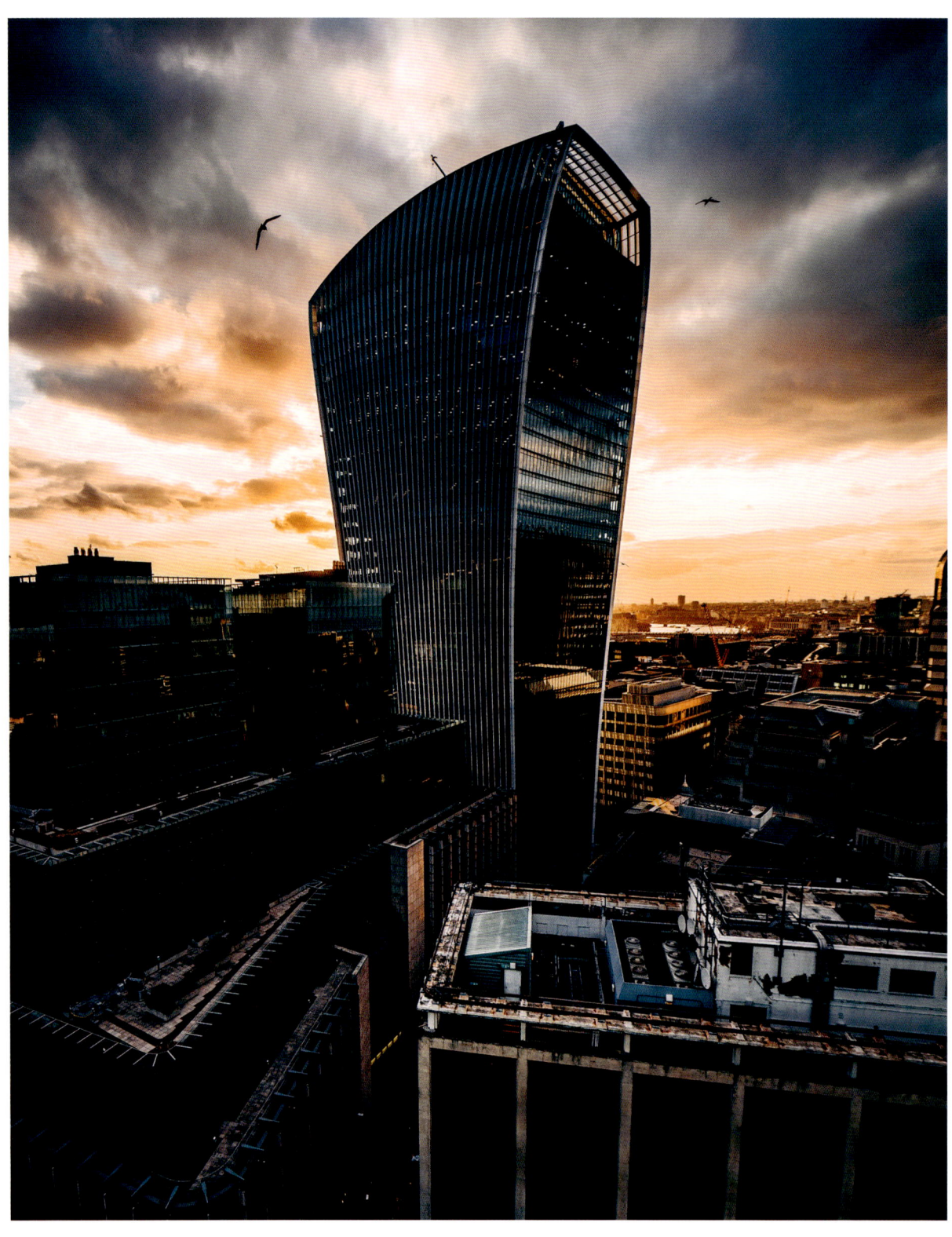

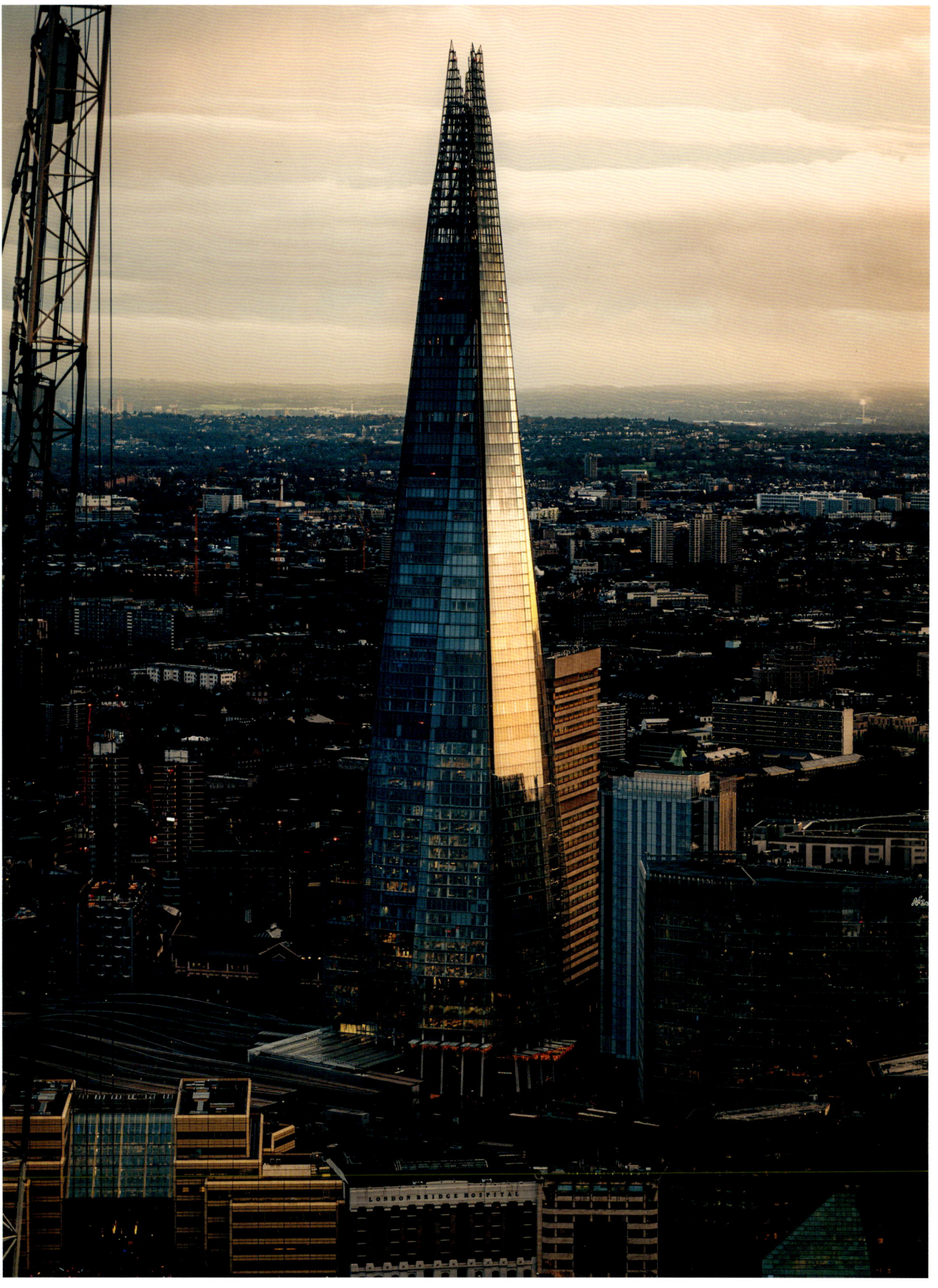

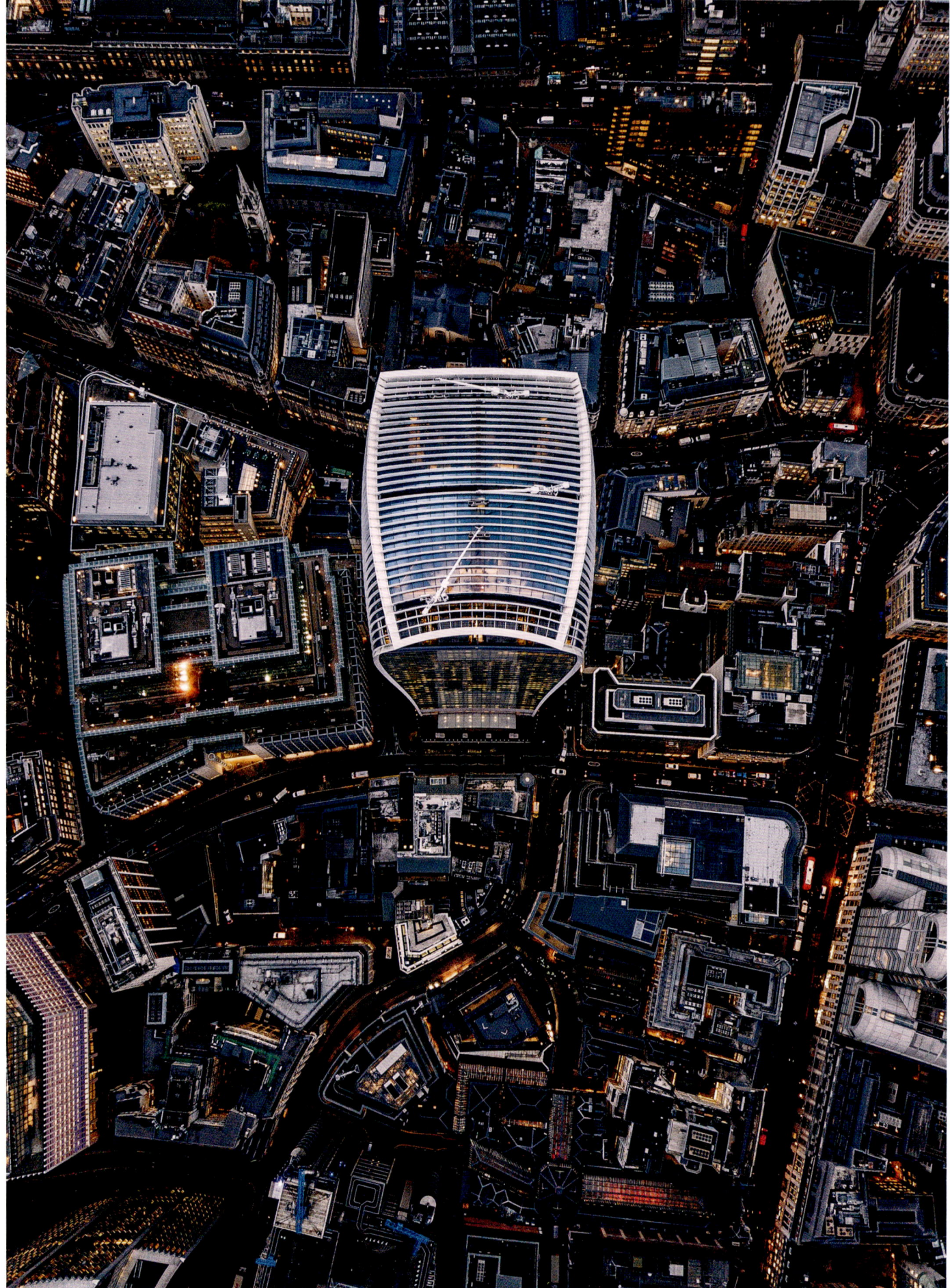

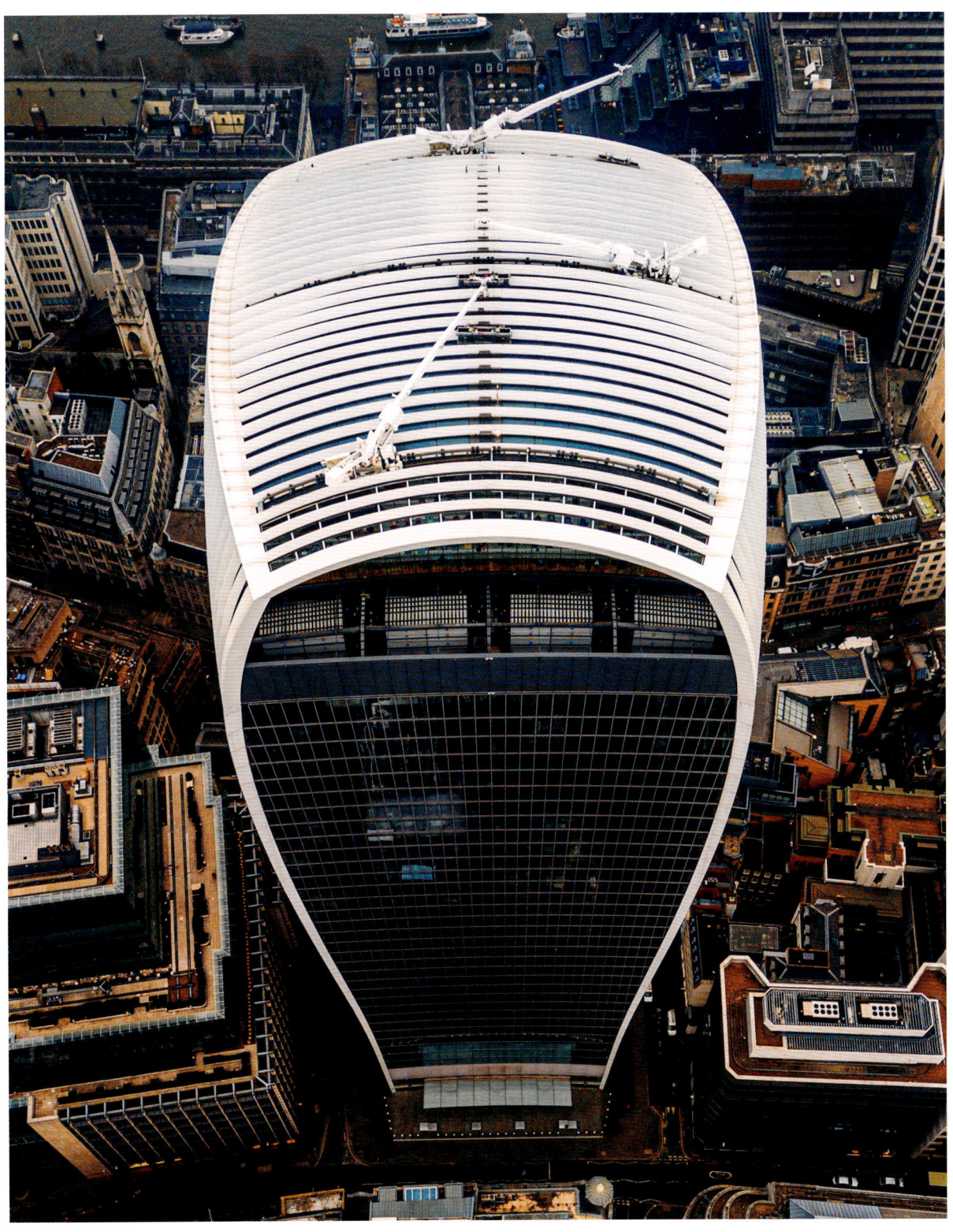

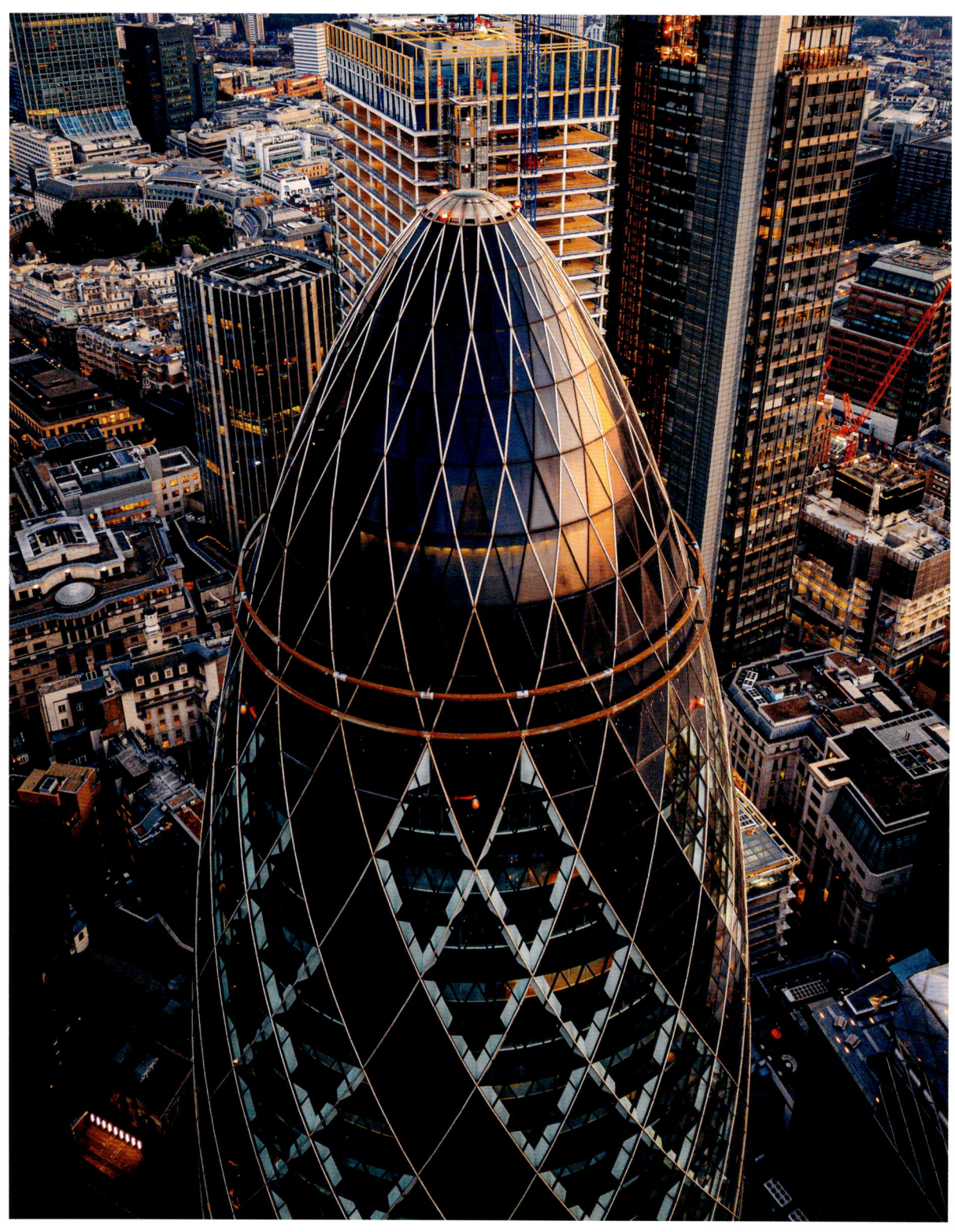

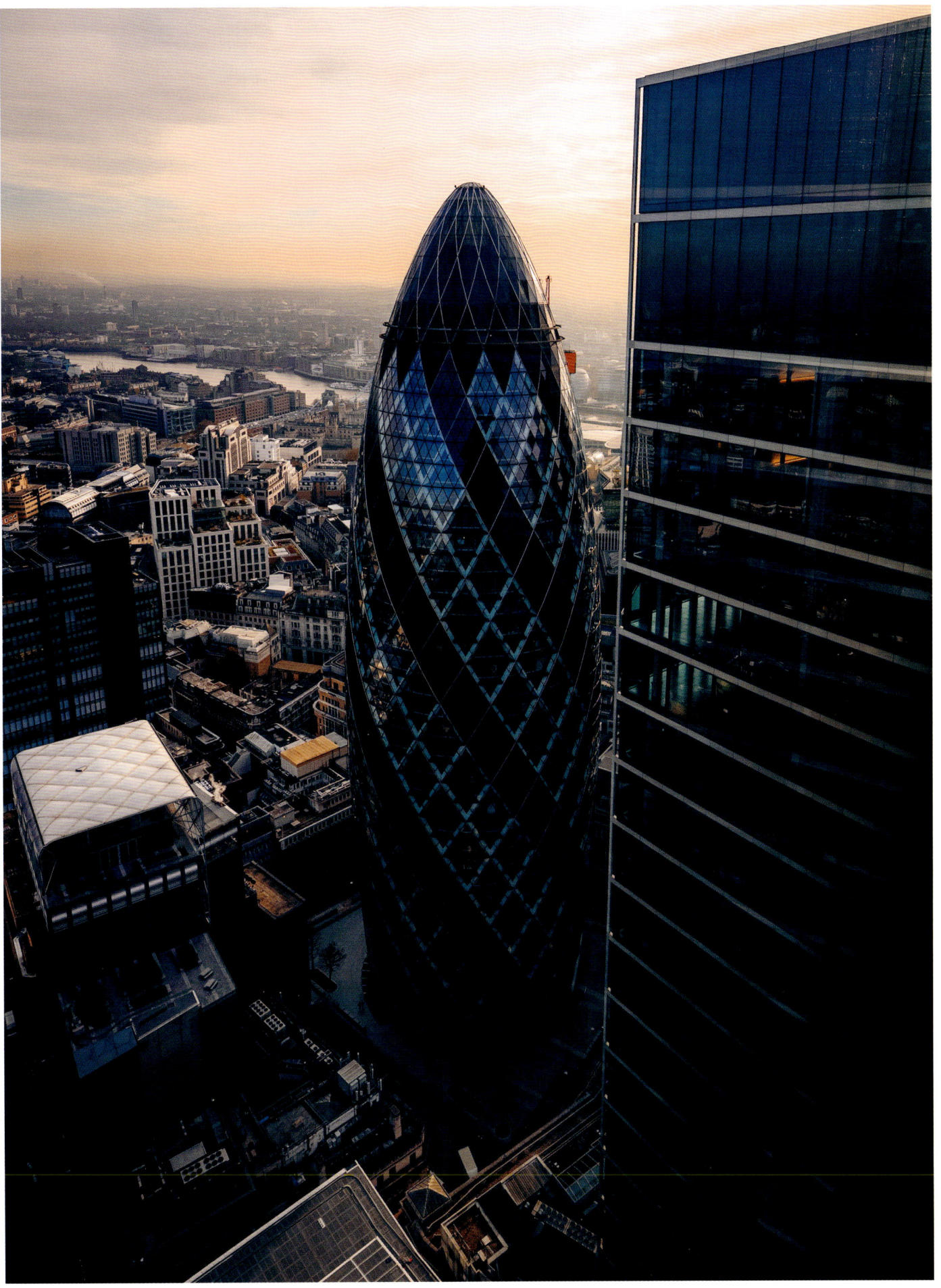

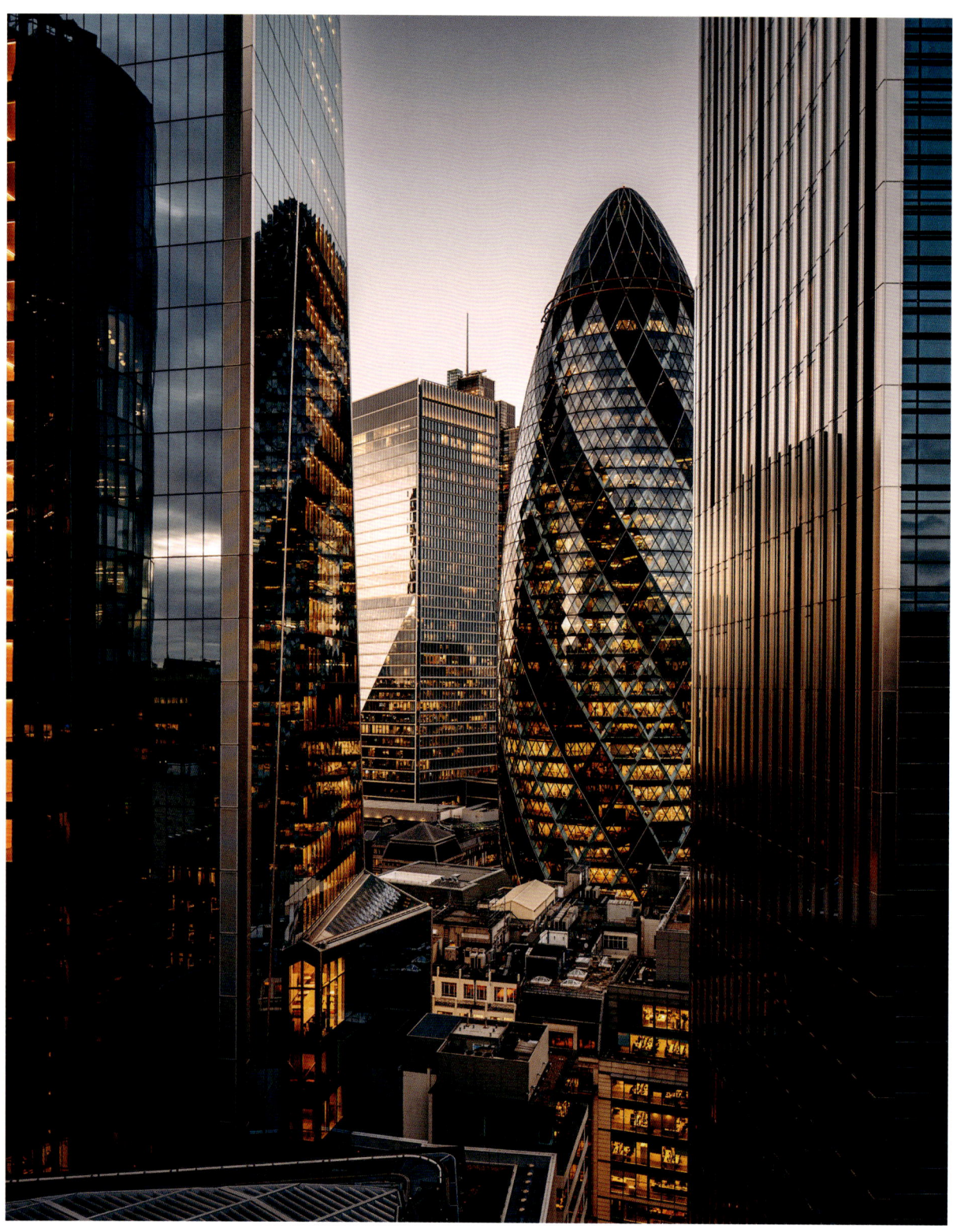

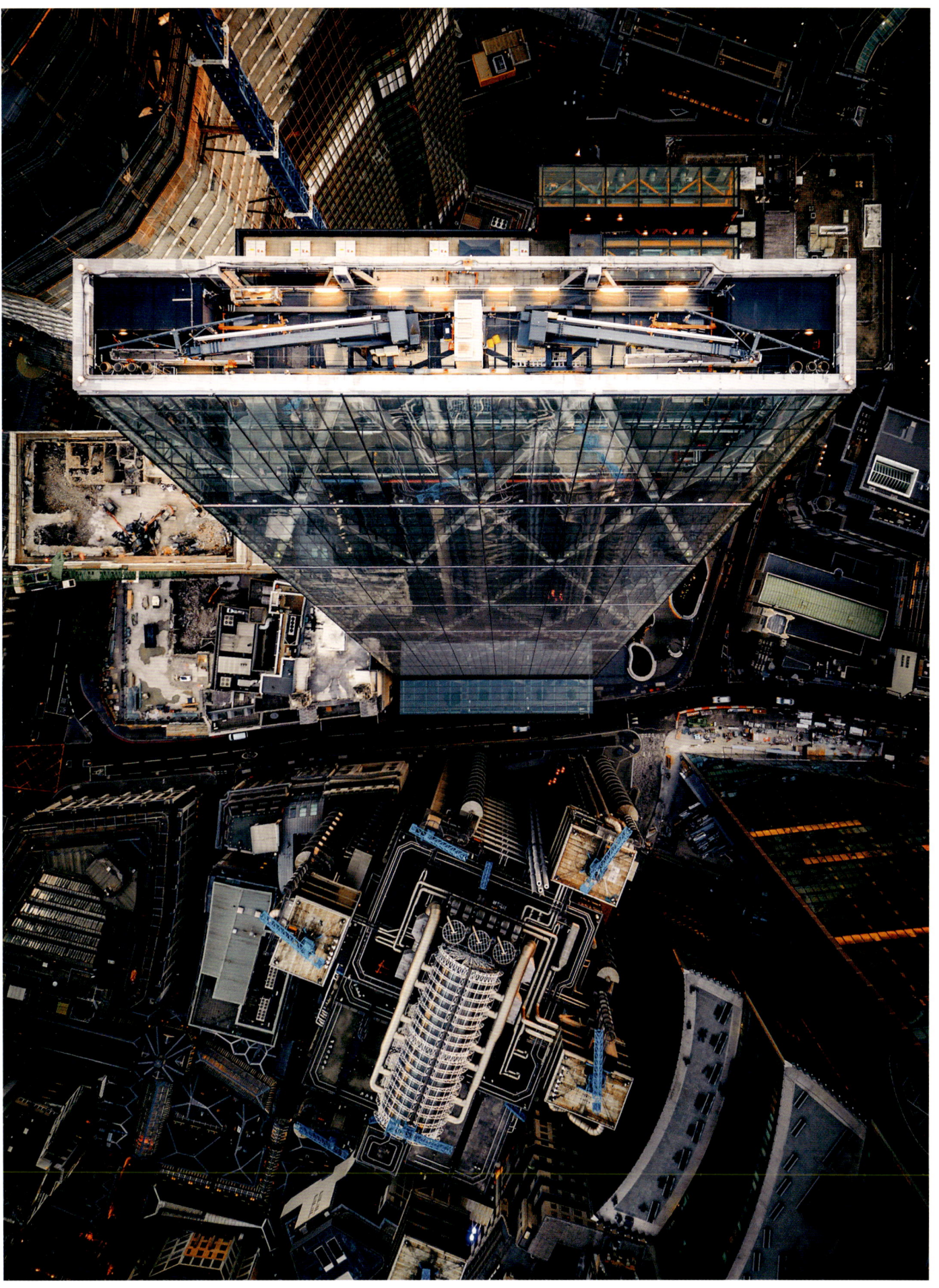

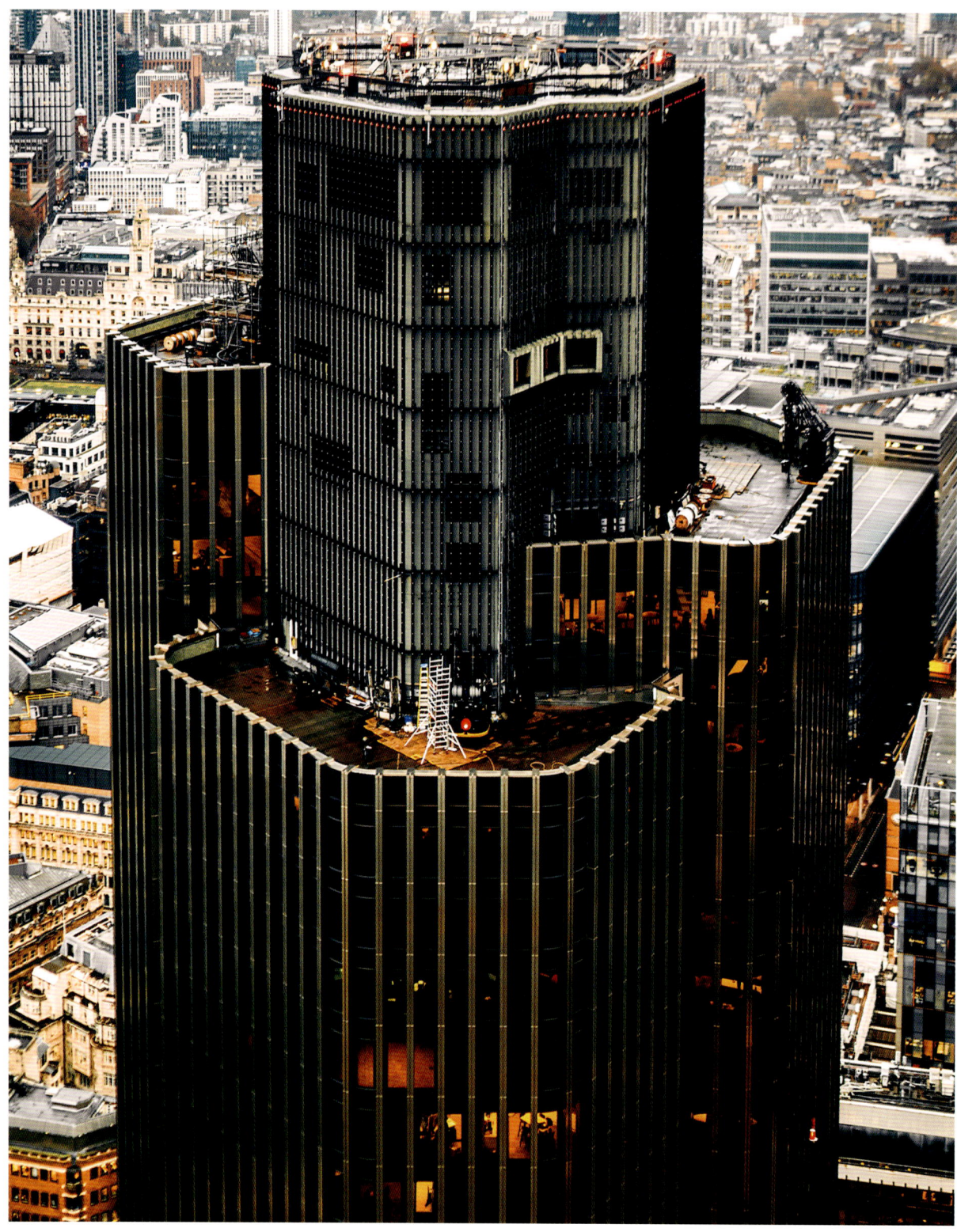

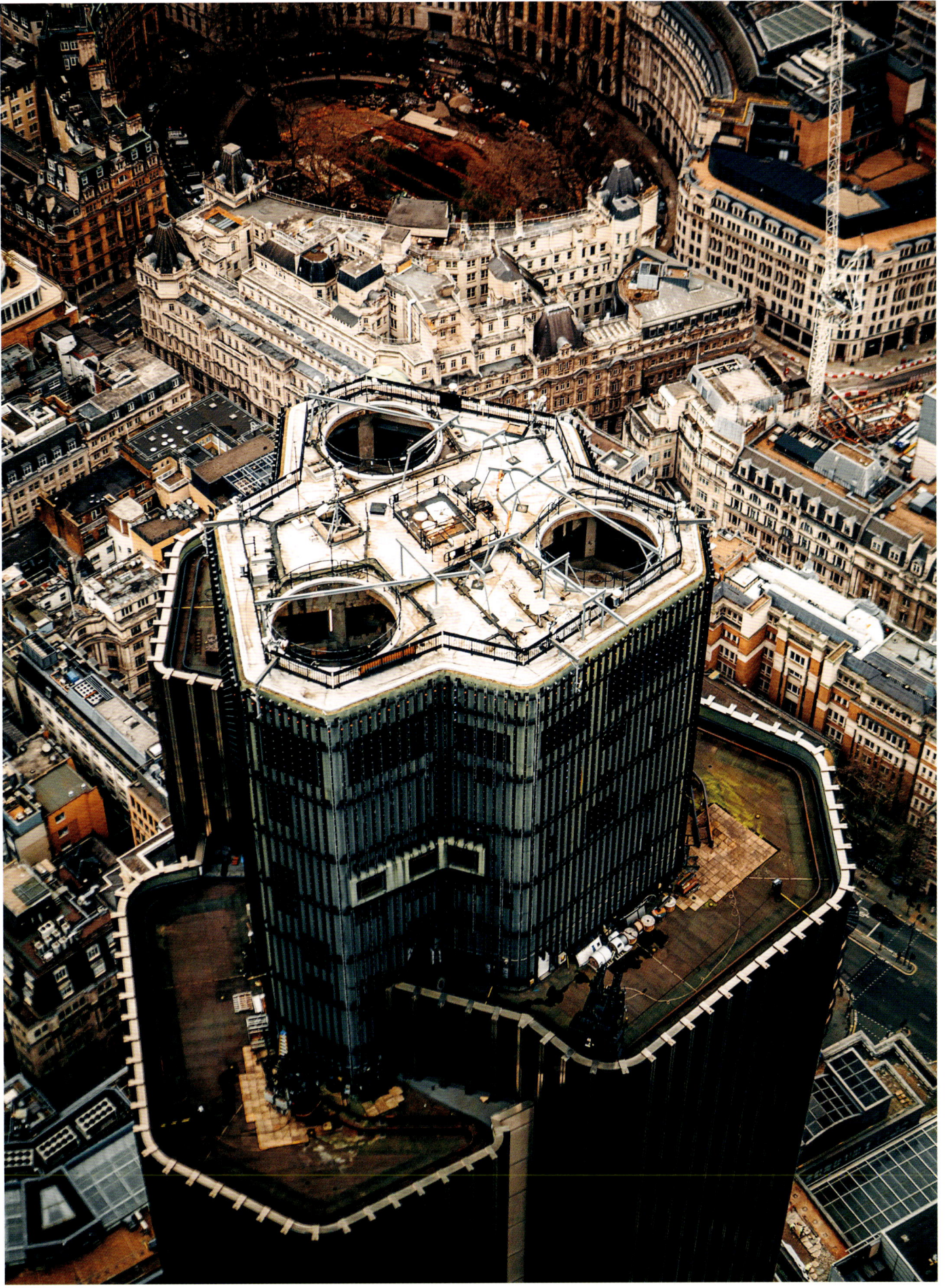

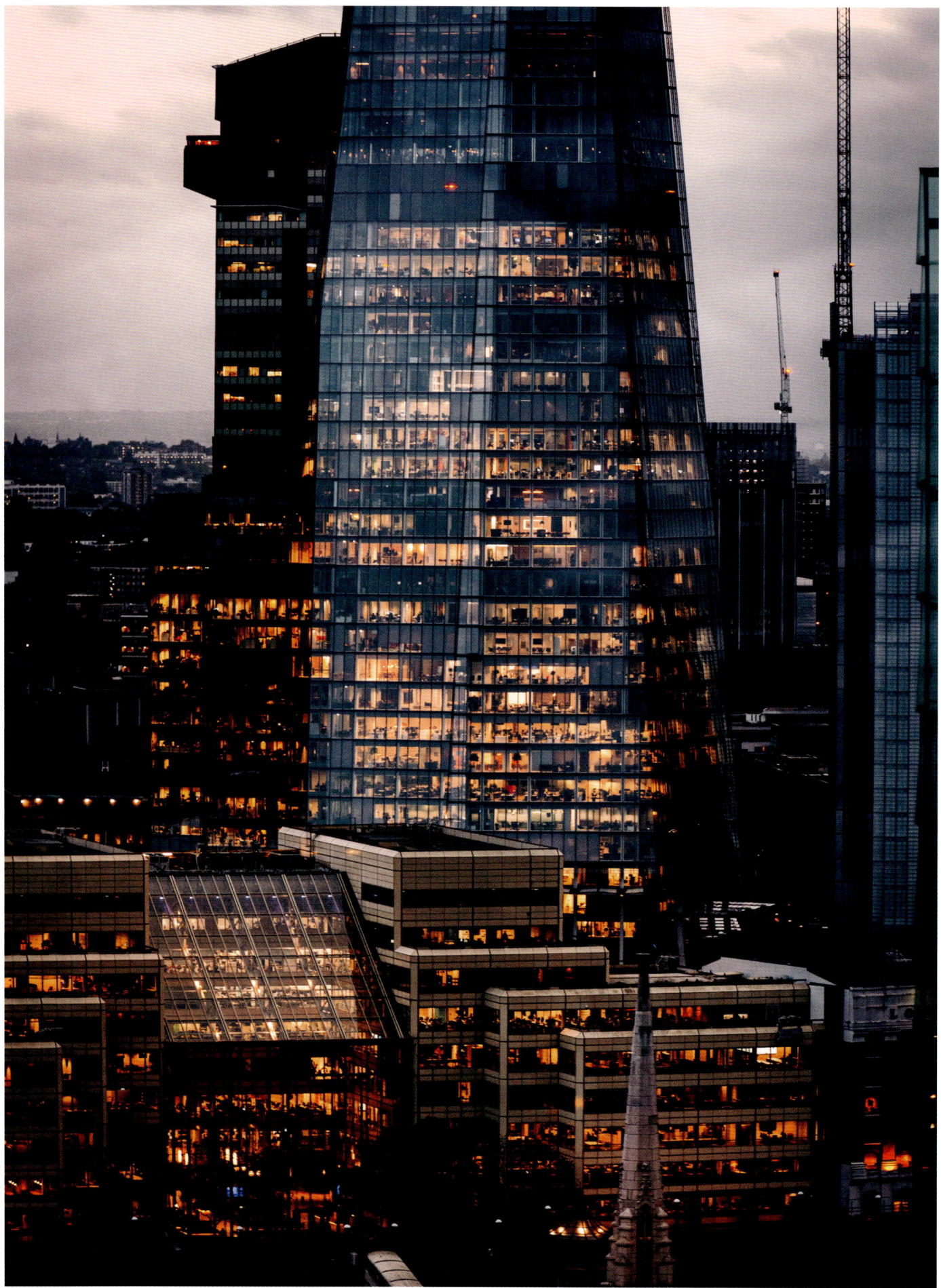

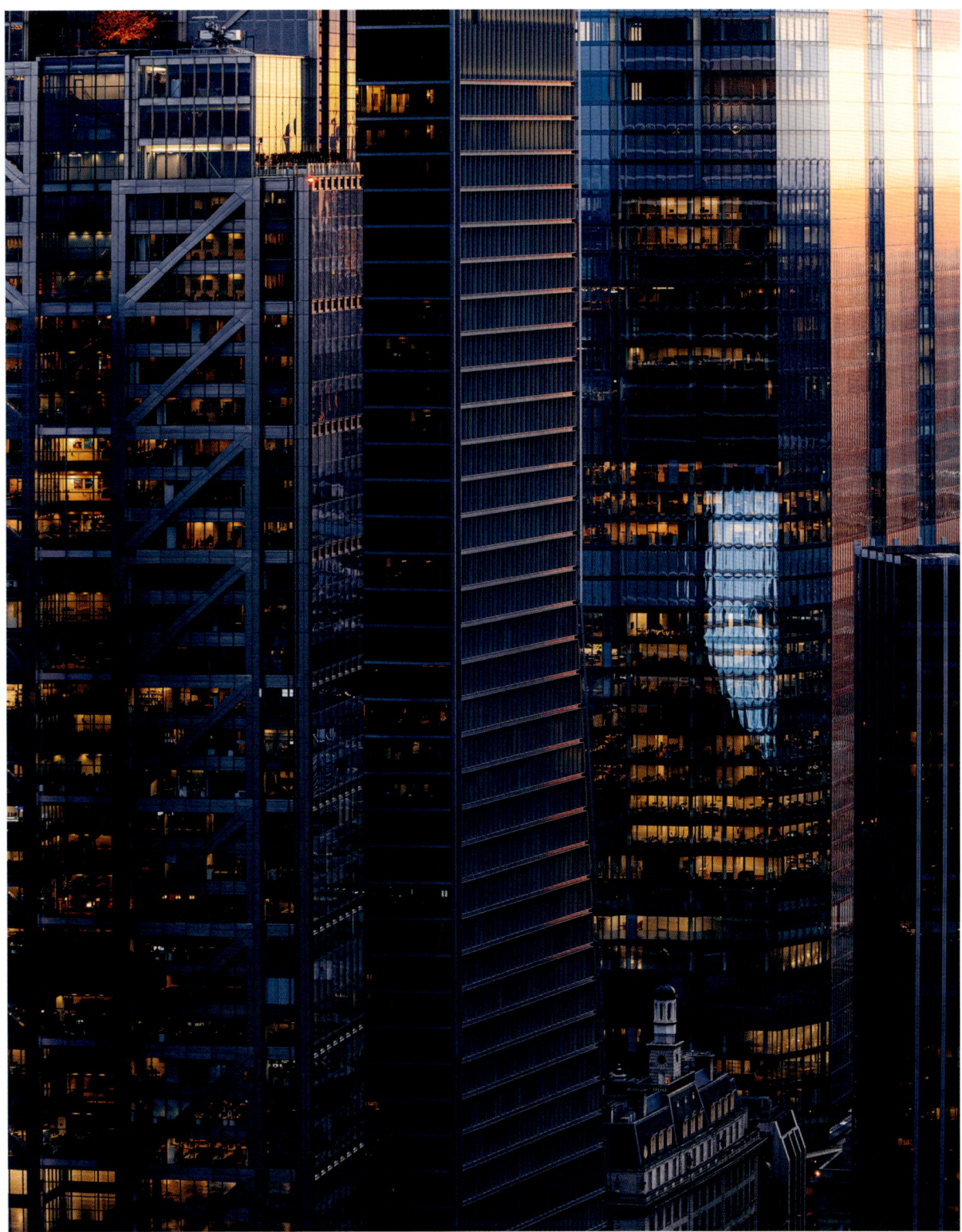

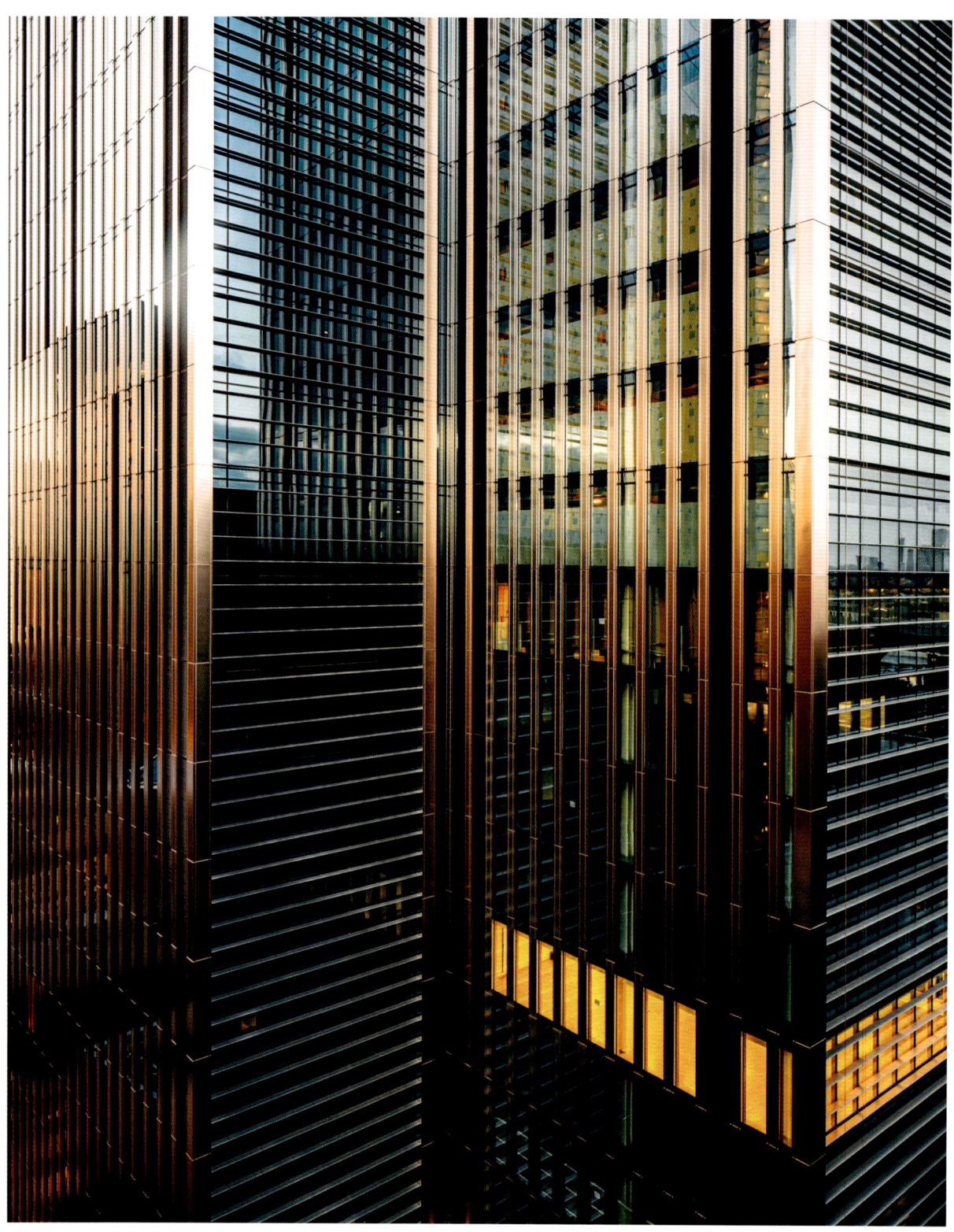

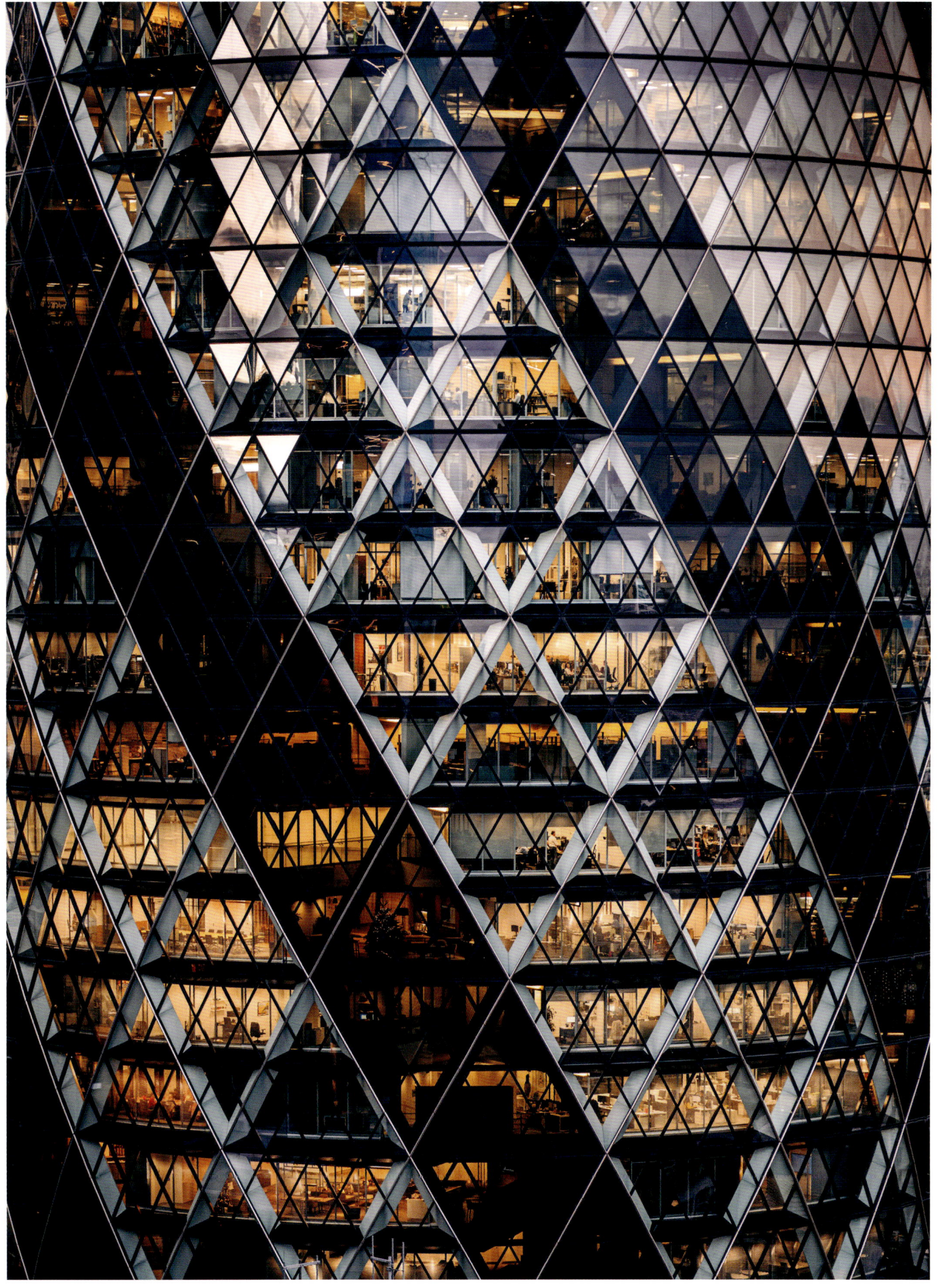

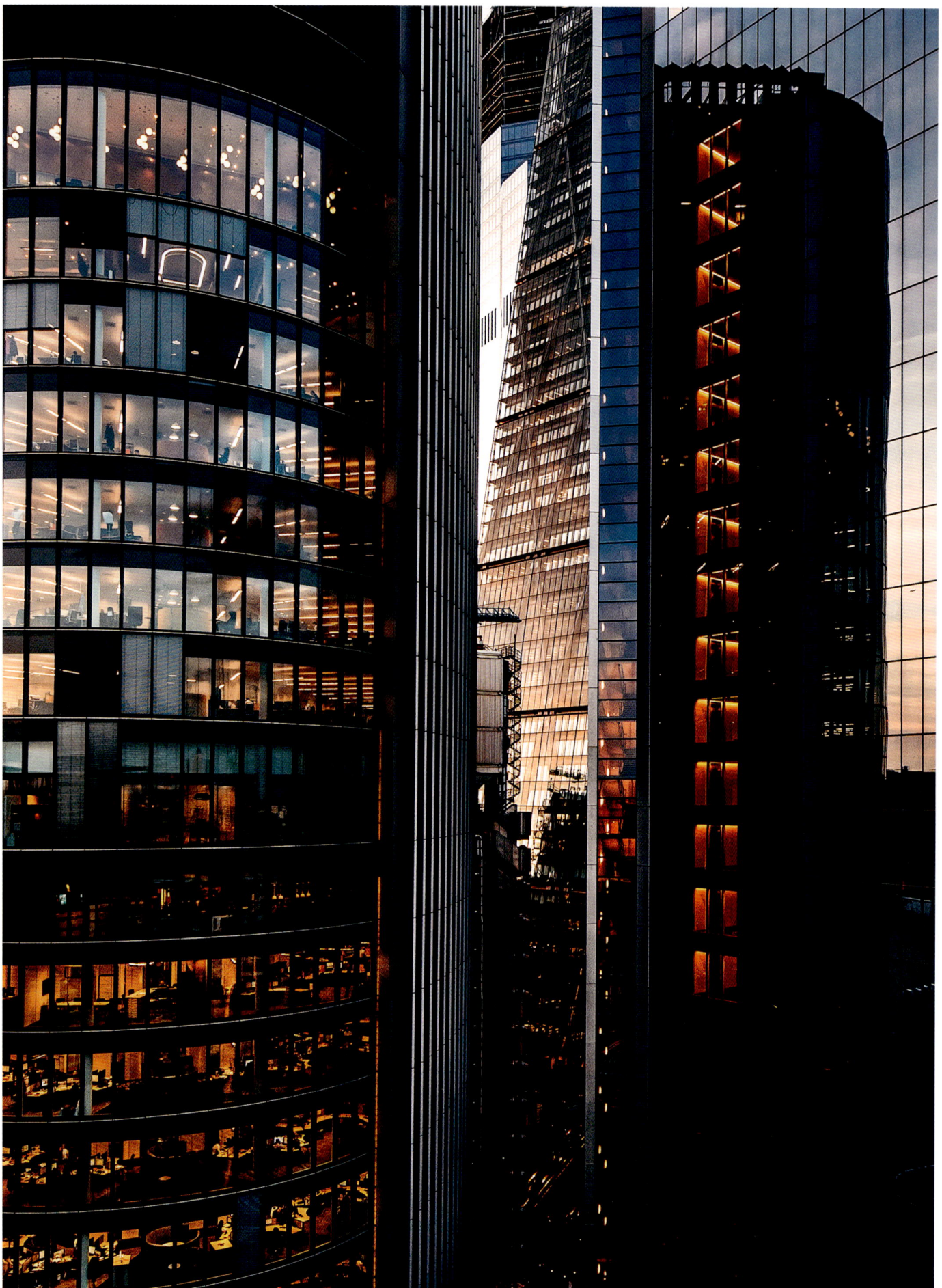

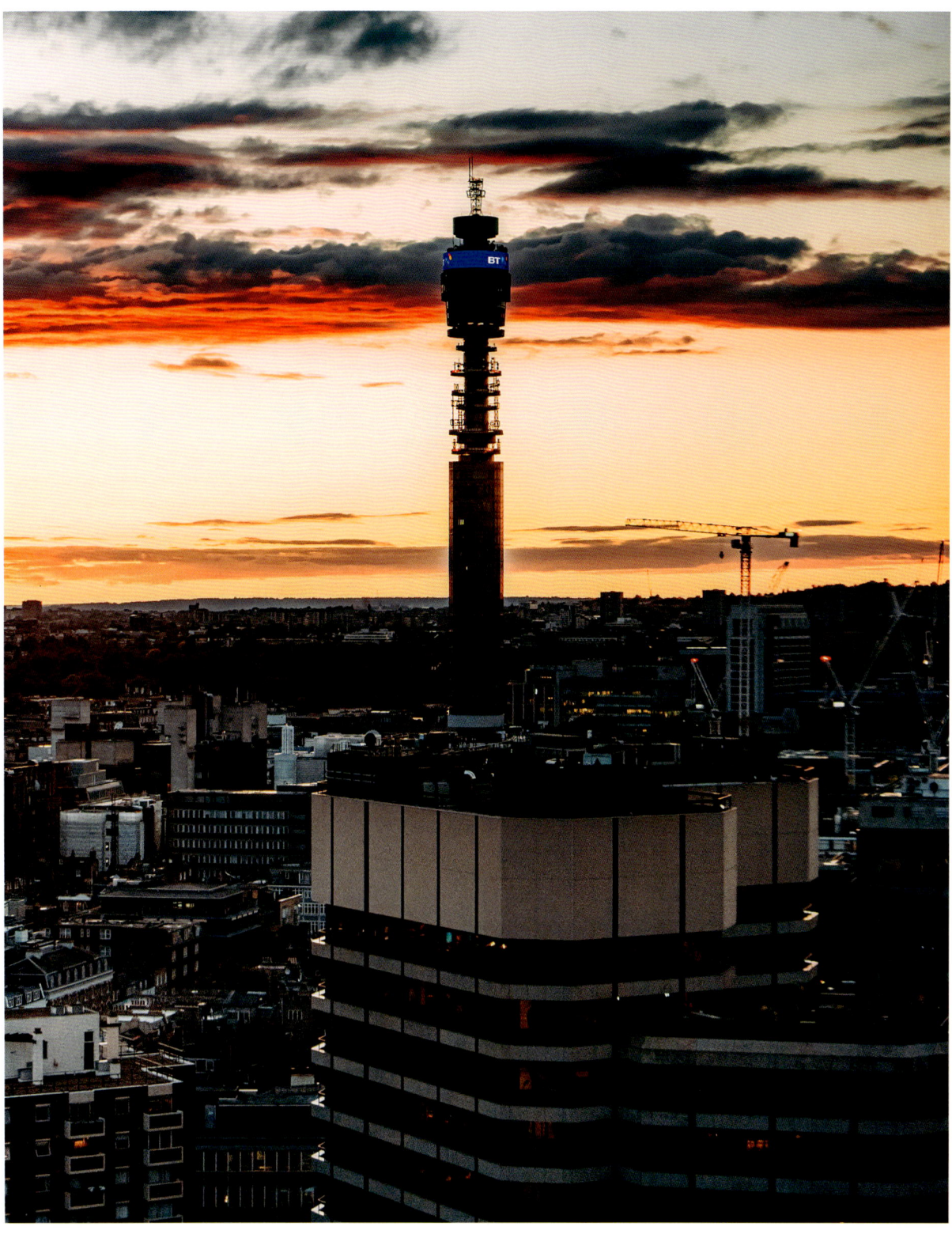

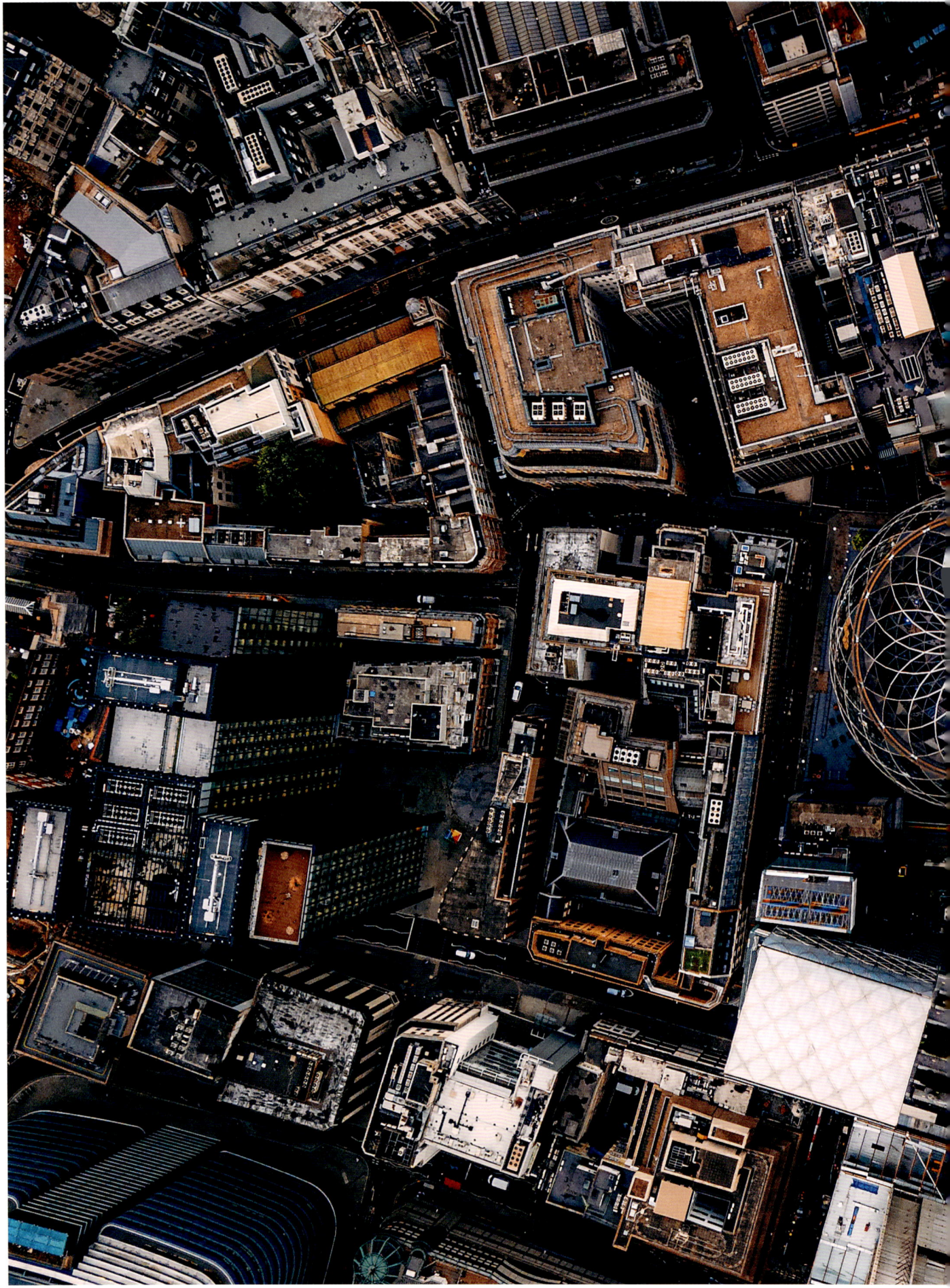

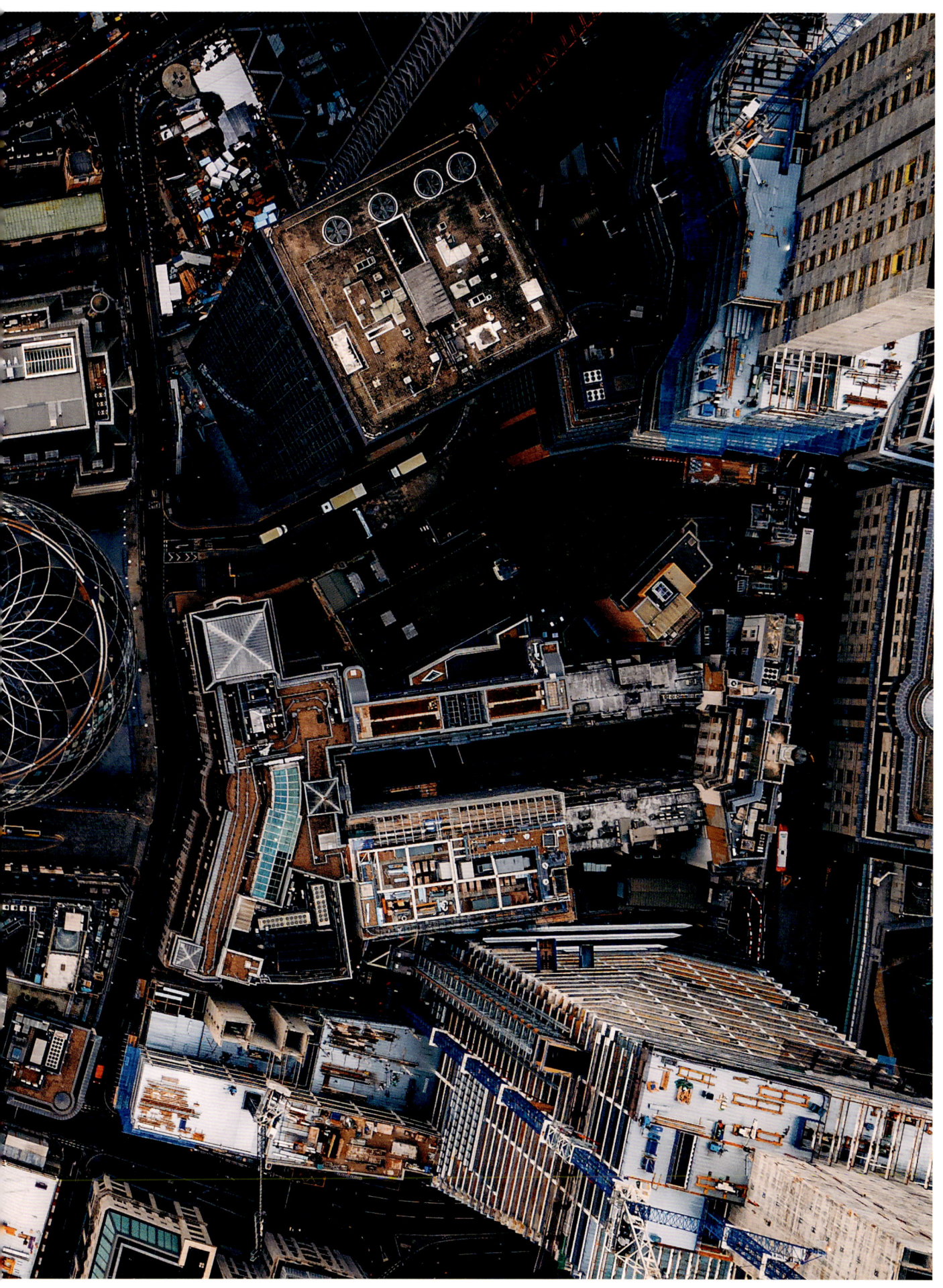

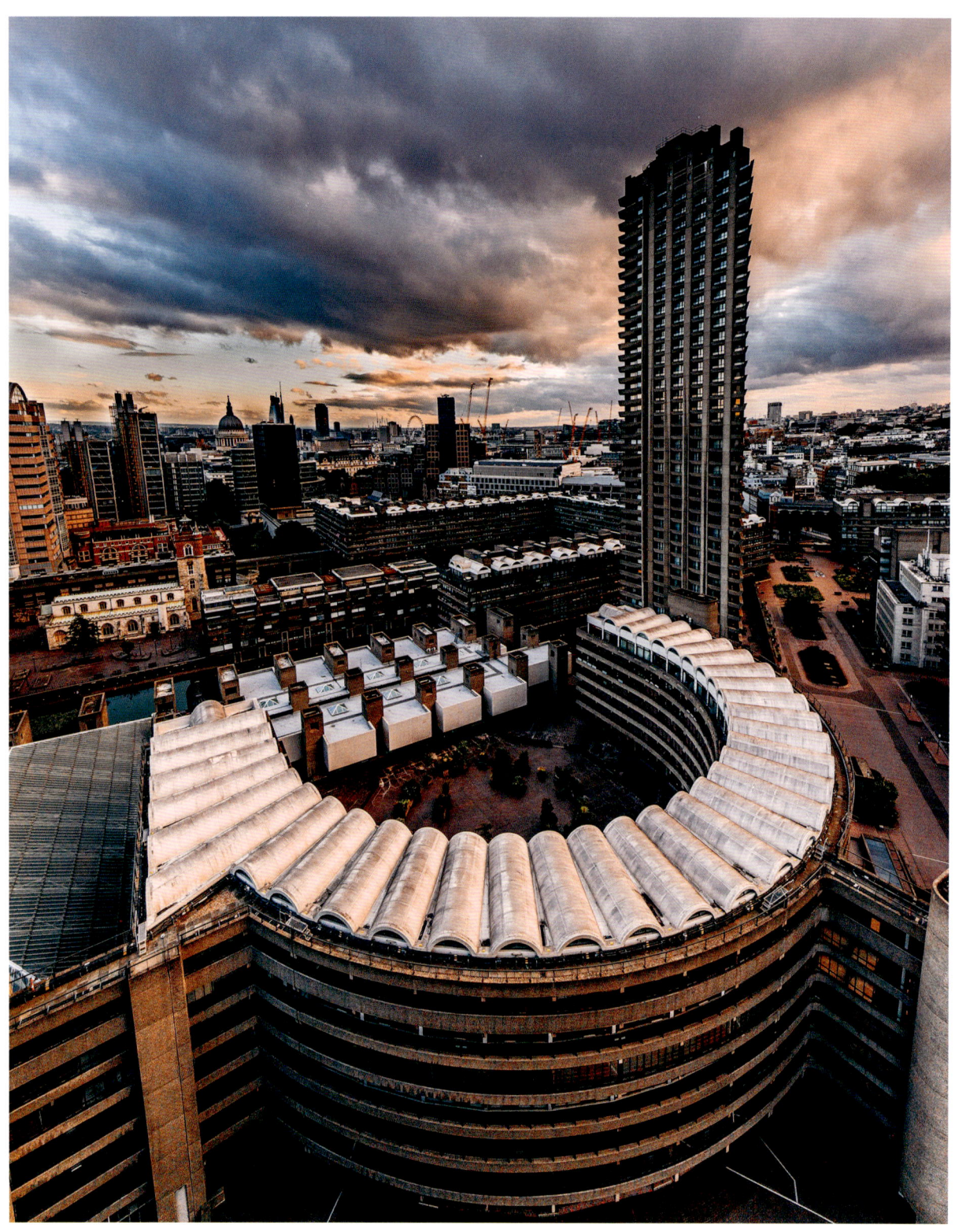

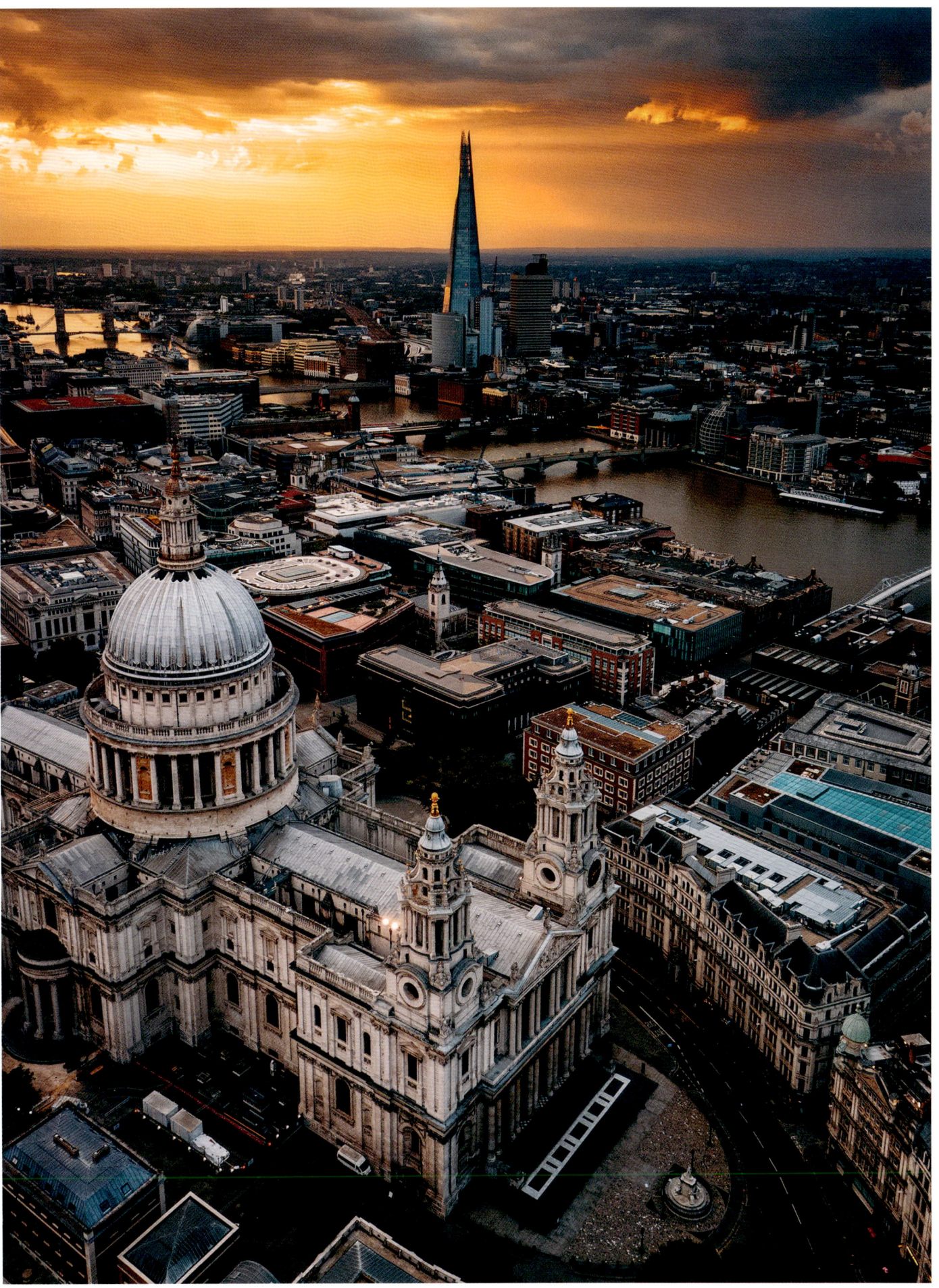

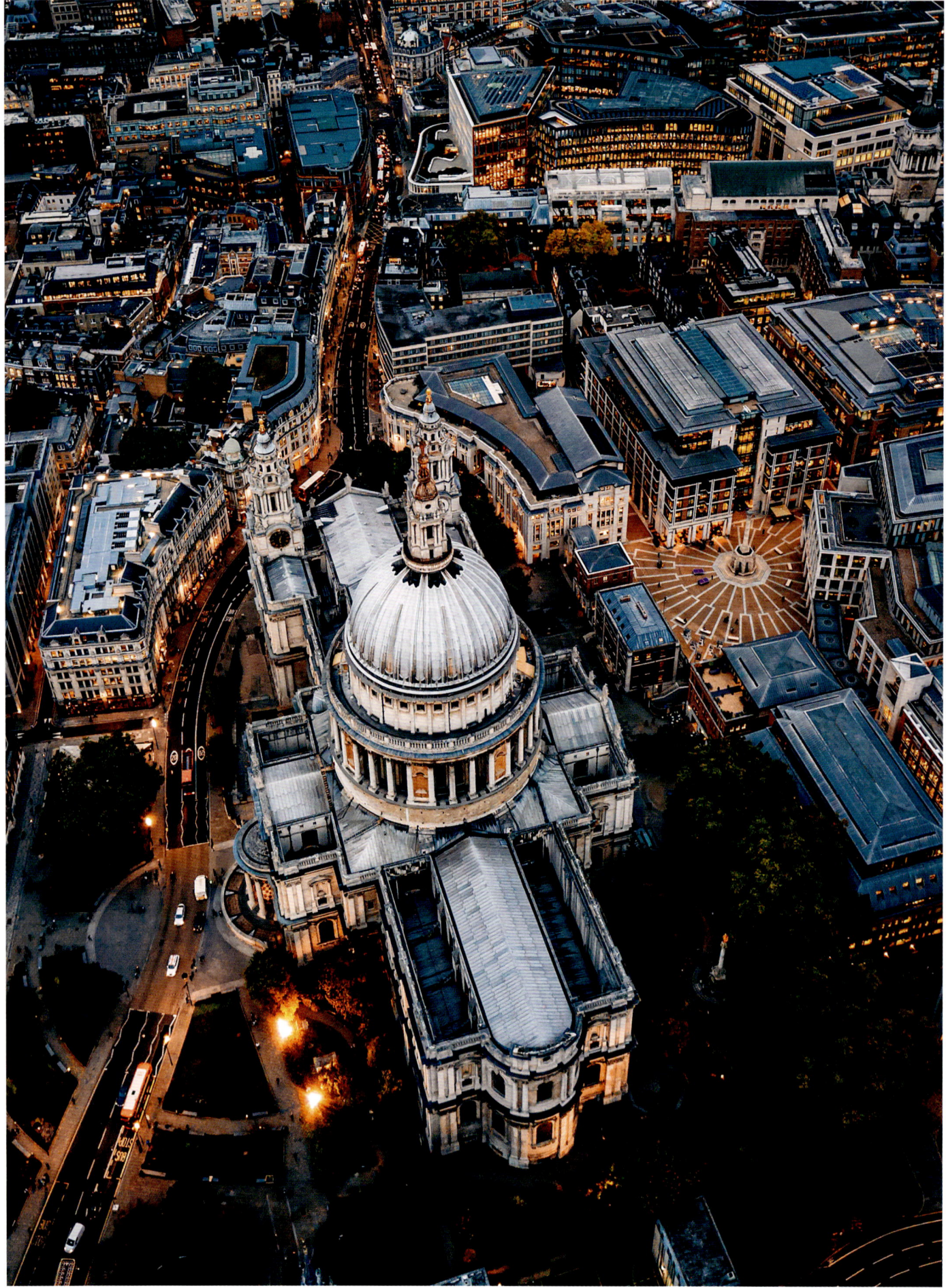

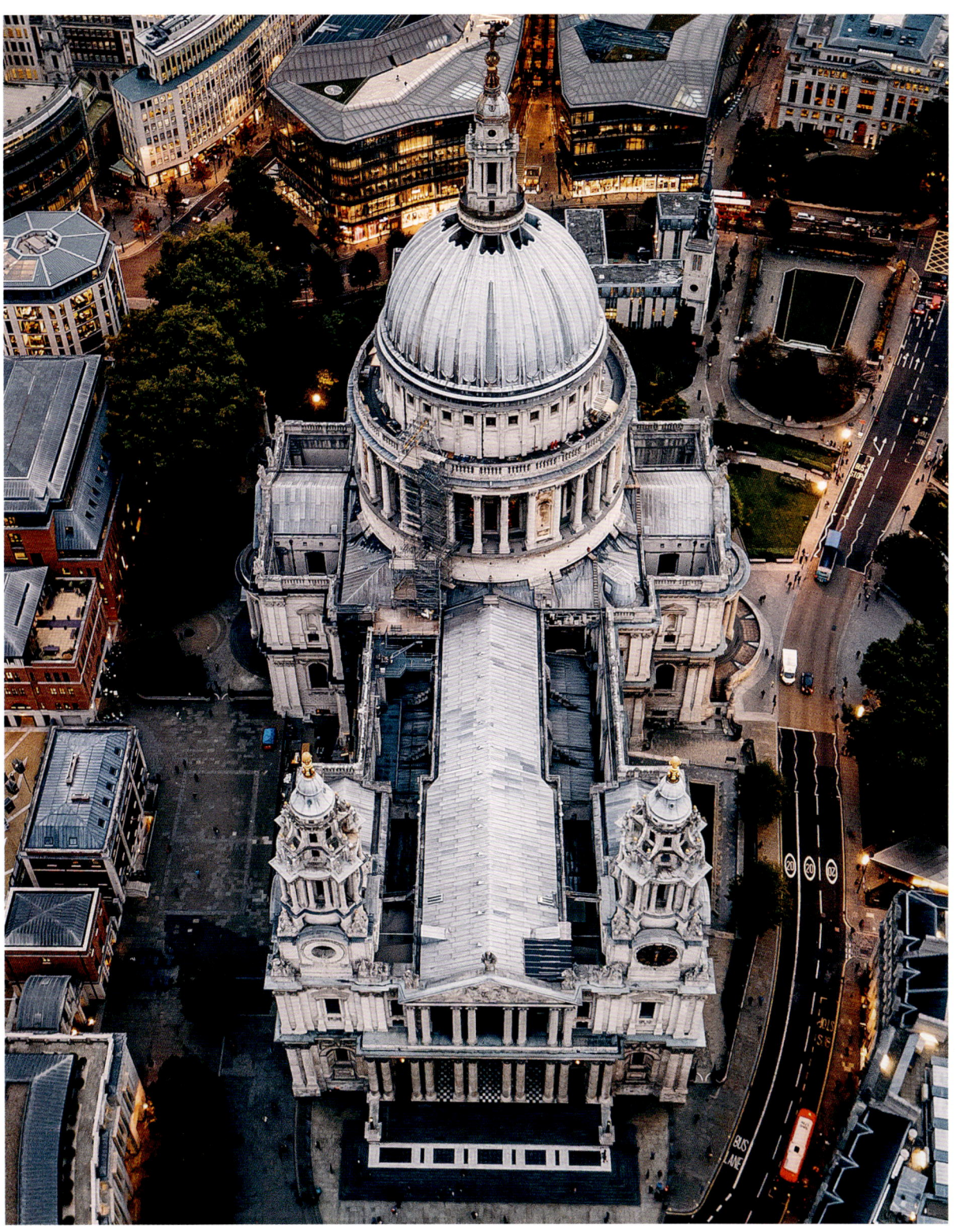

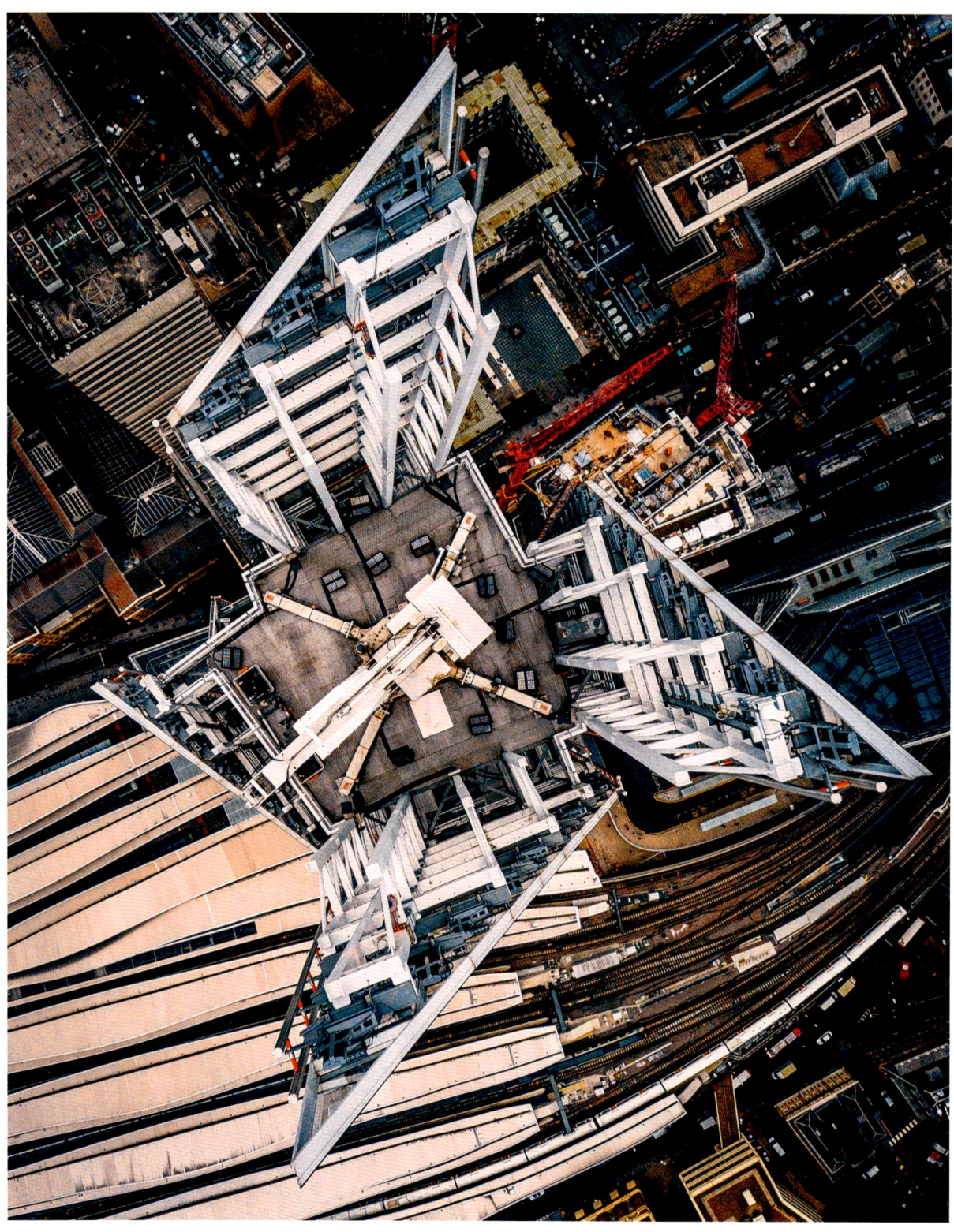

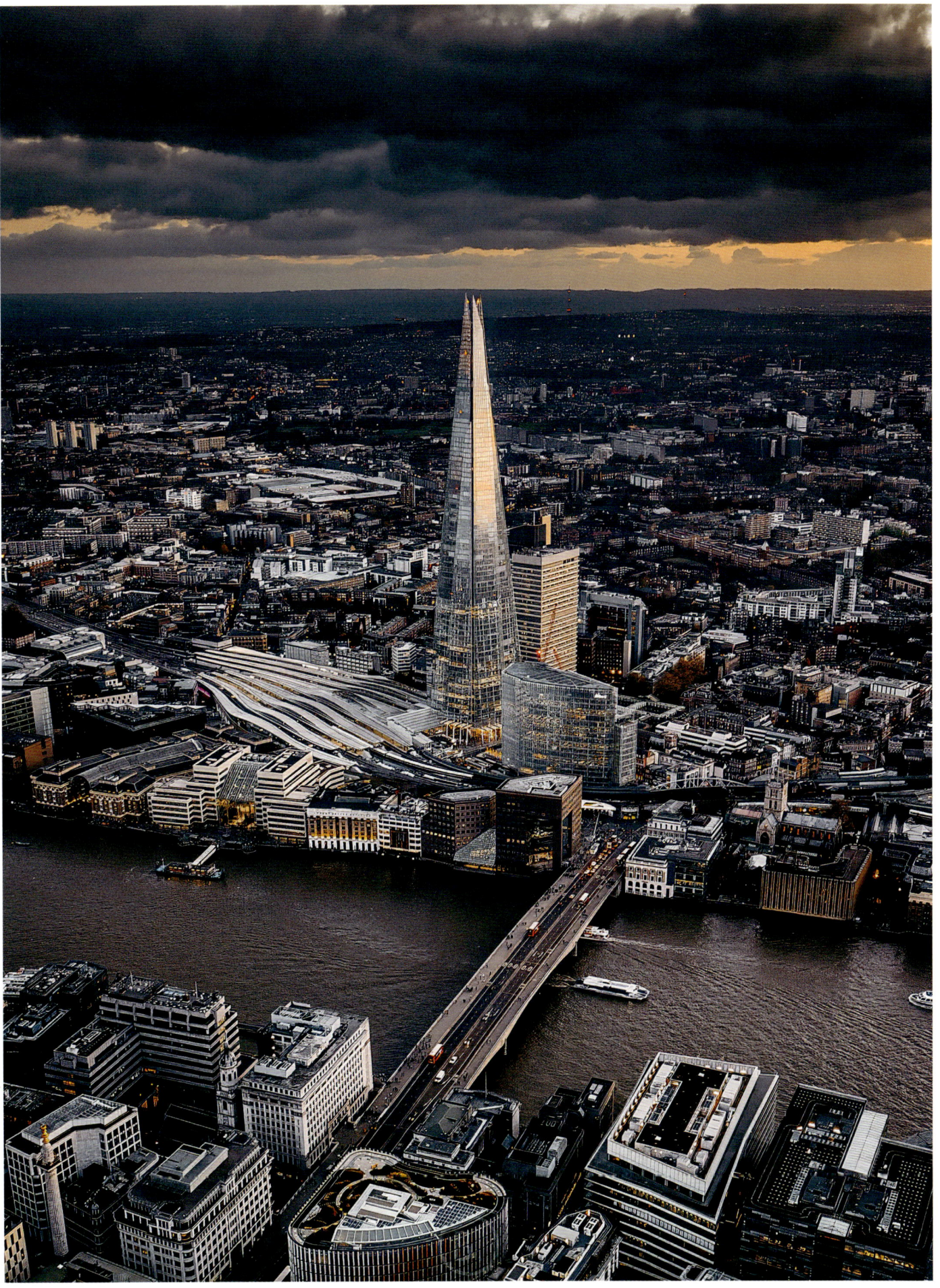

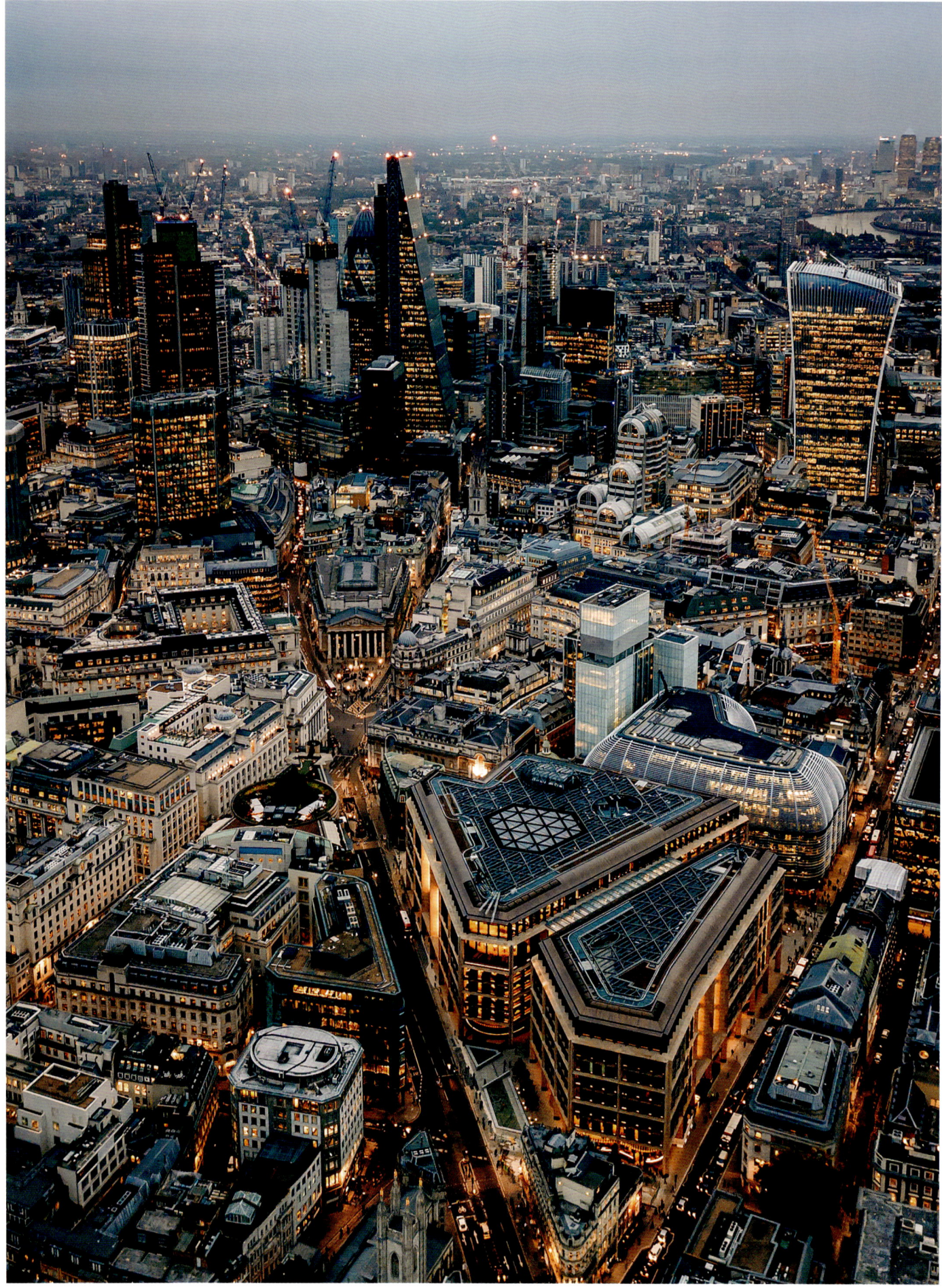

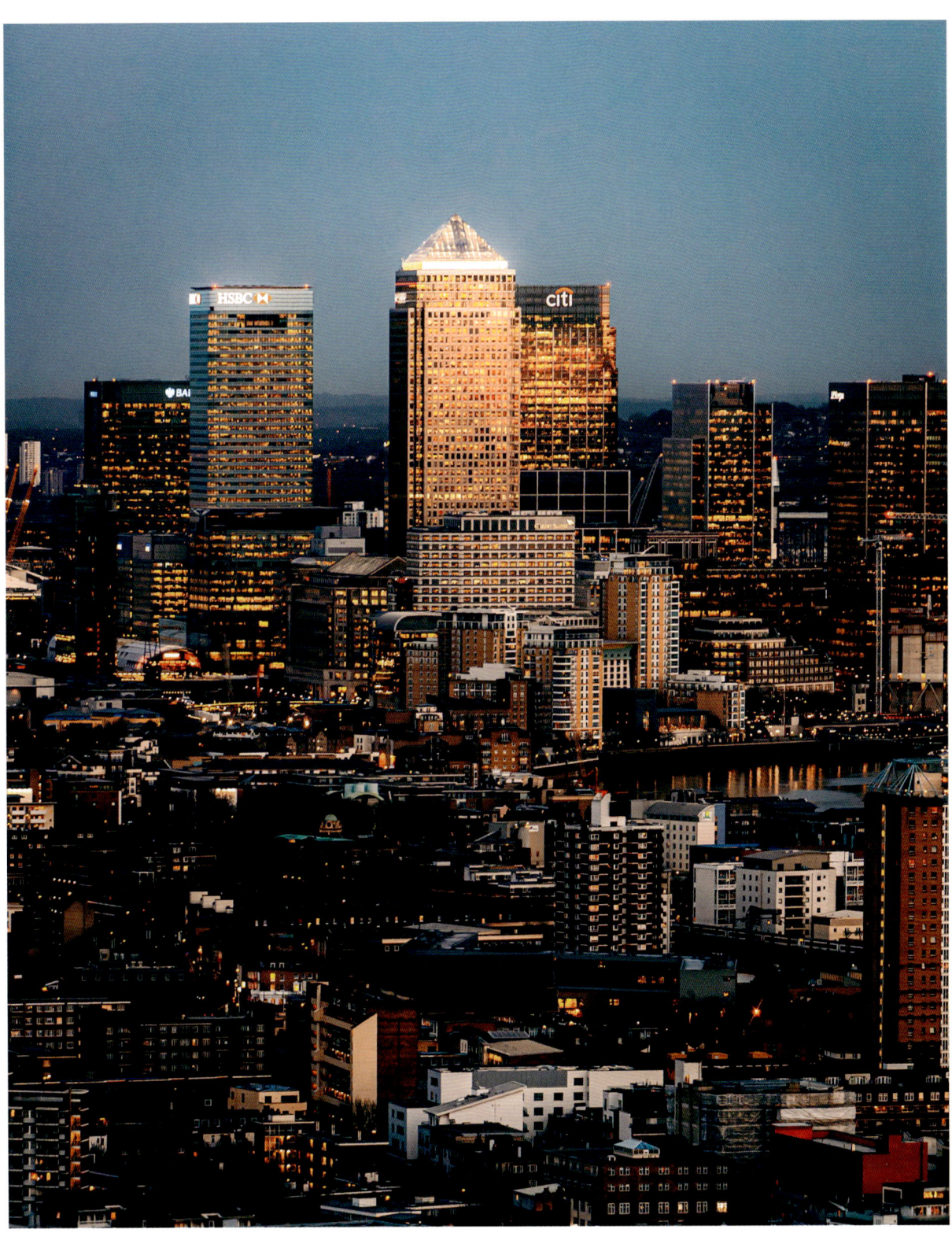

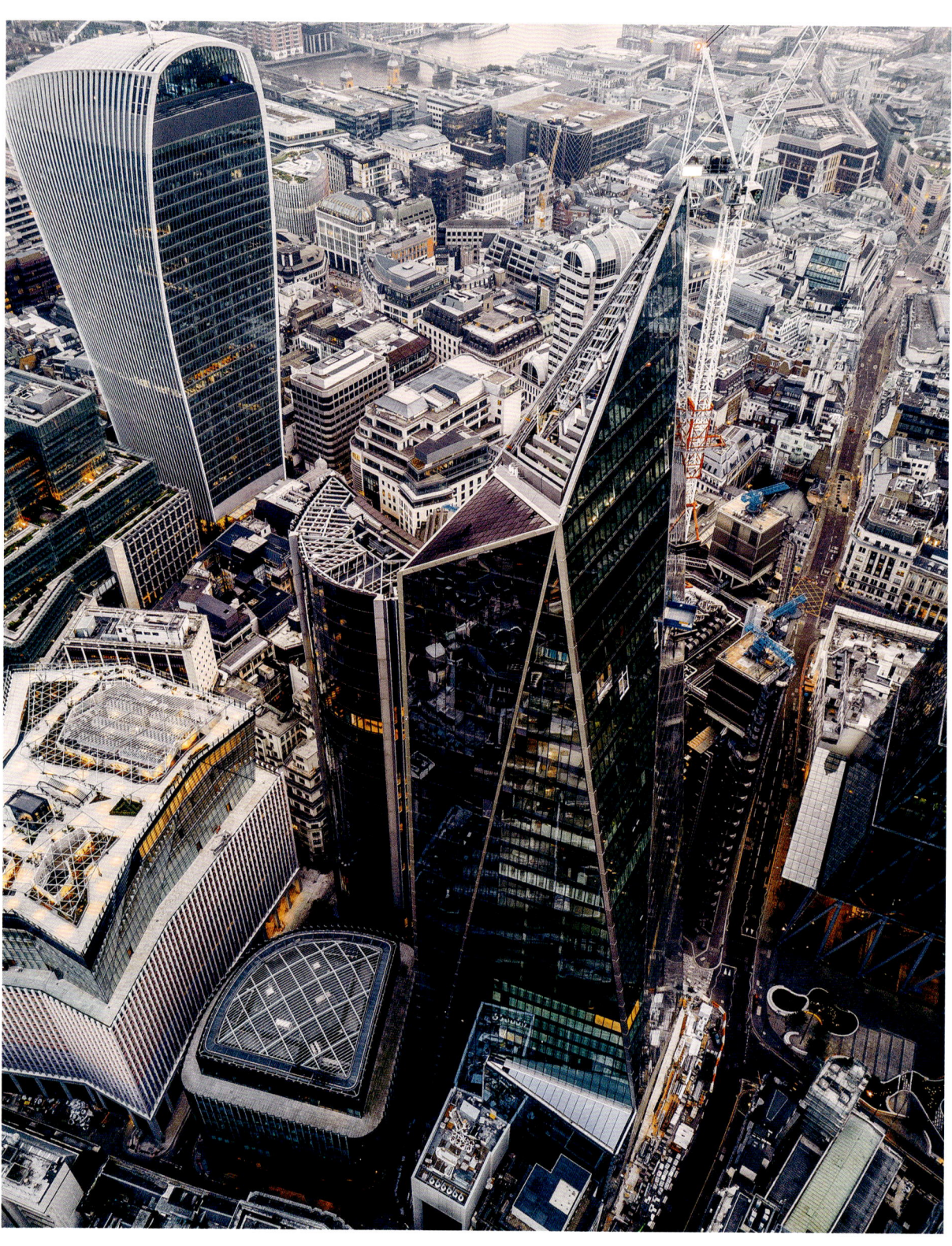

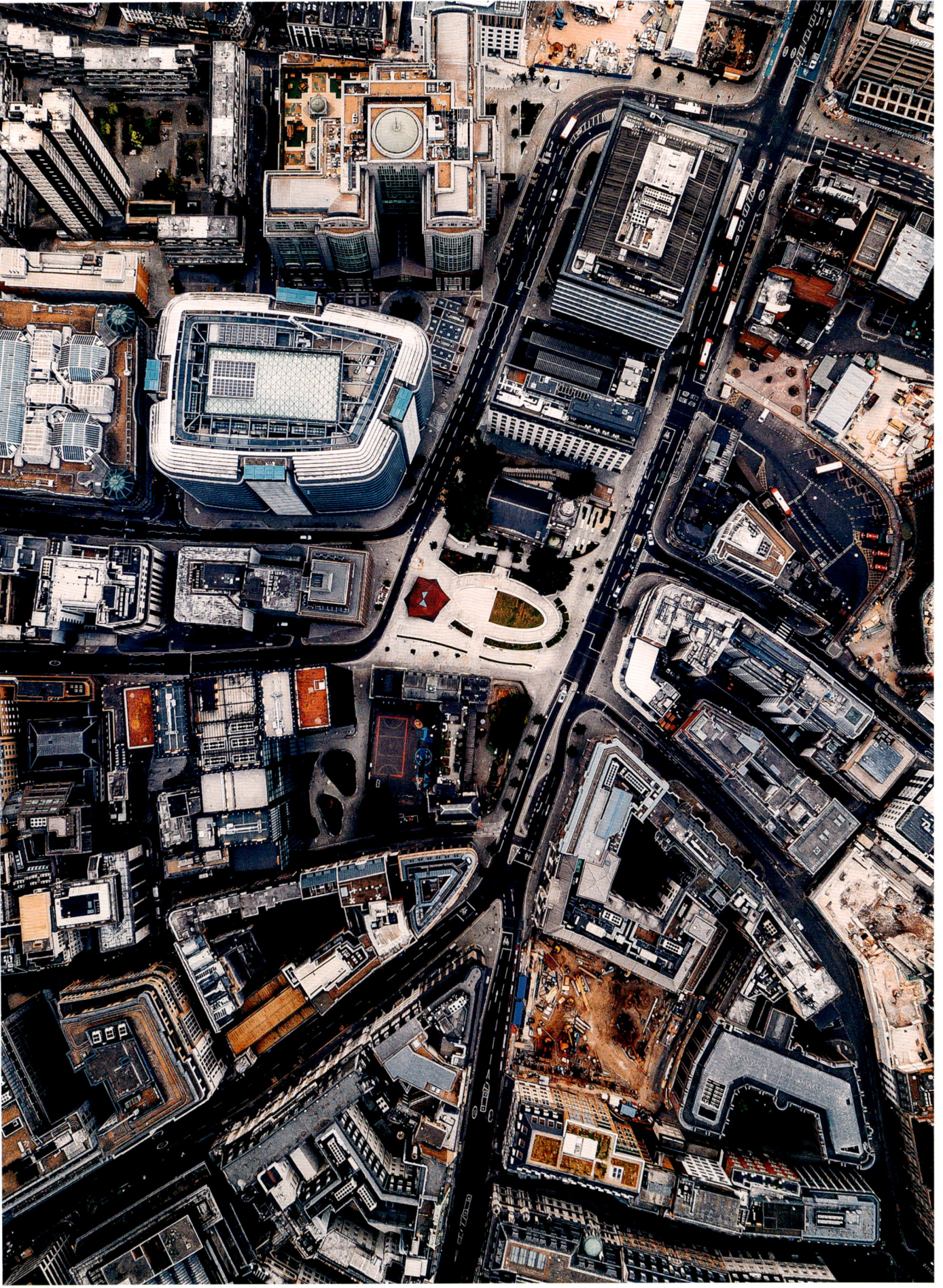

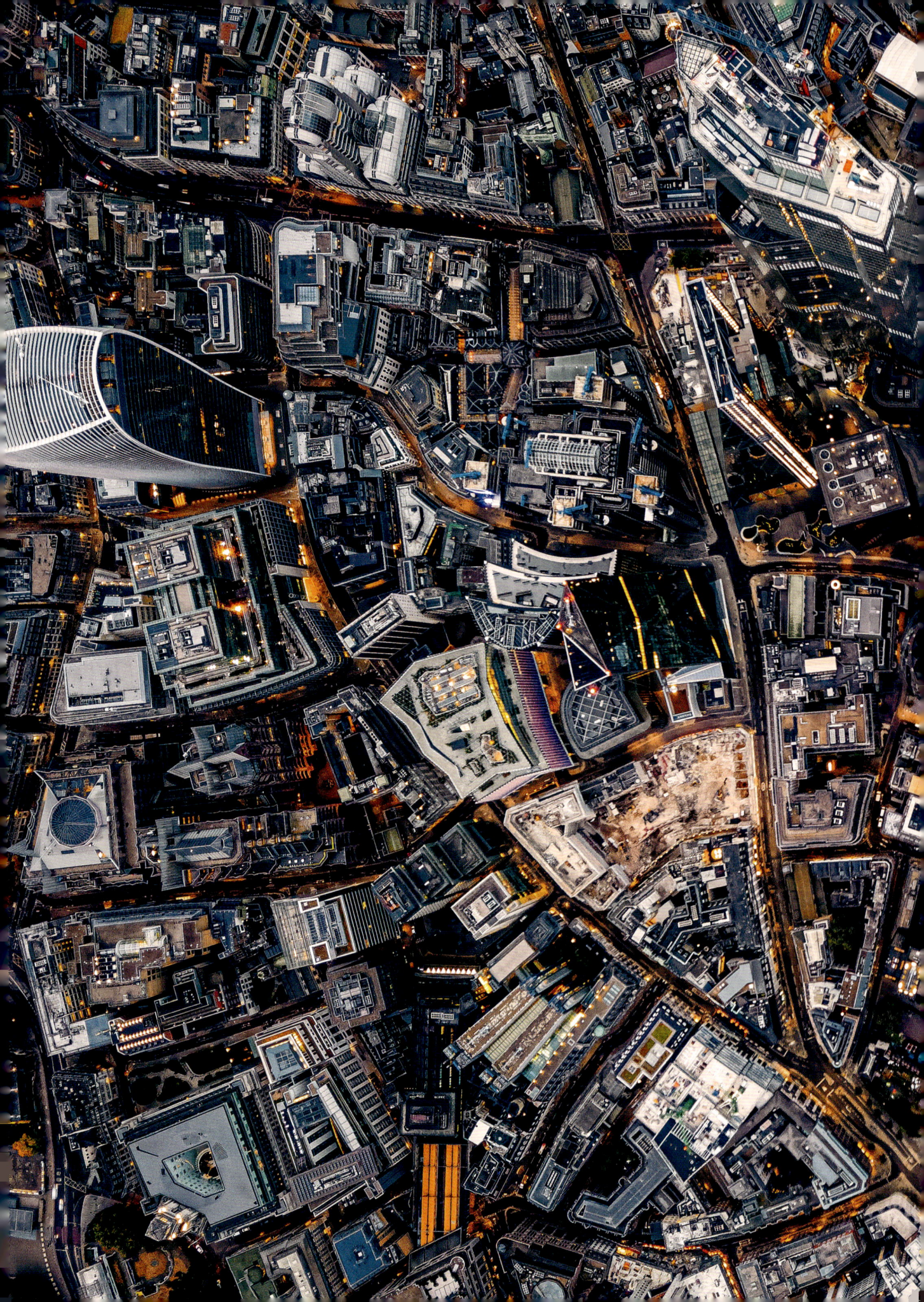

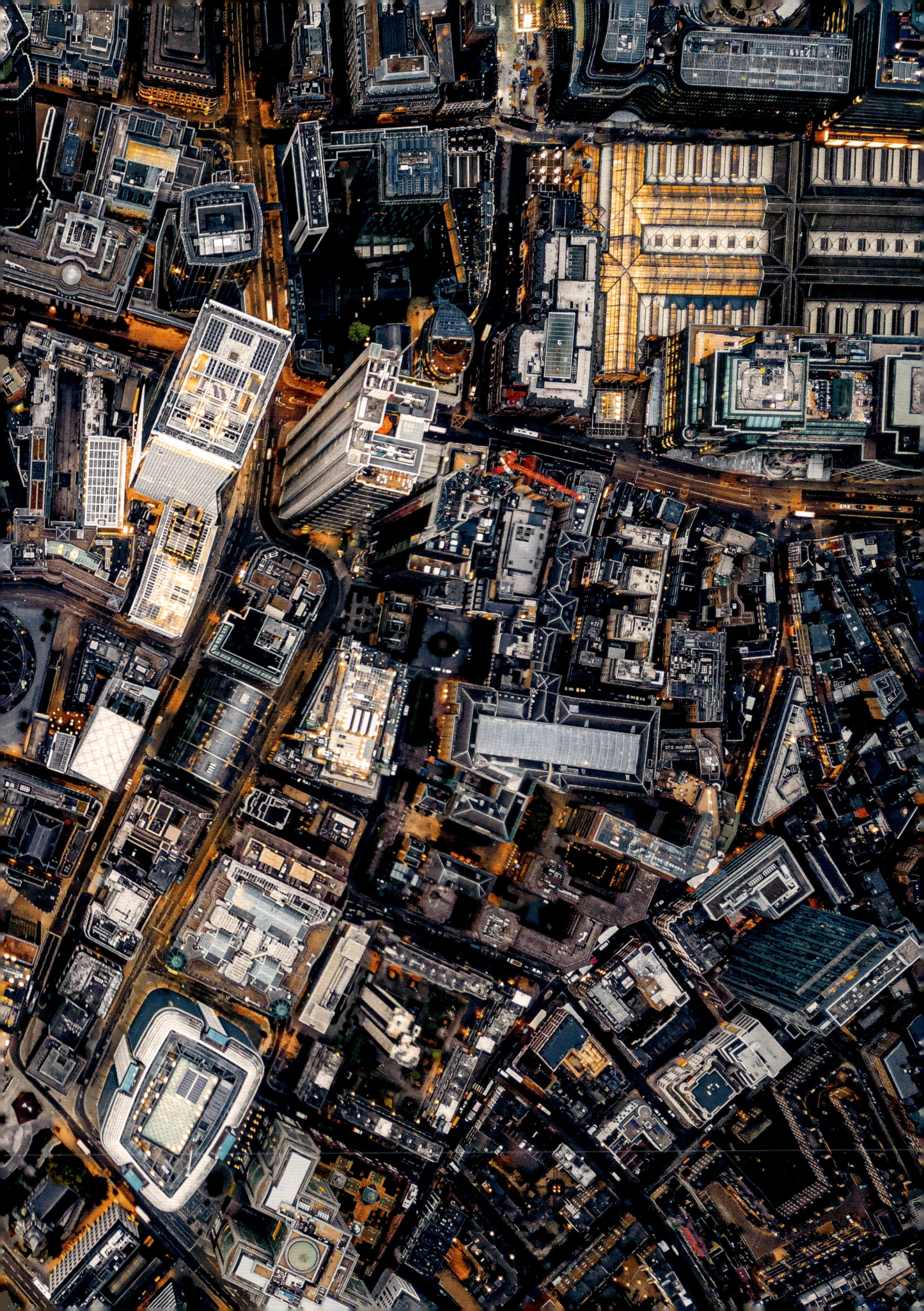

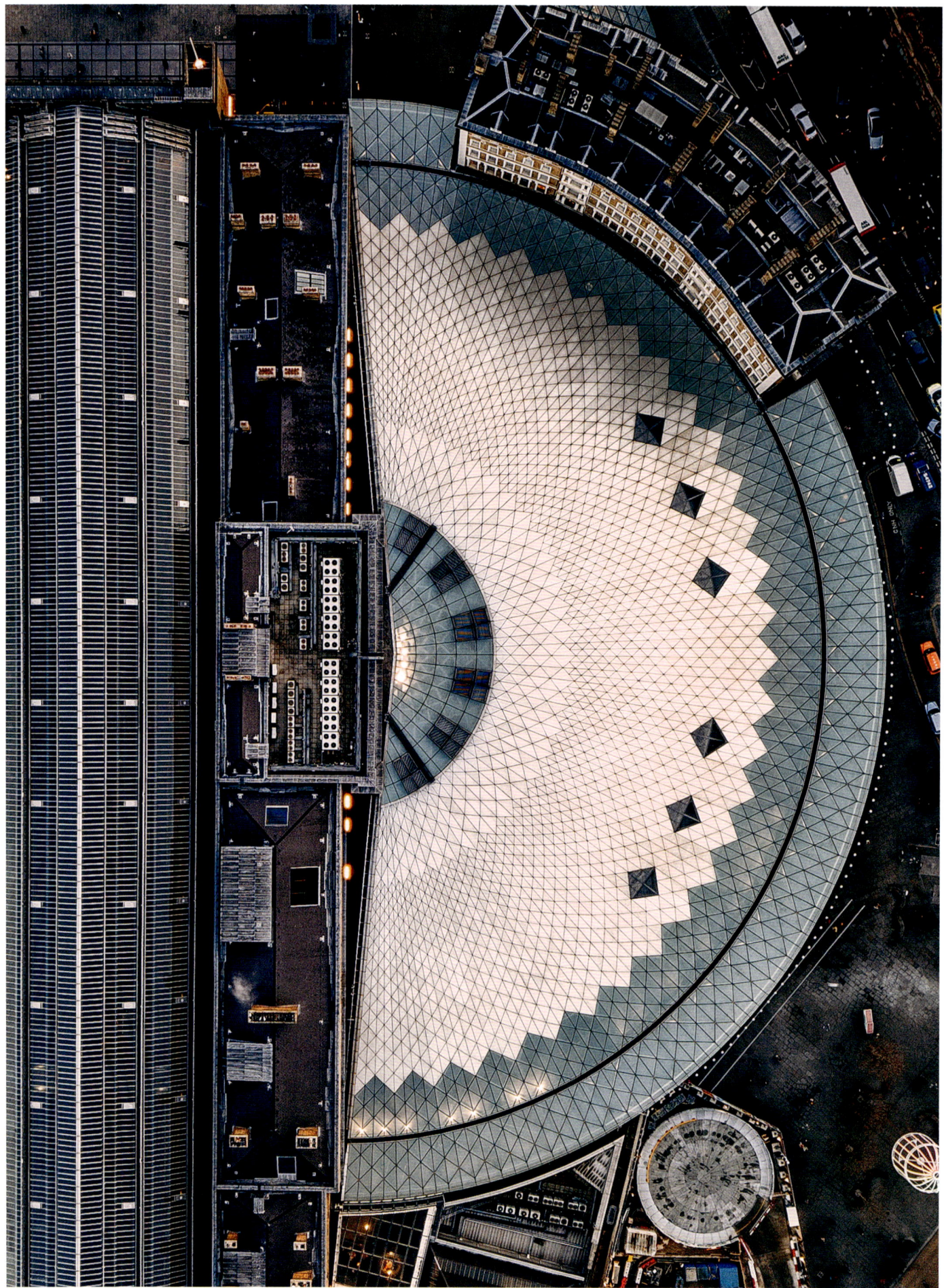

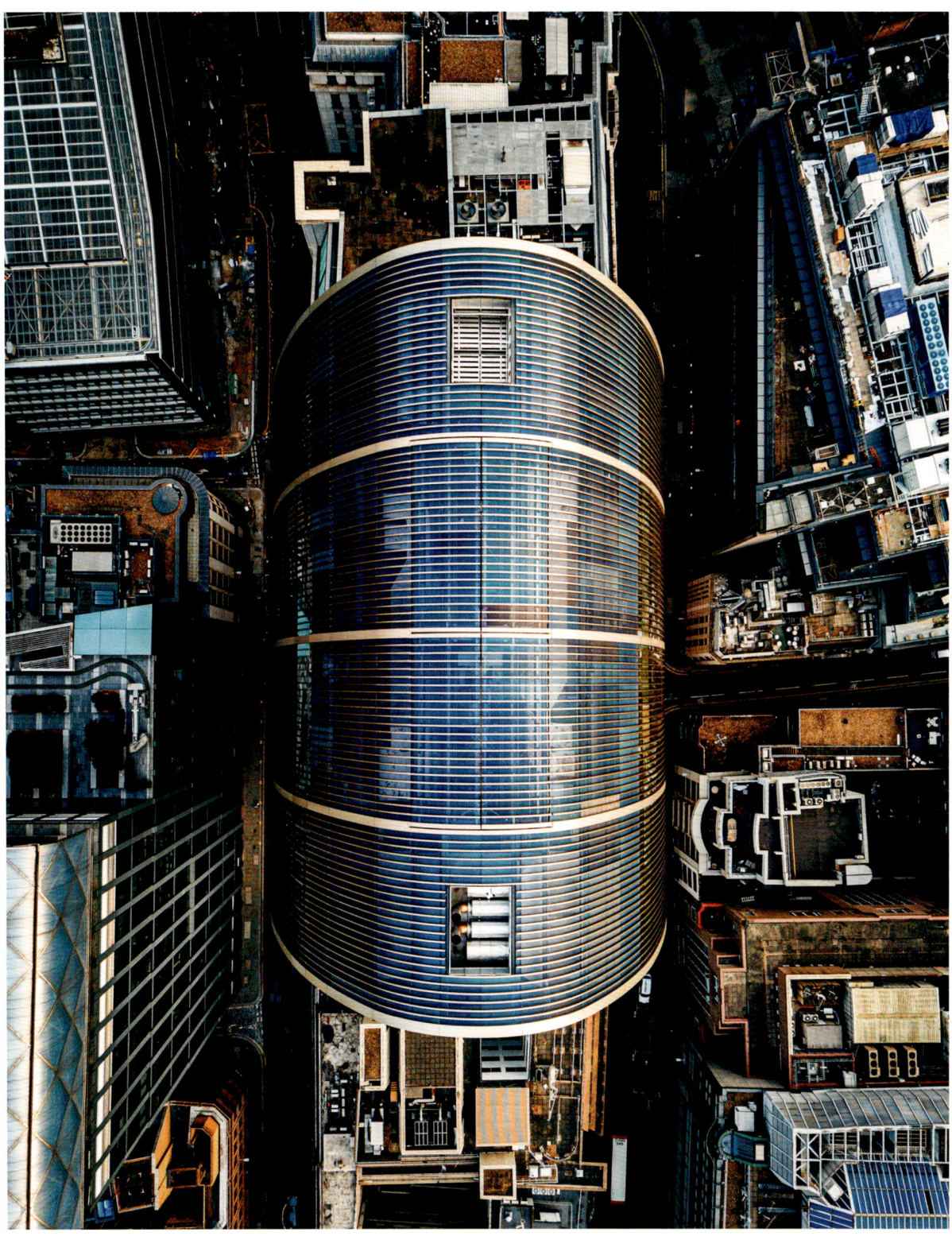

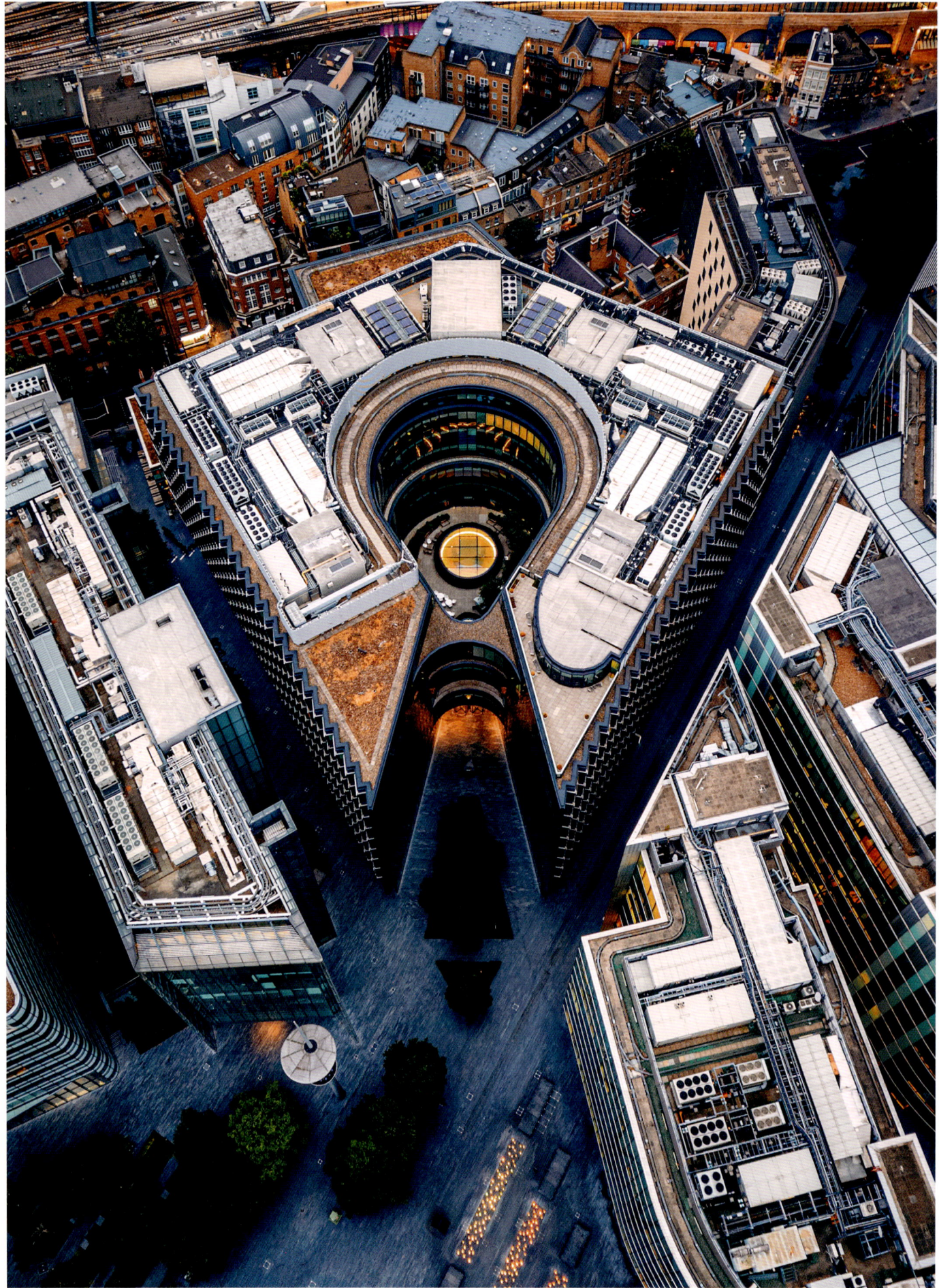

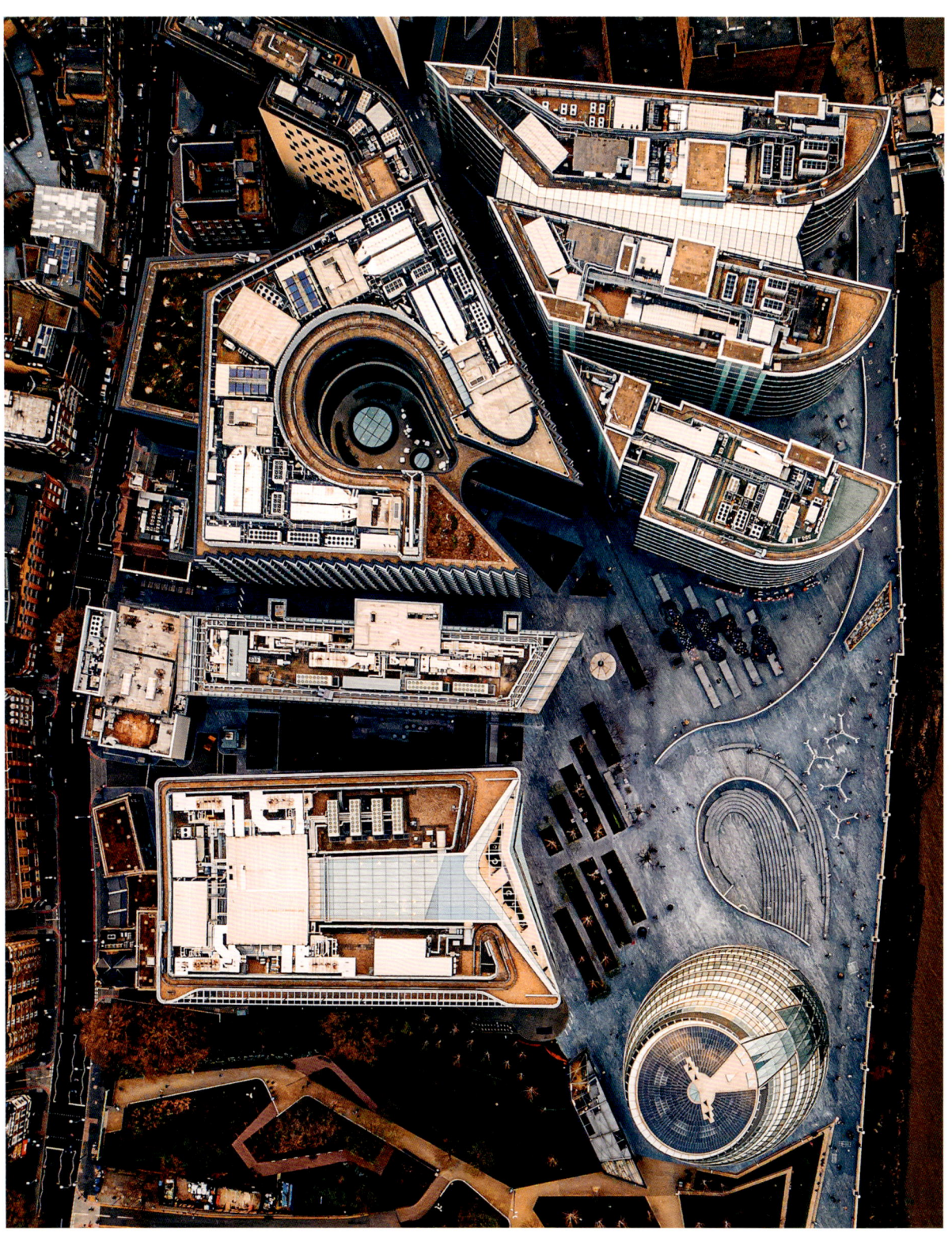

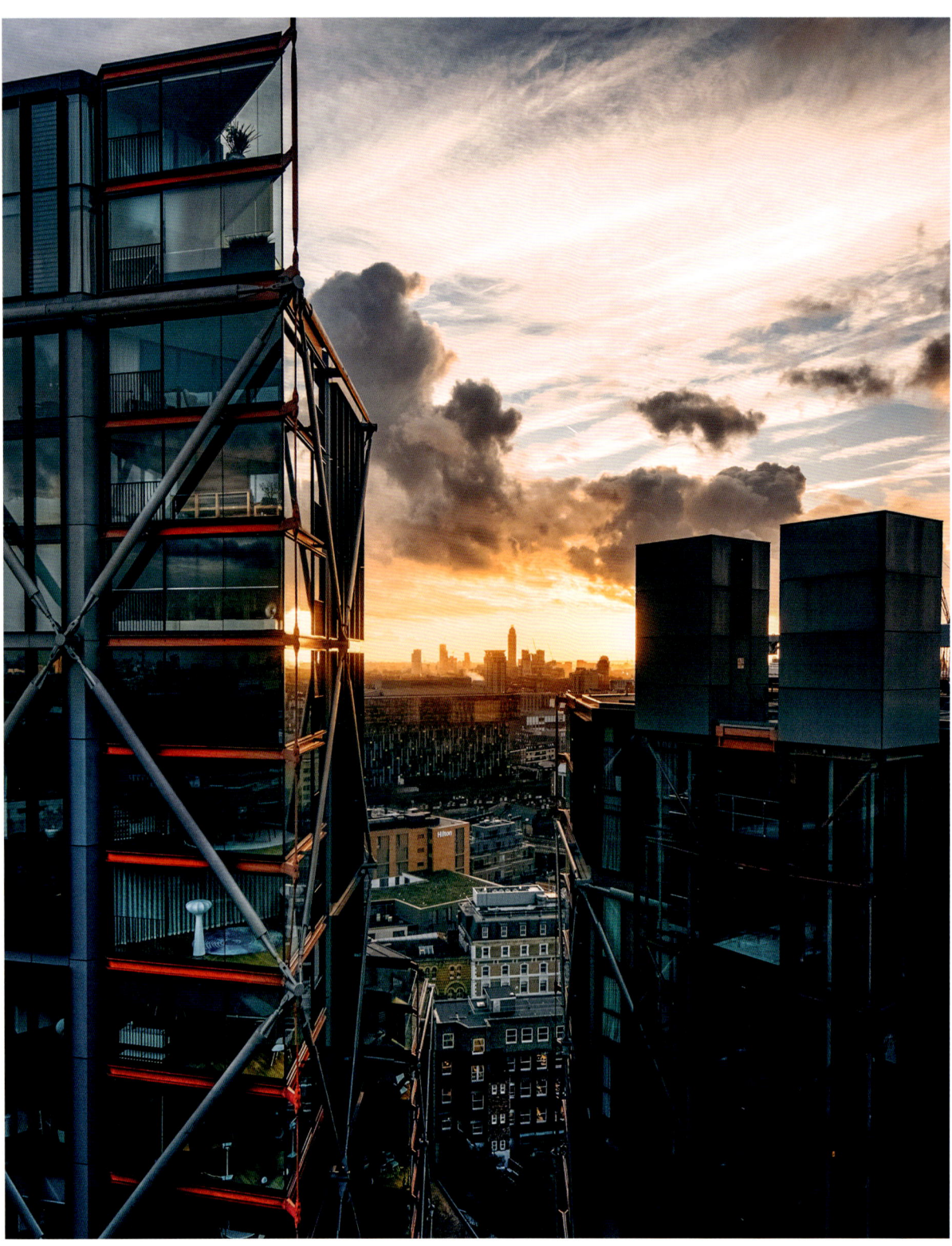

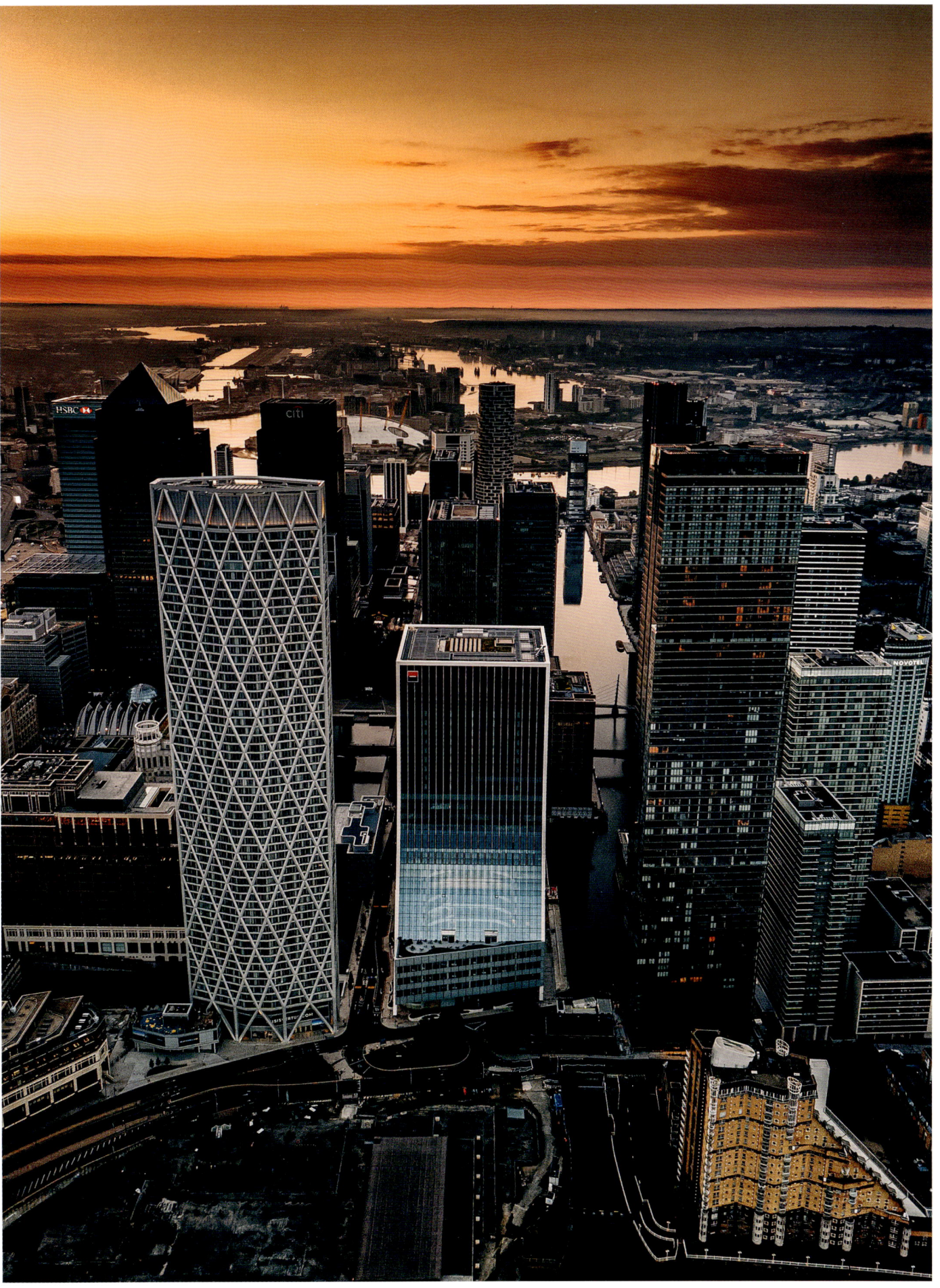

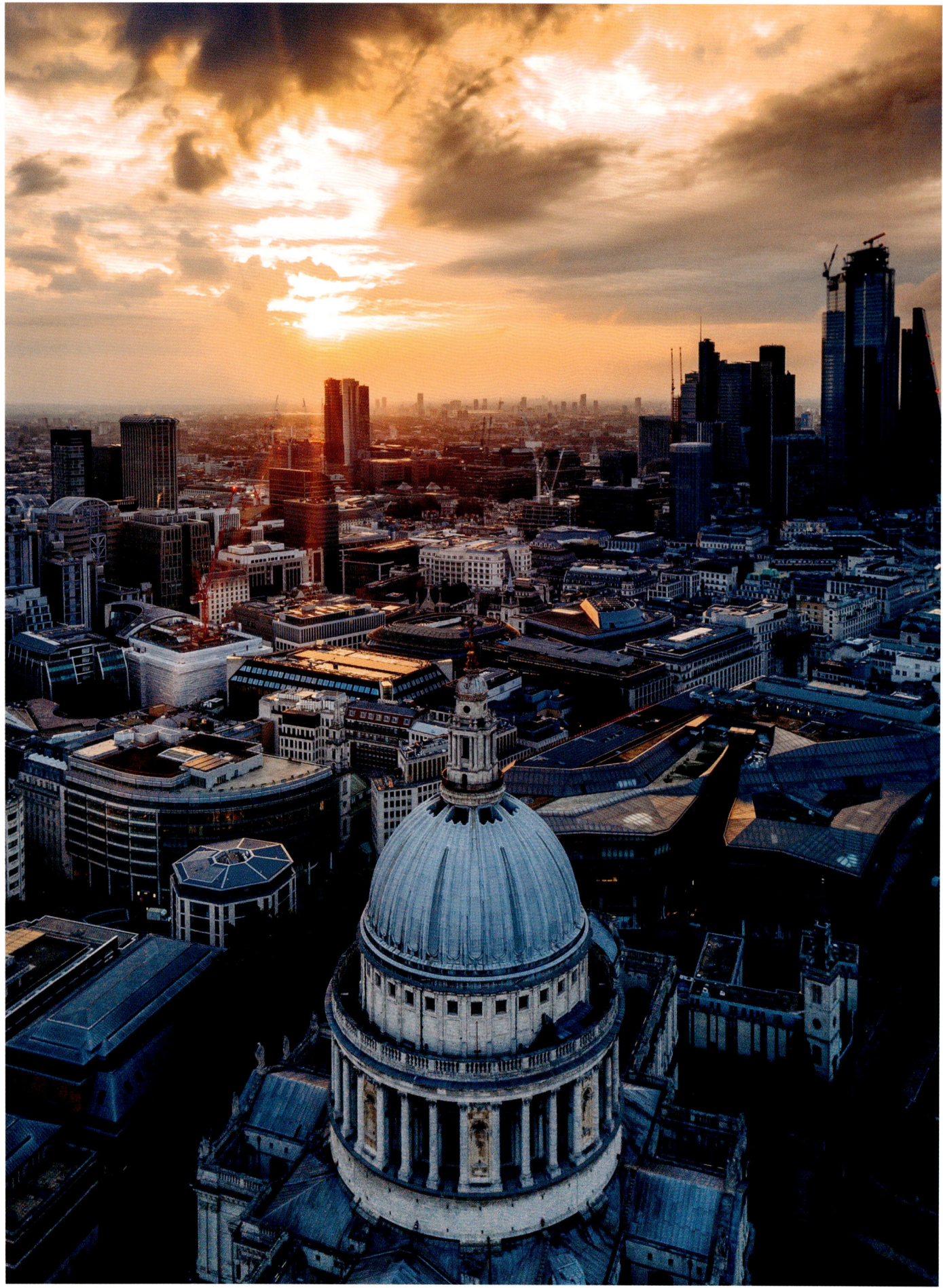

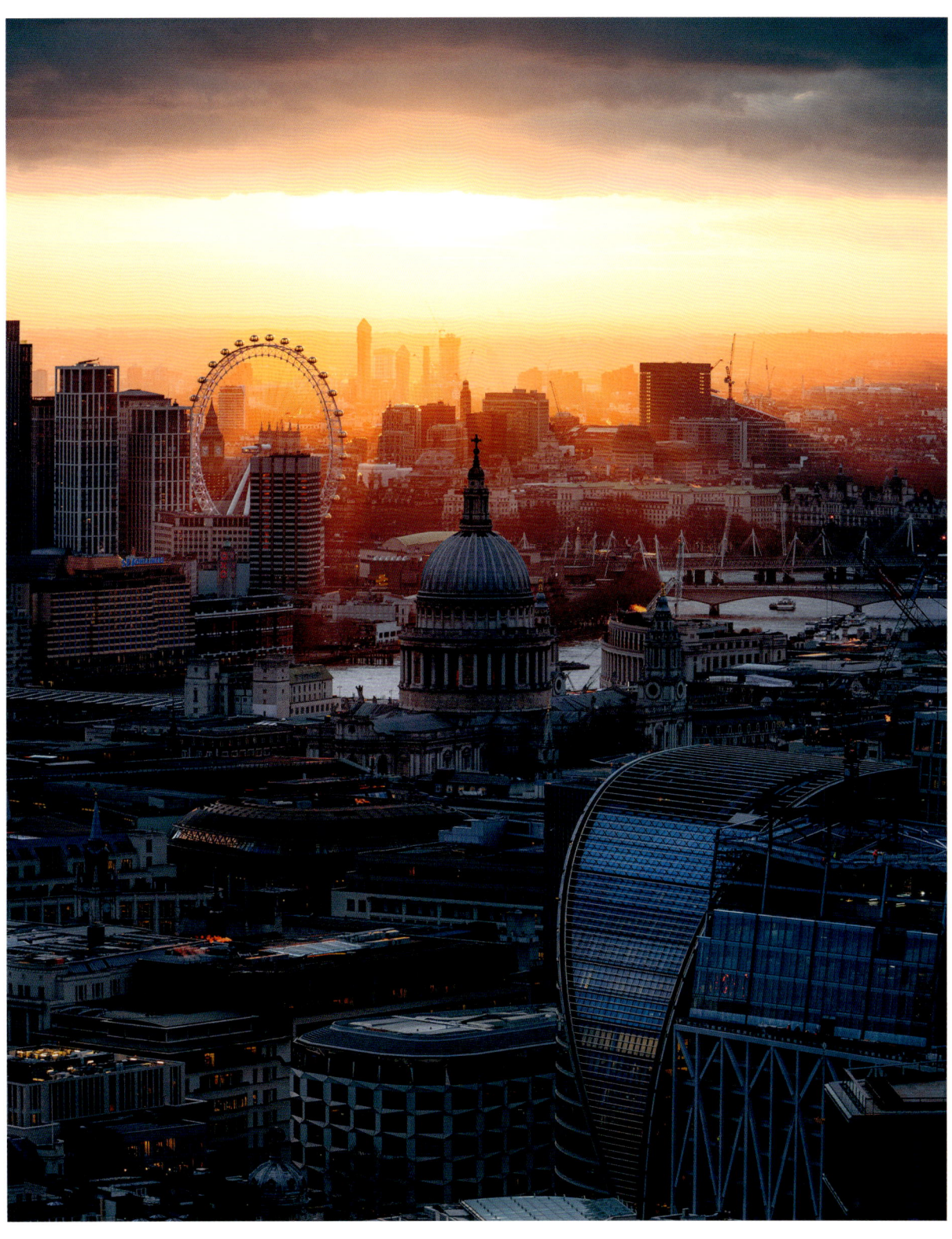

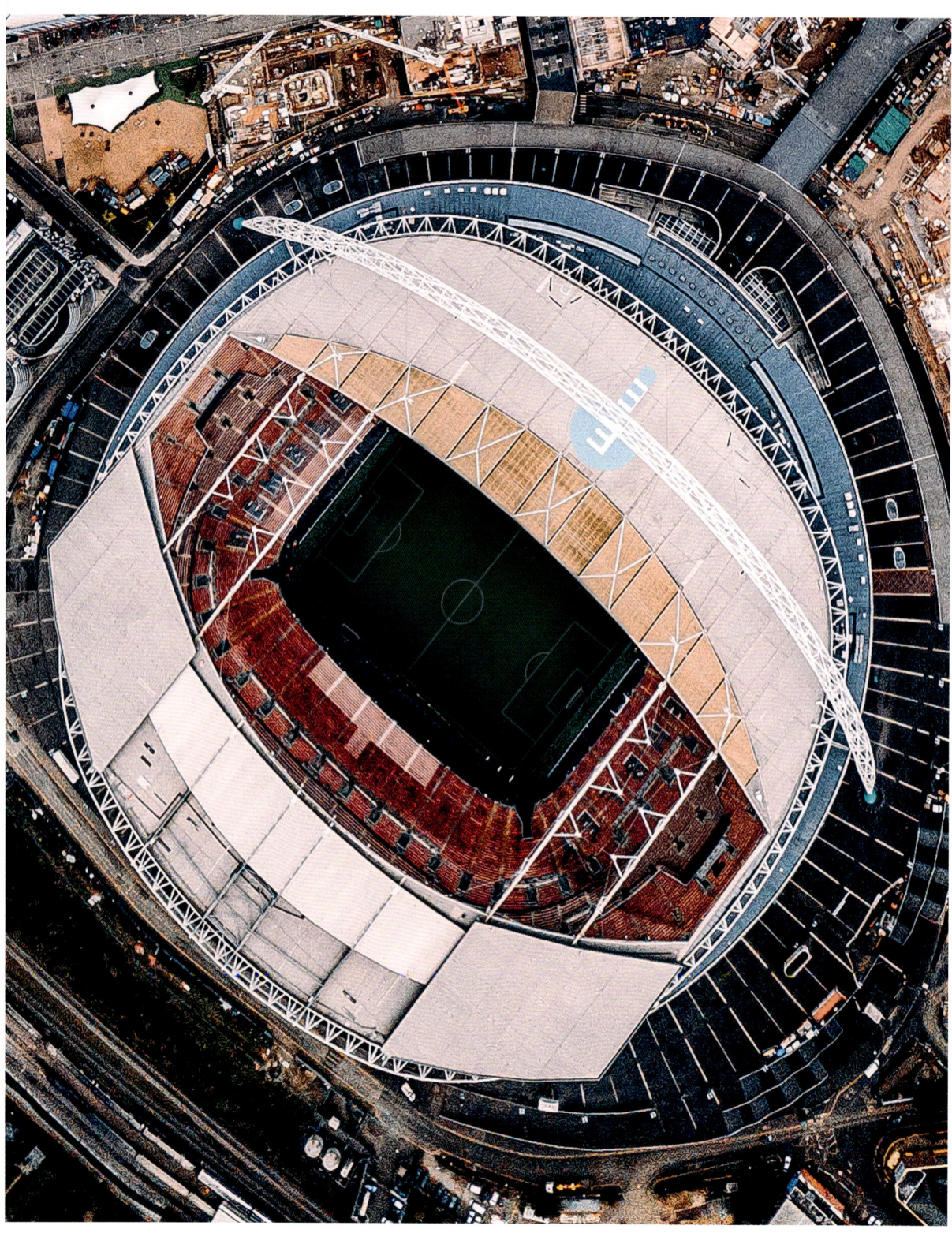

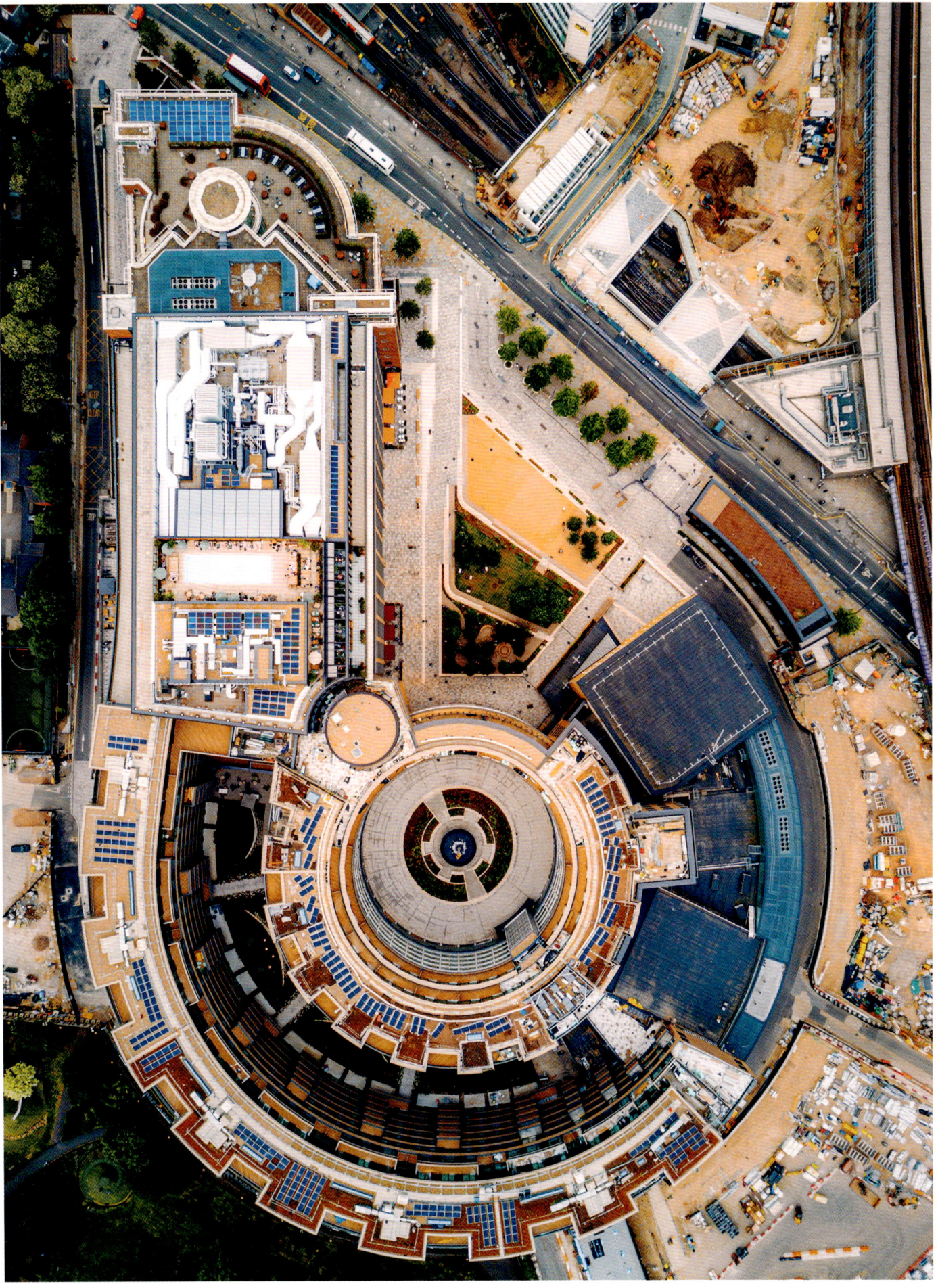

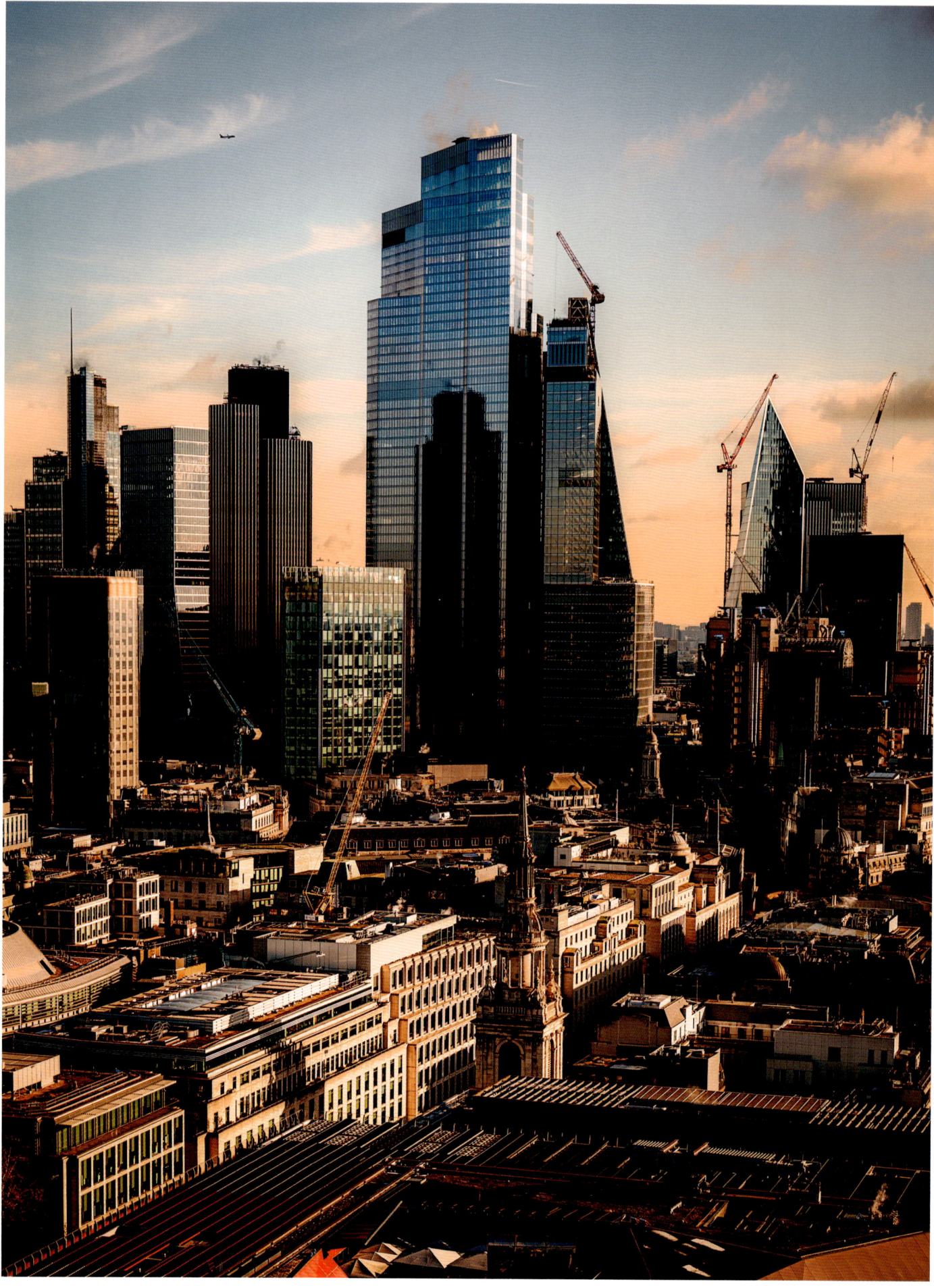

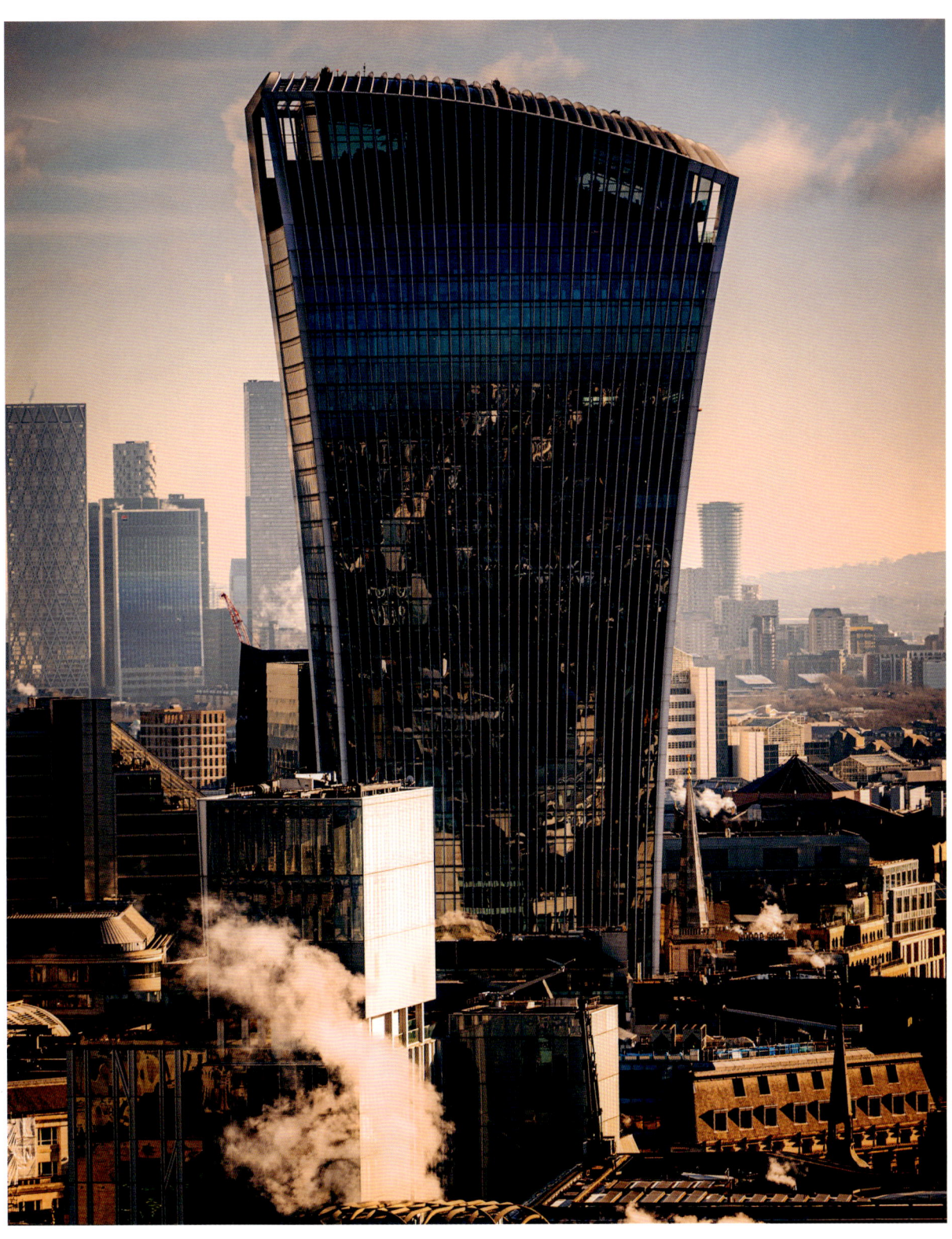

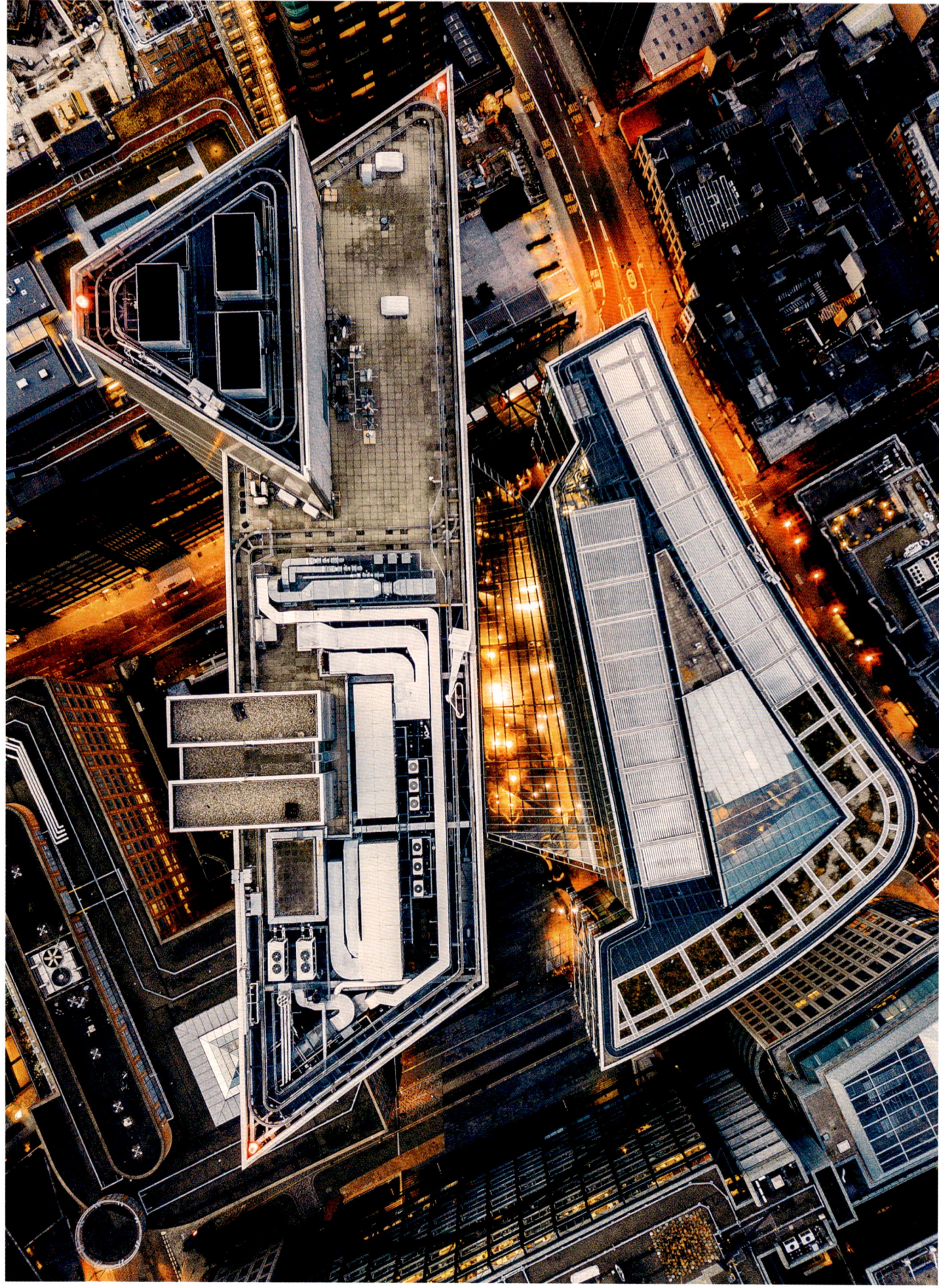

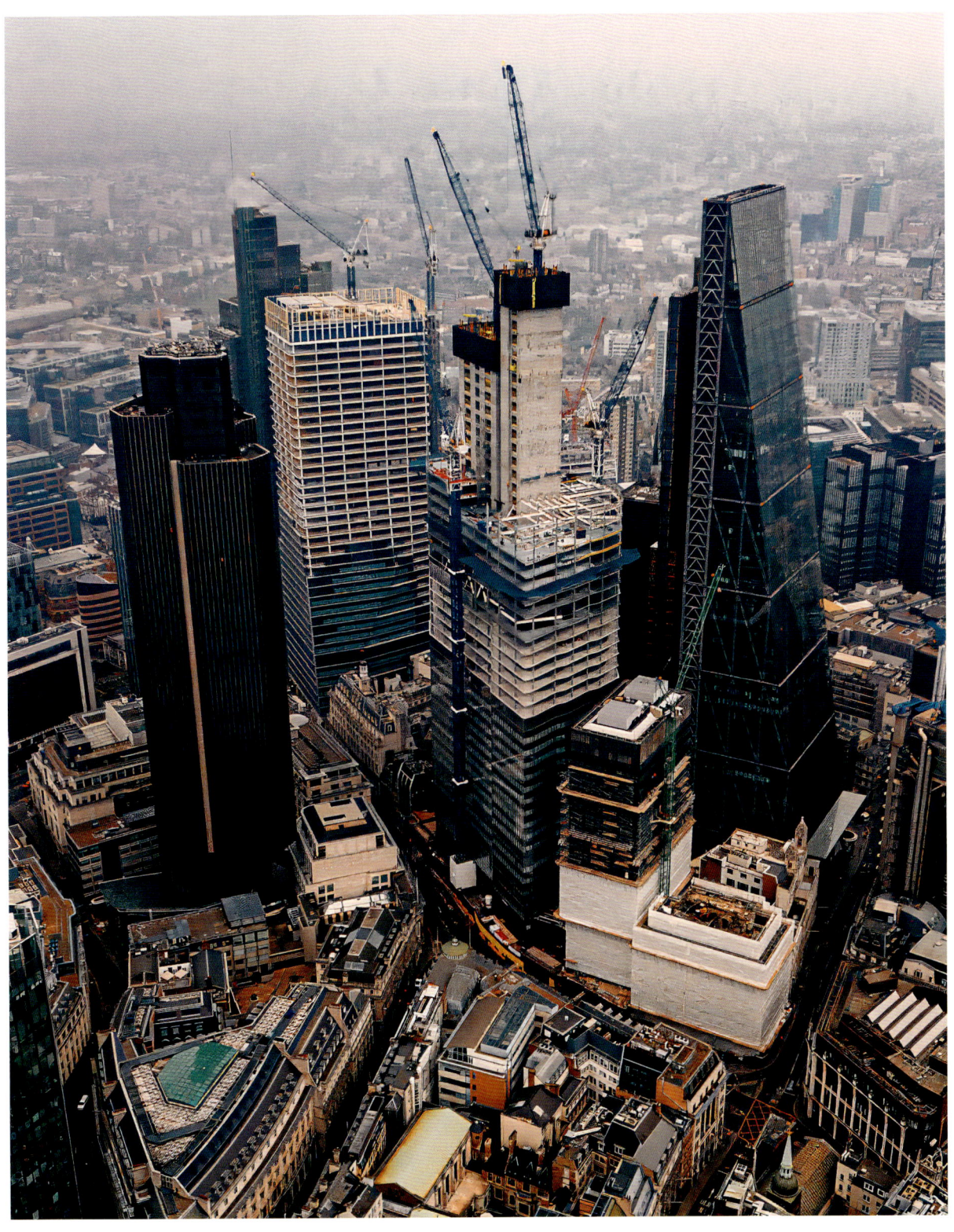

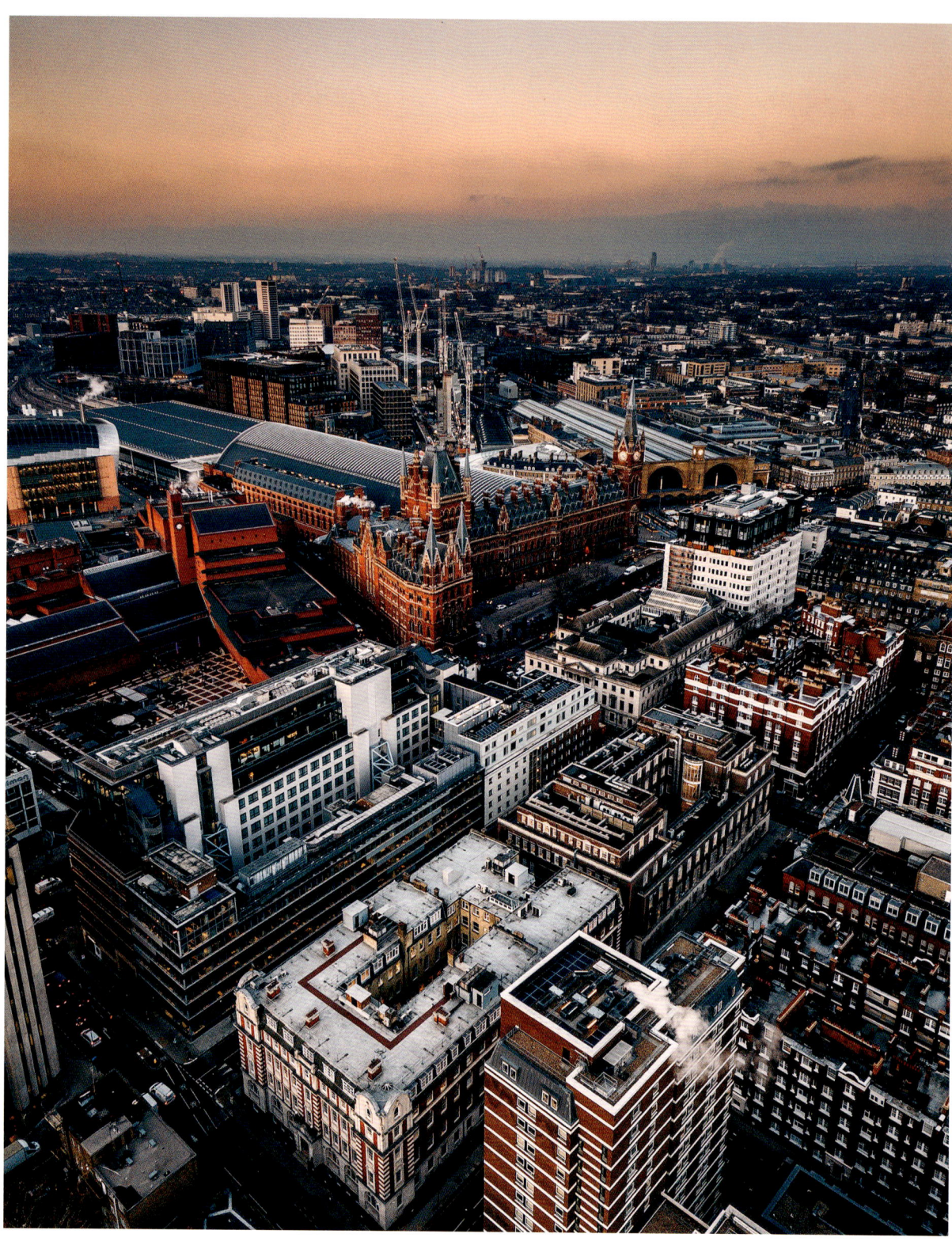

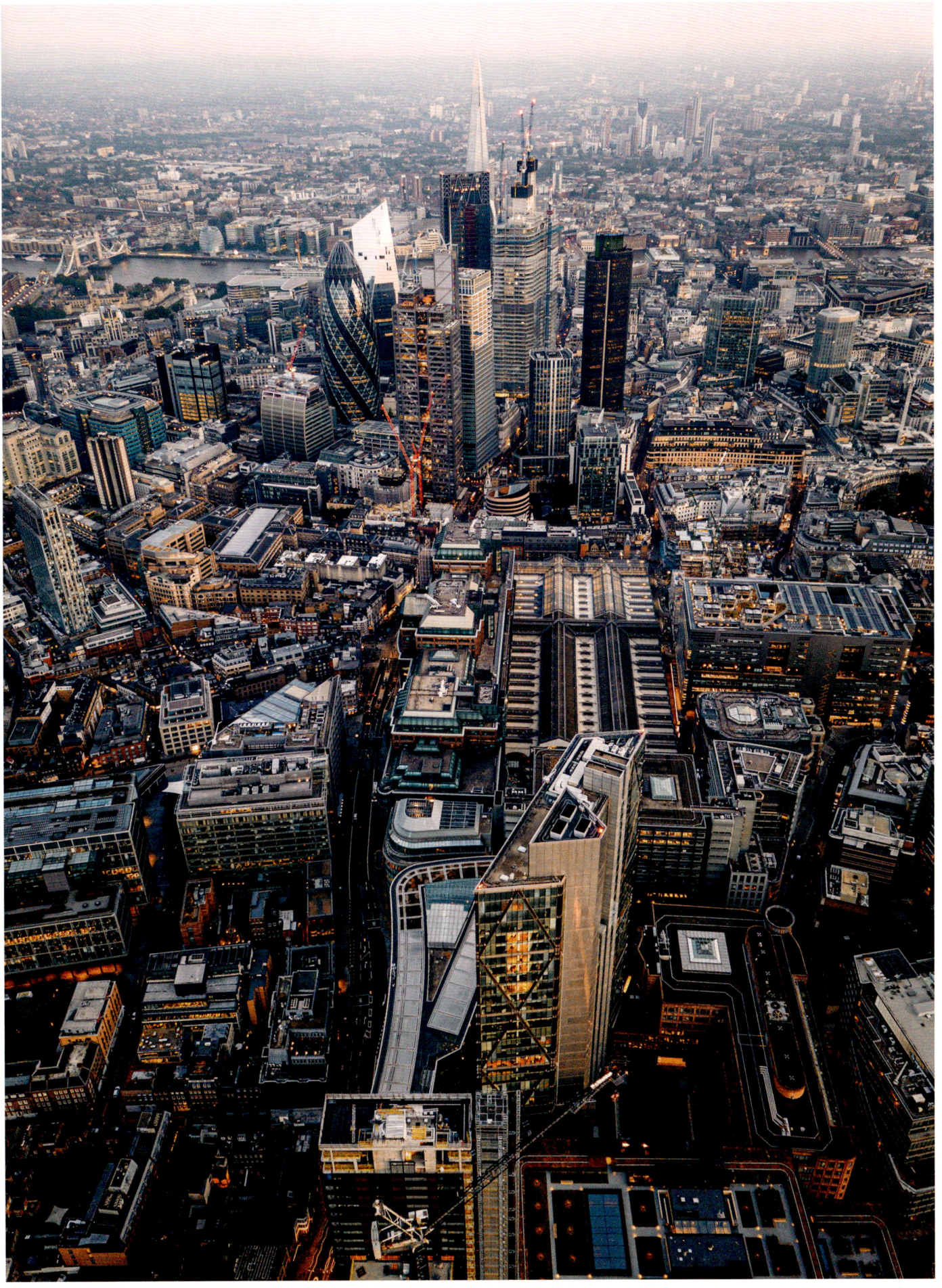

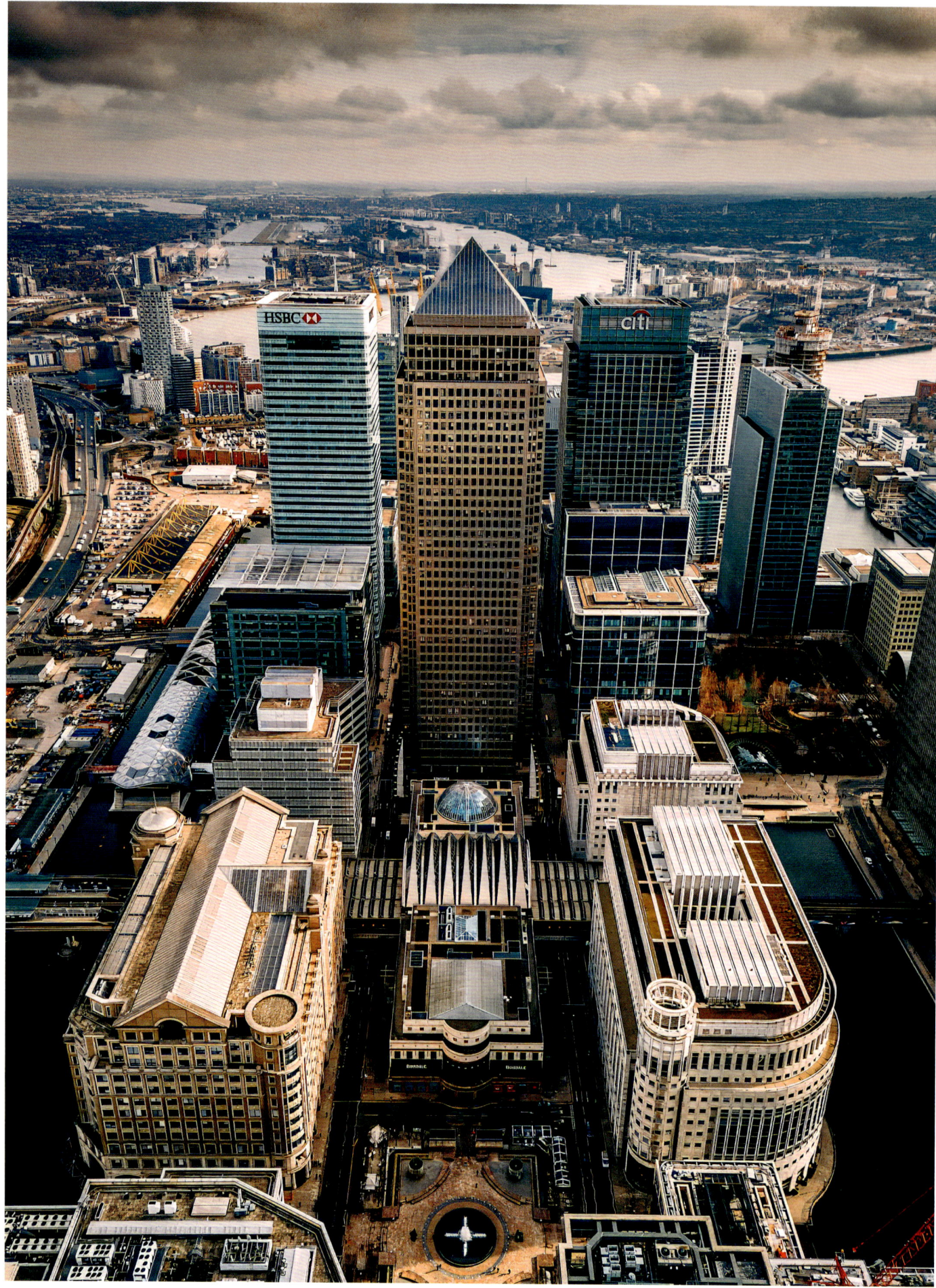

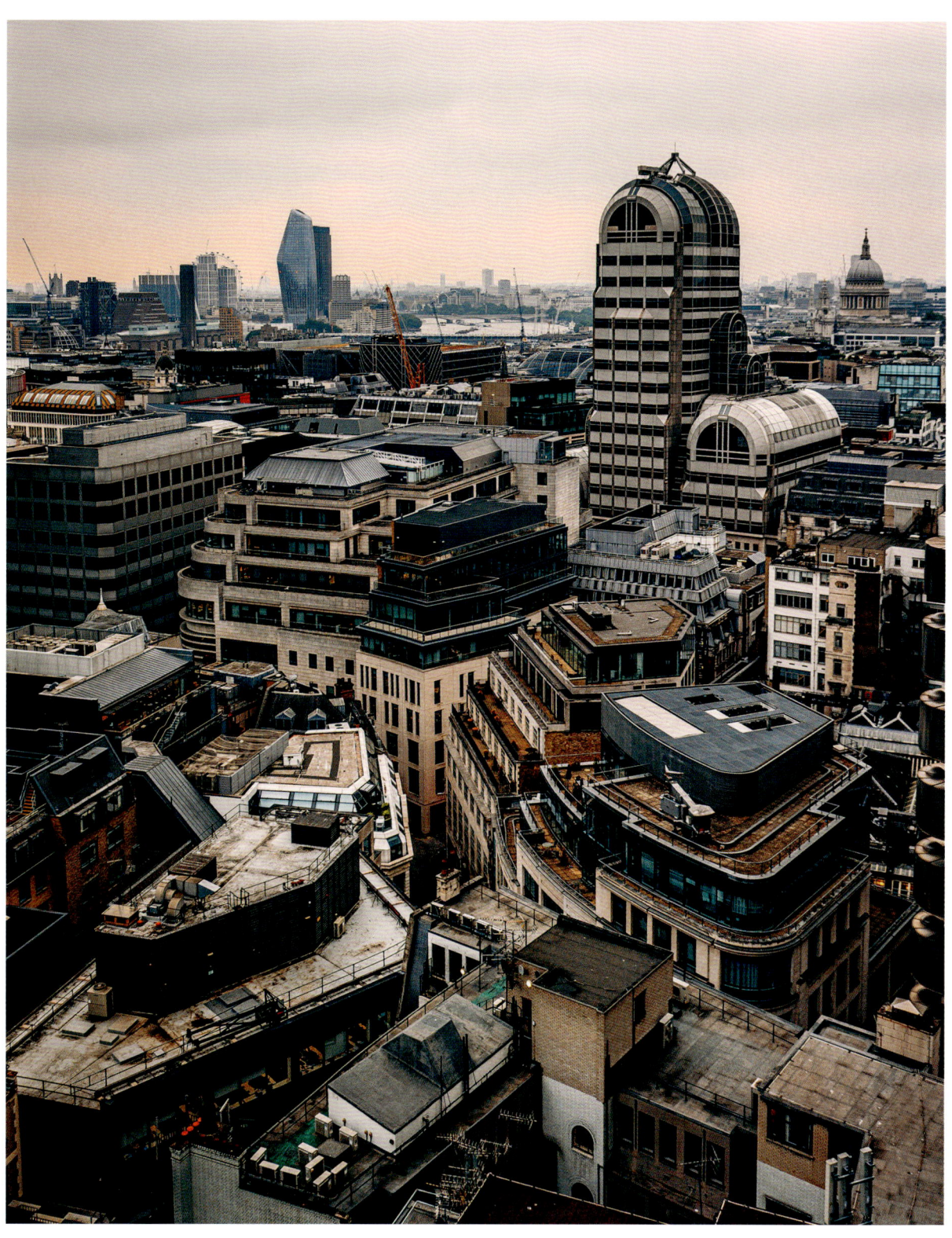

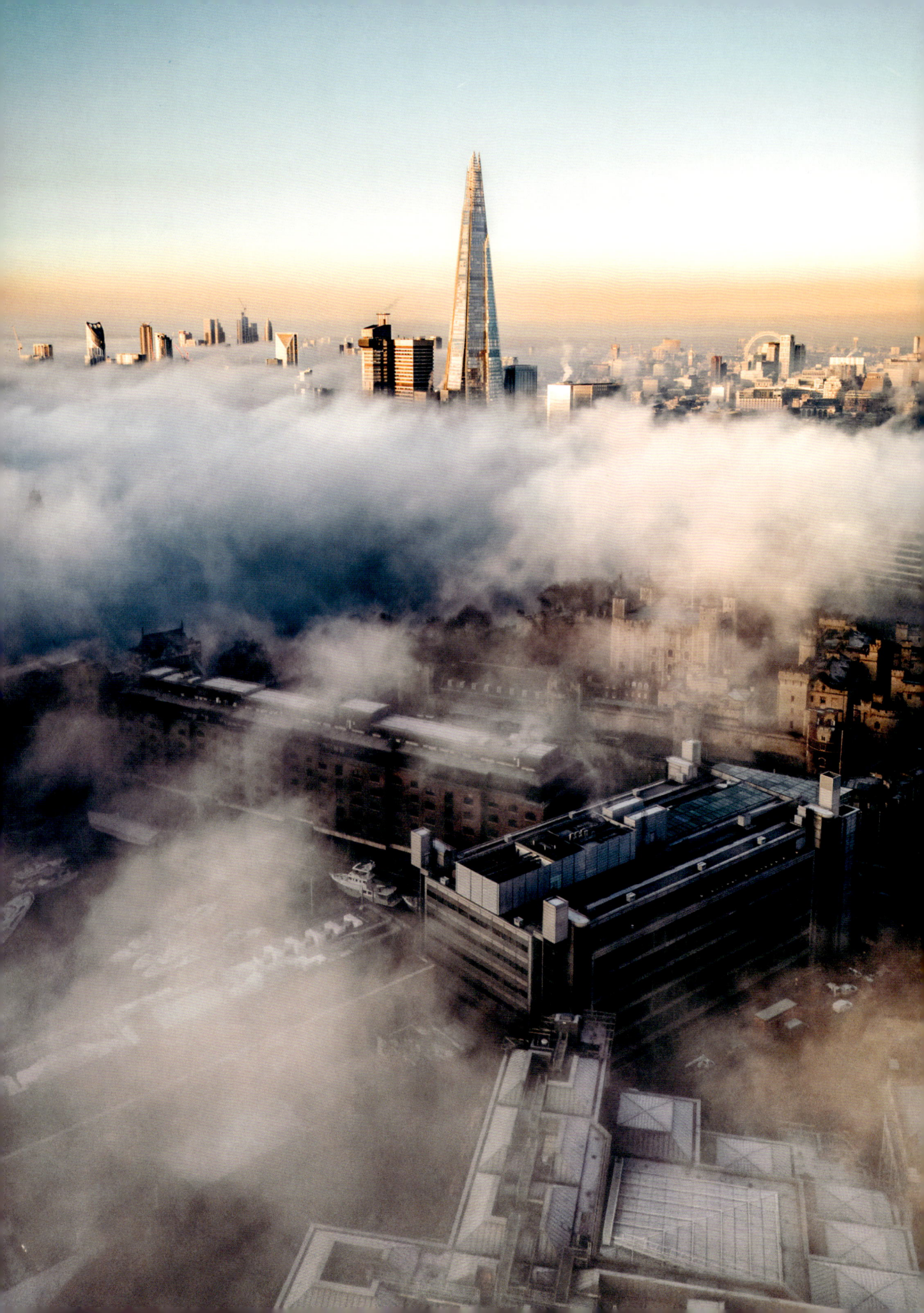

The Weather ♦ London's climate is less about extremes and more about nuance—a steady rhythm of overcast skies, crisp breezes, and the occasional golden afternoon. In a city where style is subtle and life unfolds at a considered pace, the weather behaves in much the same way: rarely dramatic and always part of the city's quiet charm. ♦ While London's winters may not be particularly snowy, when the snow does arrive, just an inch or two of precipitation can cause the city to go quiet. Trains and buses are often canceled or delayed, and in a city ill-prepared for snow clearing, sidewalks and roads can become slippery and near impossible to cross. London's snow may be brief, but it's also beautiful, leading to magical images for the photographers quick enough to capture the moment. ♦ London's foggy reputation was cemented in the 19th and early 20th centuries, not because of natural fog alone, but as a result of coal smoke. The soot and sulfur that was emitted from burning coal used in heating and factories mixed with natural fog, creating a "peasouper," so named for its greenish-yellow tint. This thick smog was toxic, and in 1952 caused the Great Smog, which lasted five days, stopped trains, cars, and public events, and caused thousands of deaths. That disaster led to the Clean Air Act of 1956, which mandated a movement towards smokeless fuels. ♦ Today's fog is cleaner, thinner, and less frequent due to air pollution controls, but it still appears, especially in autumn and winter mornings, casting a romantic mist over the city. The River Thames acts as a magnet for fog as moisture rises off the water and condenses into fog that hugs the riverbanks, masking the bases of its iconic bridges and leading to otherworldly images, particularly for aerial photographers.

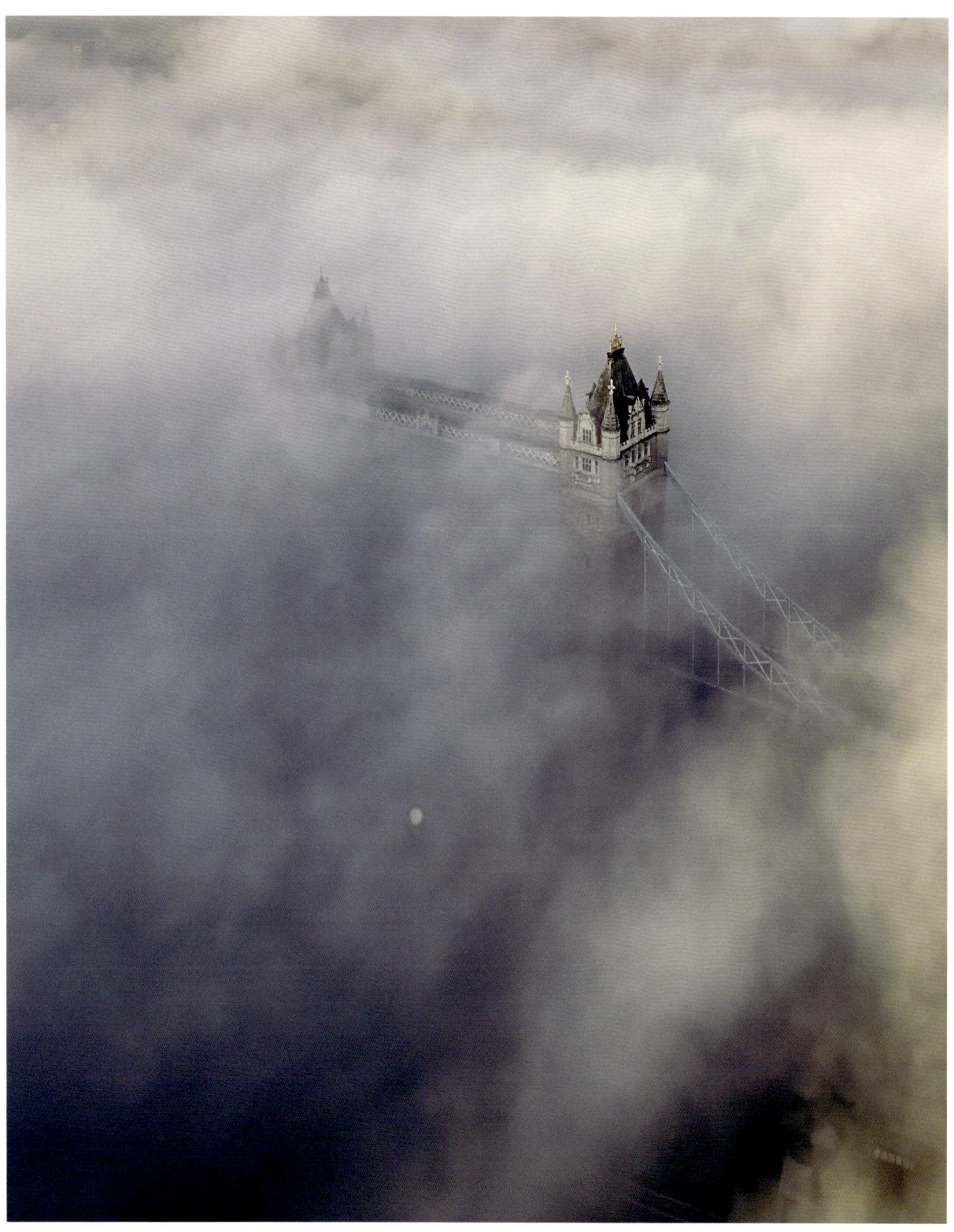

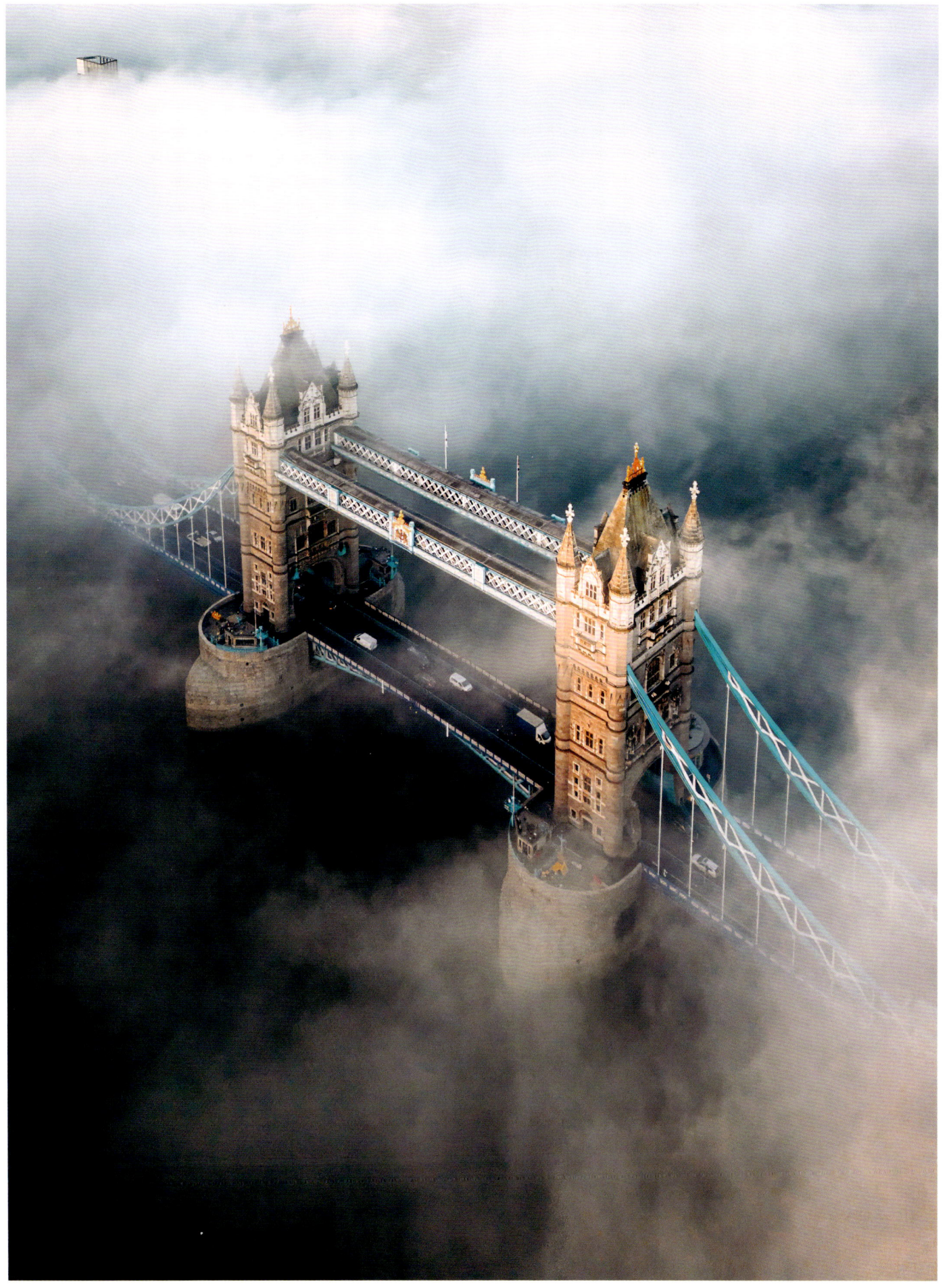

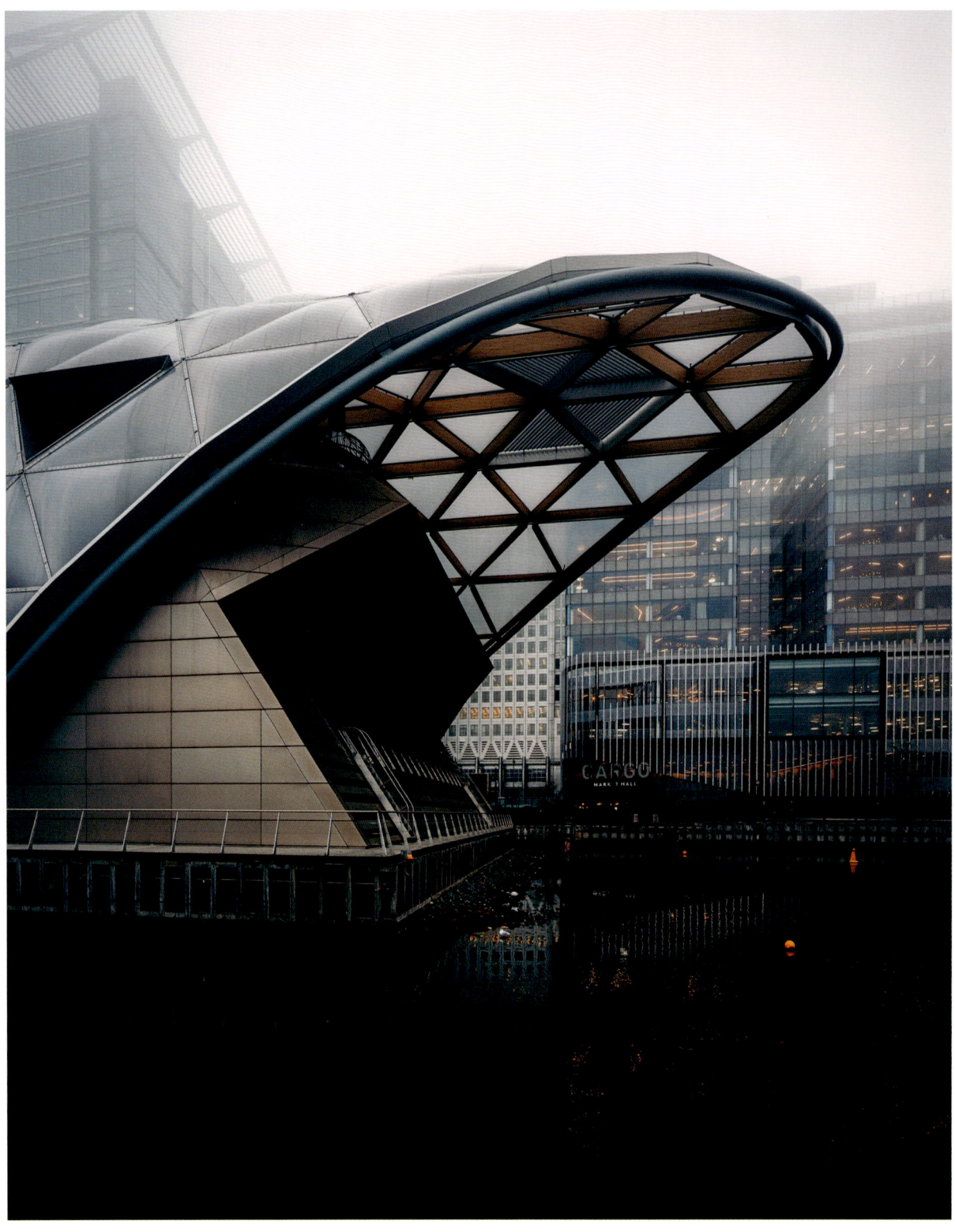

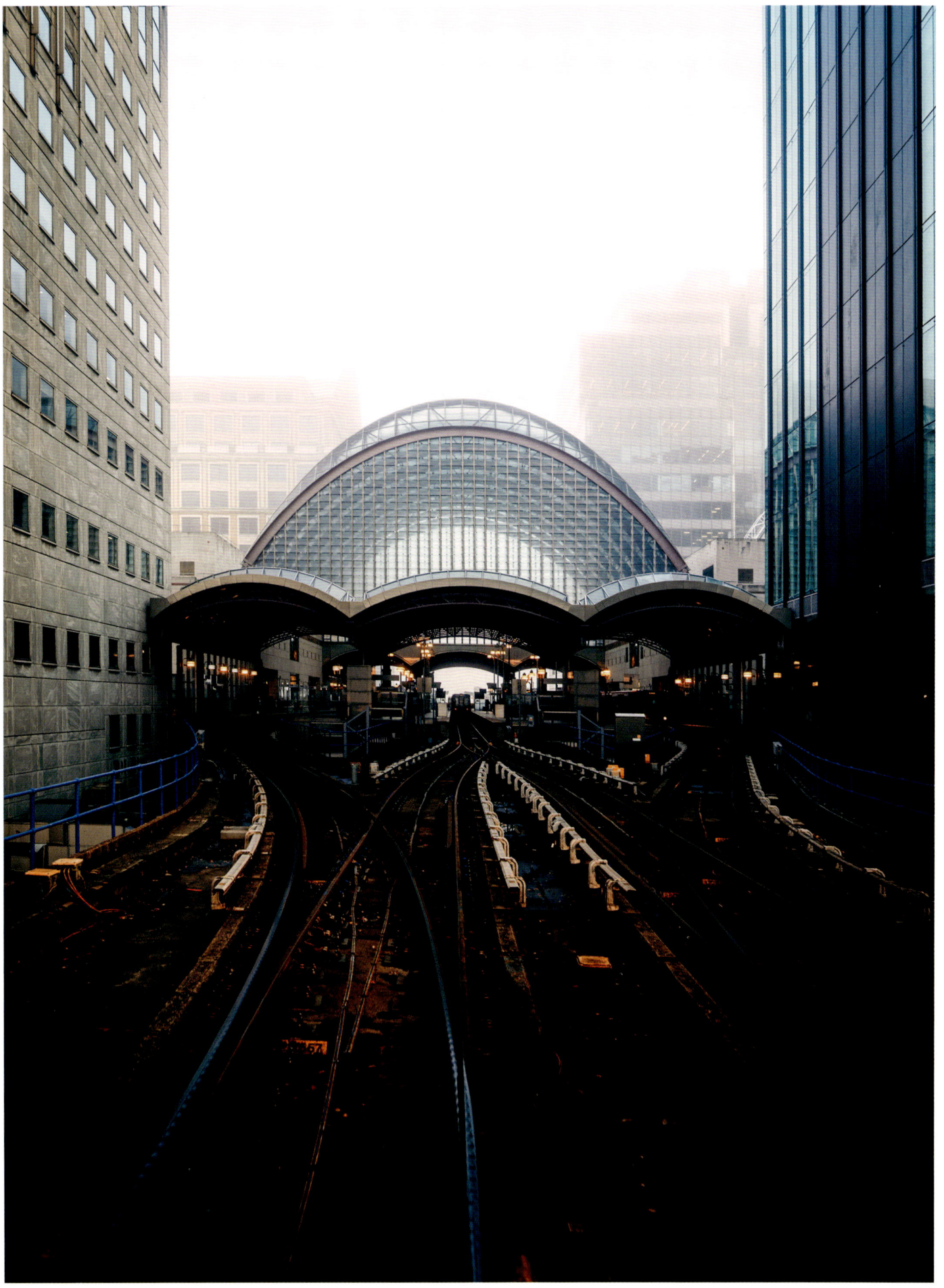

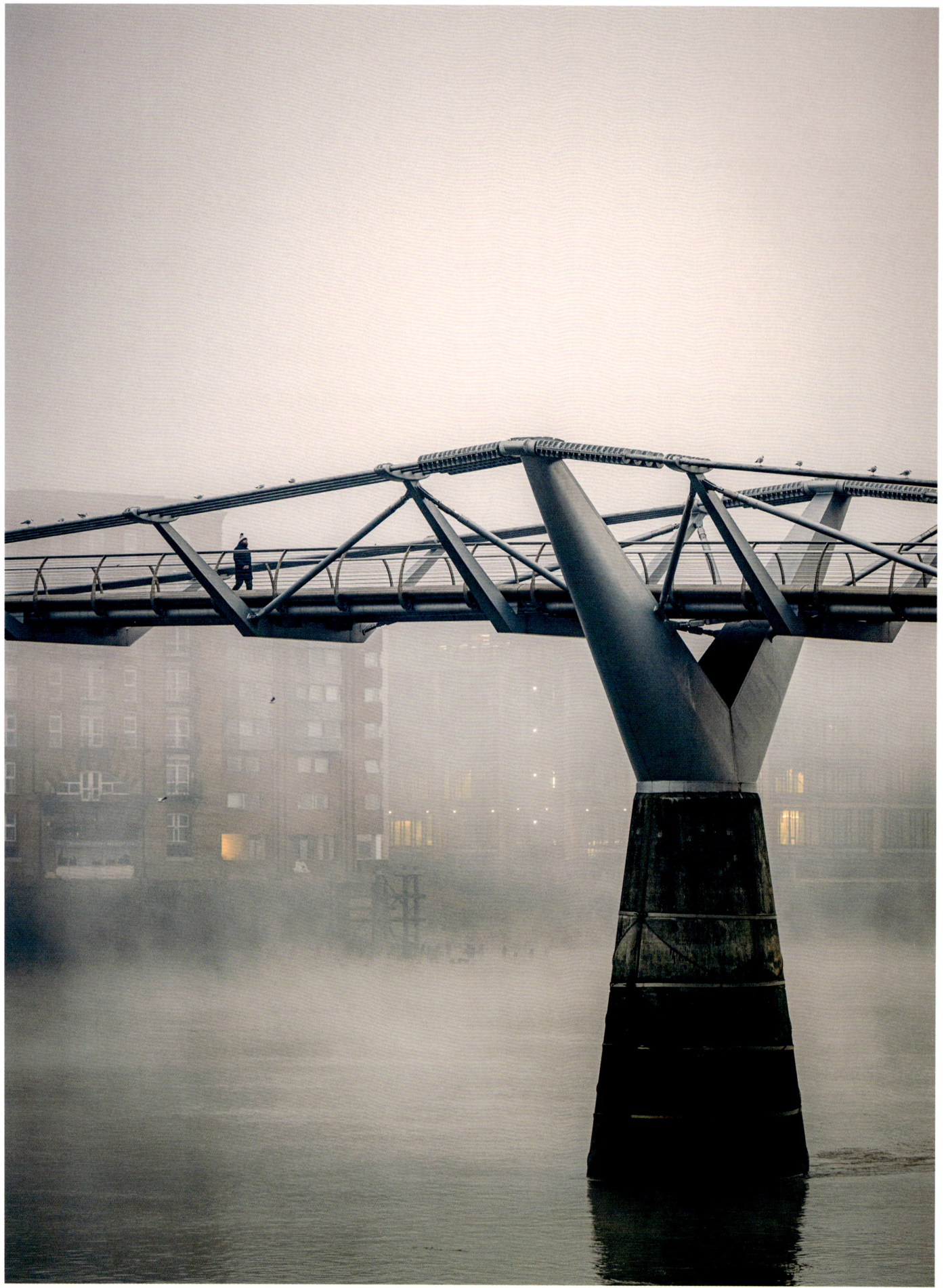

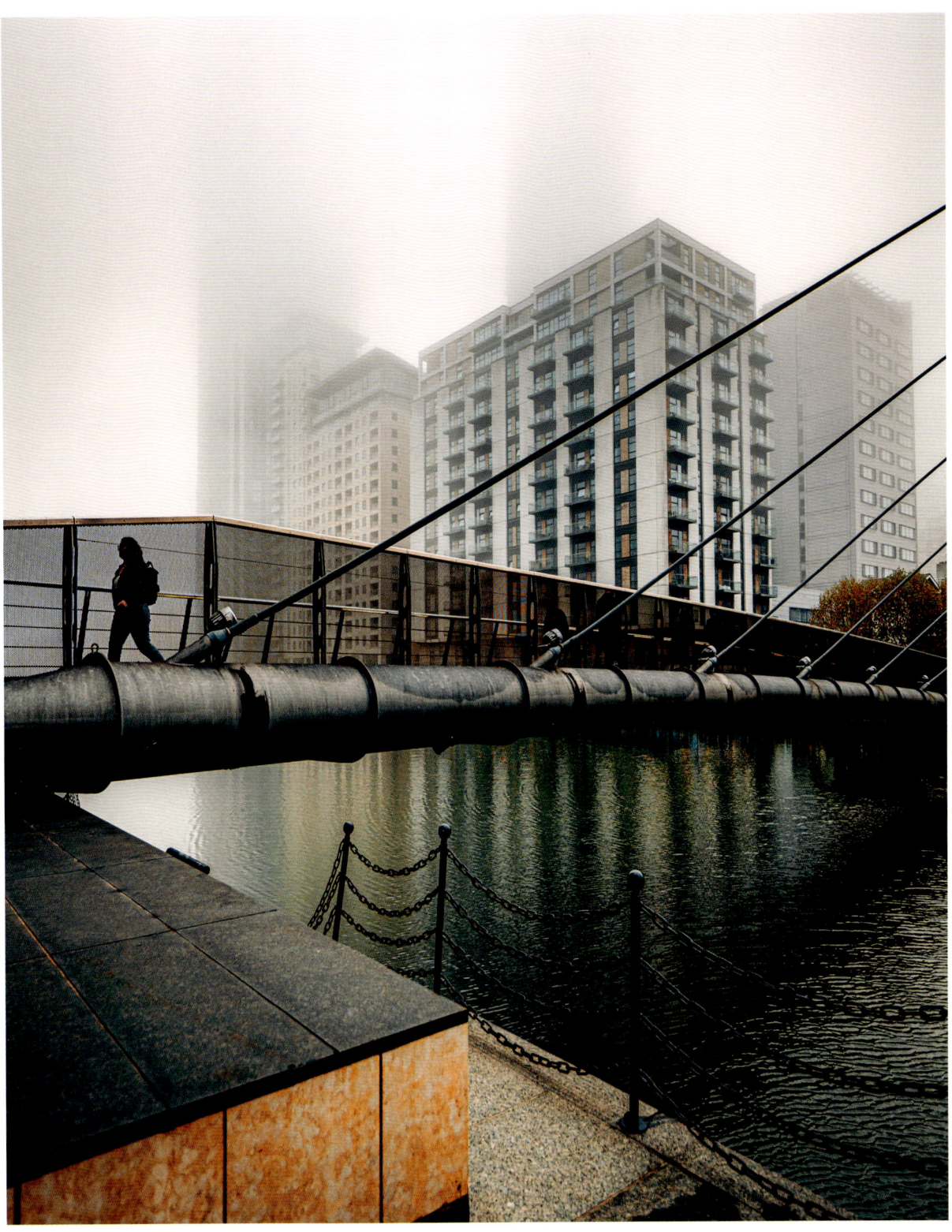

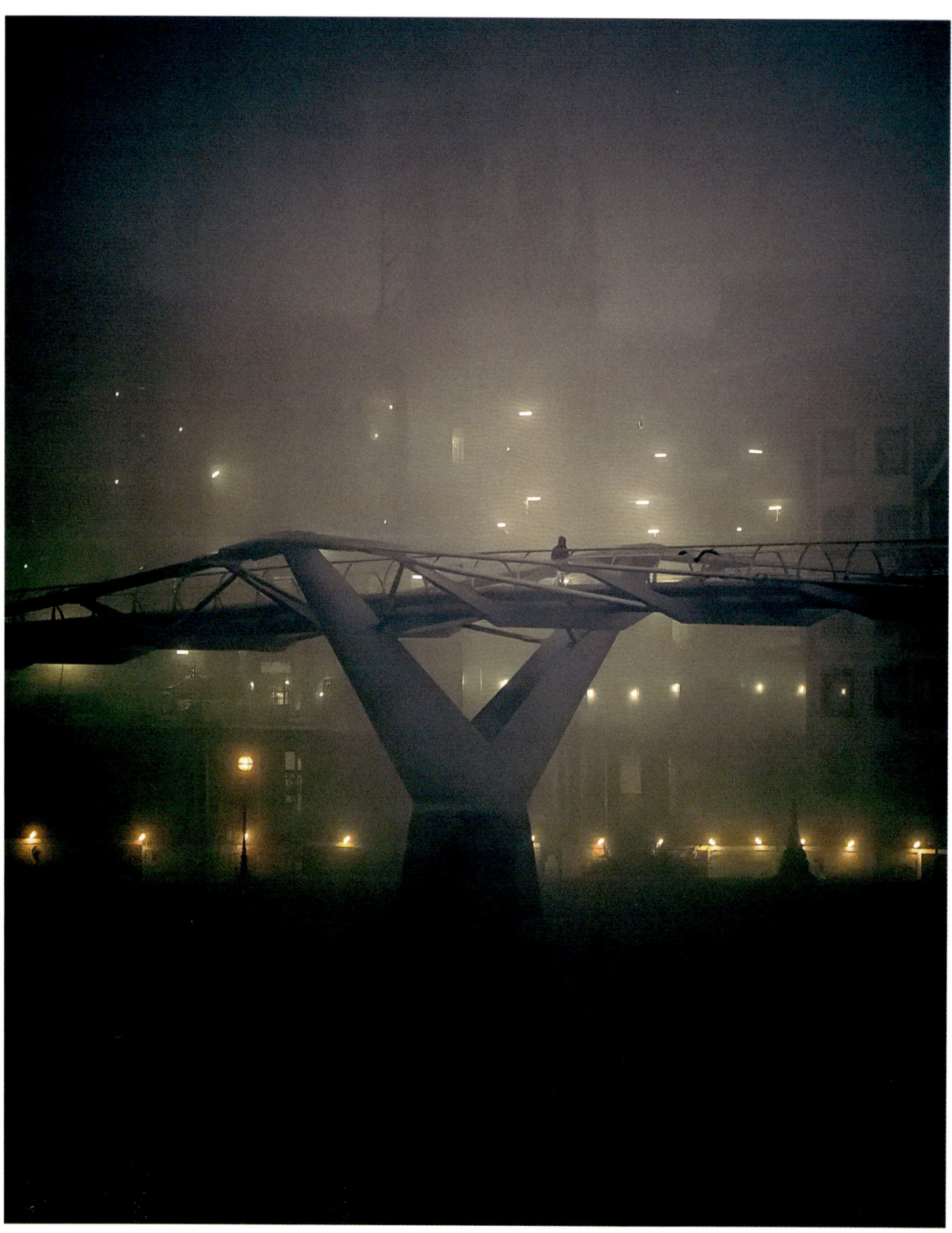

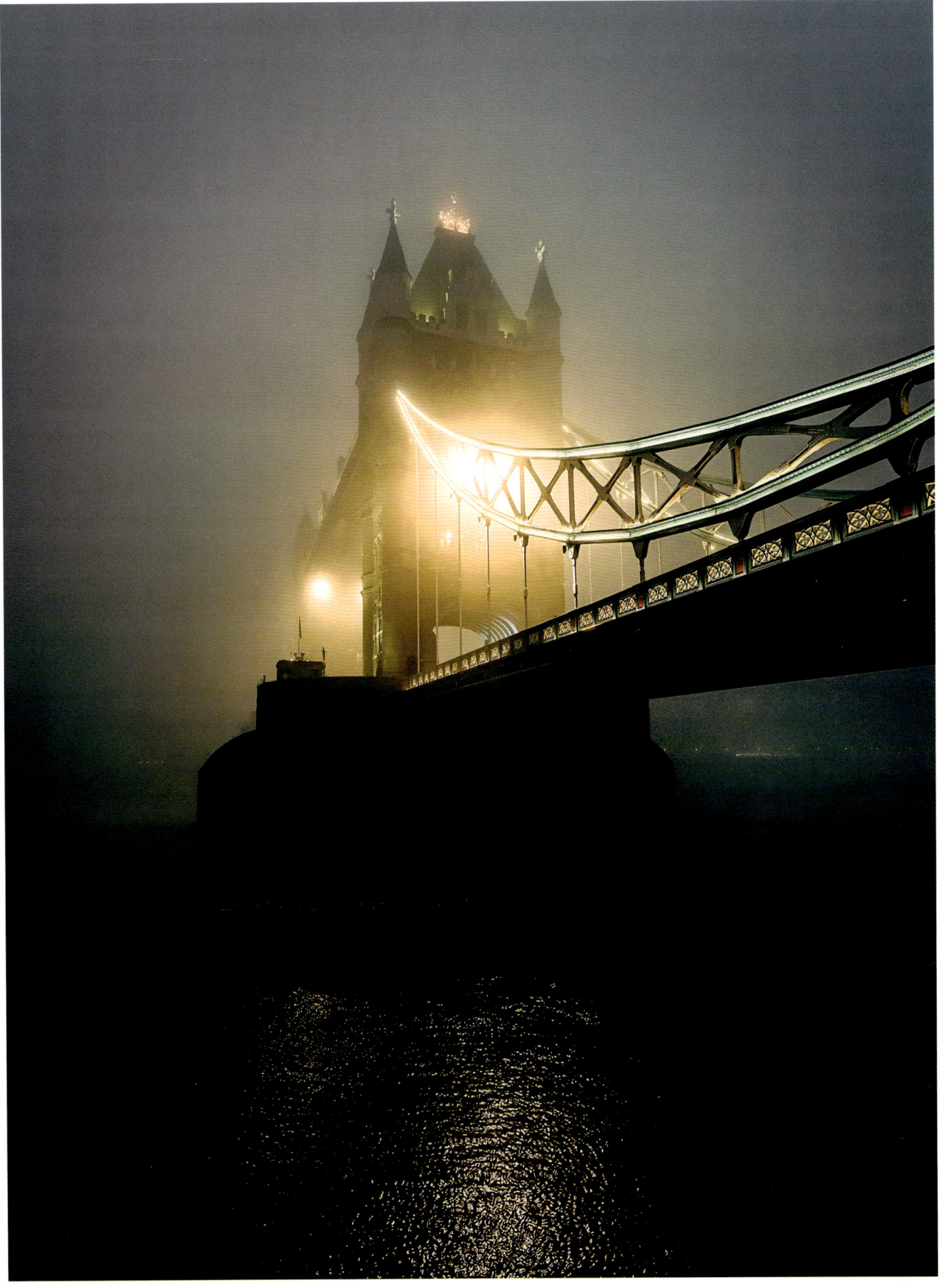

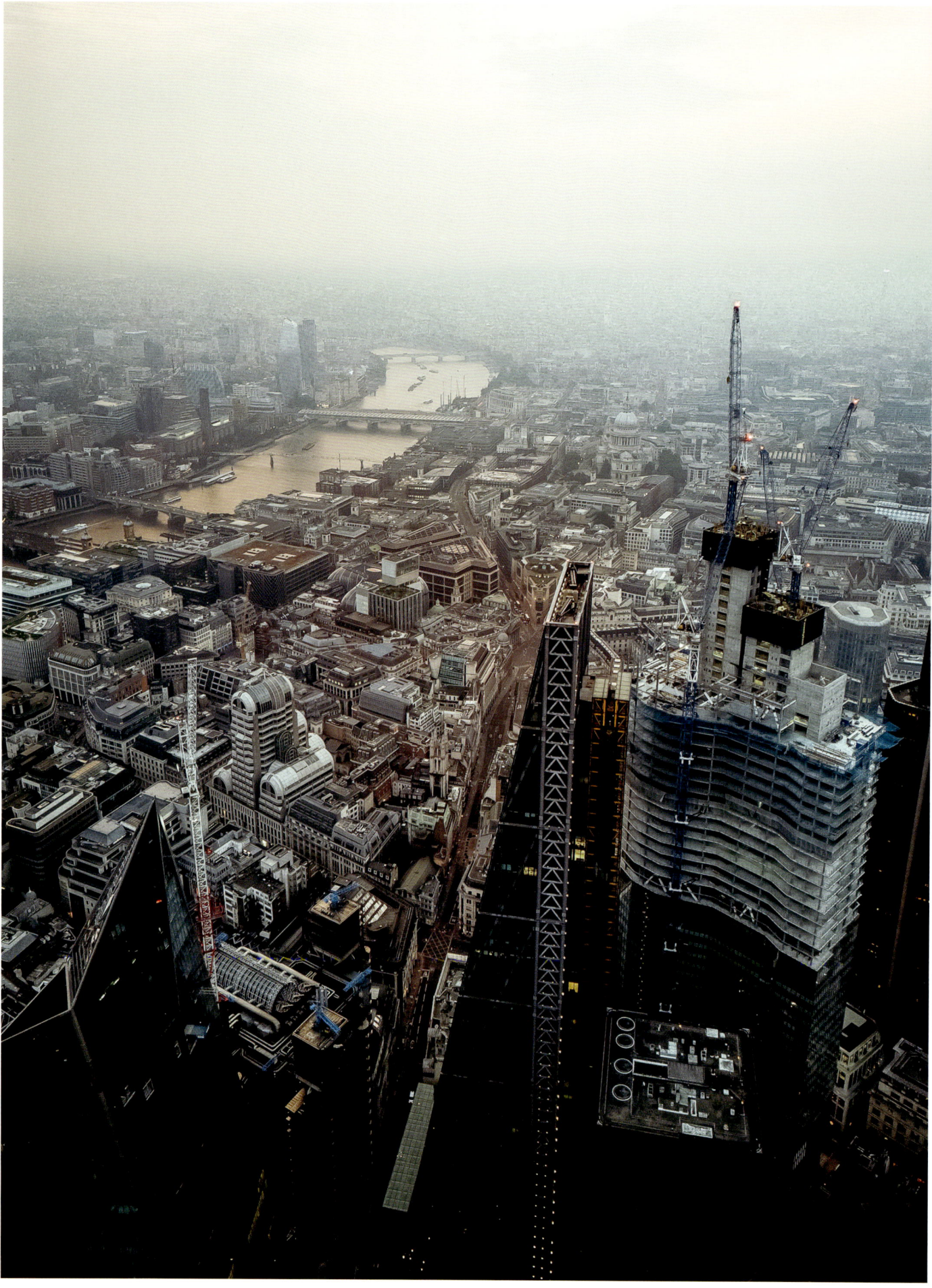

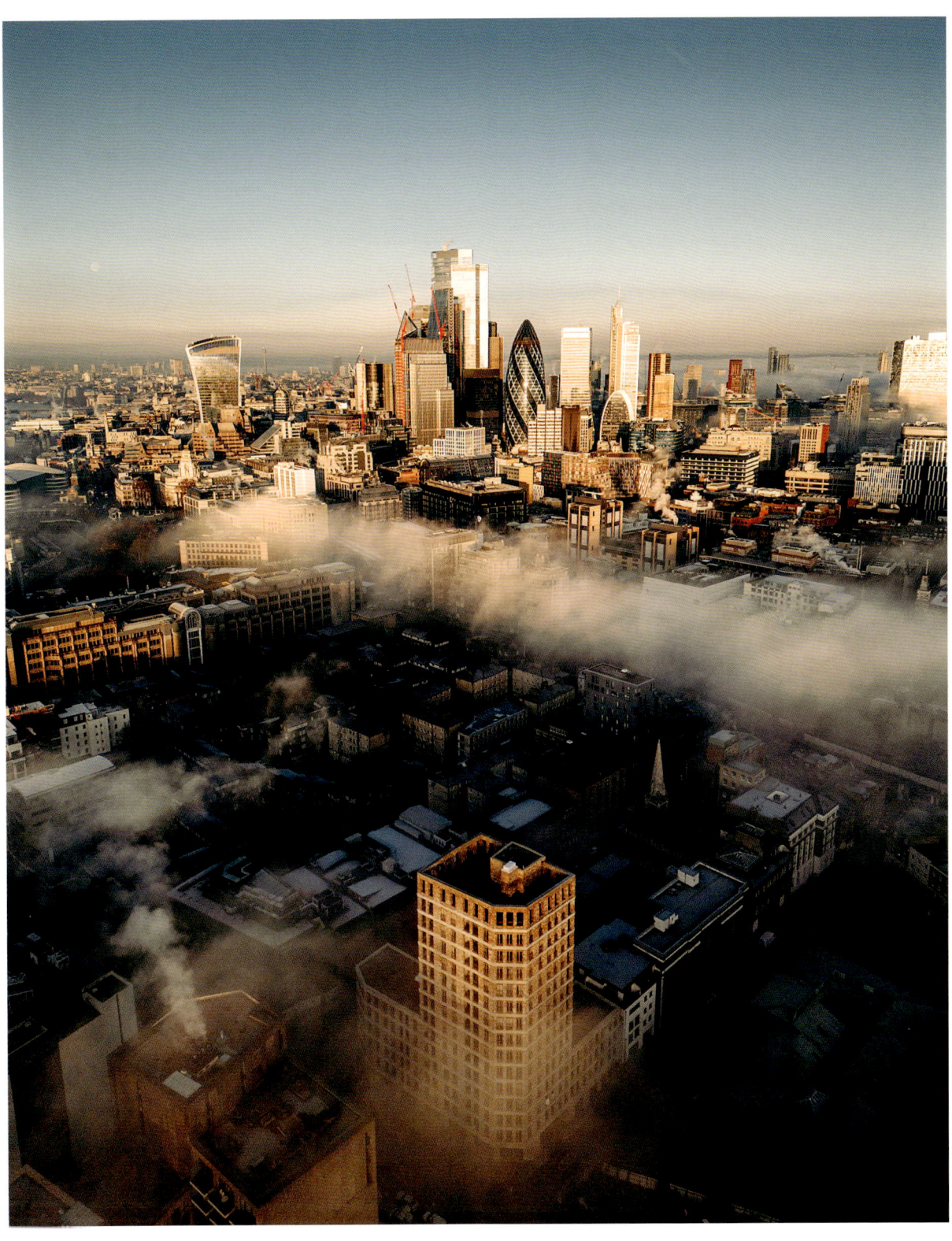

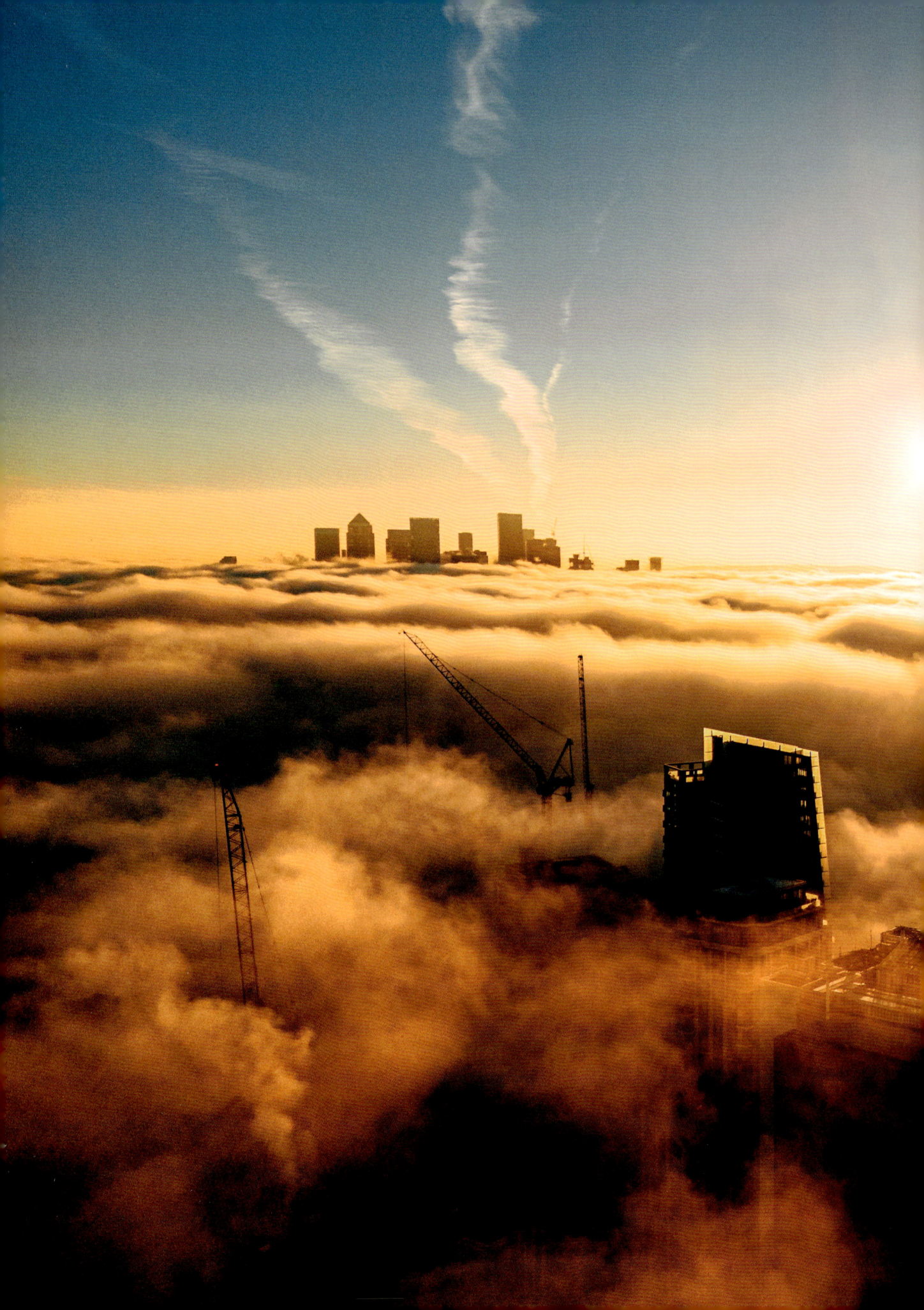

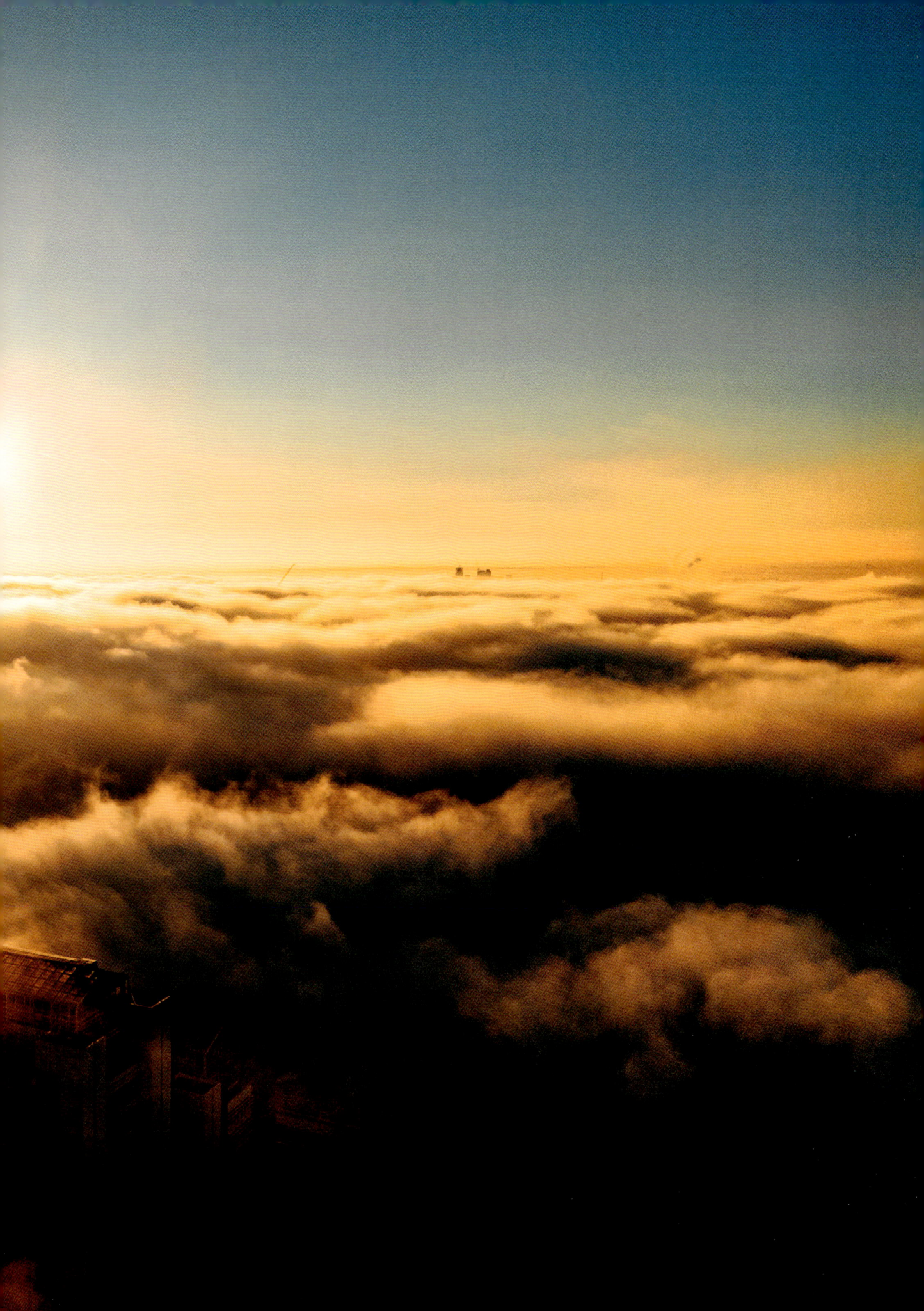

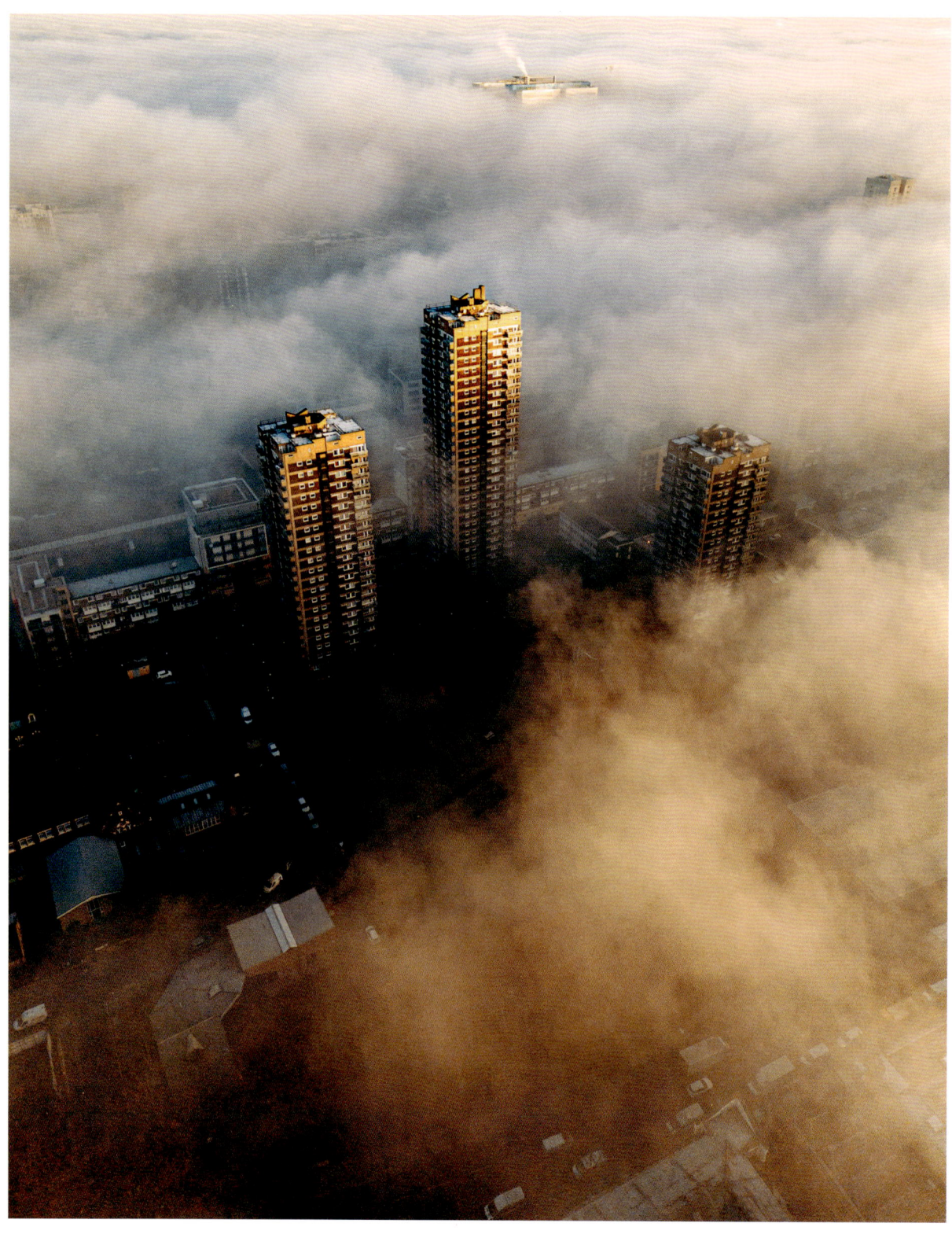

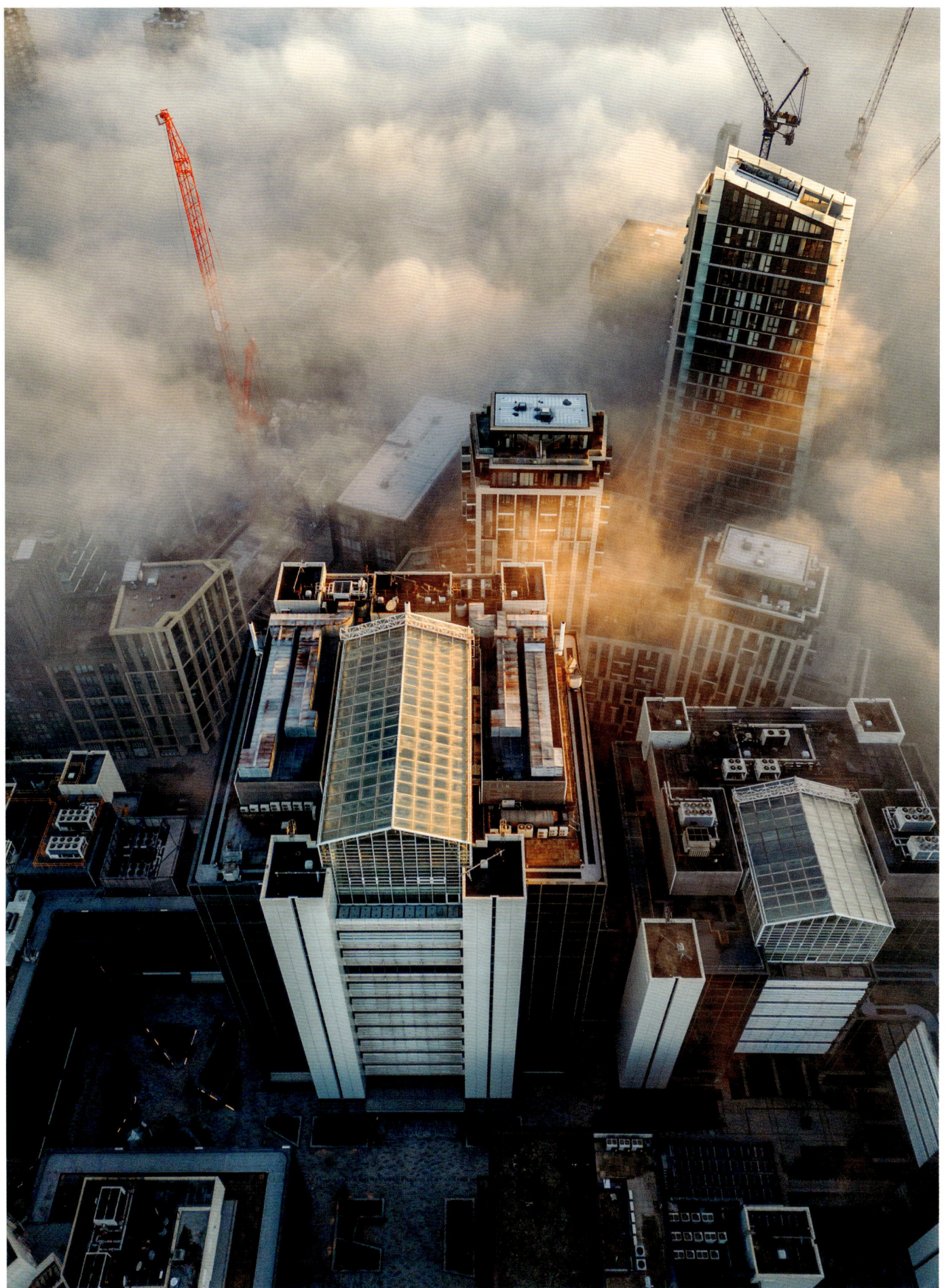

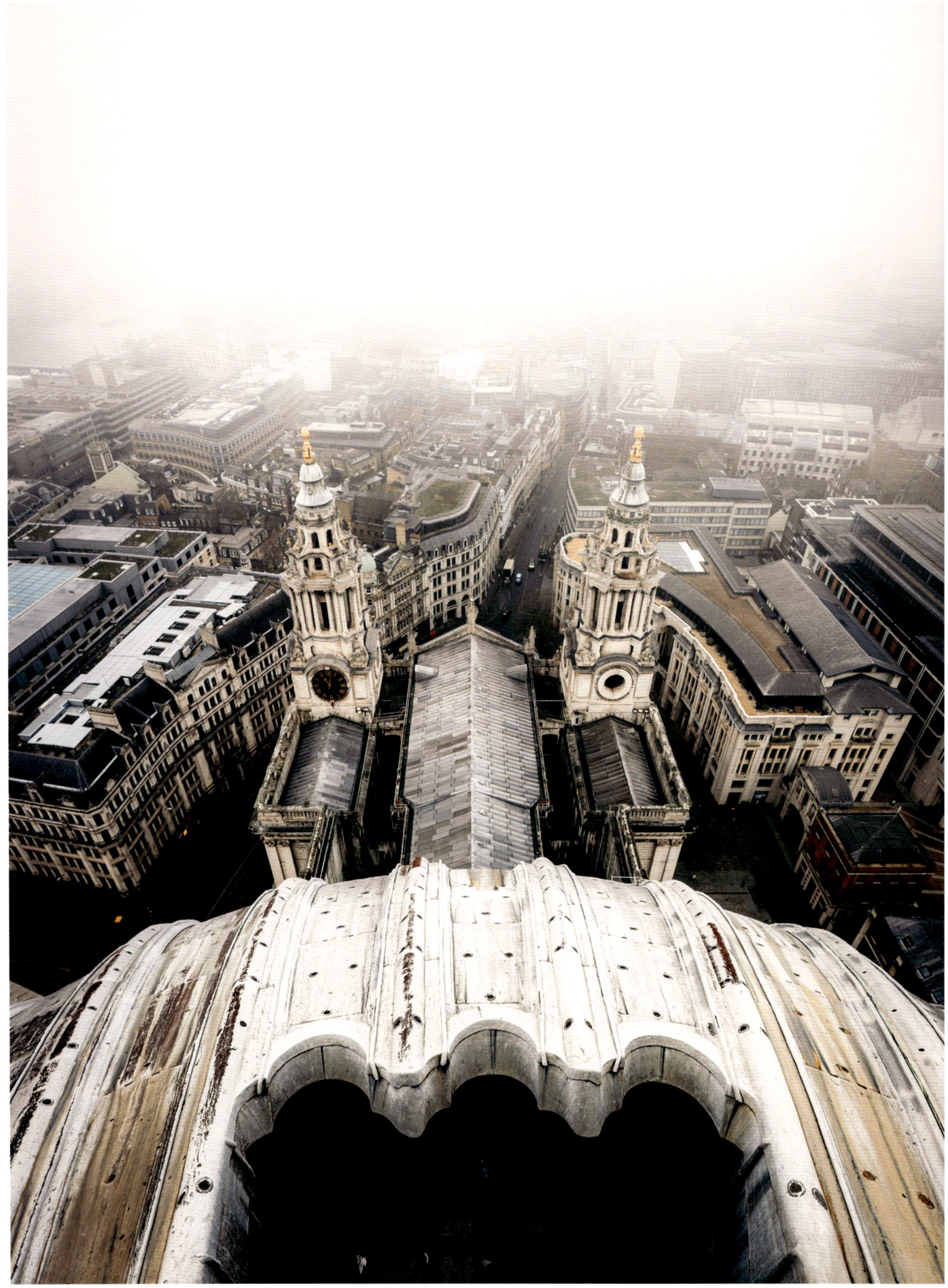

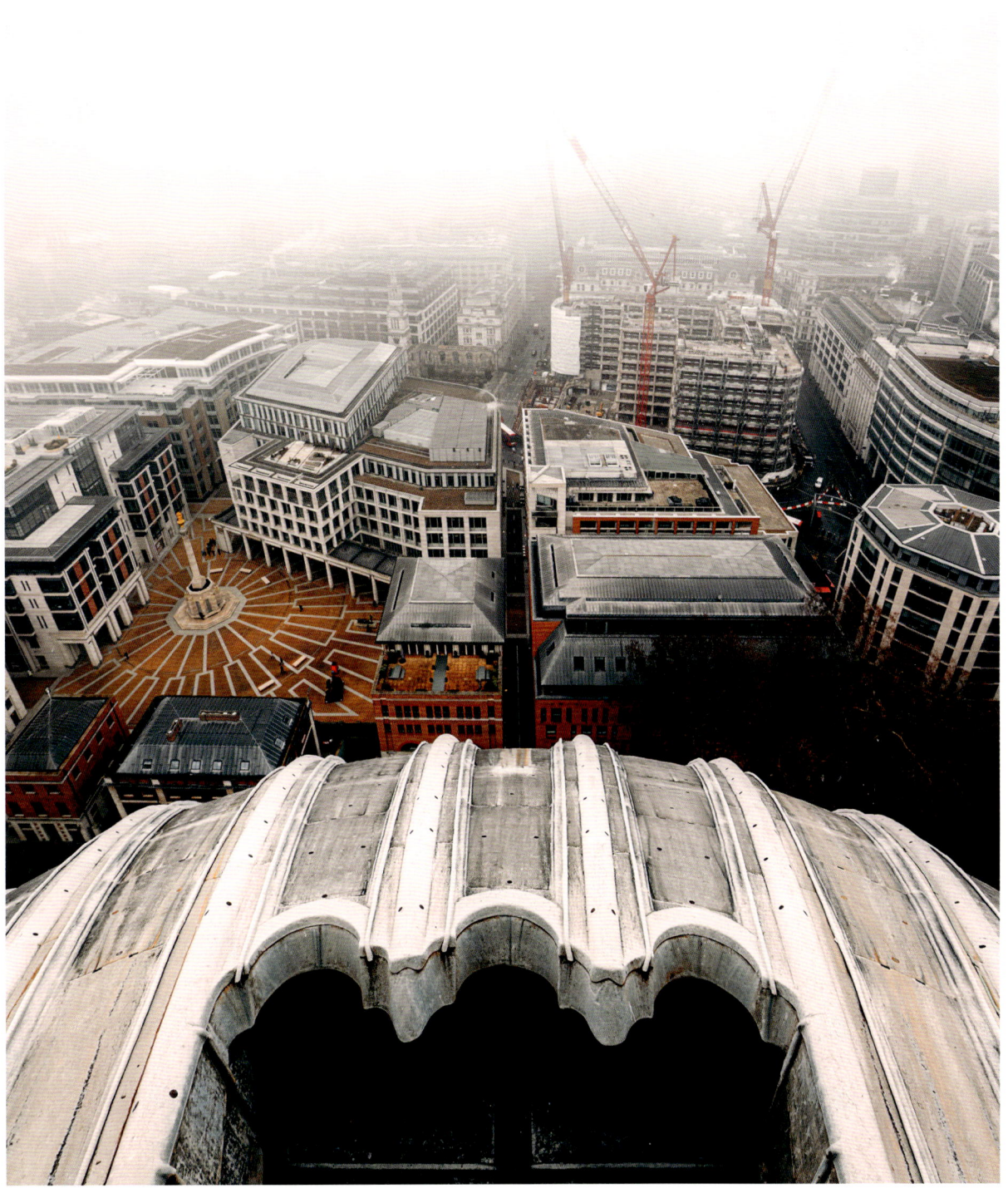

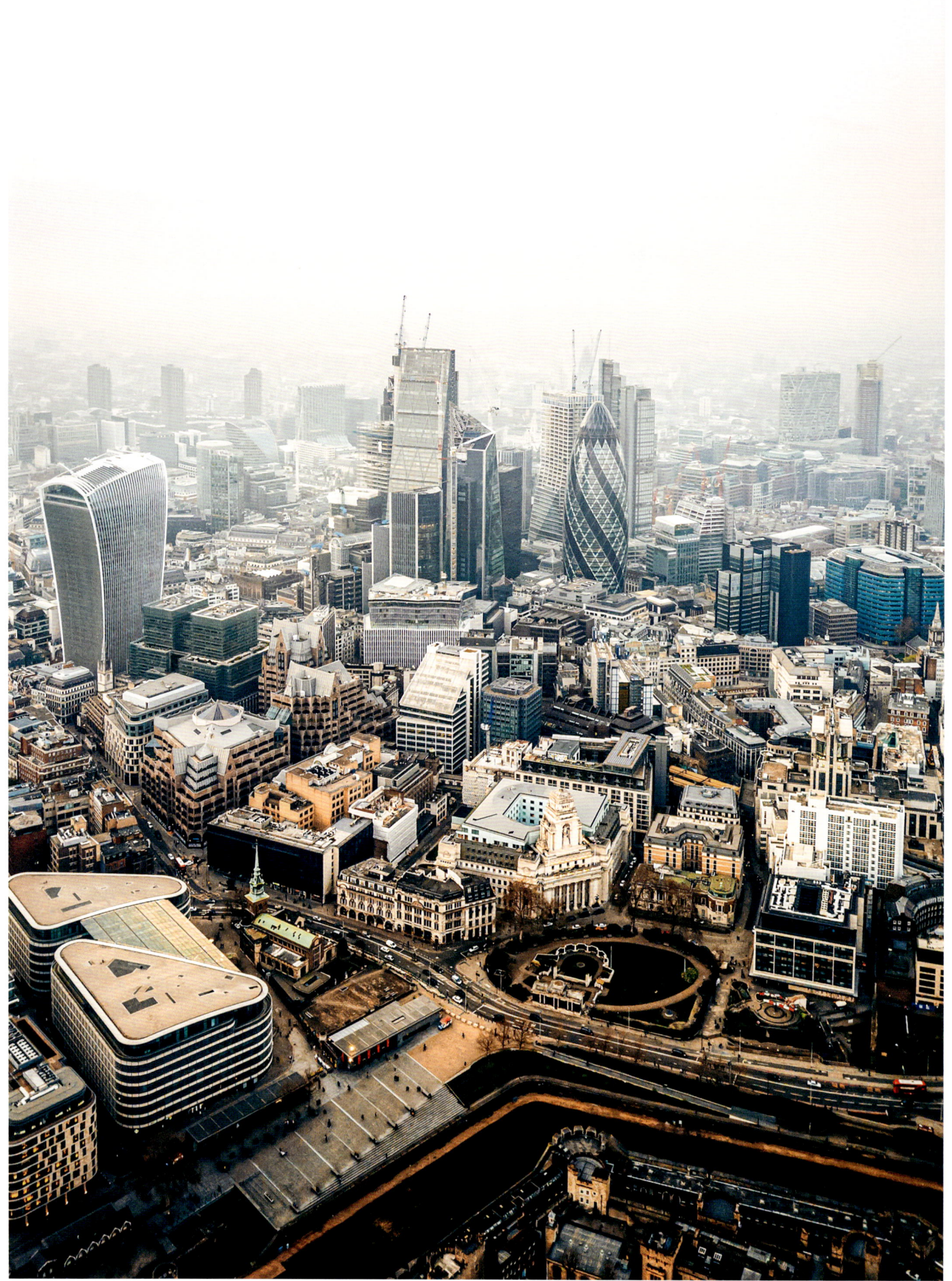

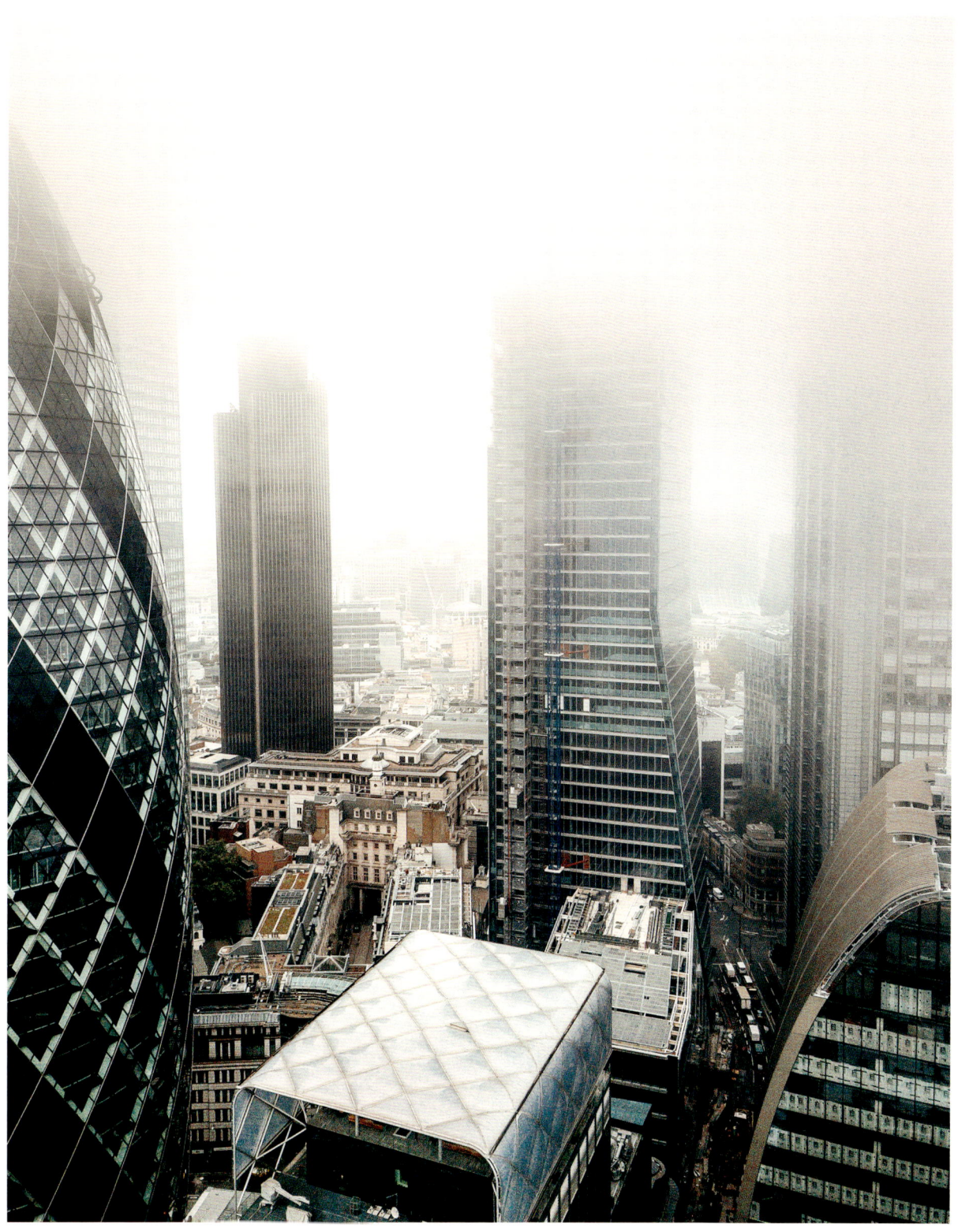

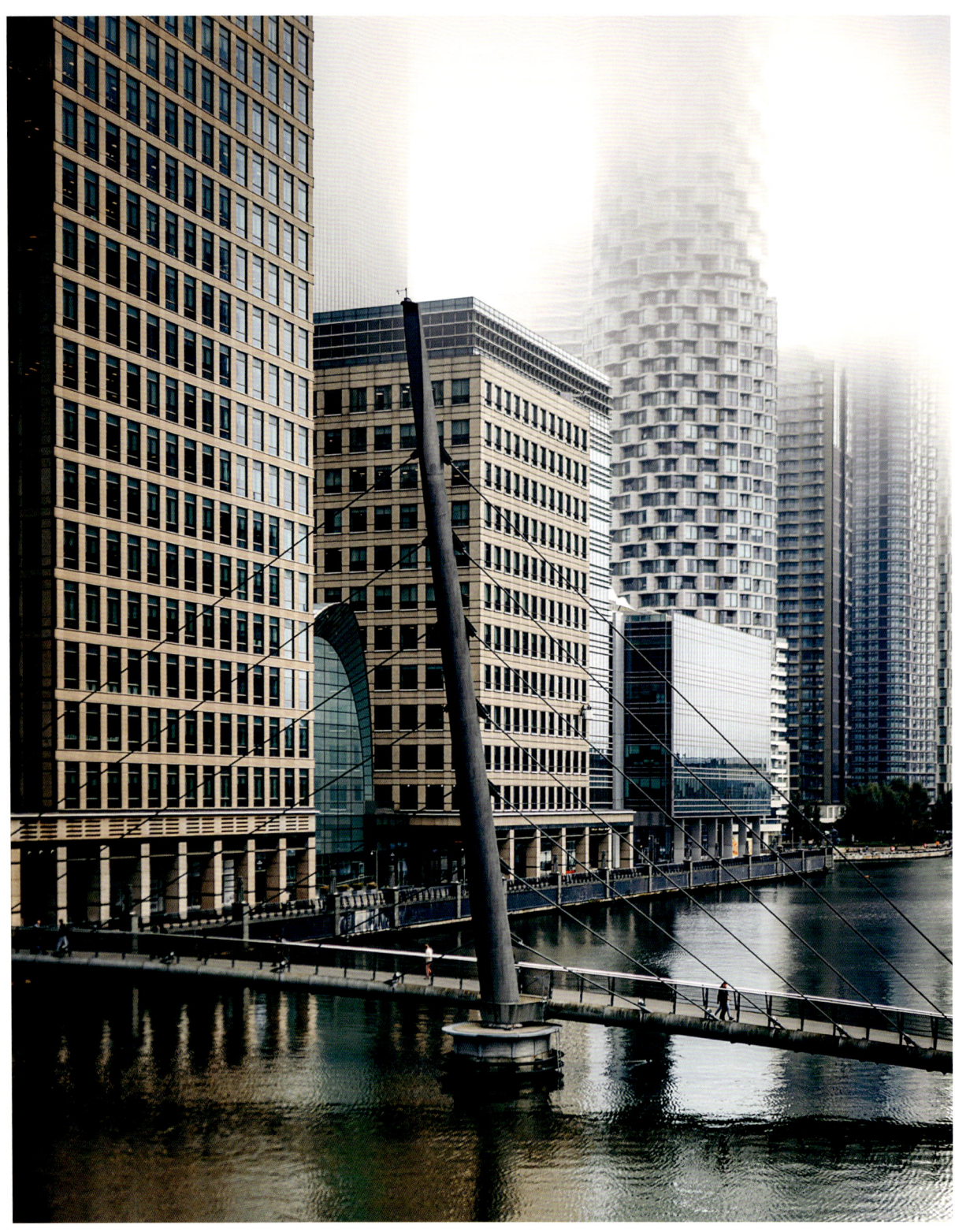

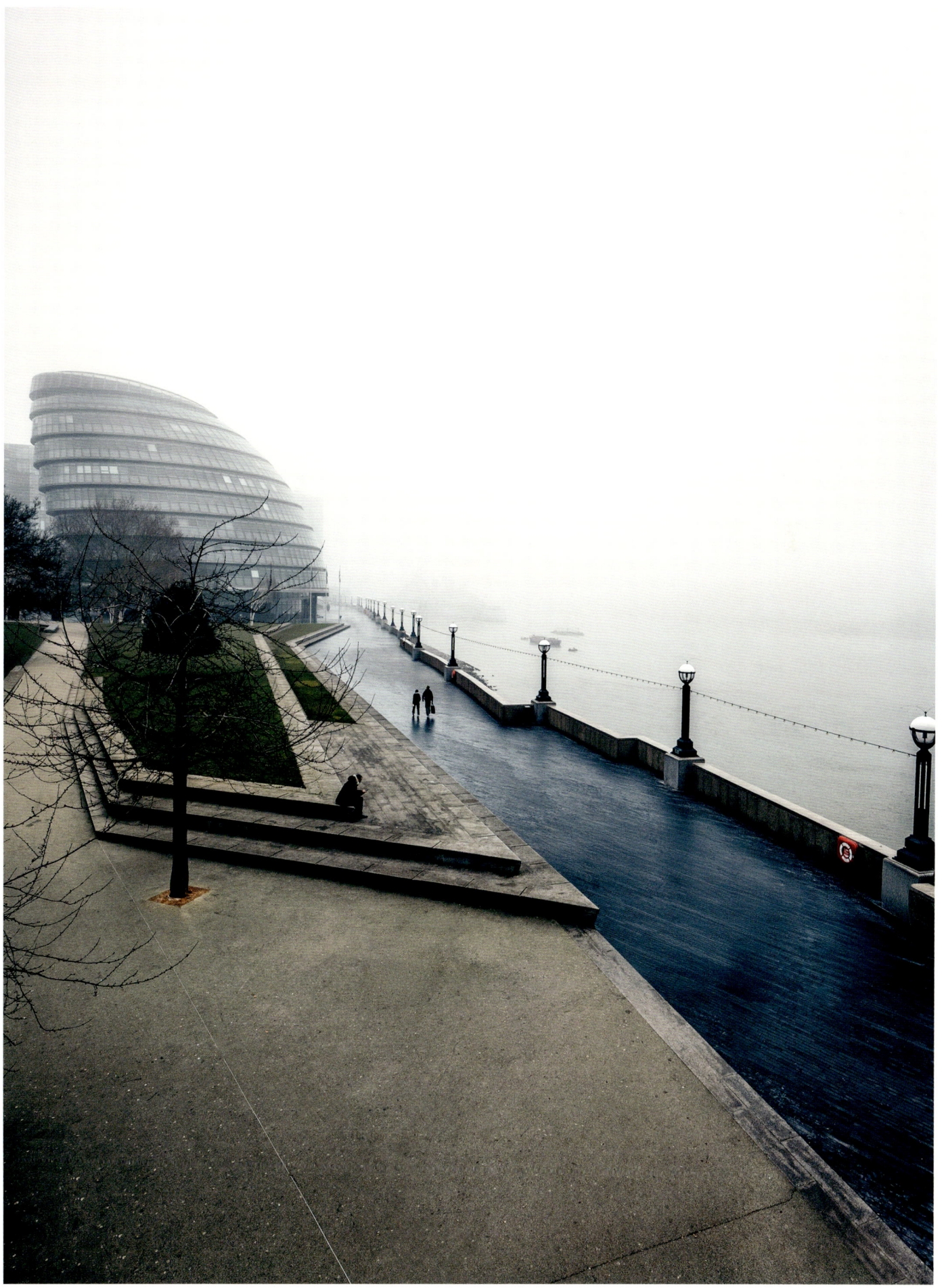

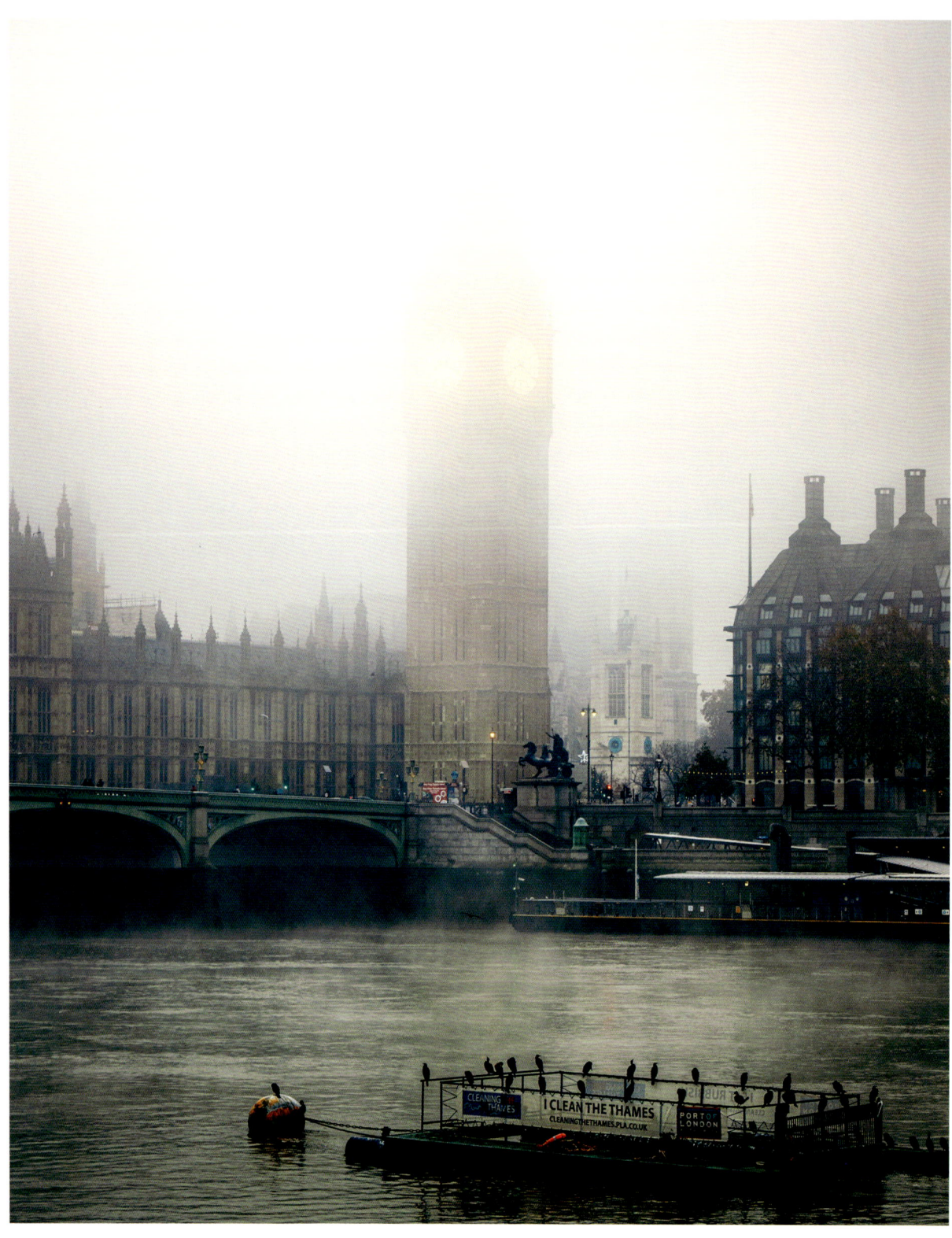

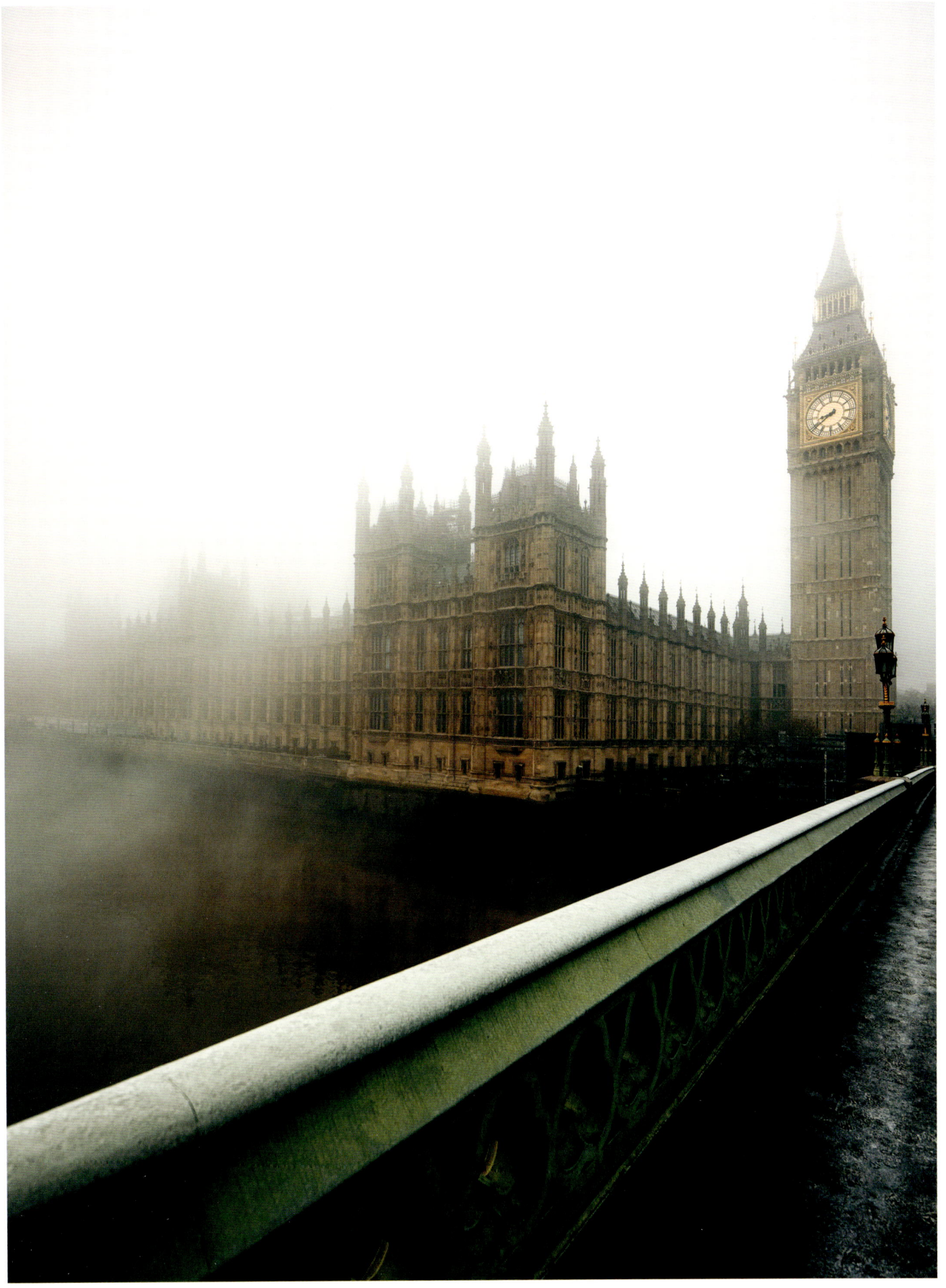

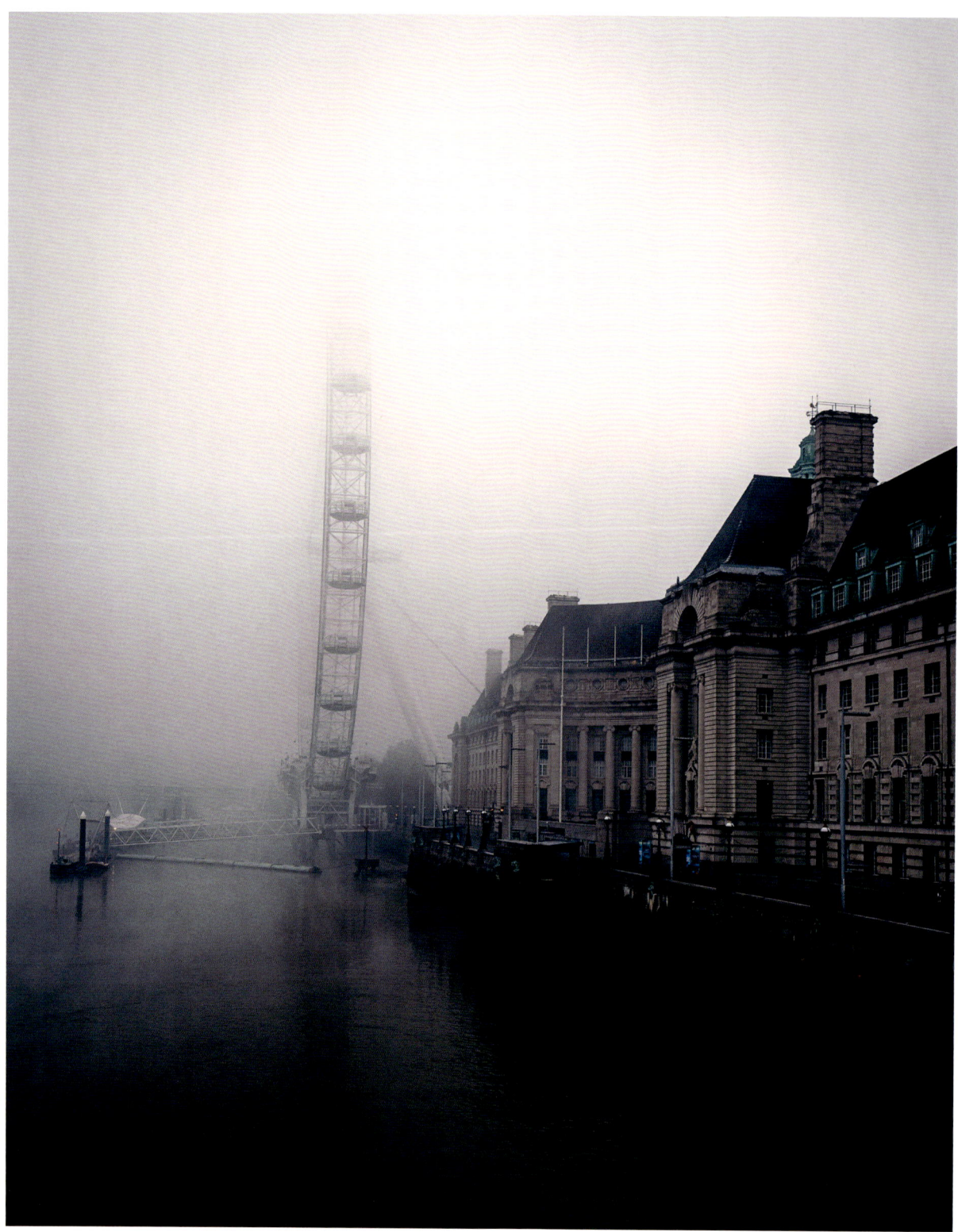

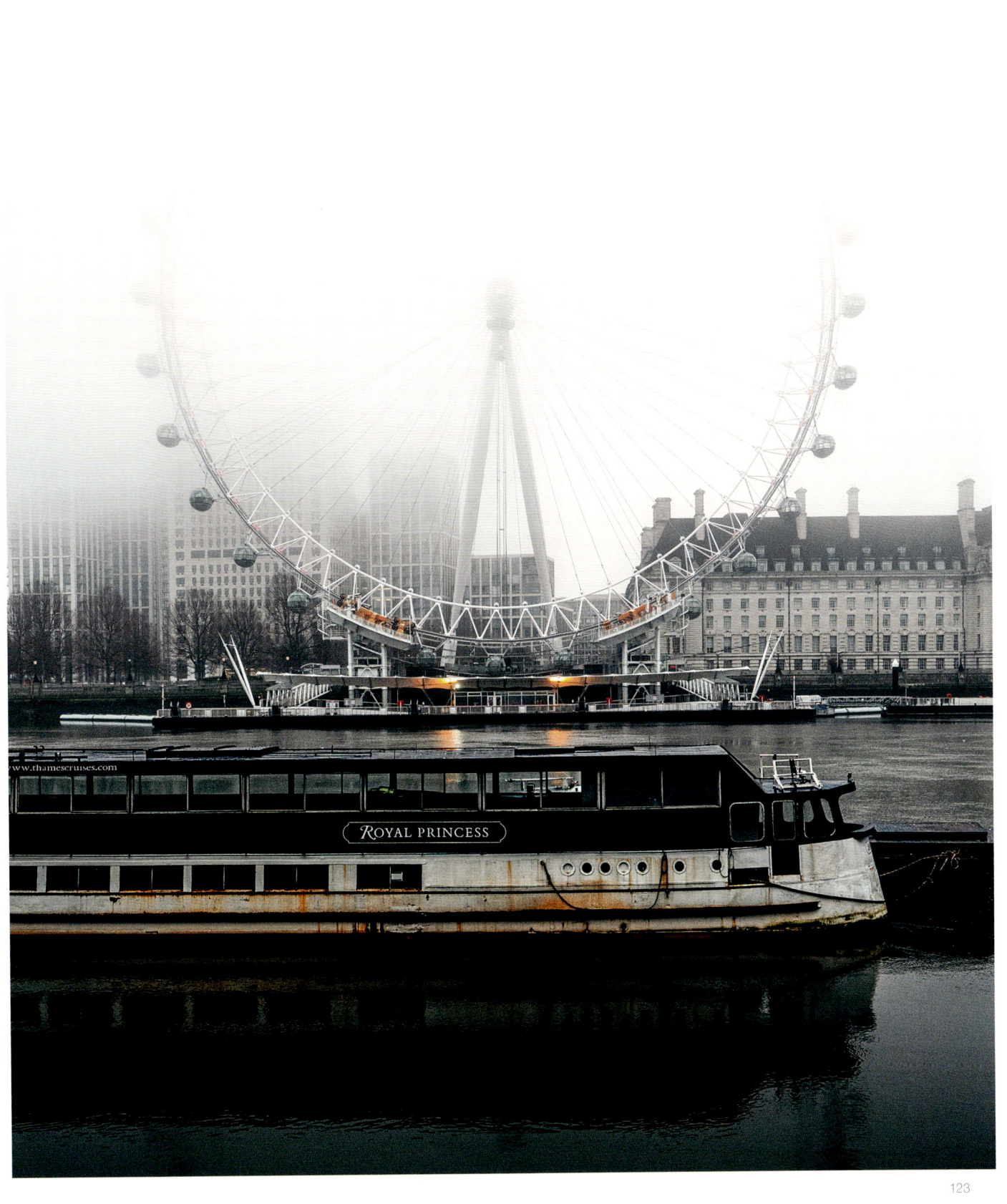

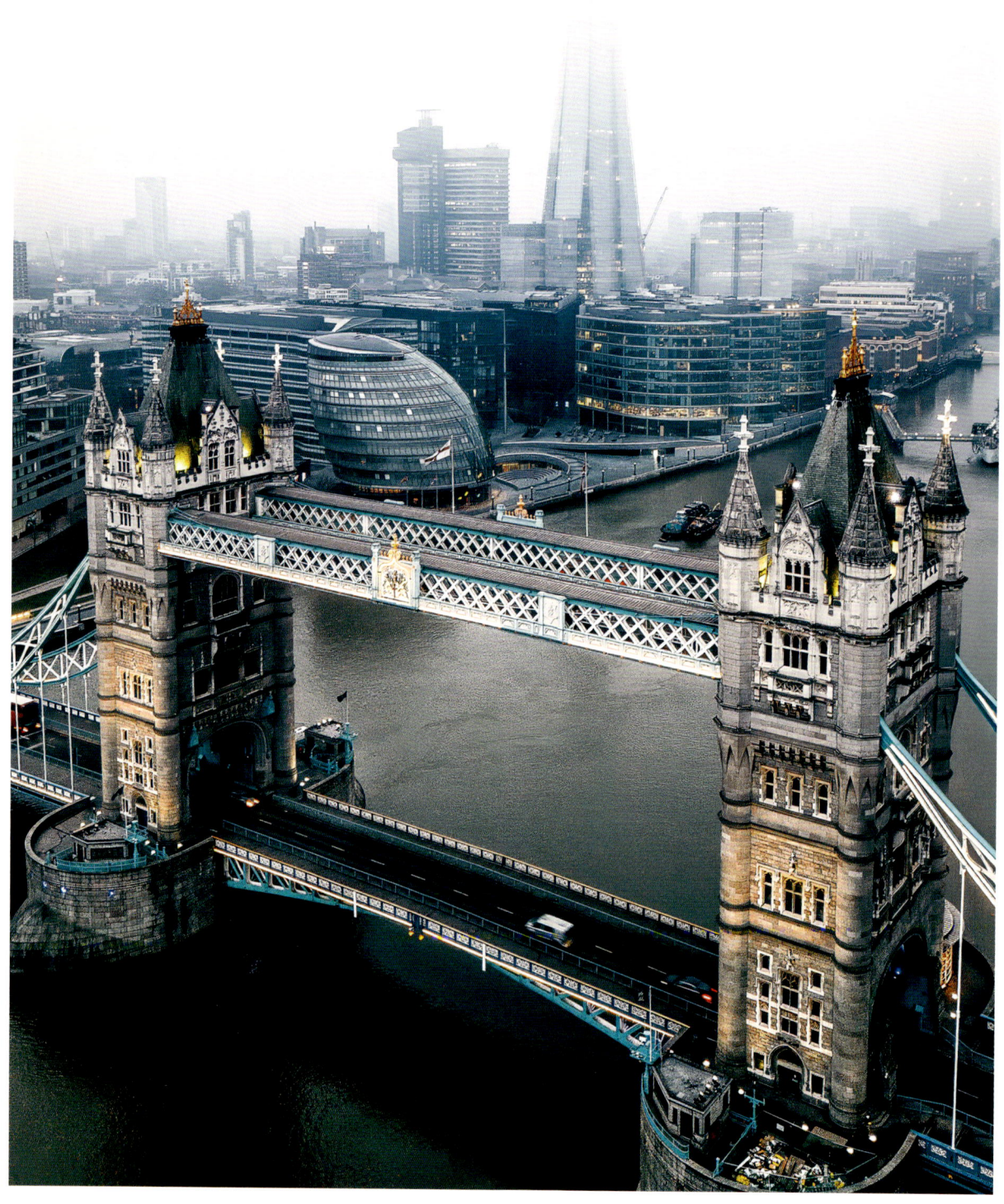

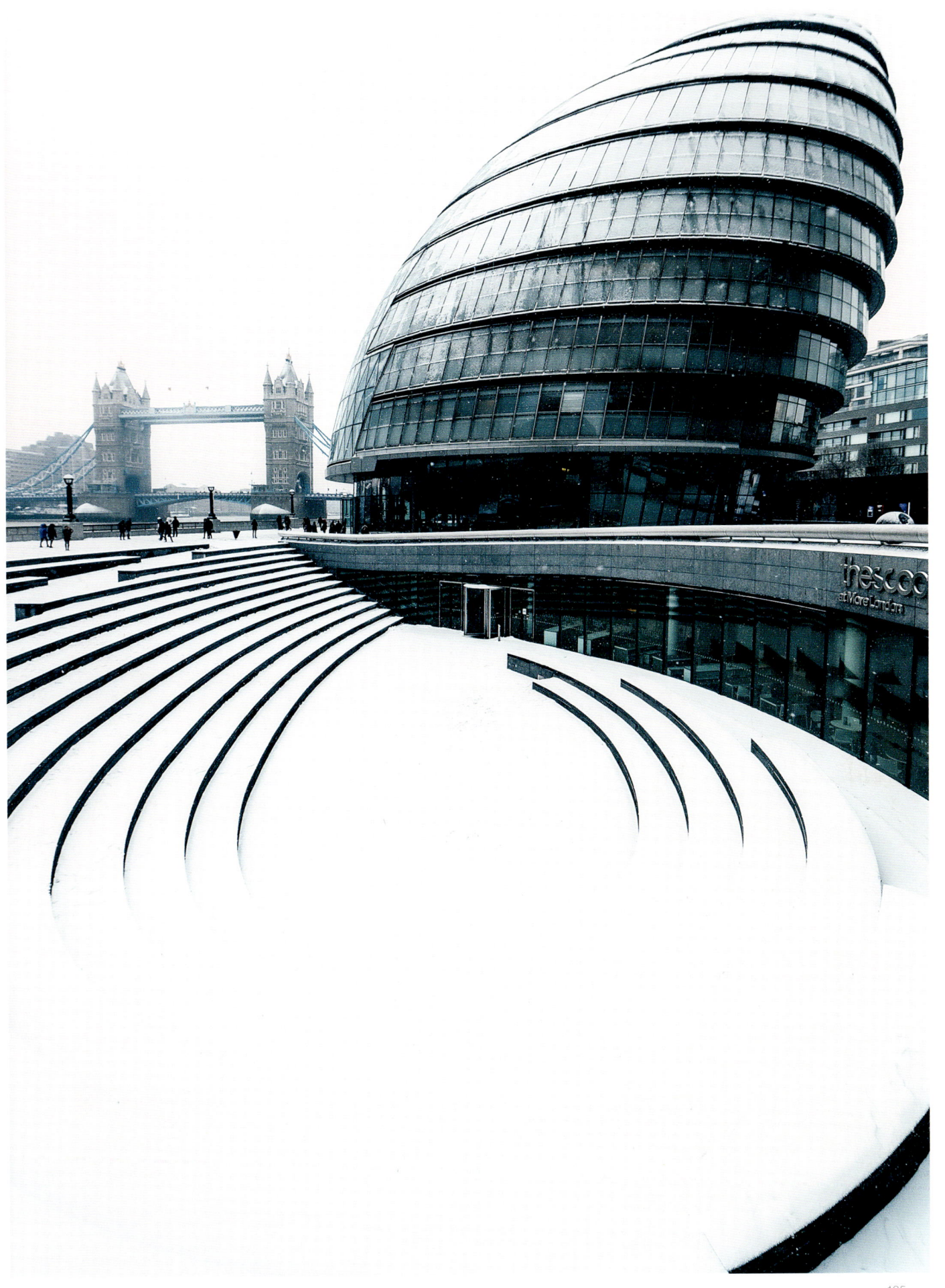

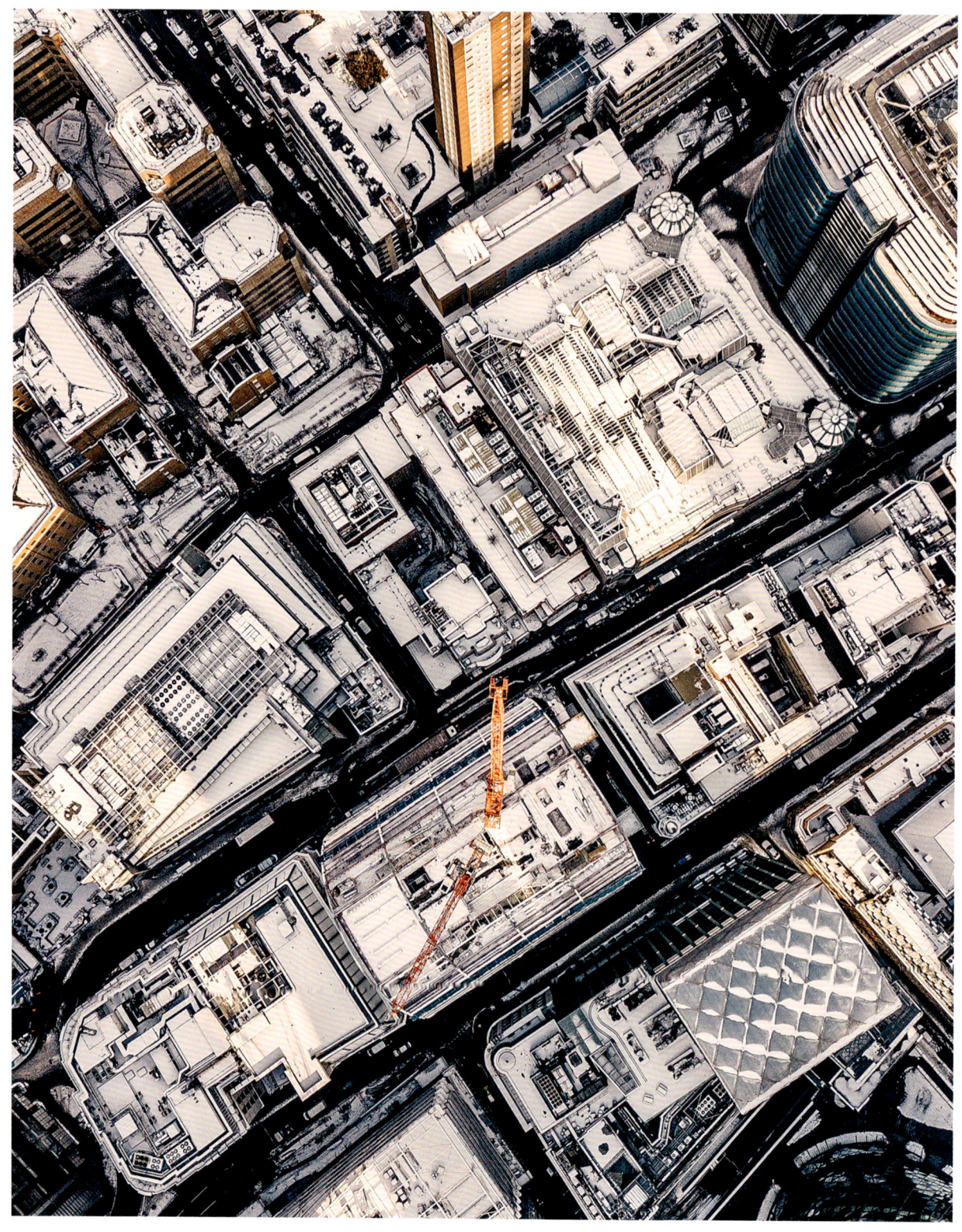

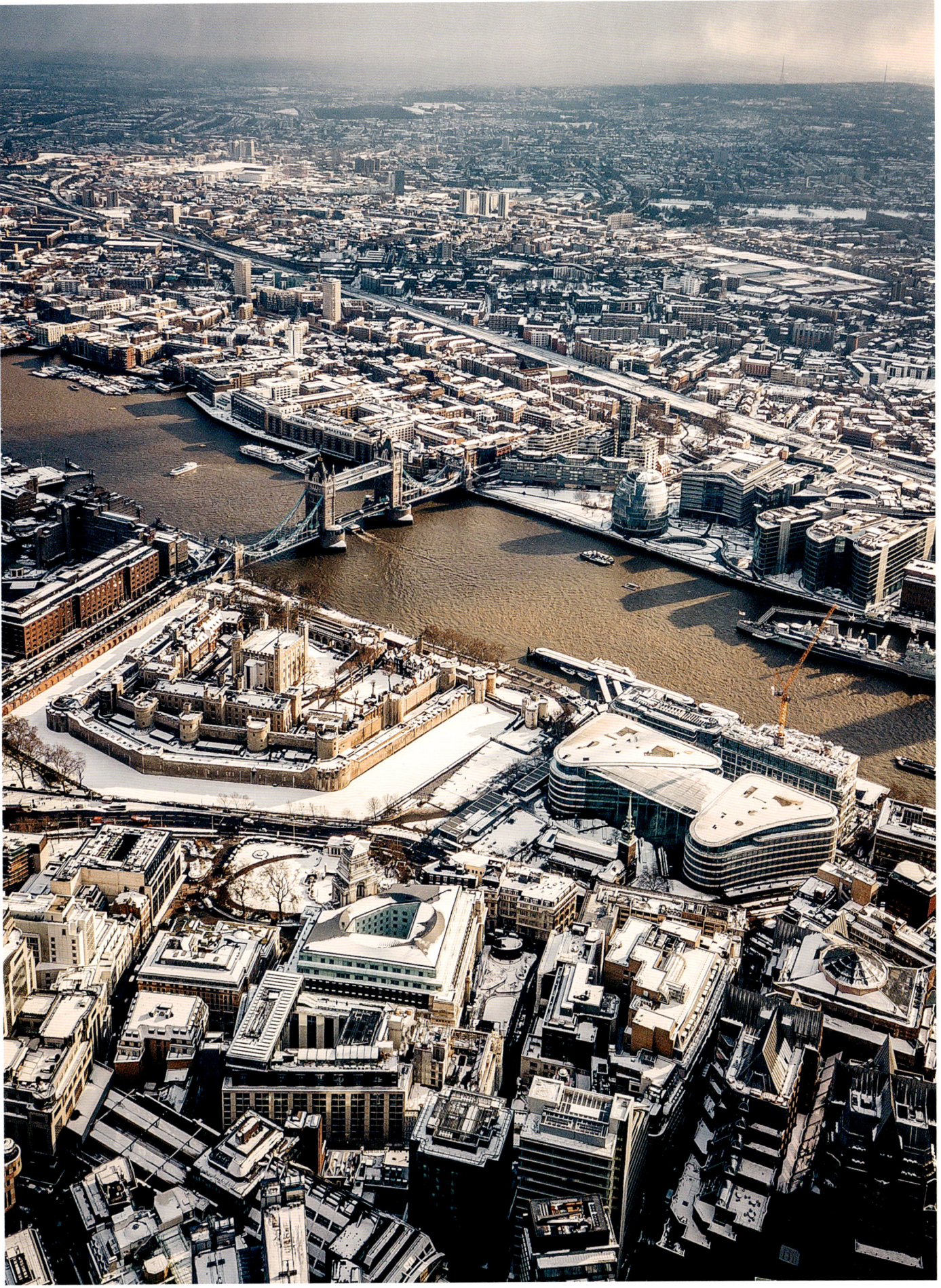

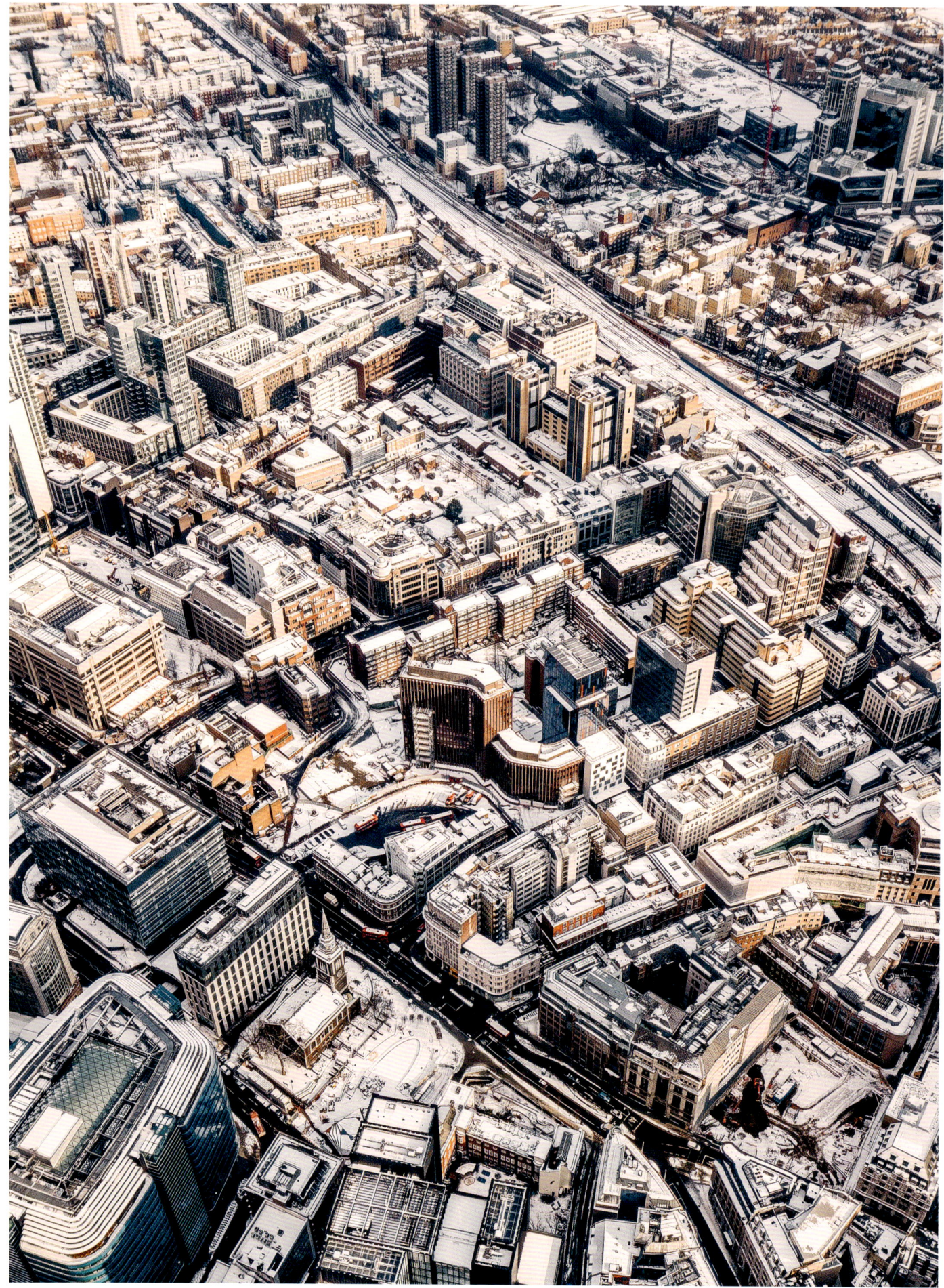

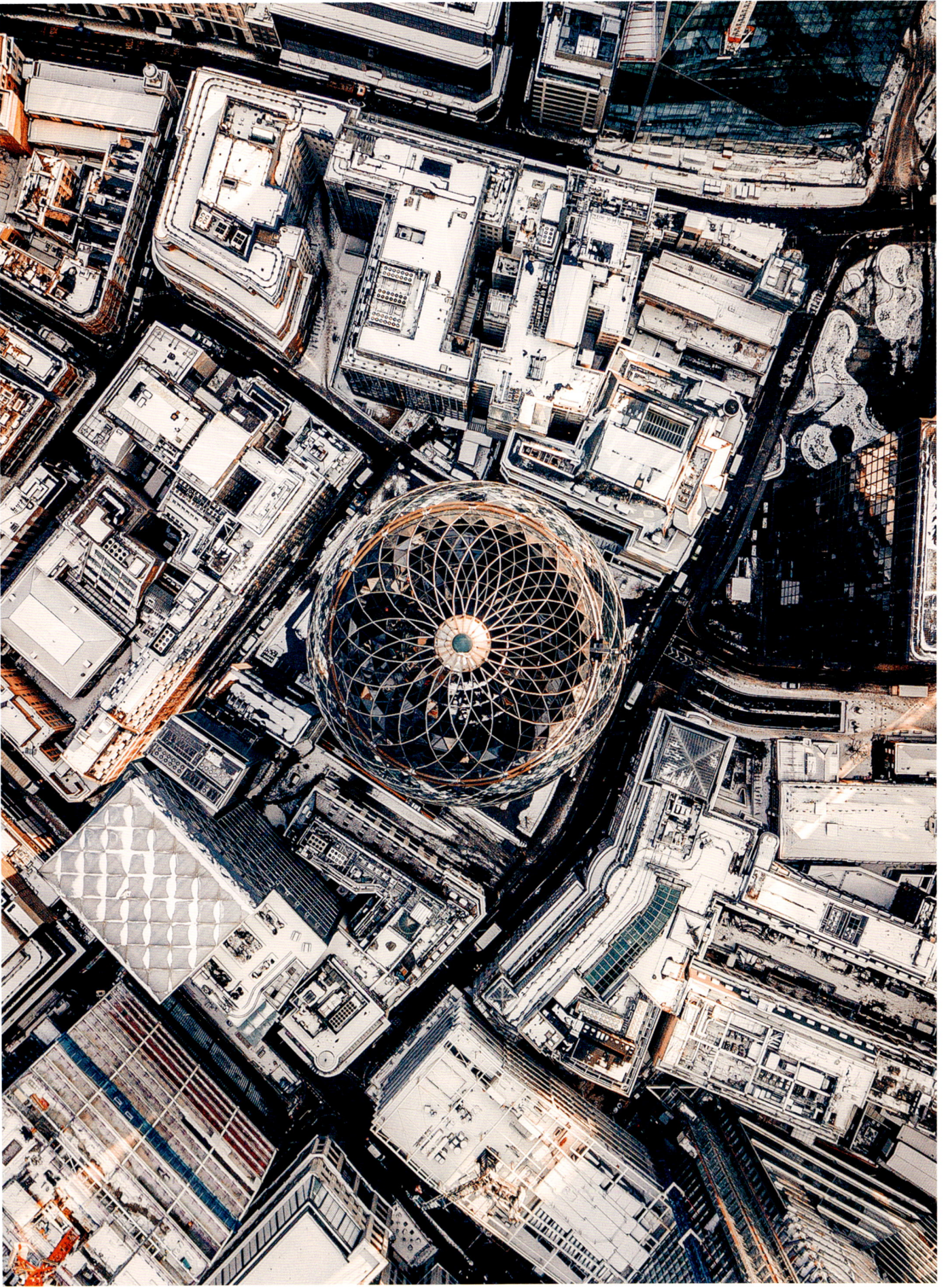

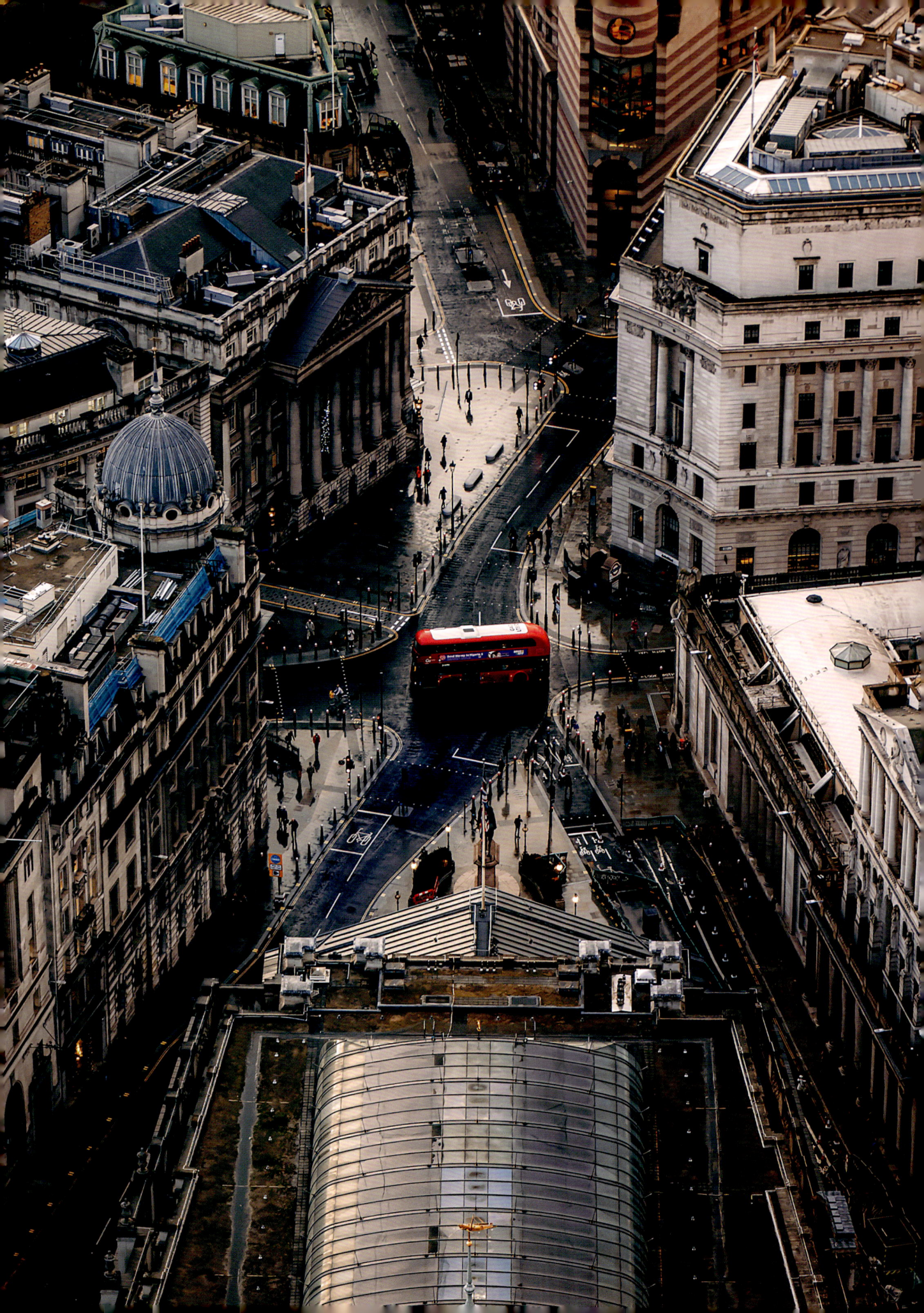

City Planning ♦ London is truly a city of contrasts: old and new, orderly and chaotic, traditional and modern. It is said that London grew, not by planning, but by swallowing up the countryside village by village. The evidence is in the complexity of London's meandering streets, where modern structures sit quite comfortably next to 18th-century Georgian architecture. ♦ After the Great Fire of London in 1666 destroyed nearly a third of the city, it was proposed that London be rebuilt on a grid system. That plan was roundly rejected, paving the way for today's at-times chaotic maze of streets with their baffling tendency to change names or direction without much warning. ♦ Perhaps no one understands this complex web better than London cabbies. To earn the right to sit behind the wheel of one of London's iconic black cabs, aspiring drivers must learn the 25,000 streets and 20,000 points of interest in central London, and the fastest routes between them. The test is called "The Knowledge" and is universally known as one of the hardest exams in the world. ♦ And yet, despite its tangled streets, London is one of the world's most walkable cities. A wrong turn can lead to provocative street art in the Waterloo Tunnel, medieval architecture in the City, and historic pubs tuckered away on the most unassuming corners. London is a city that reveals itself ever so slowly, making it a mecca for photographers.

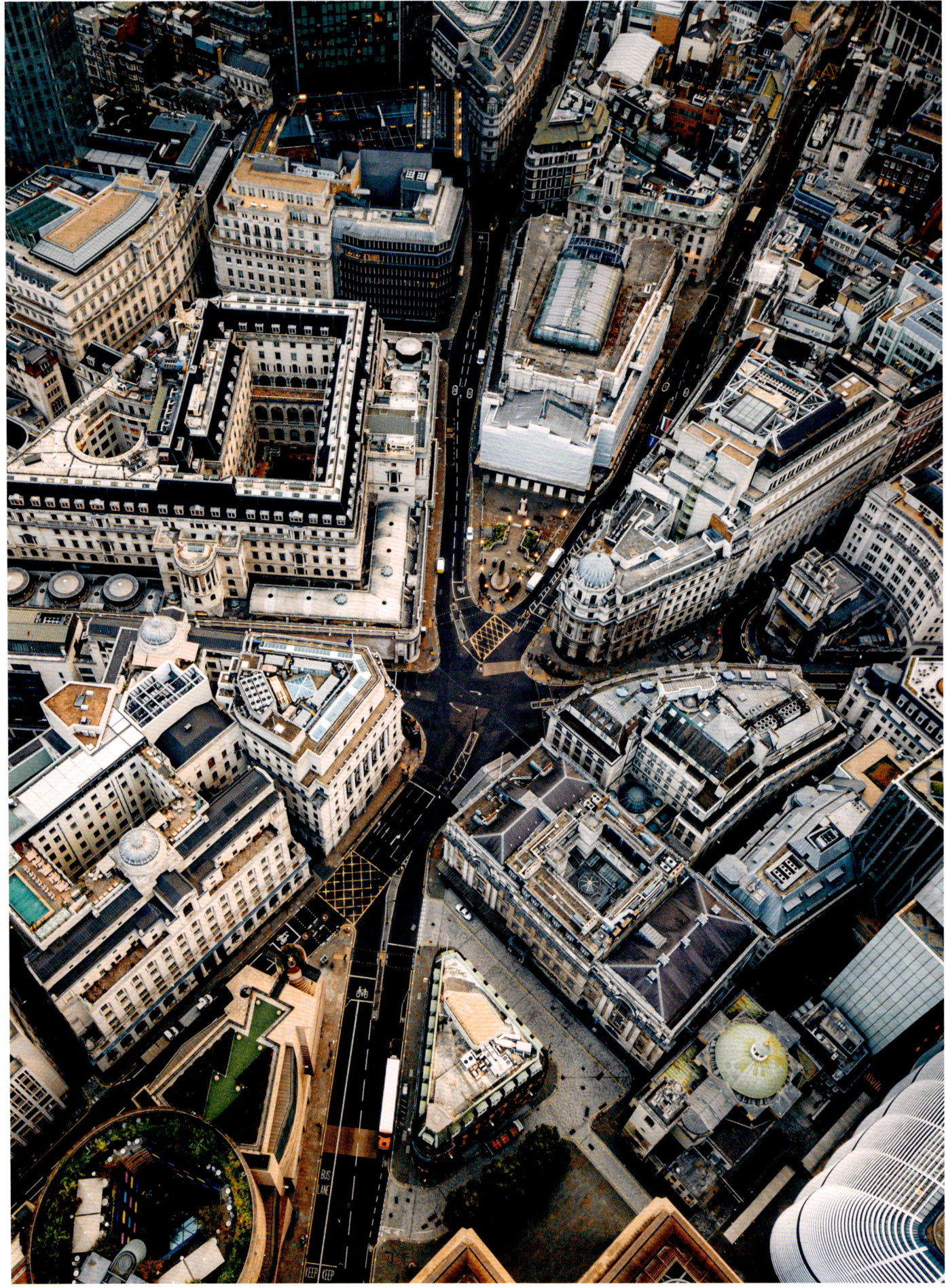

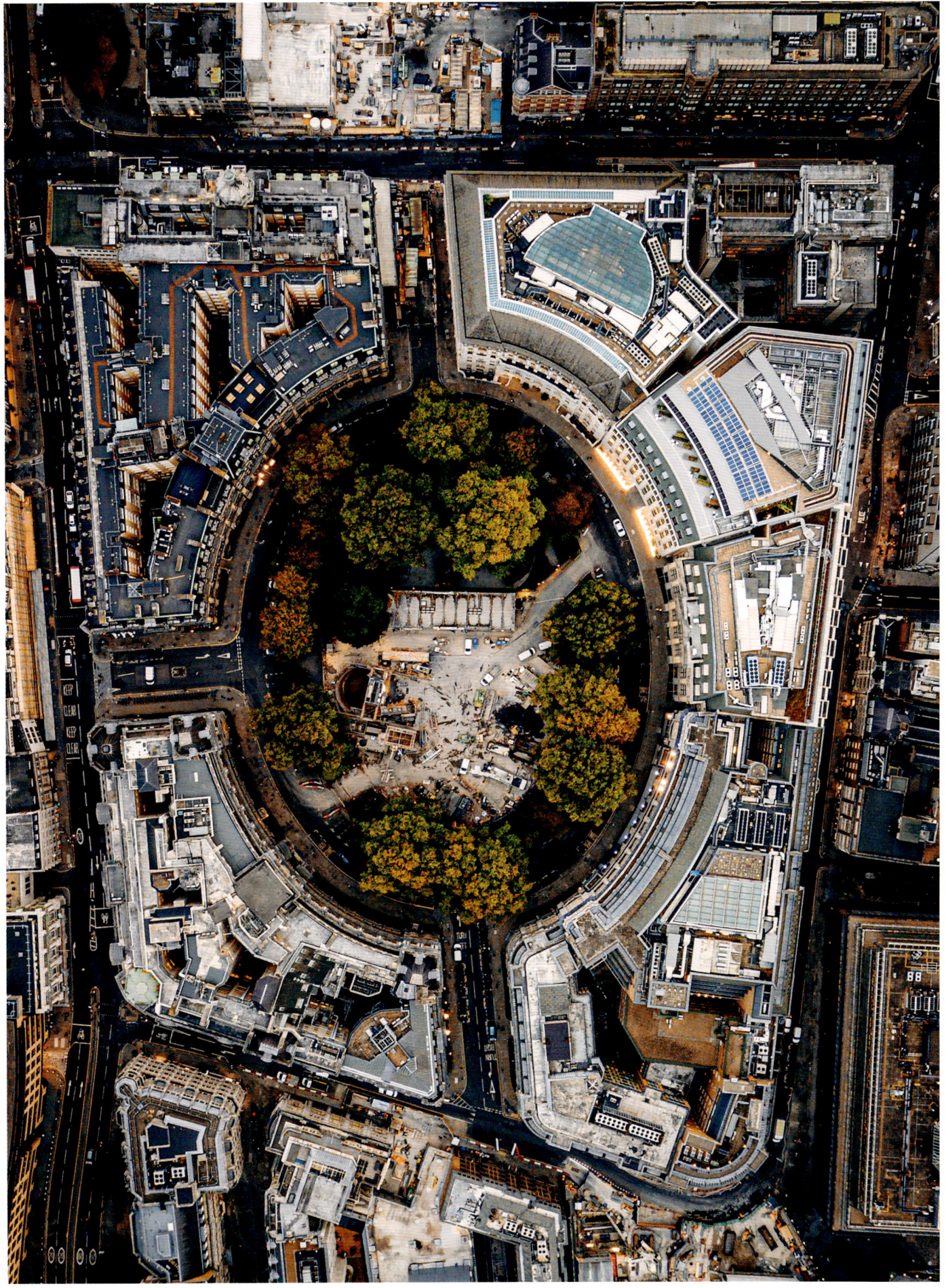

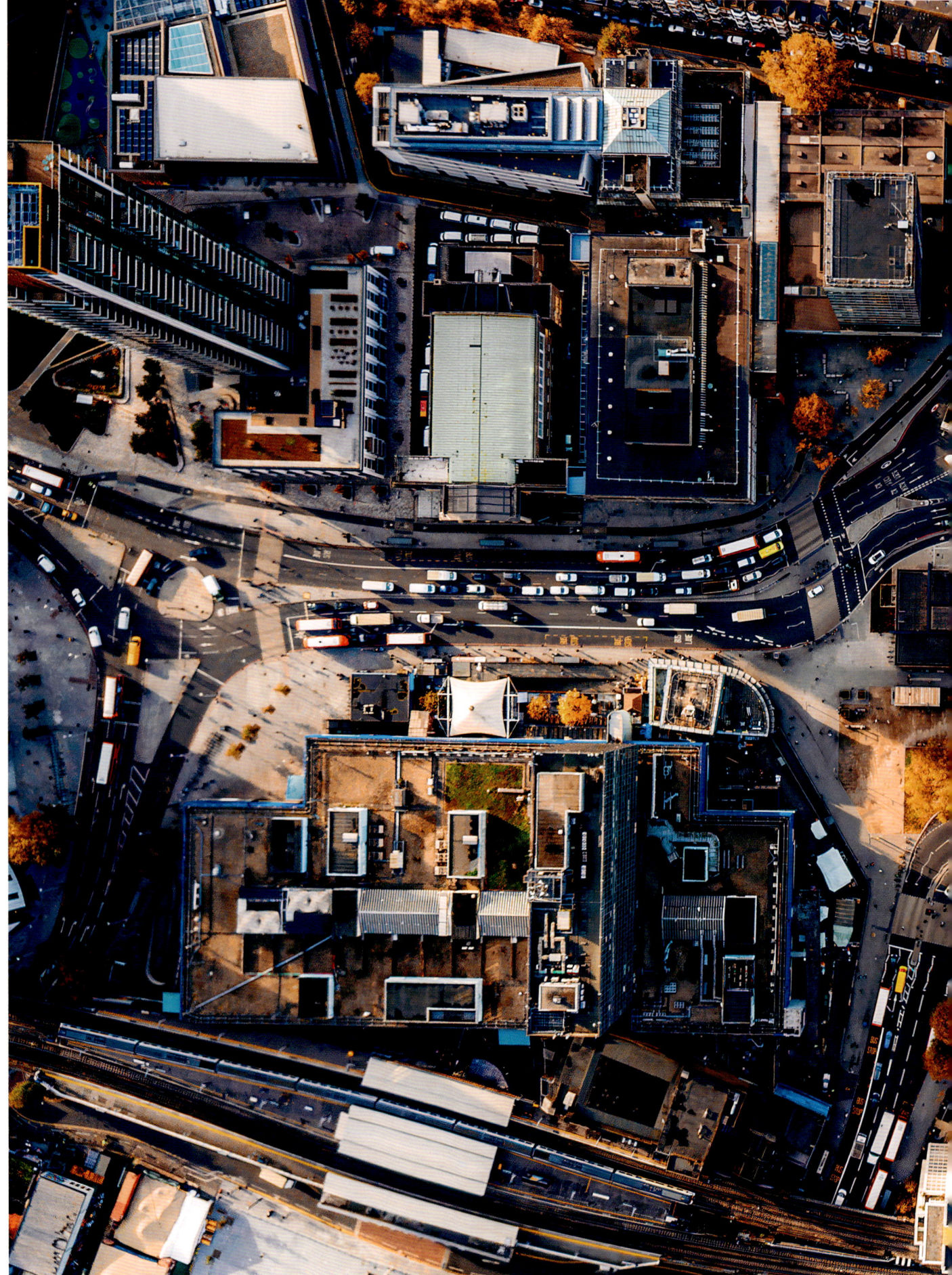

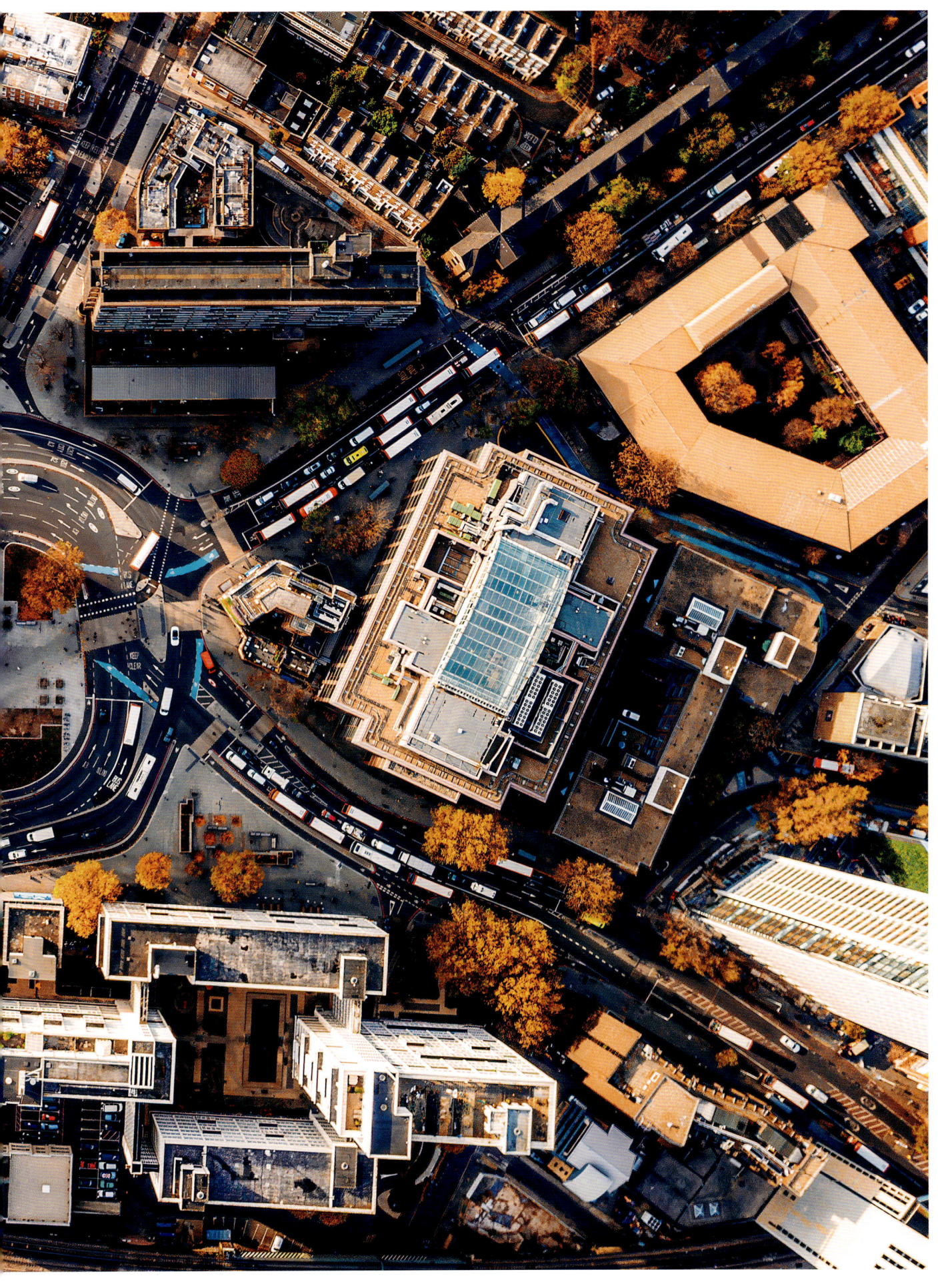

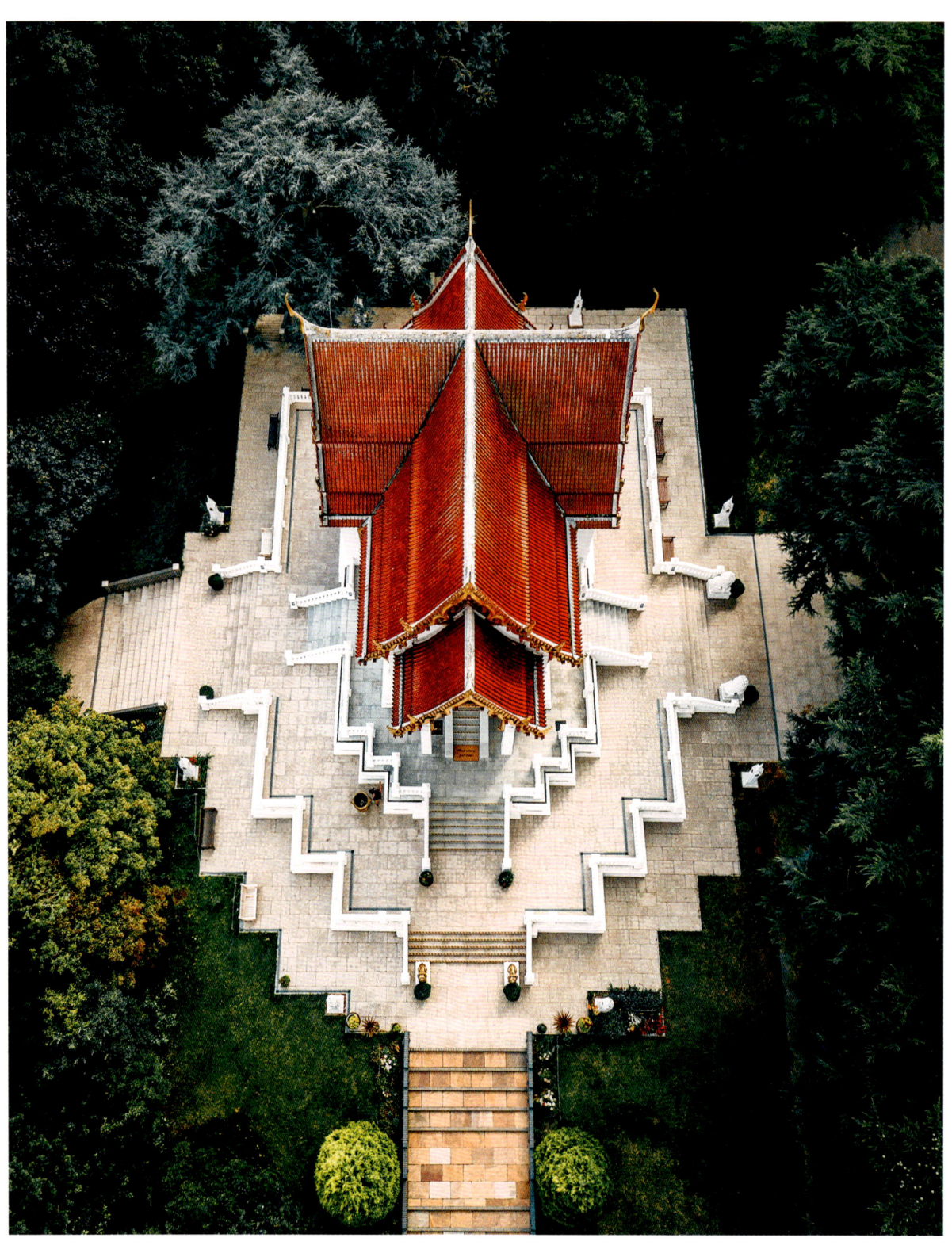

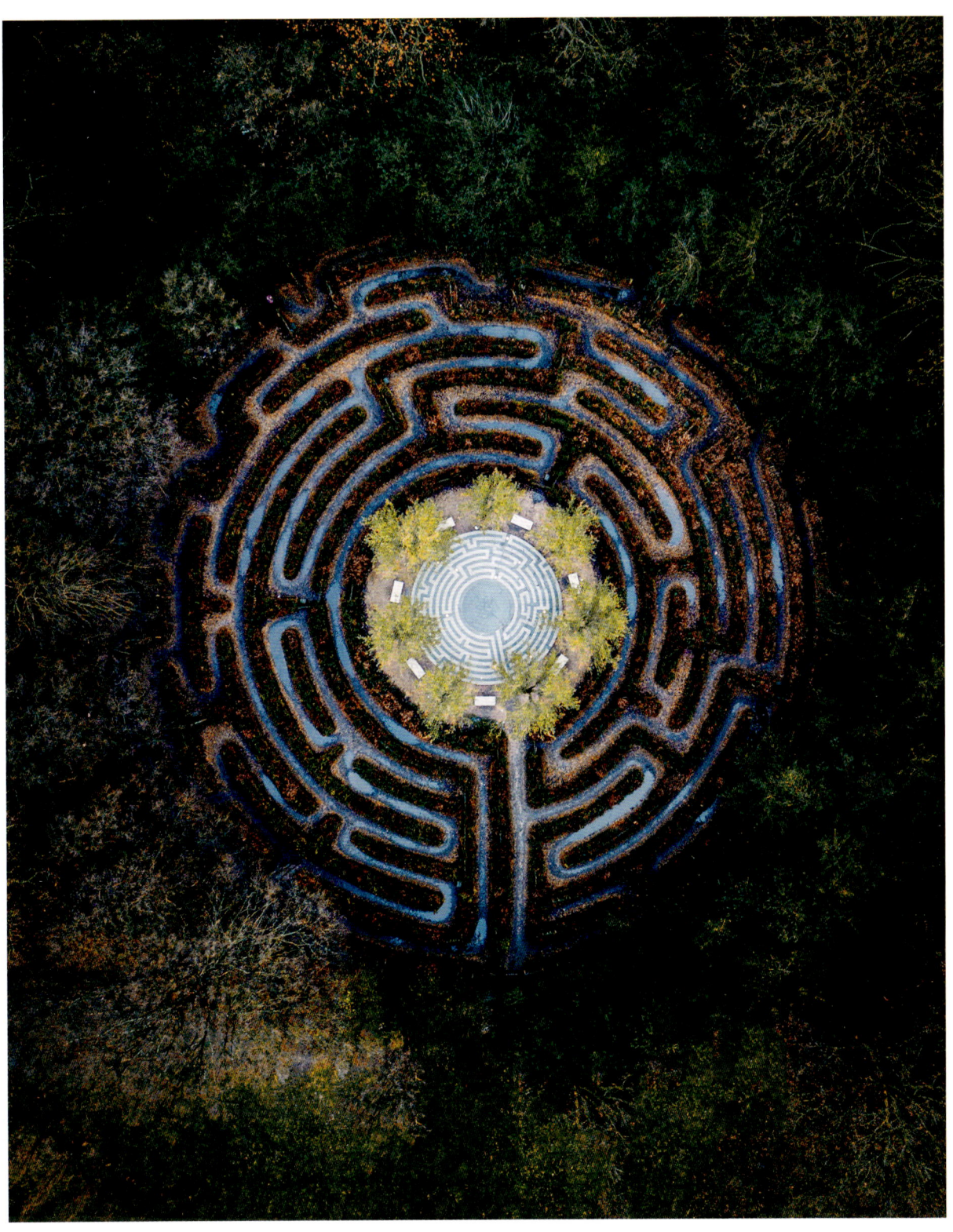

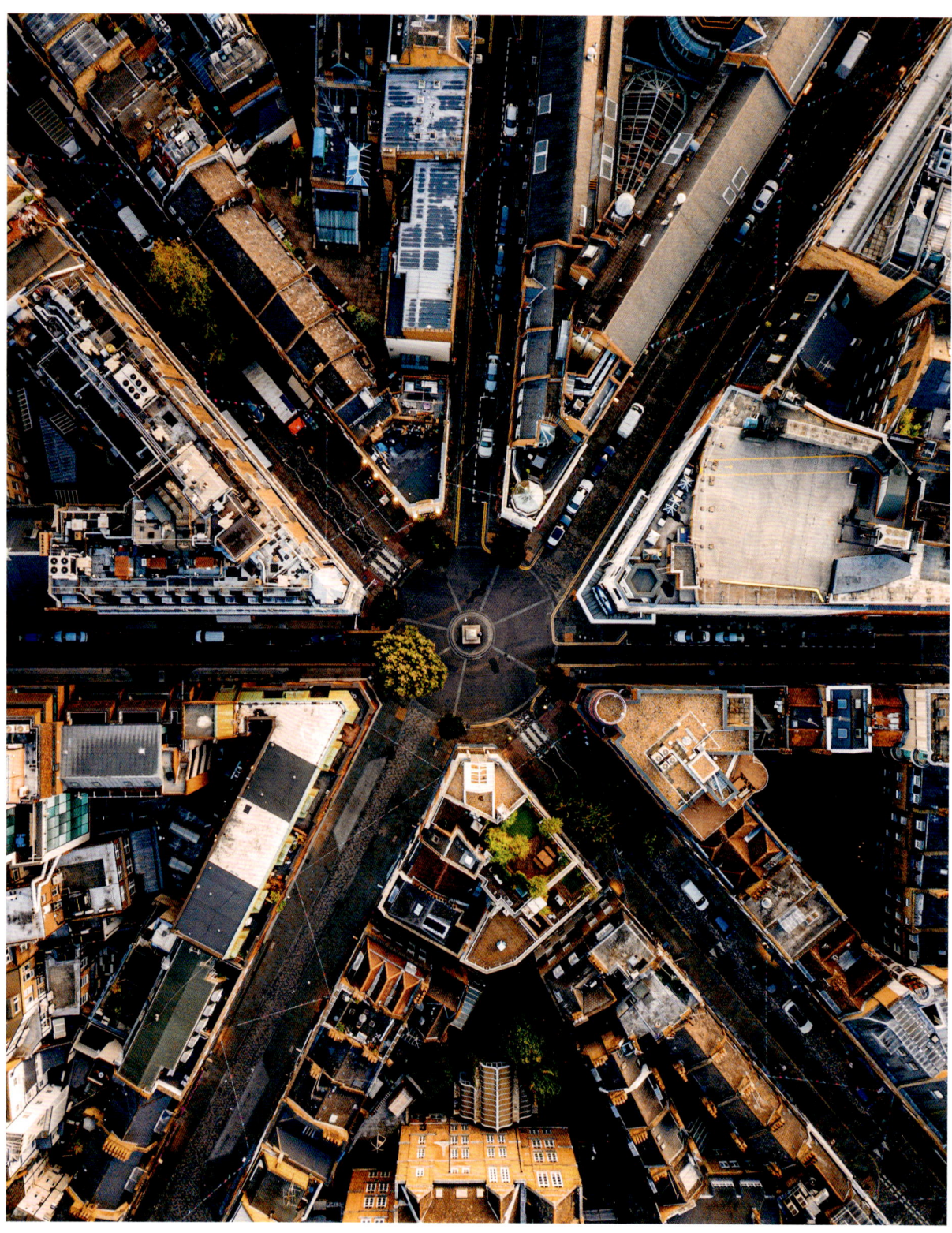

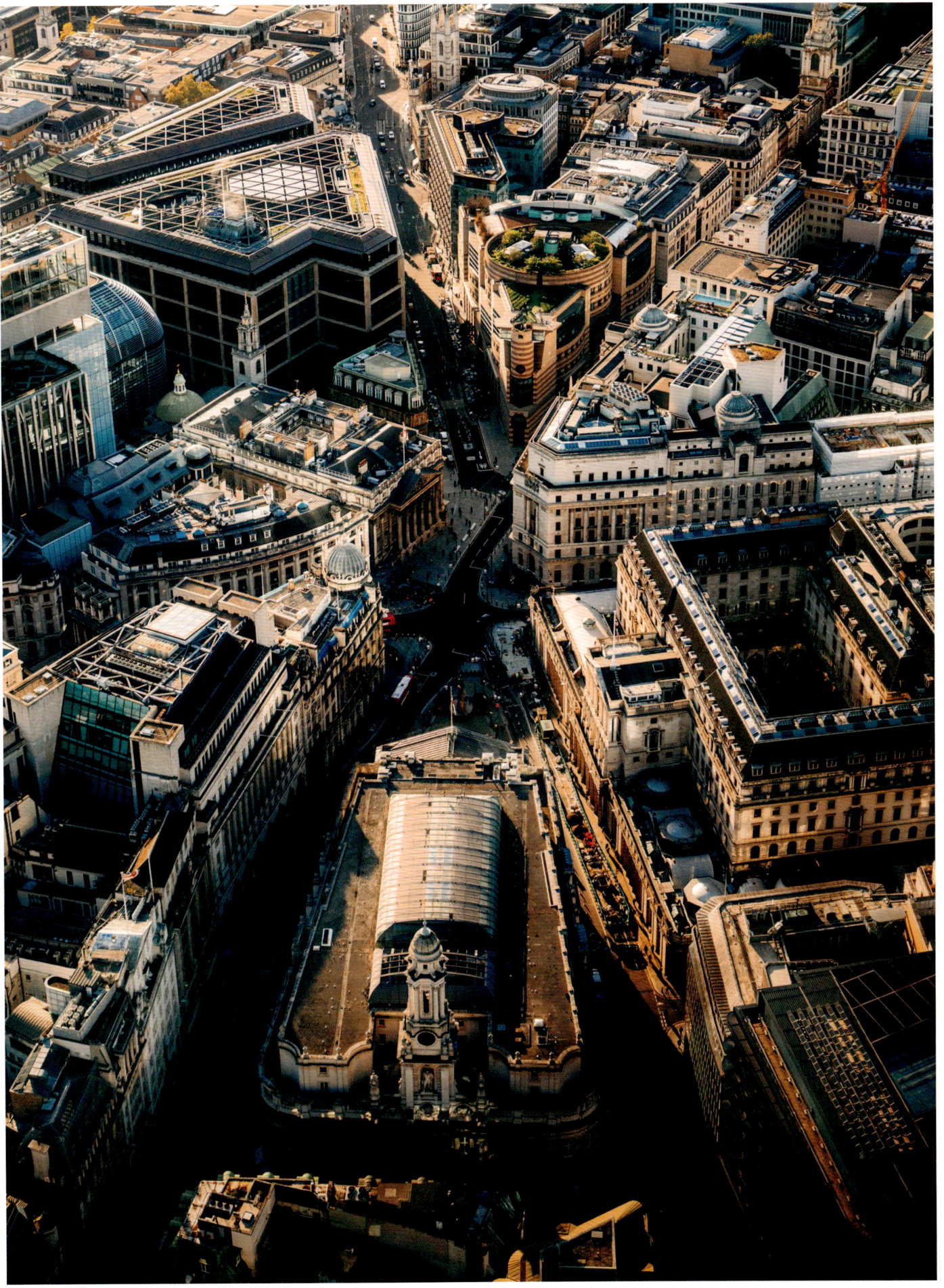

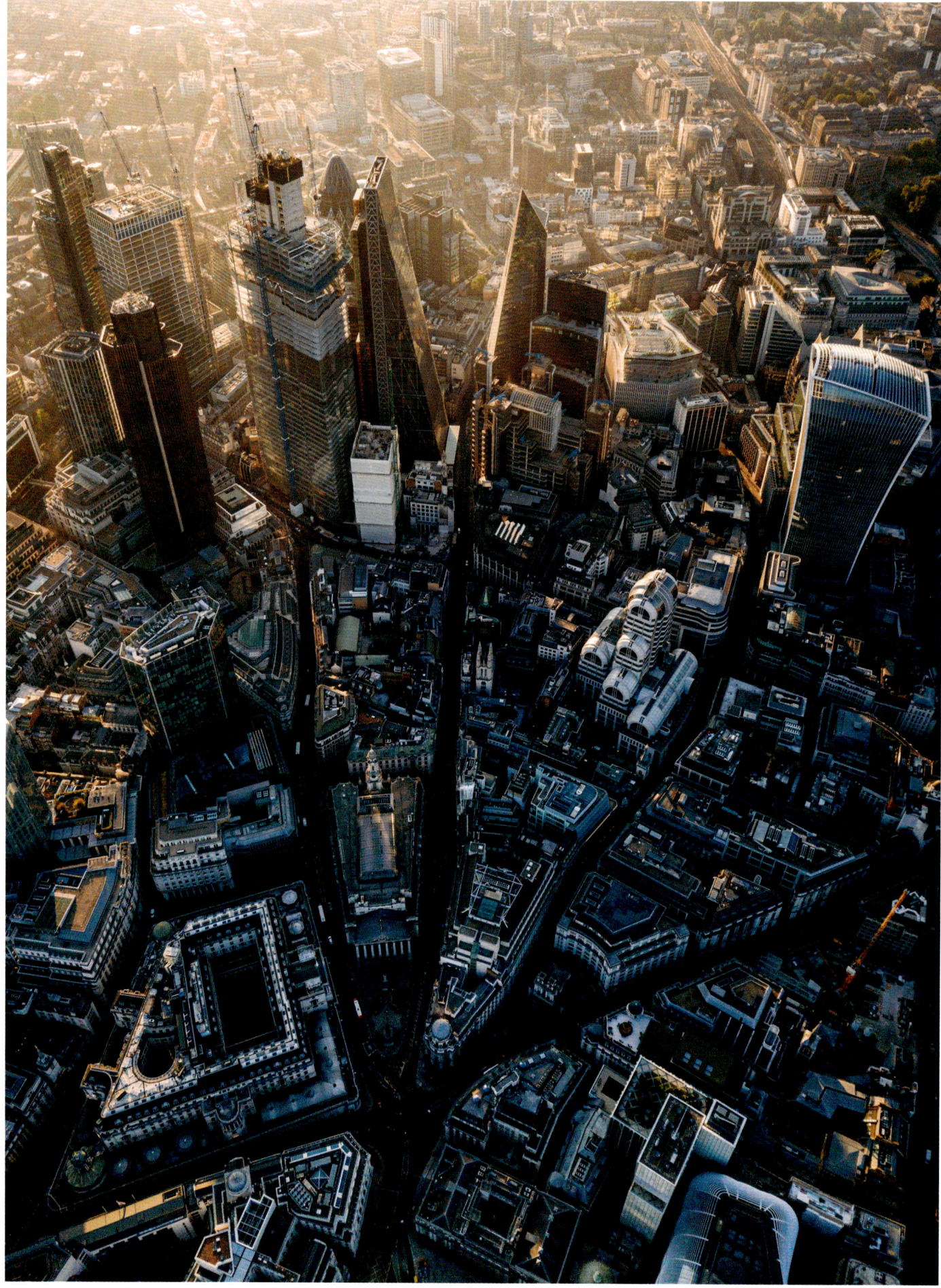

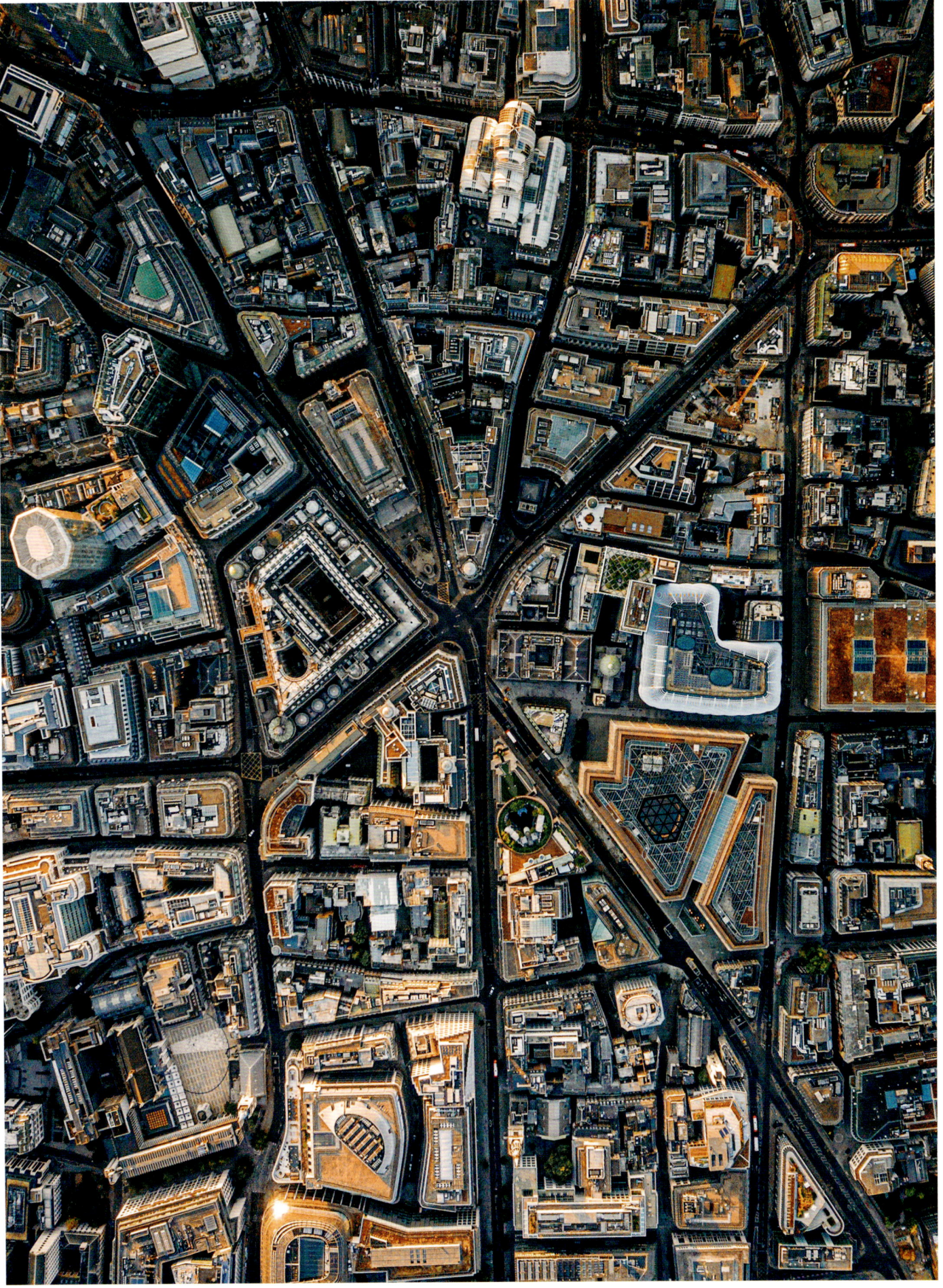

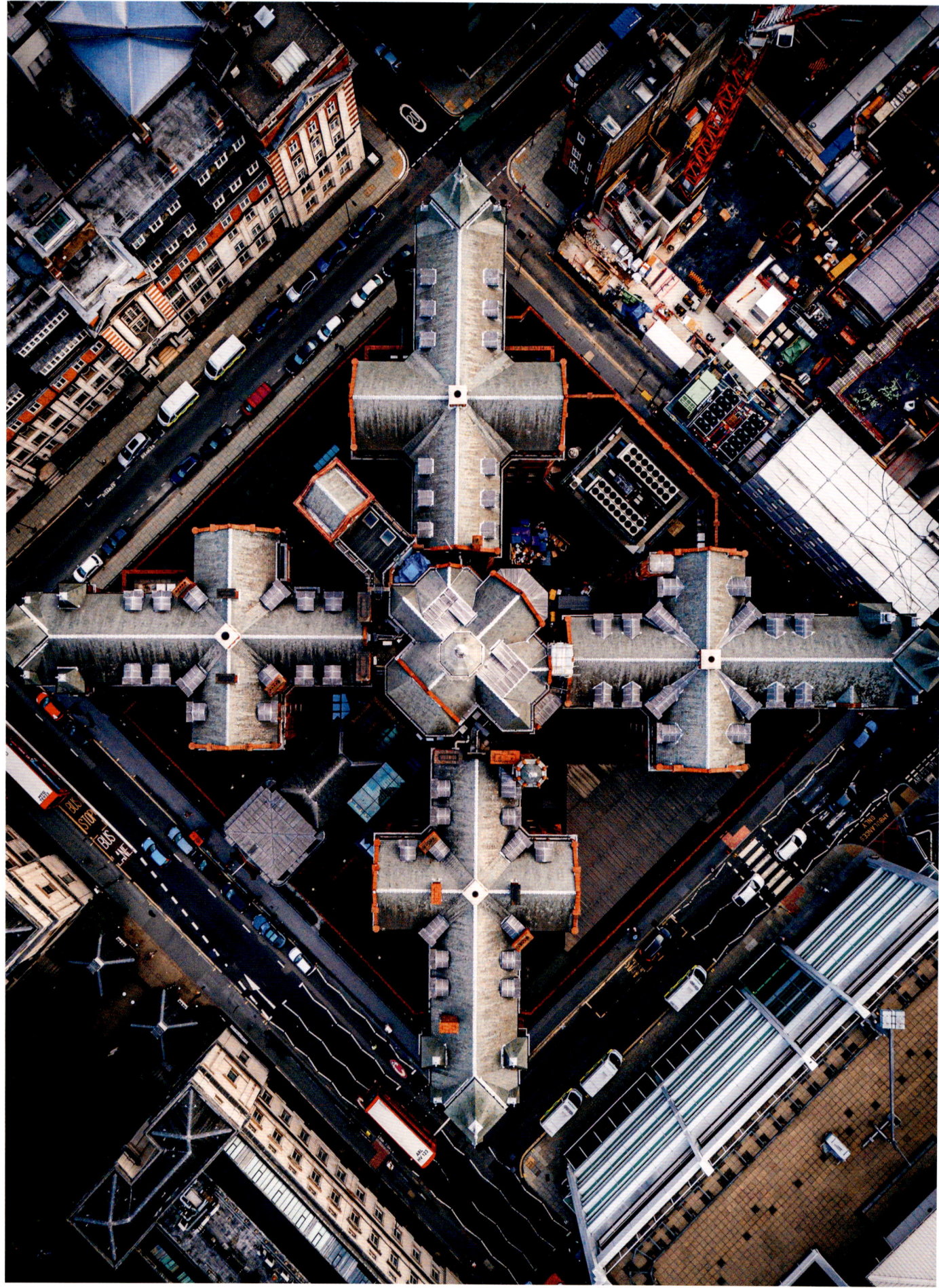

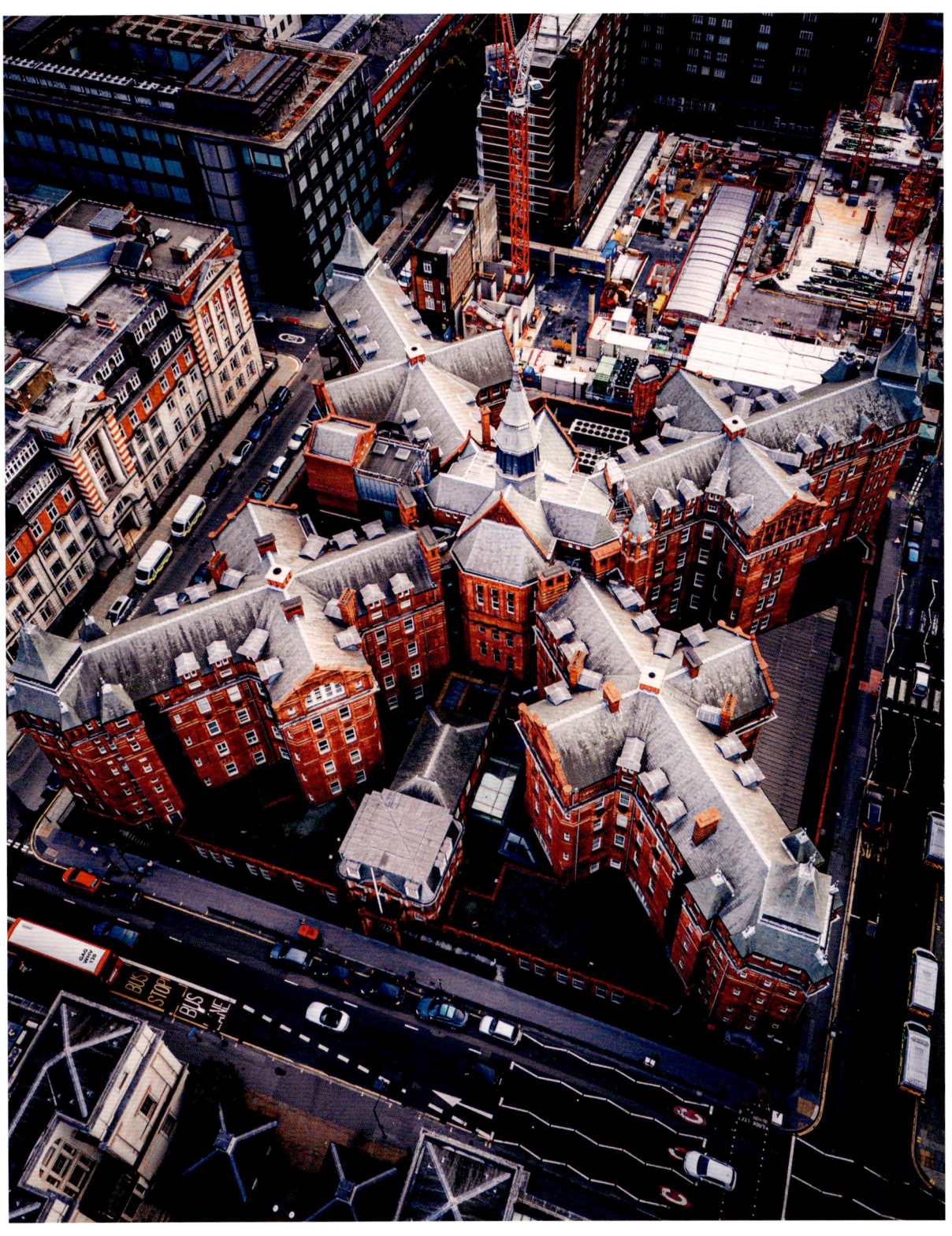

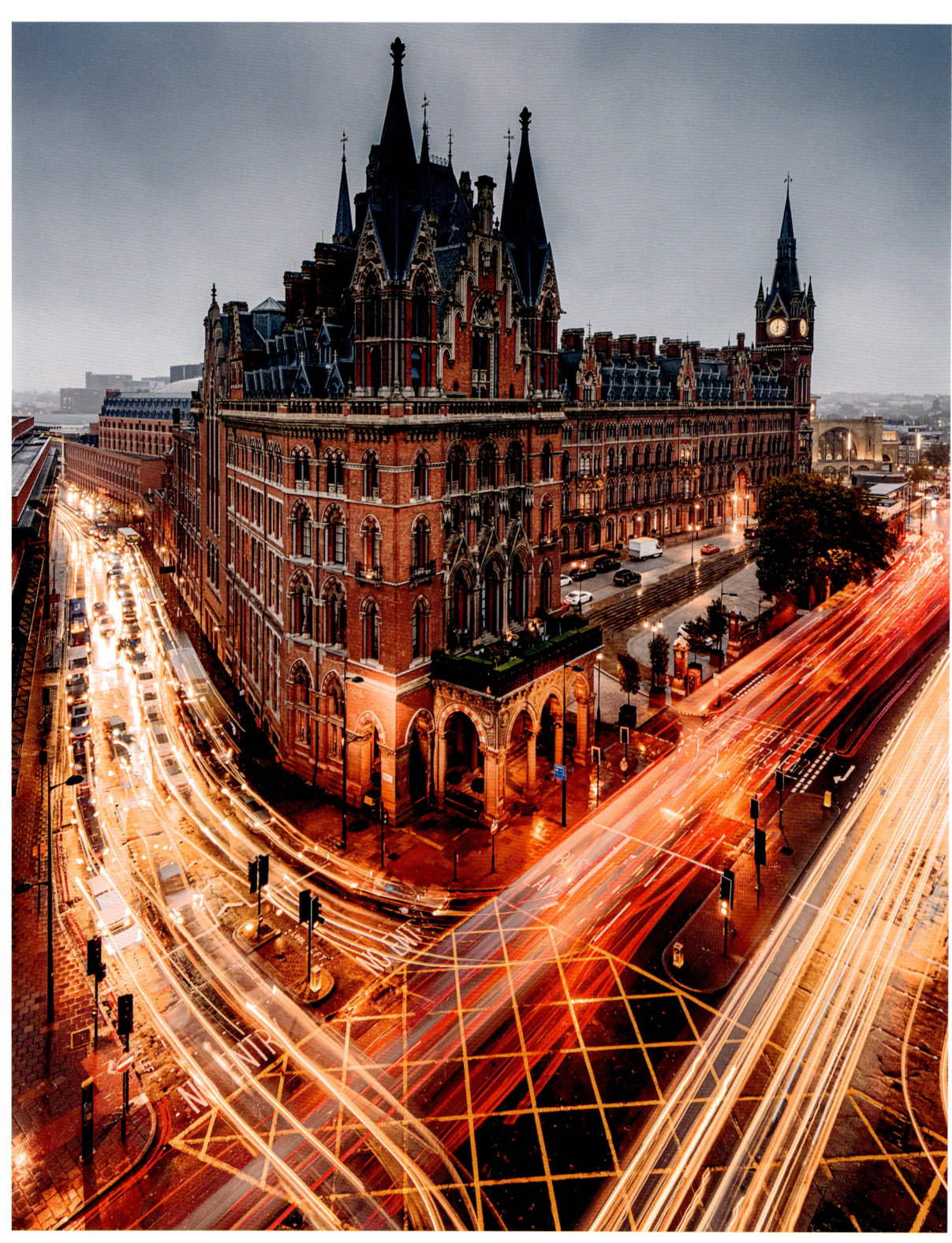

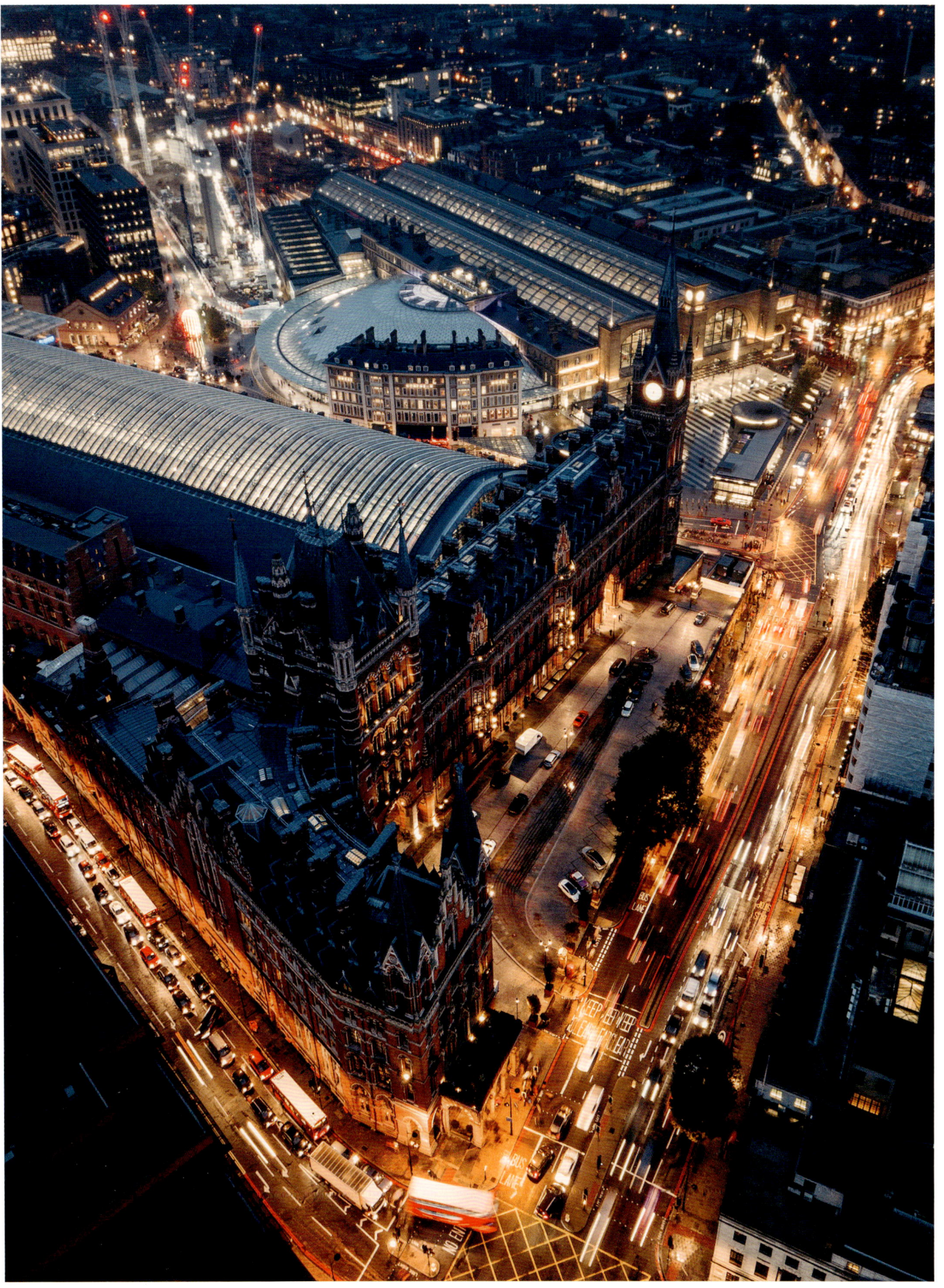

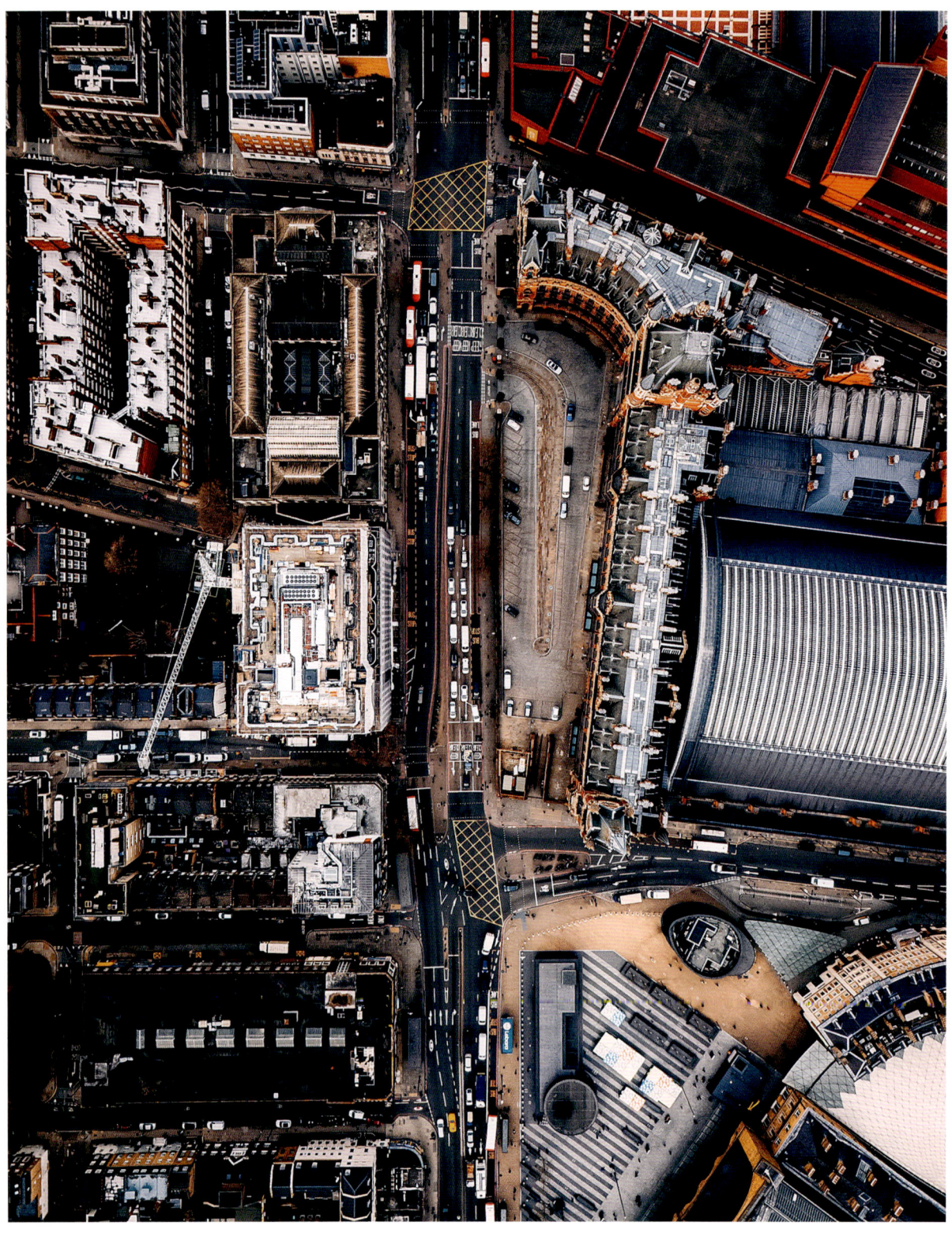

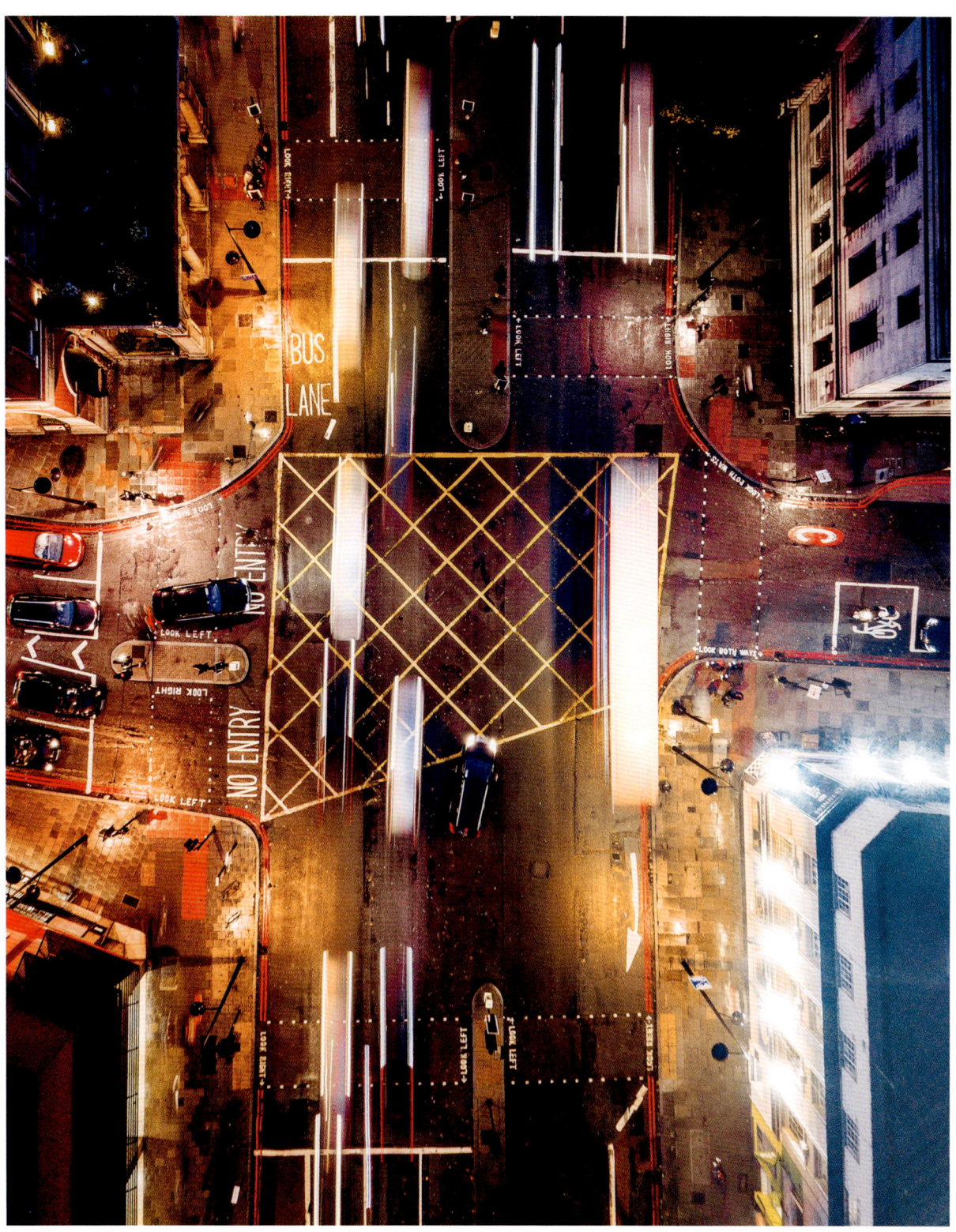

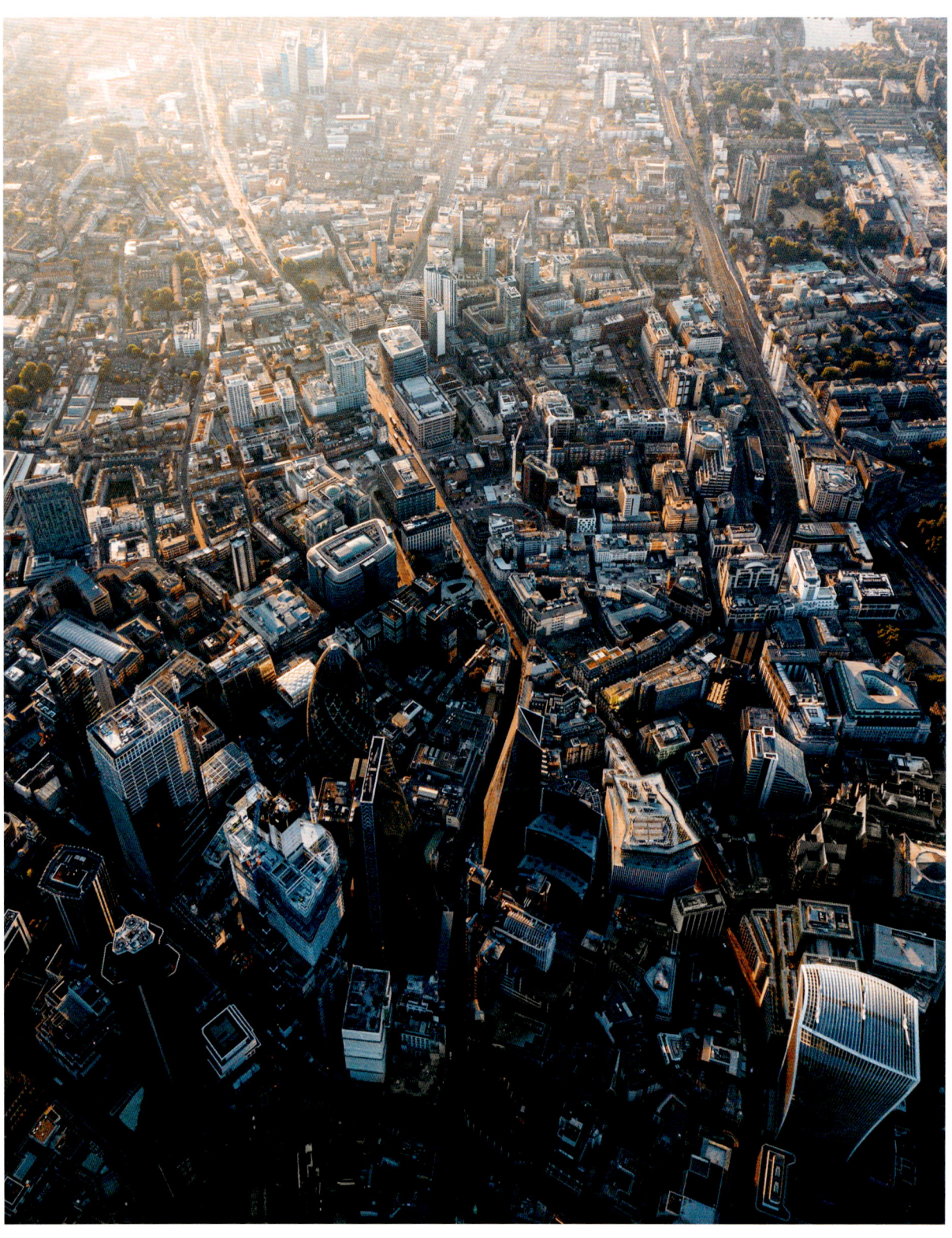

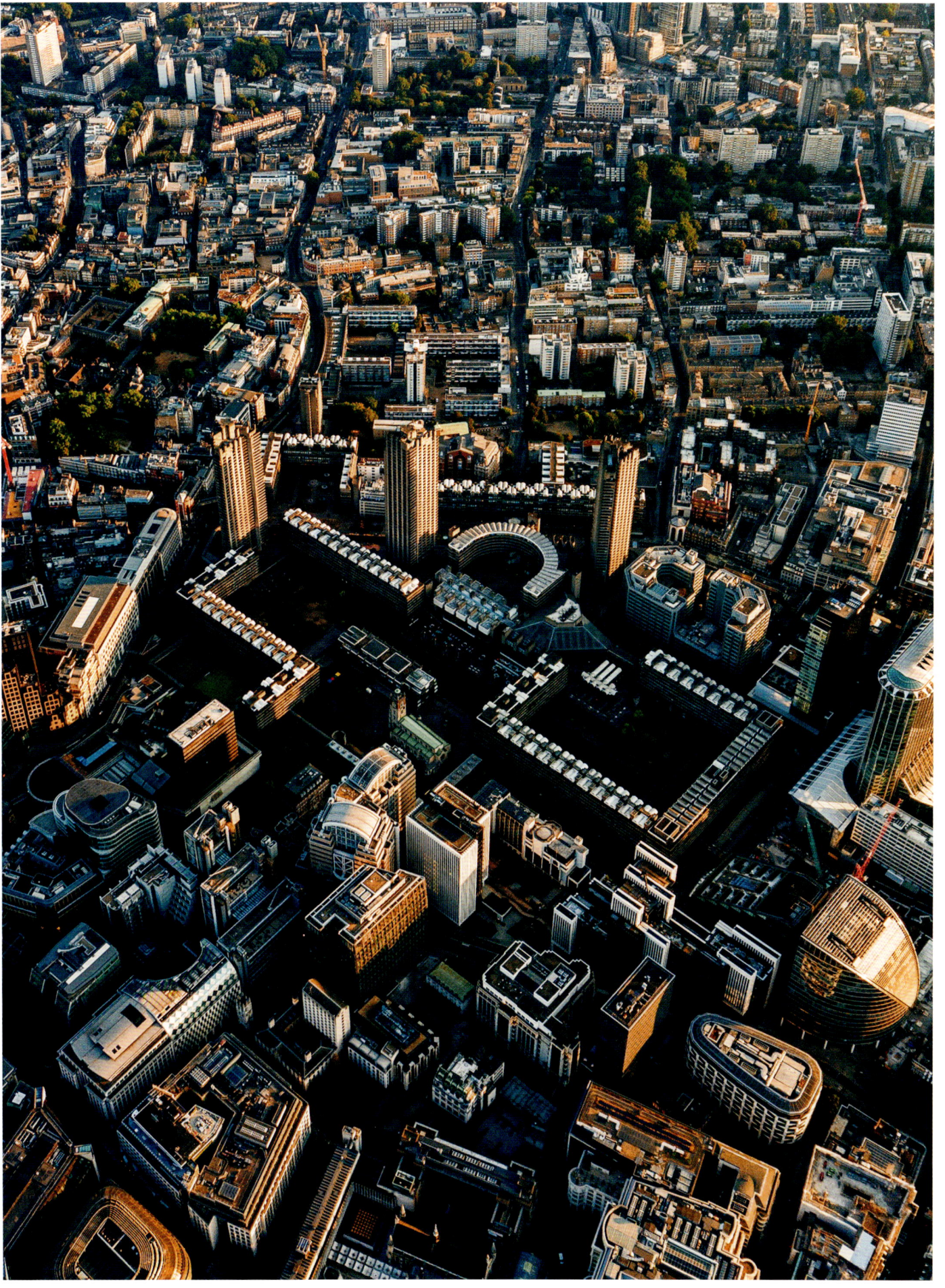

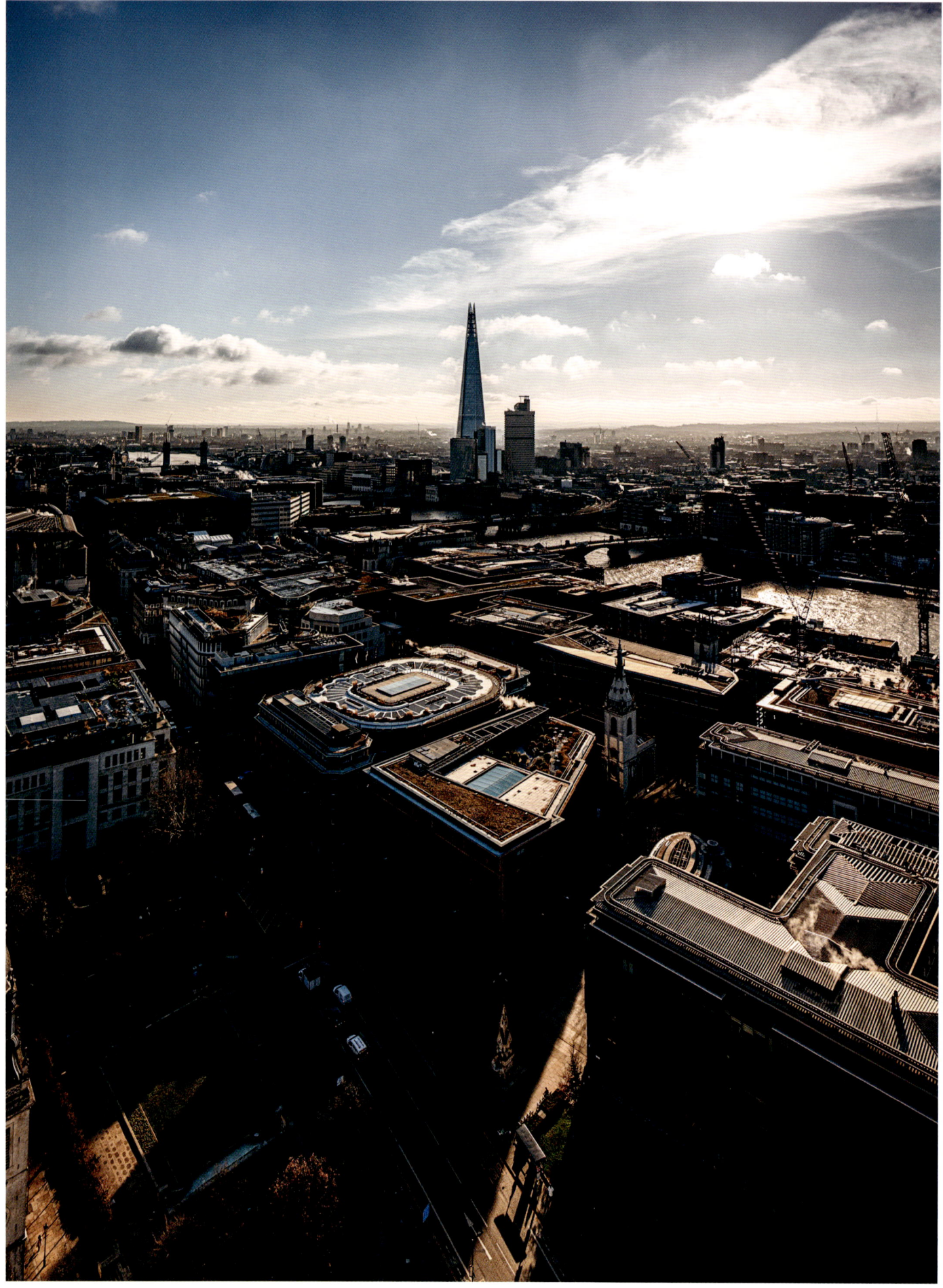

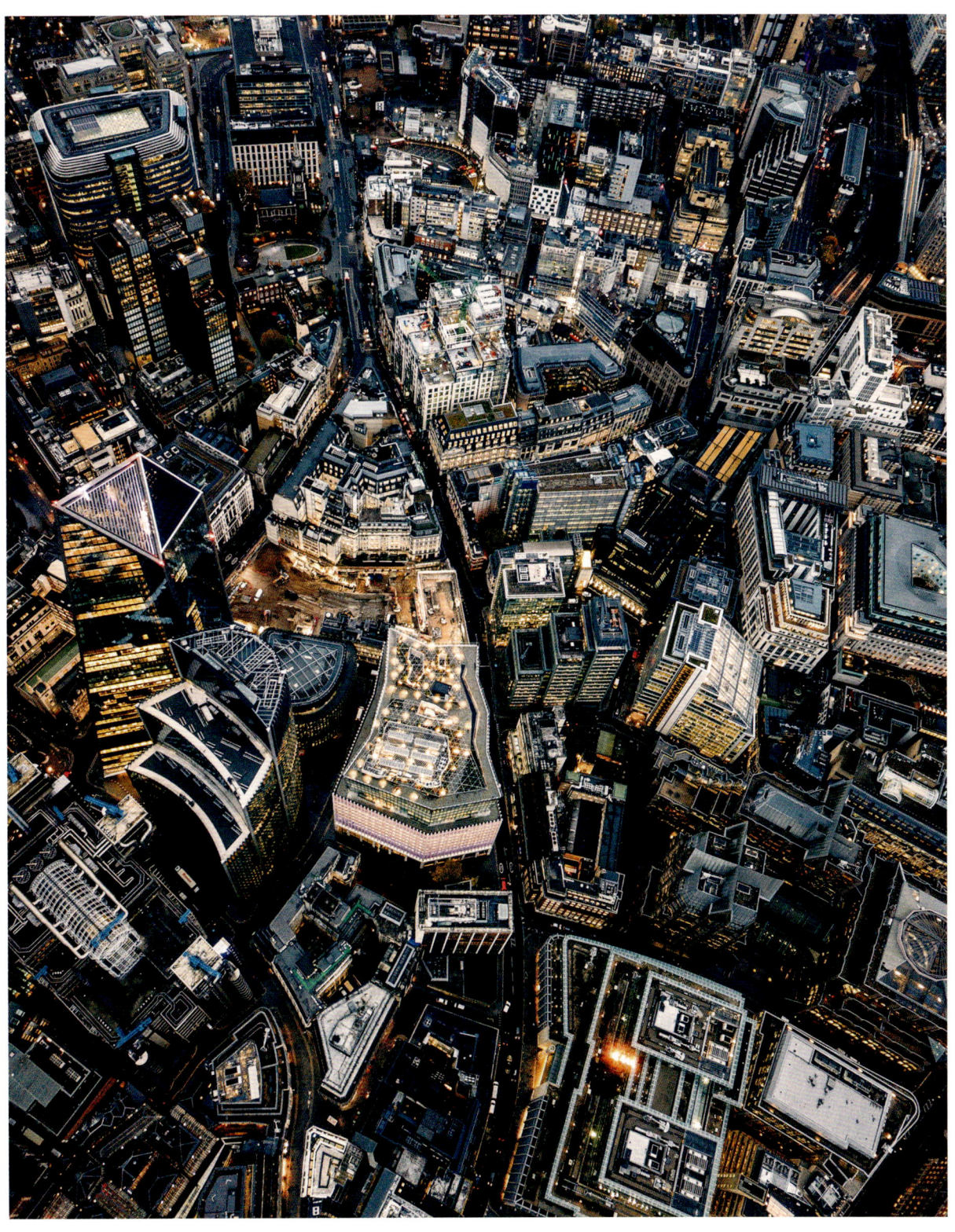

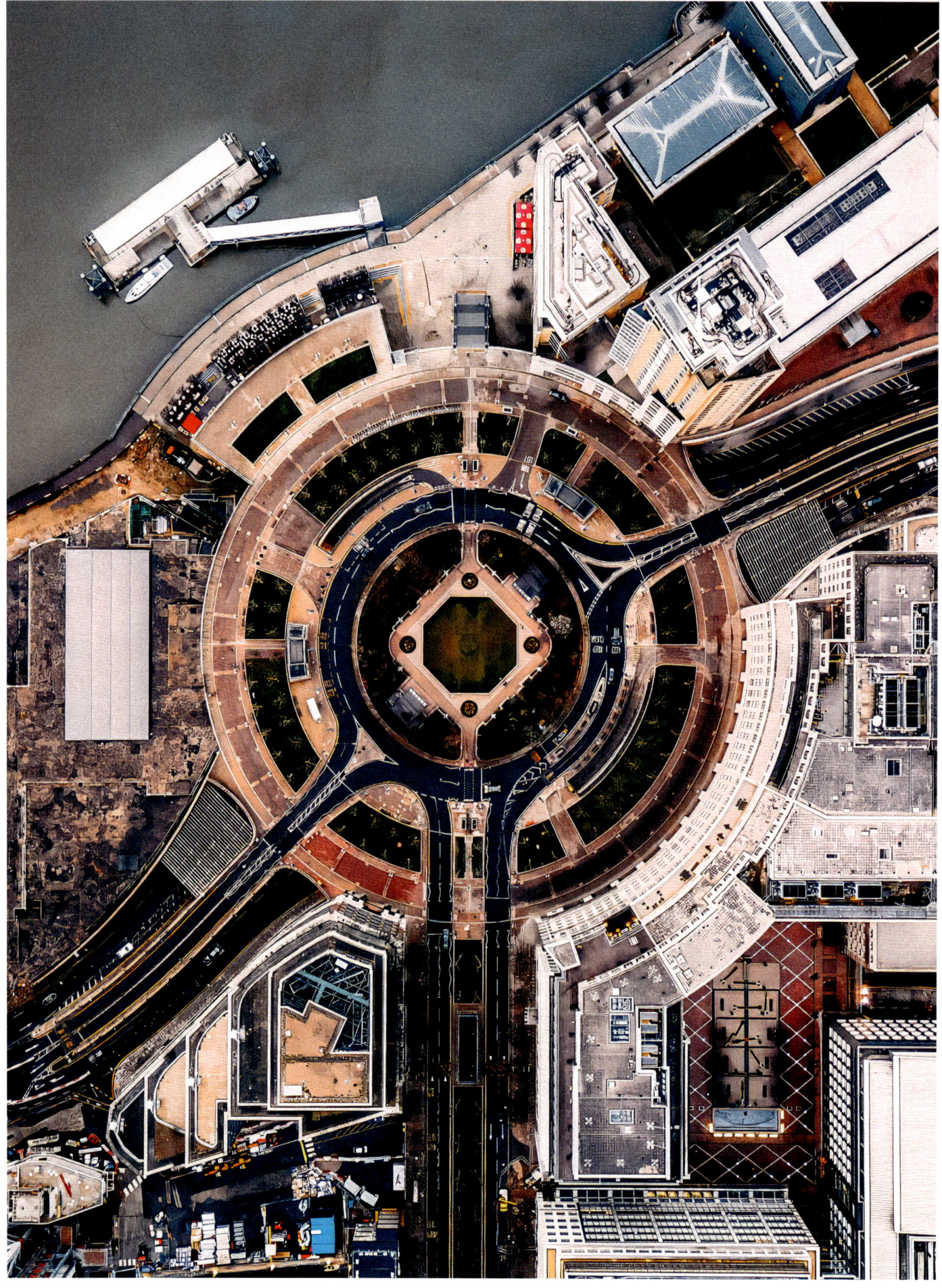

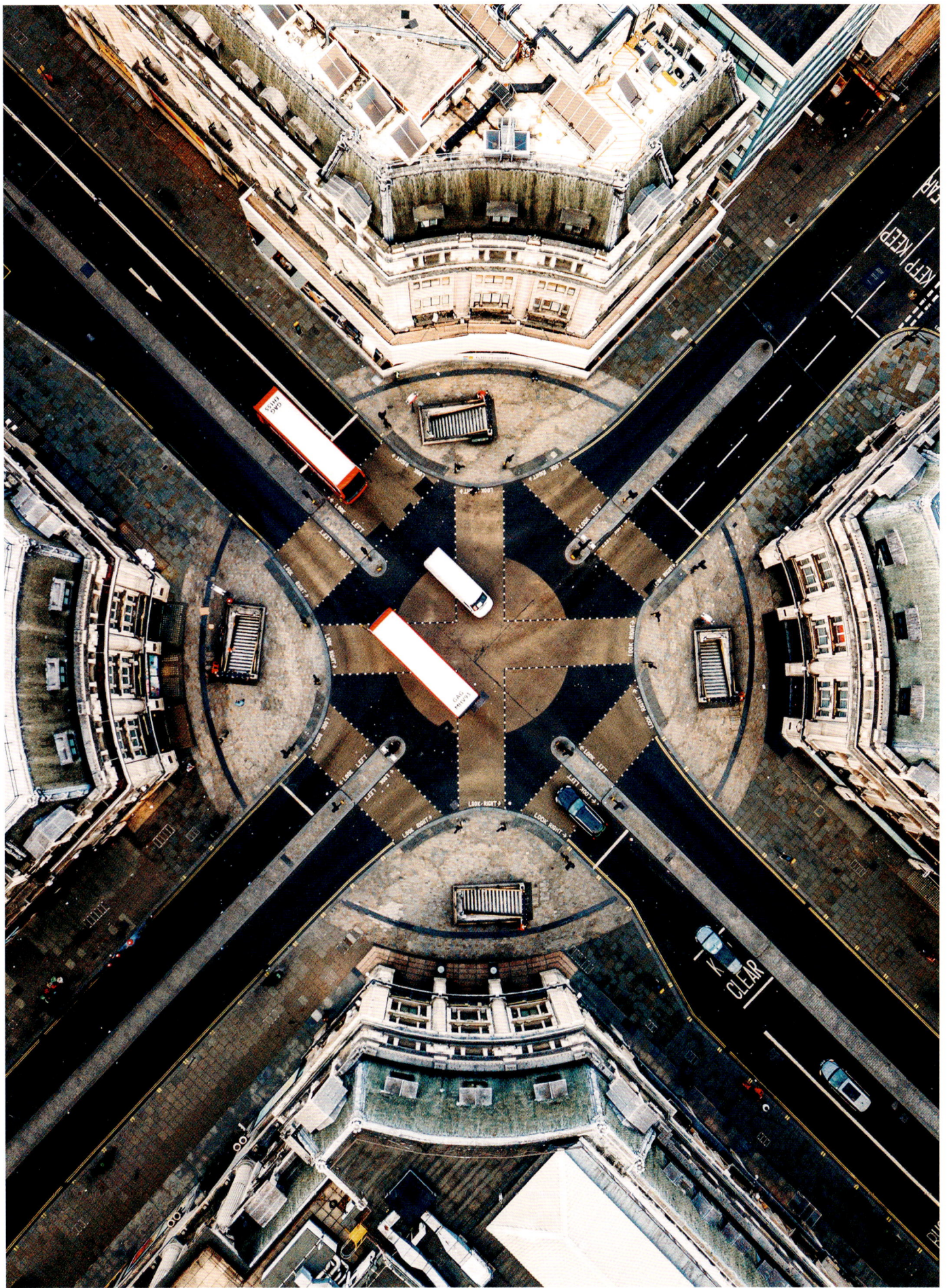

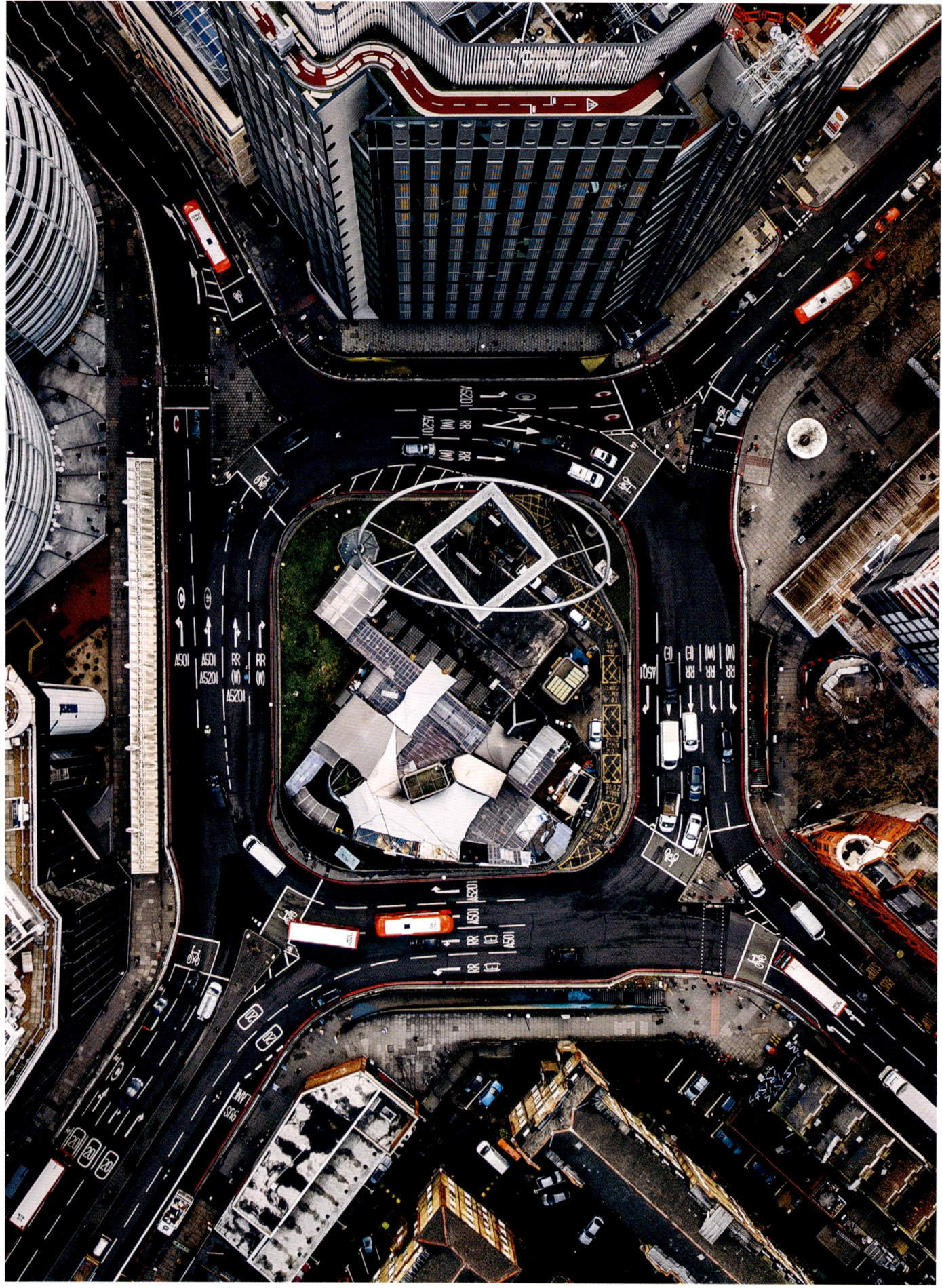

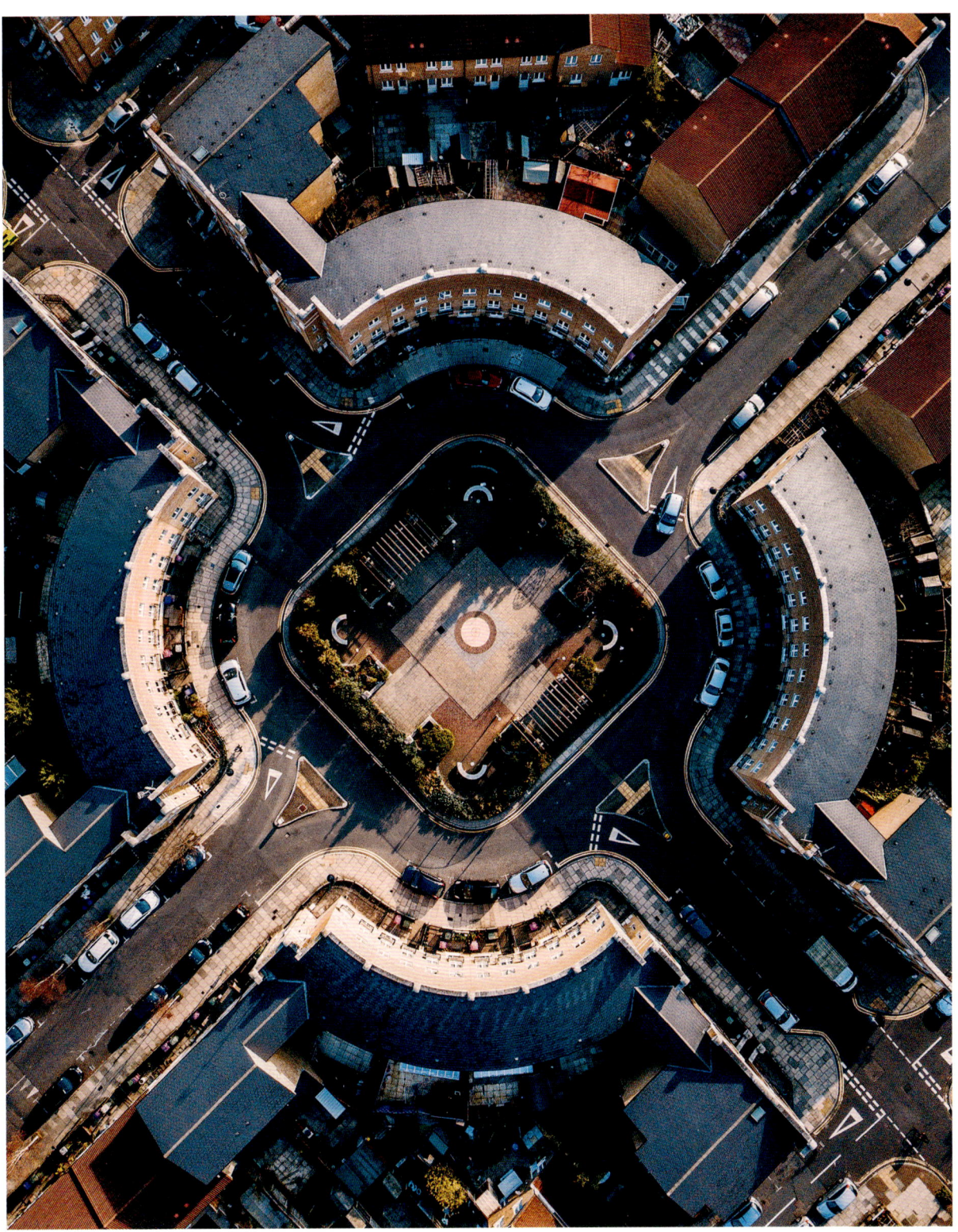

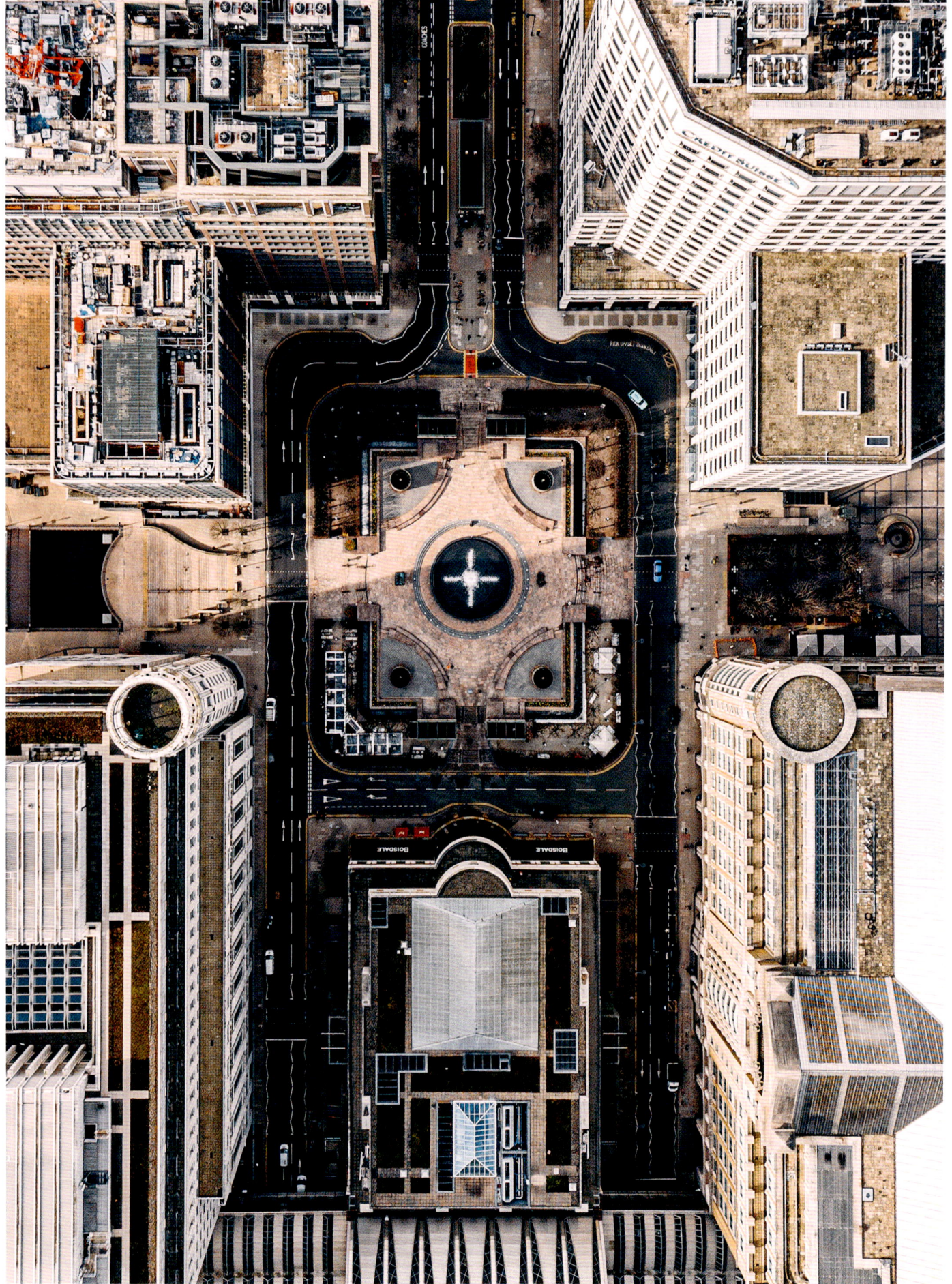

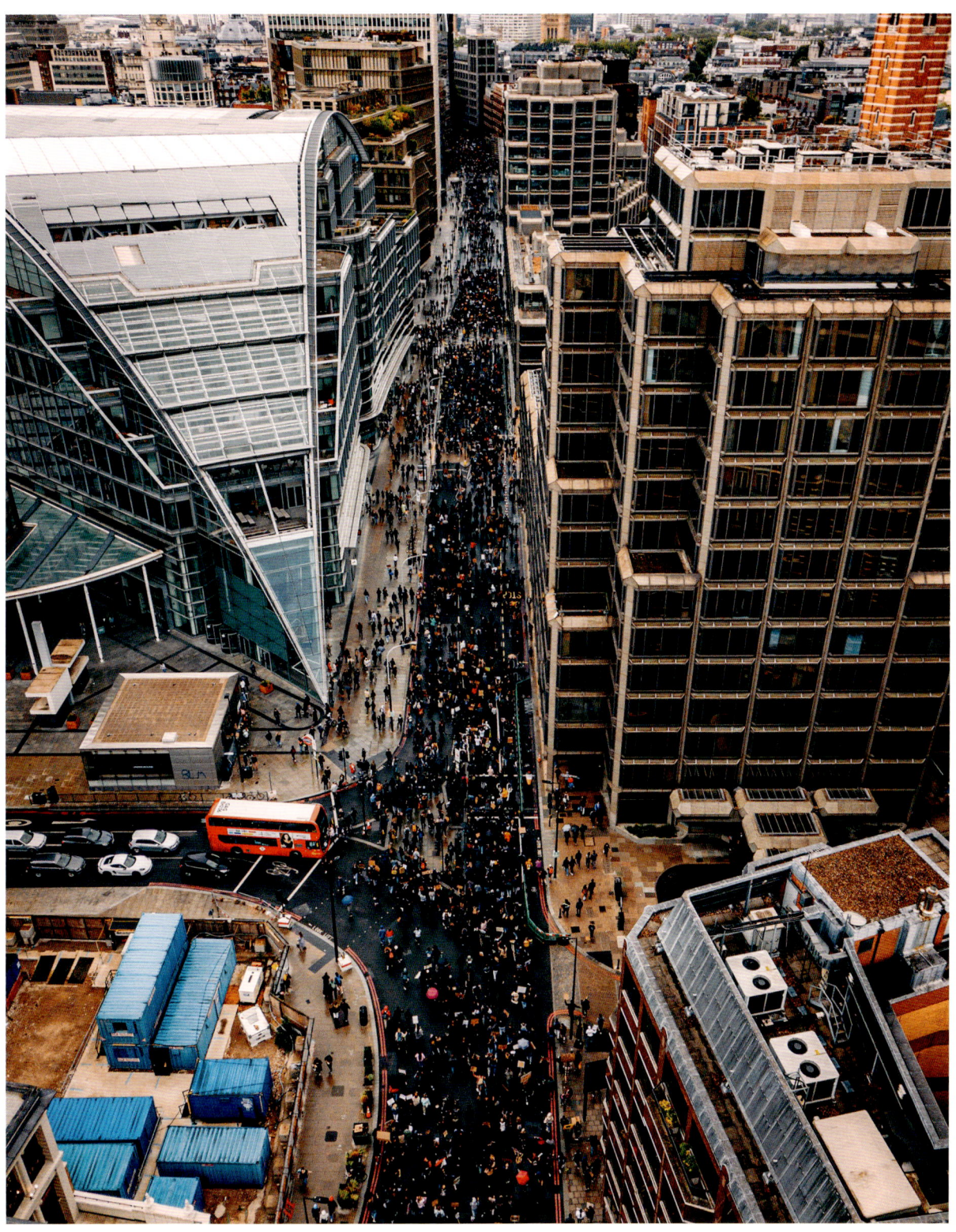

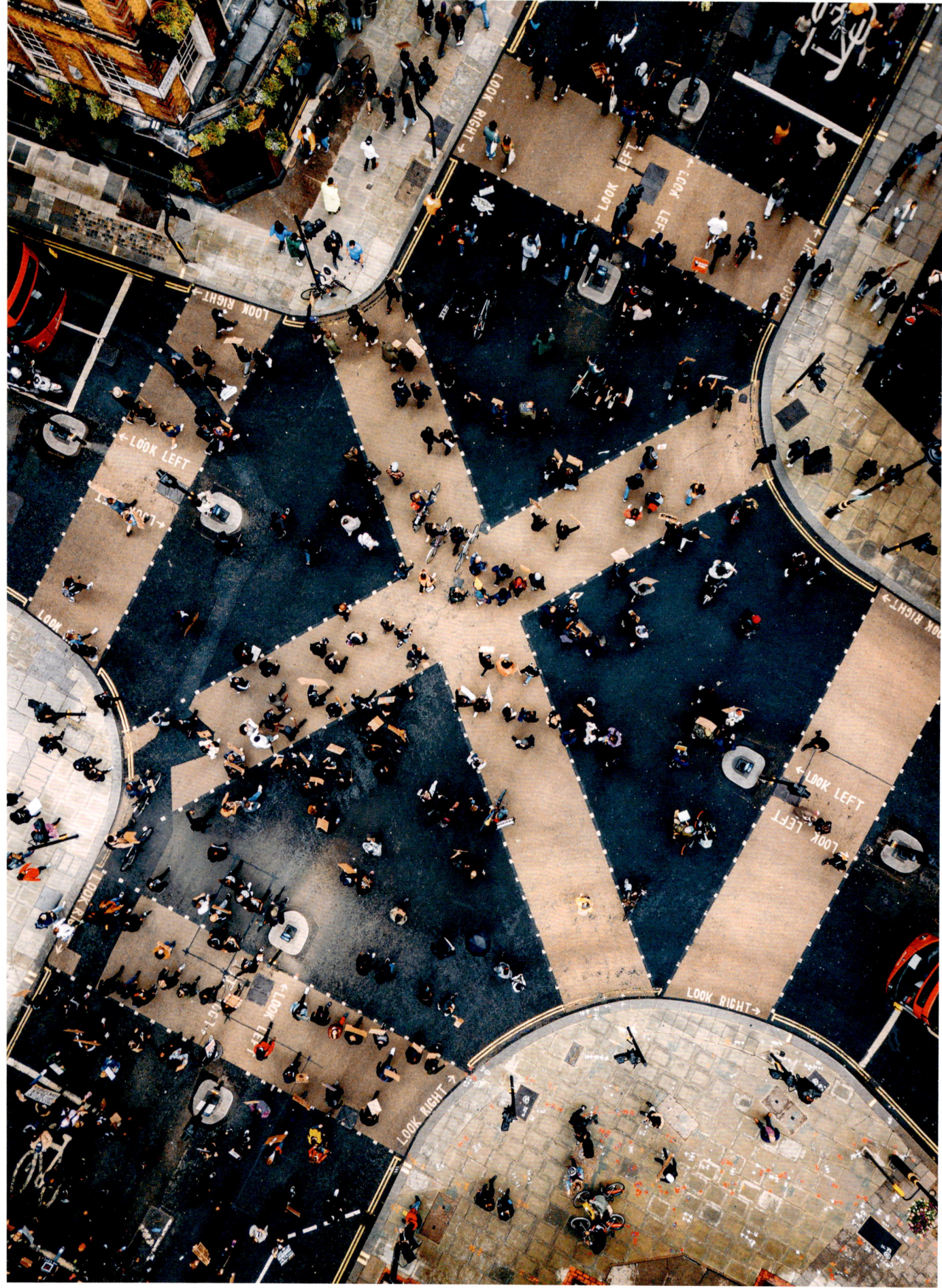

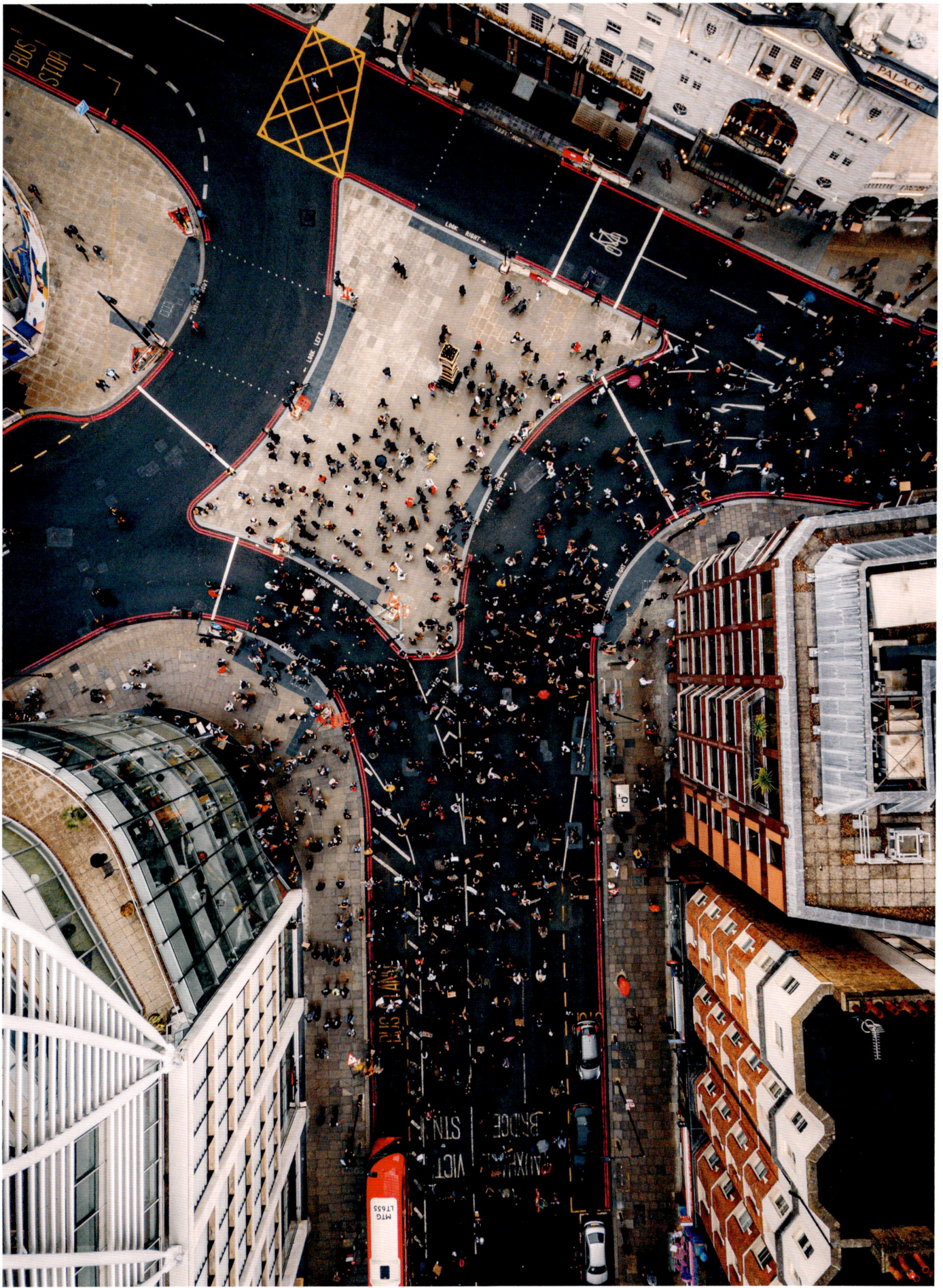

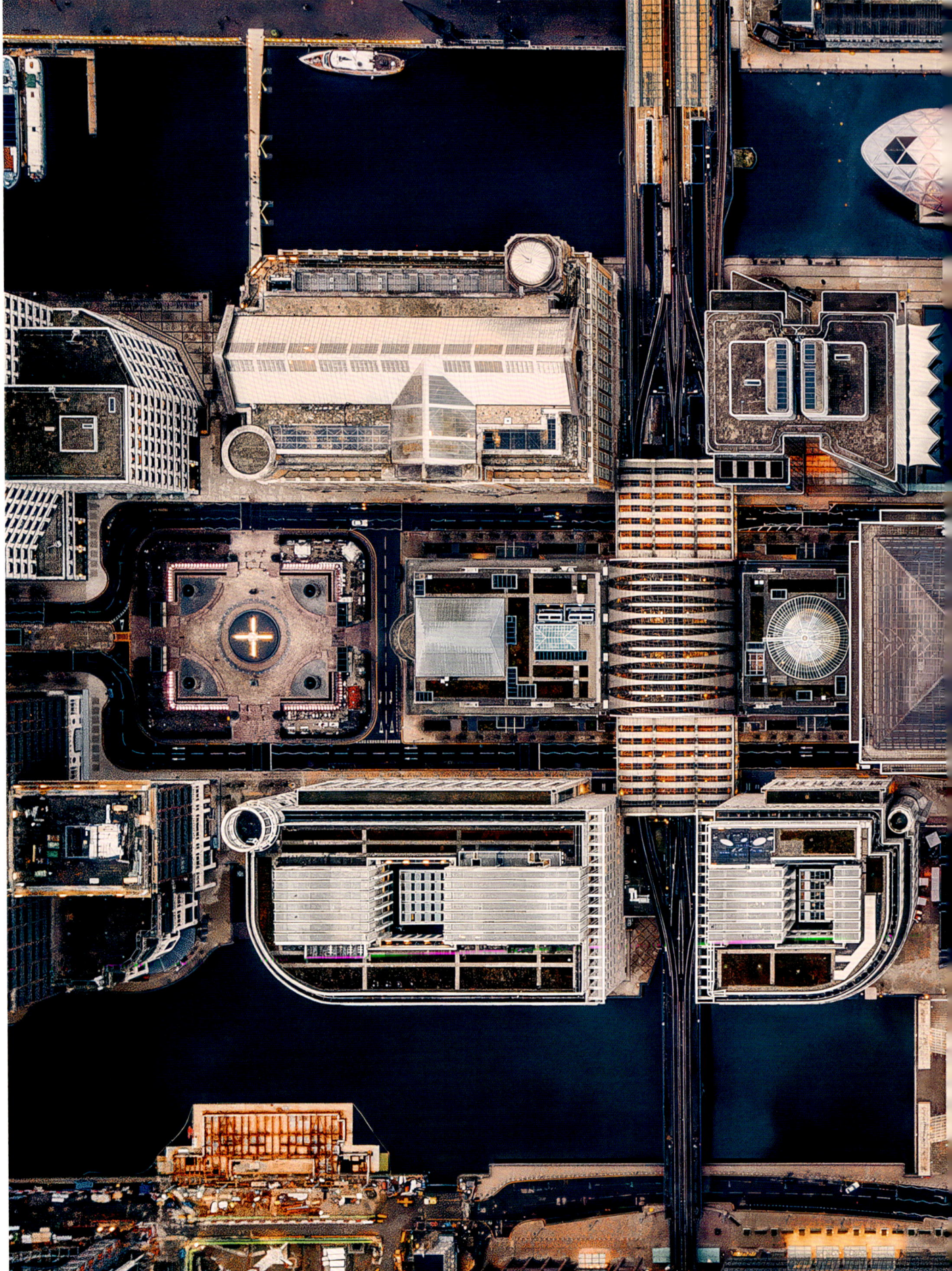

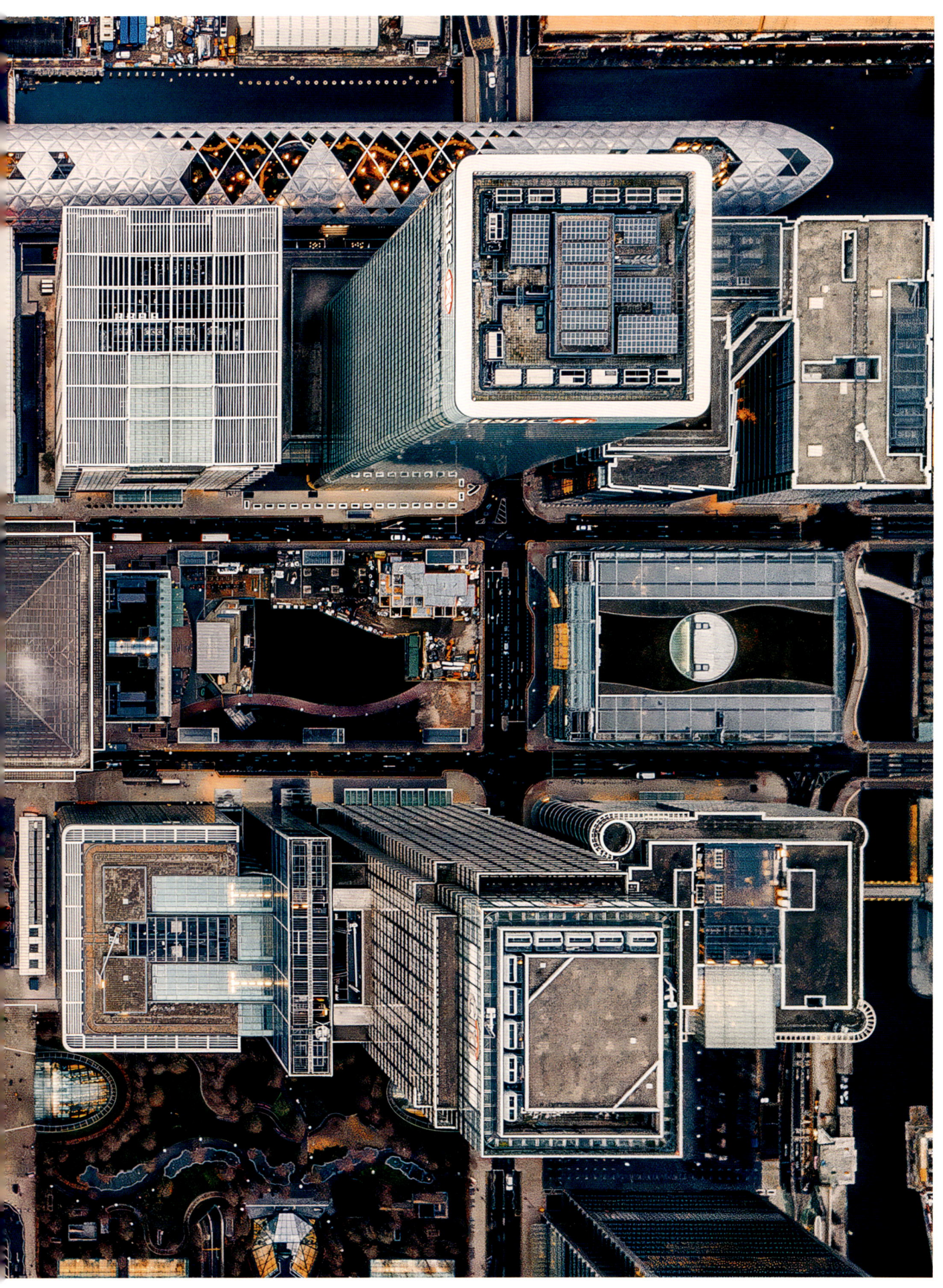

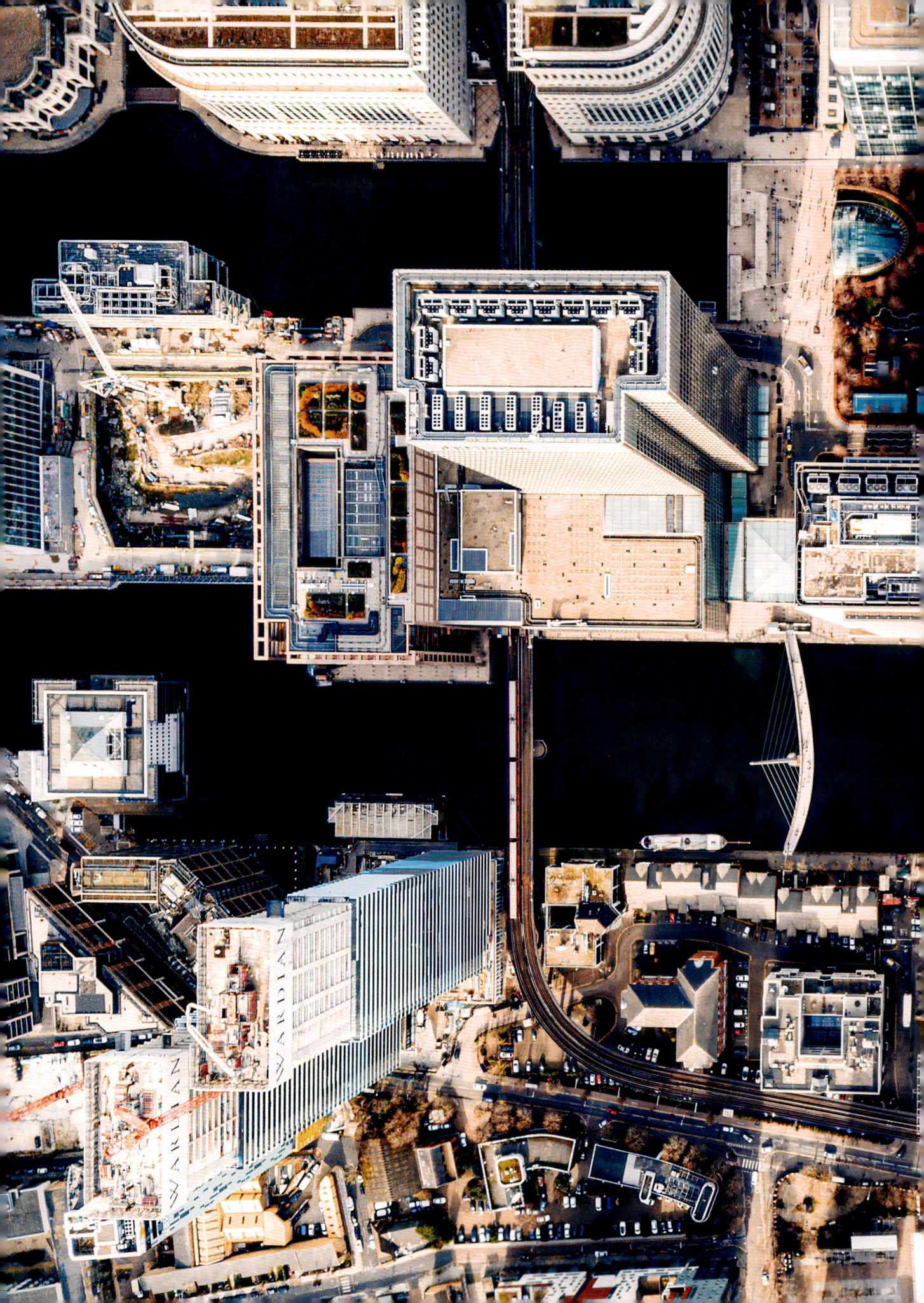

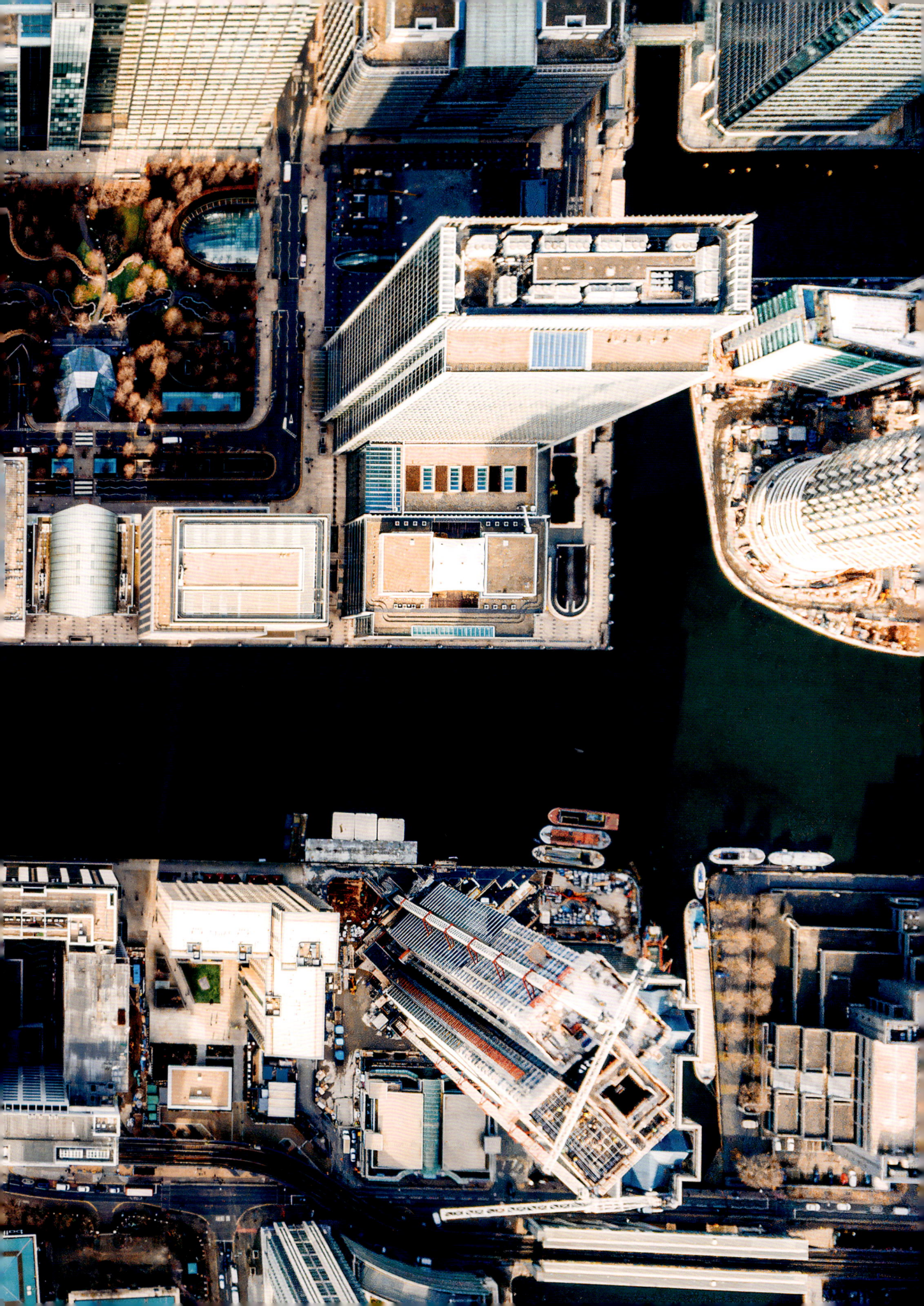

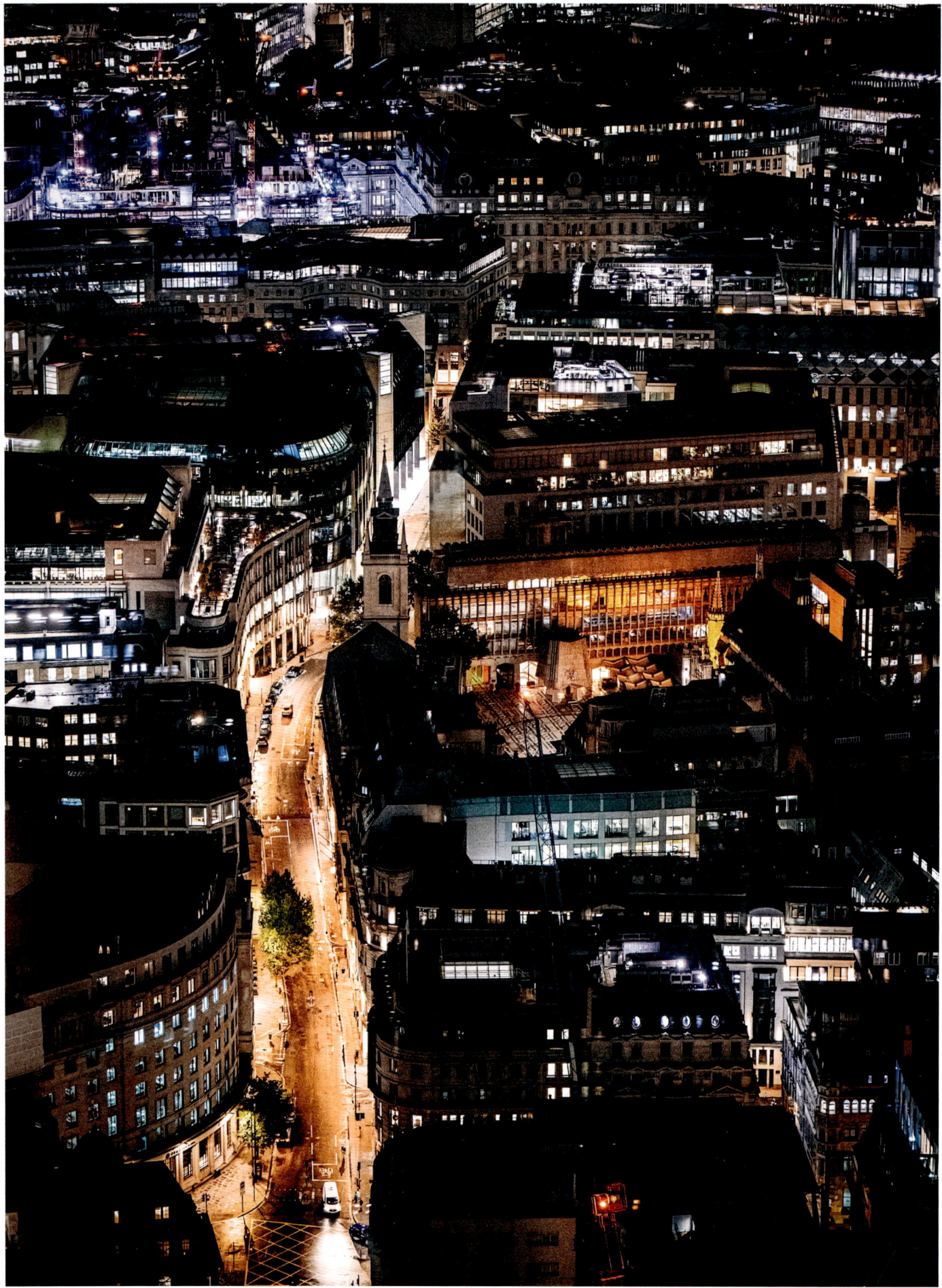

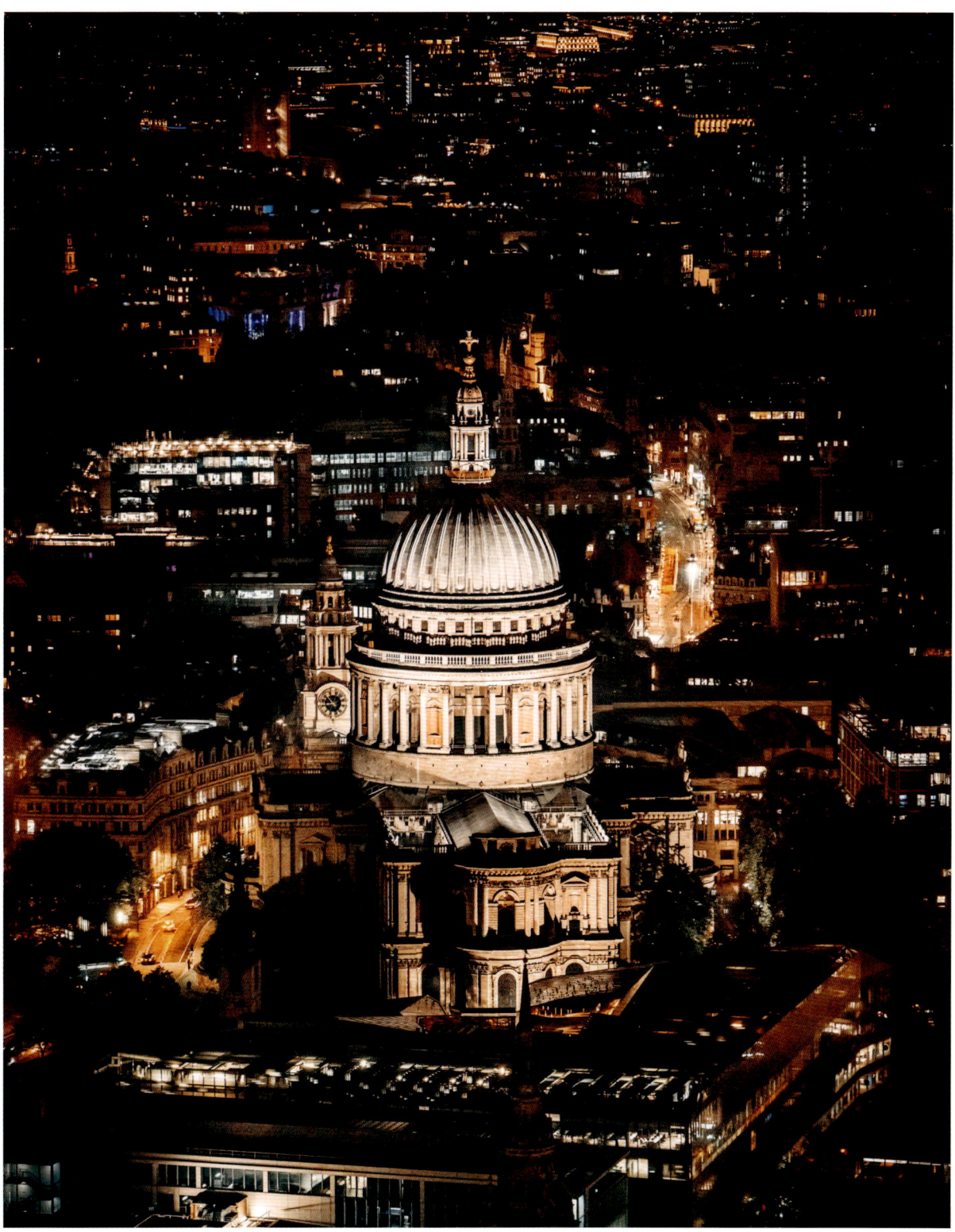

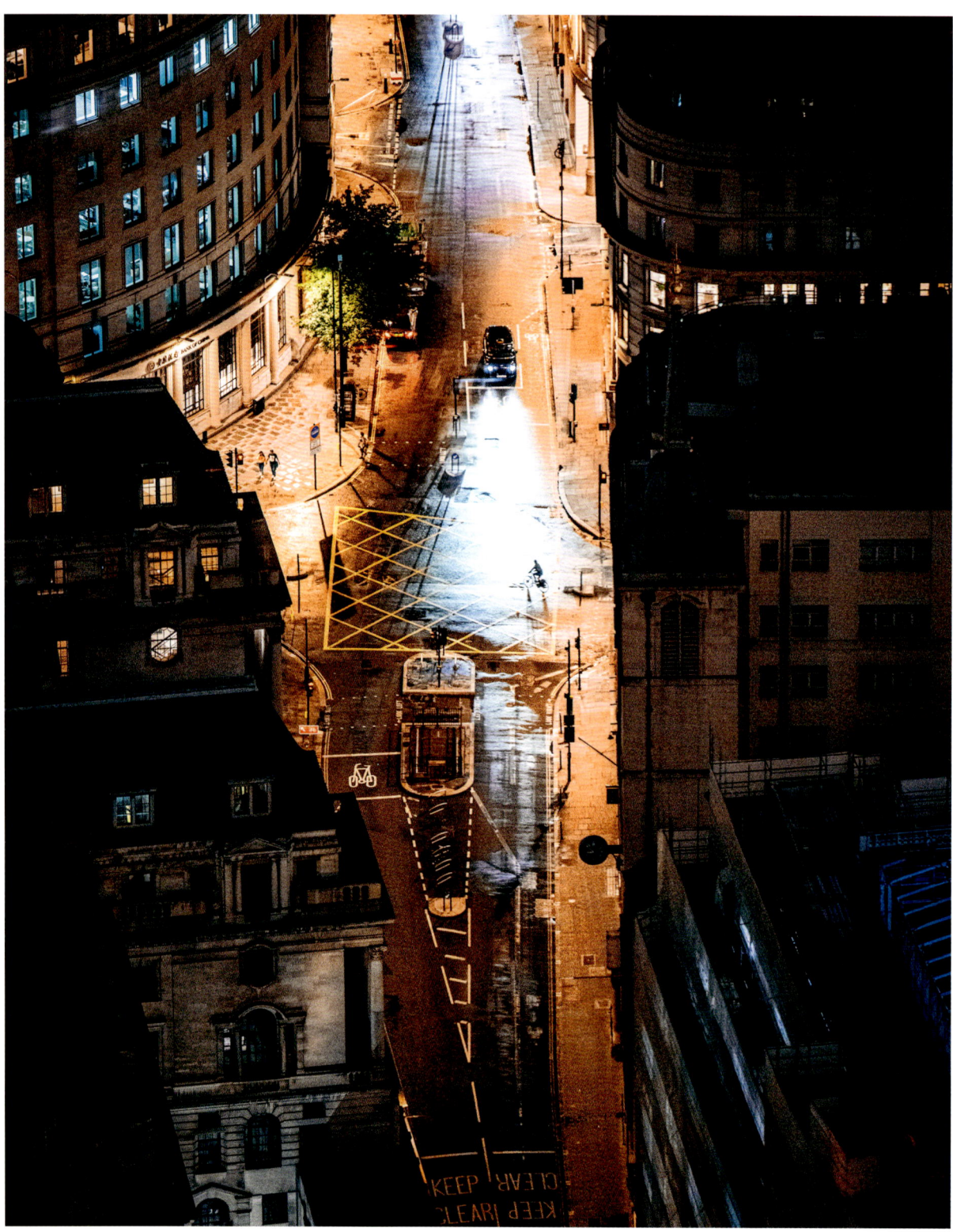

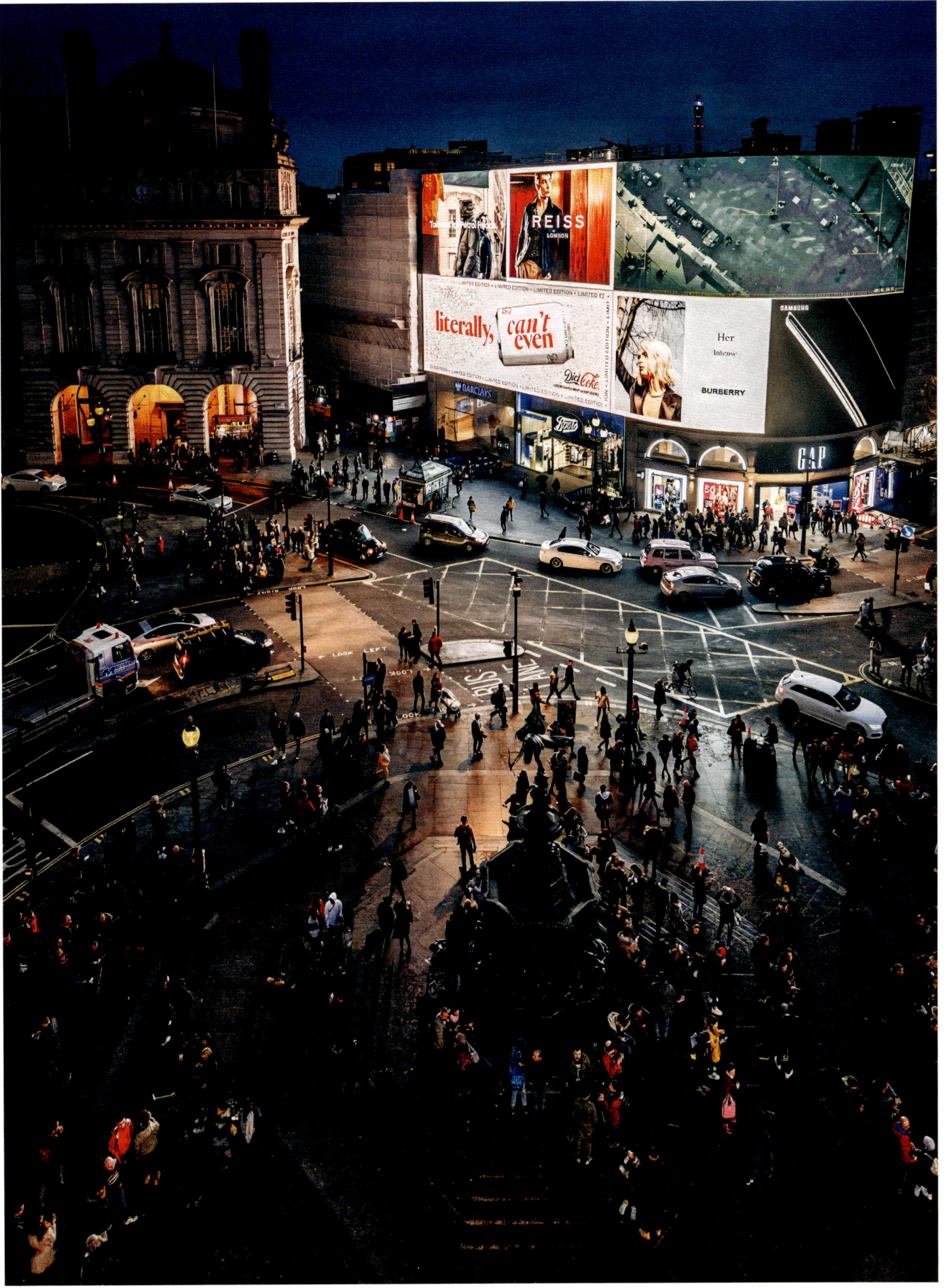

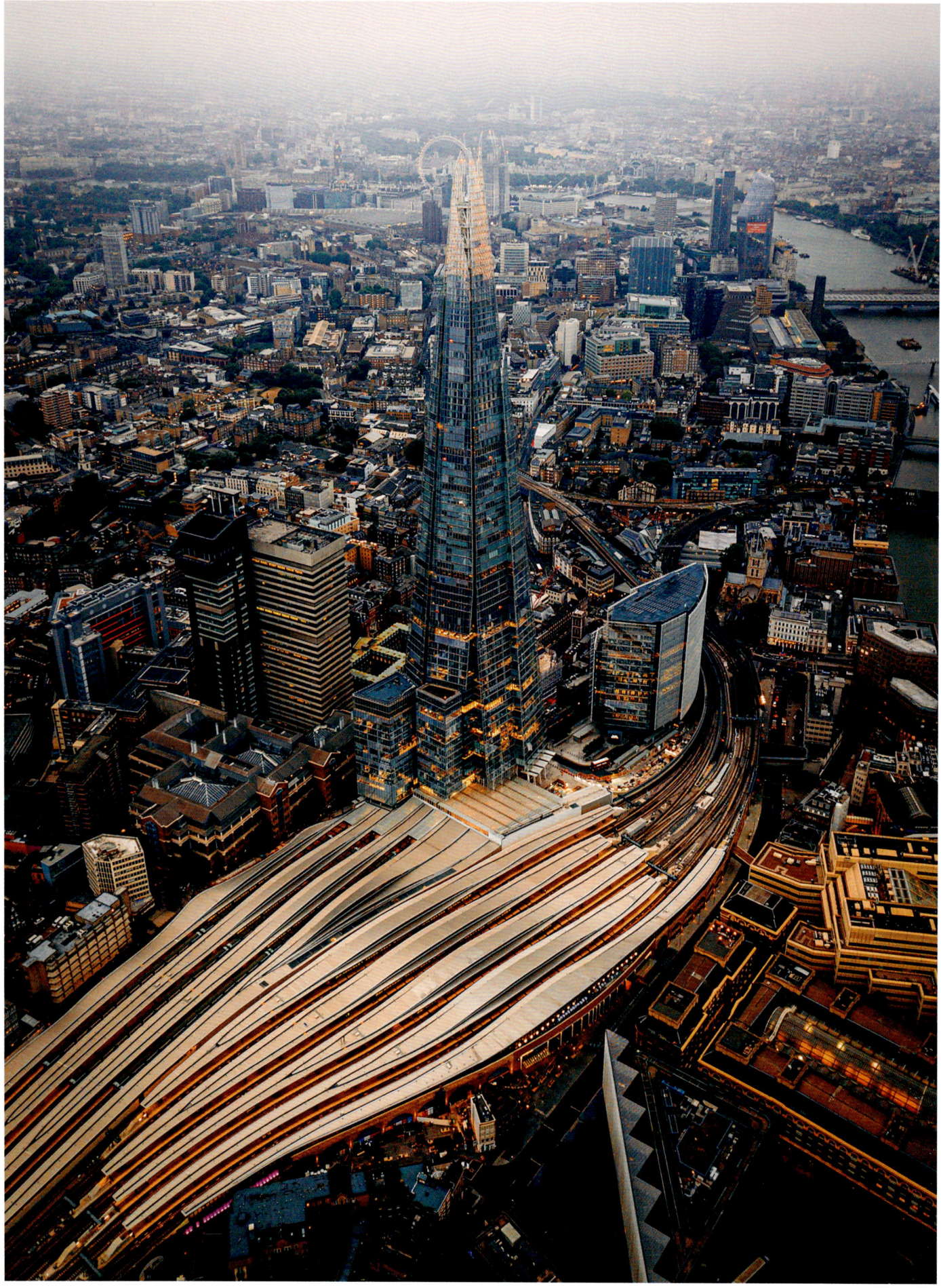

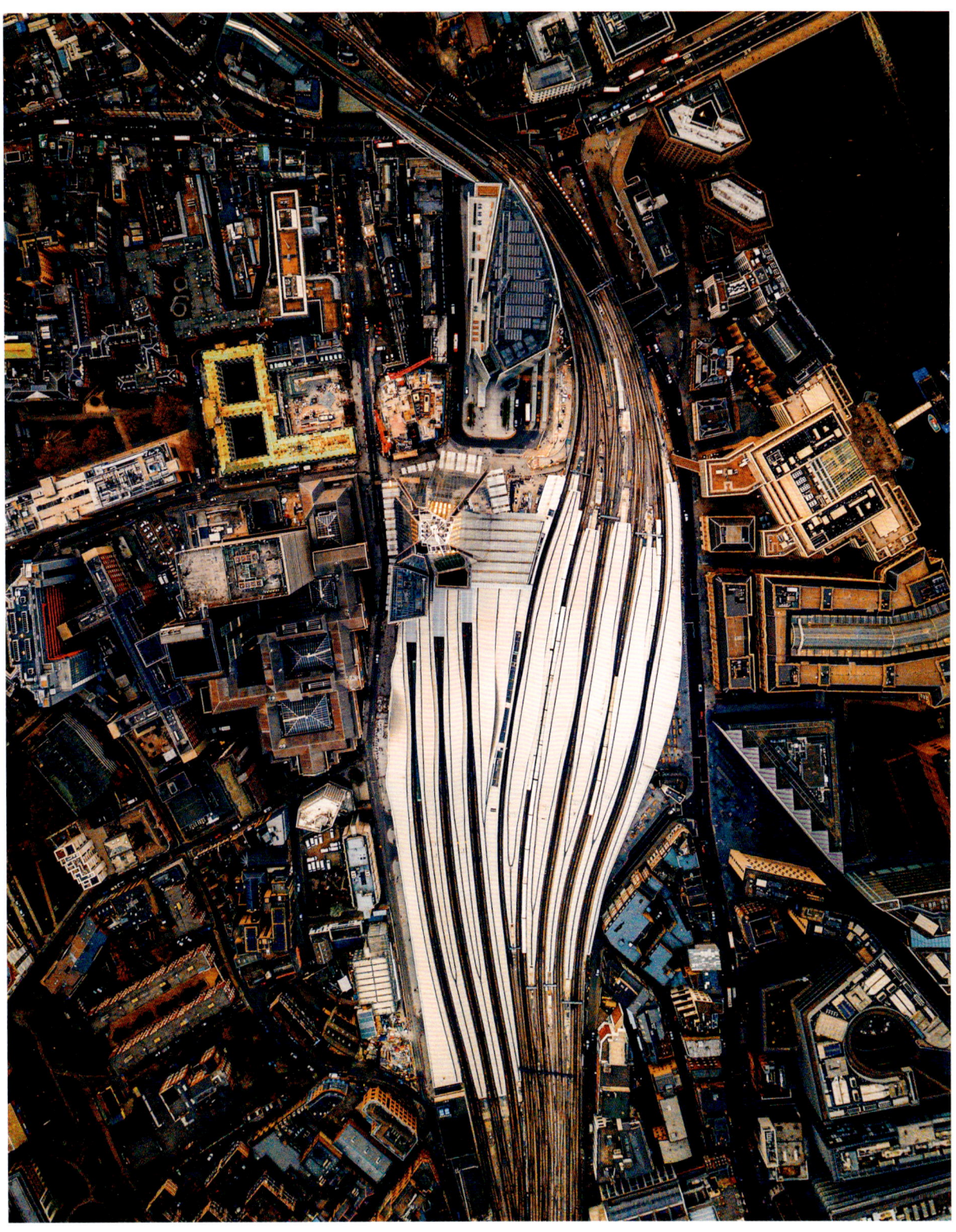

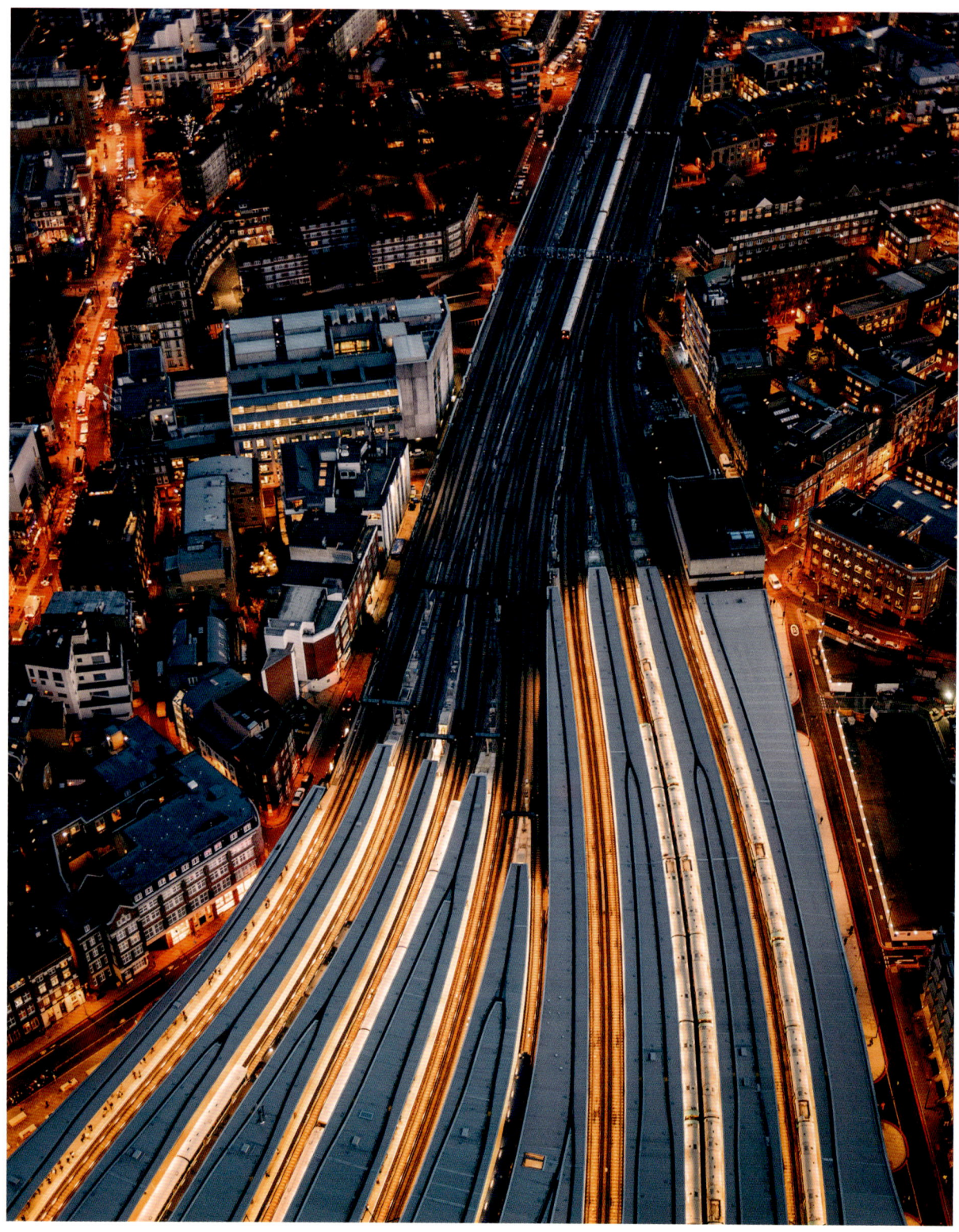

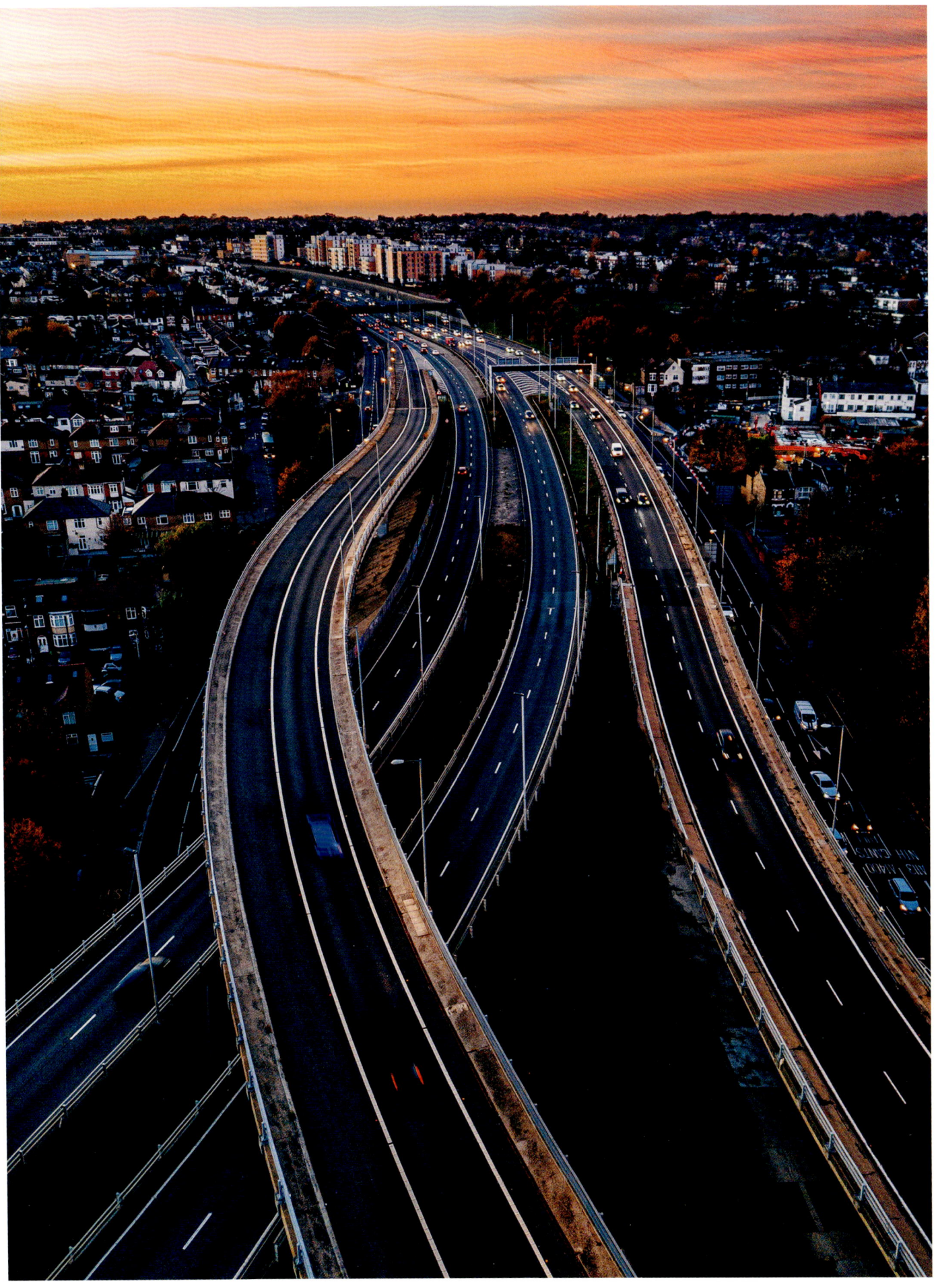

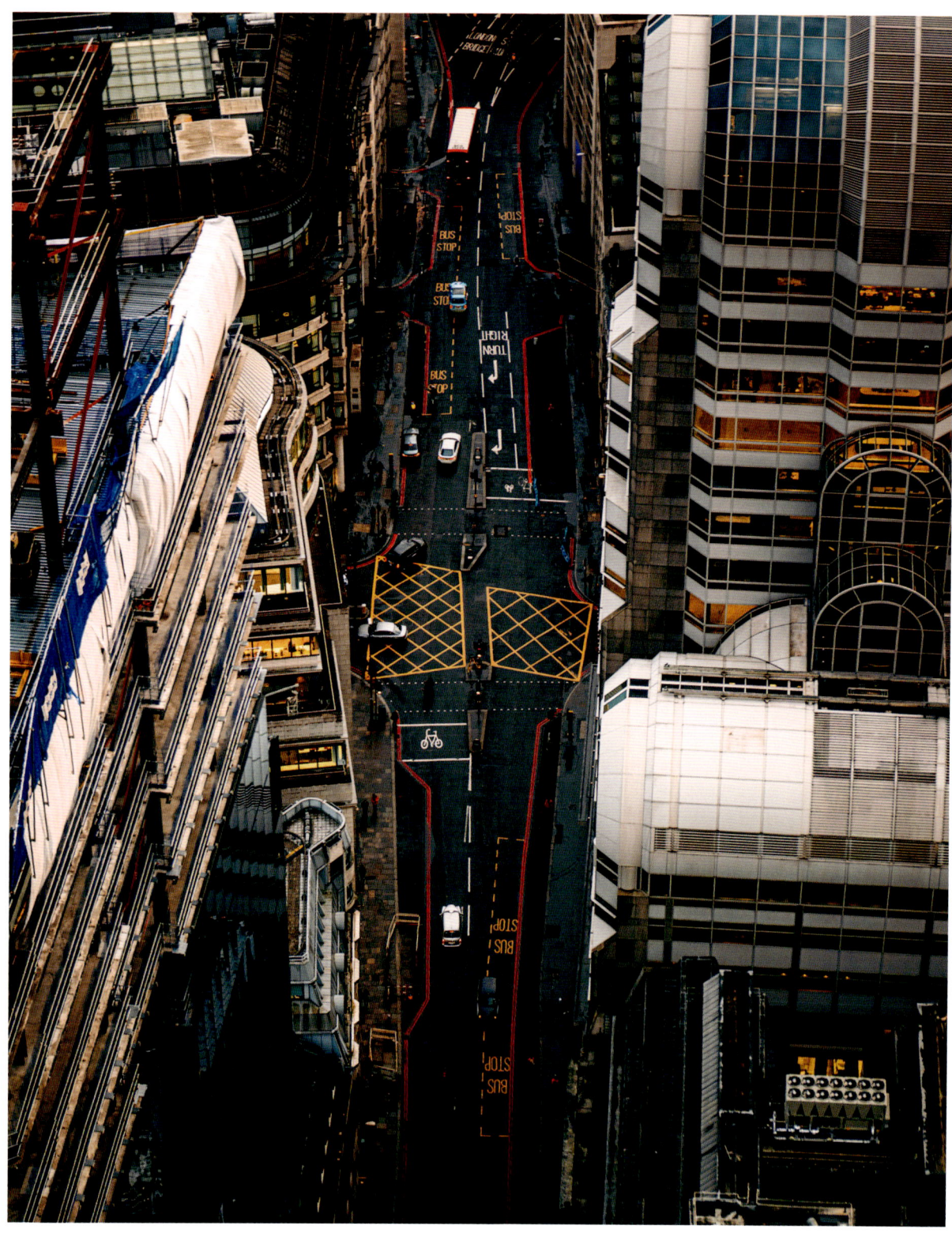

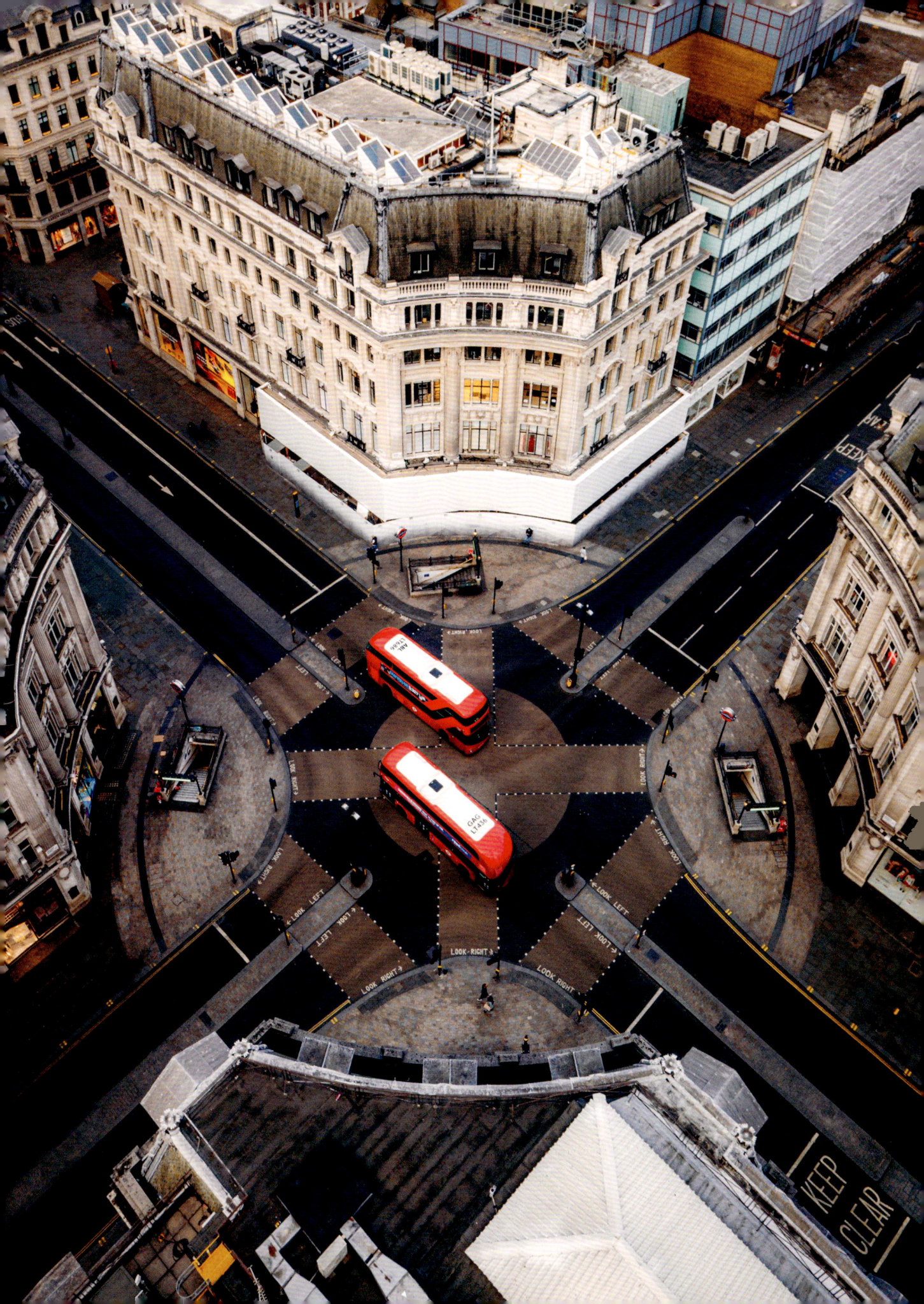

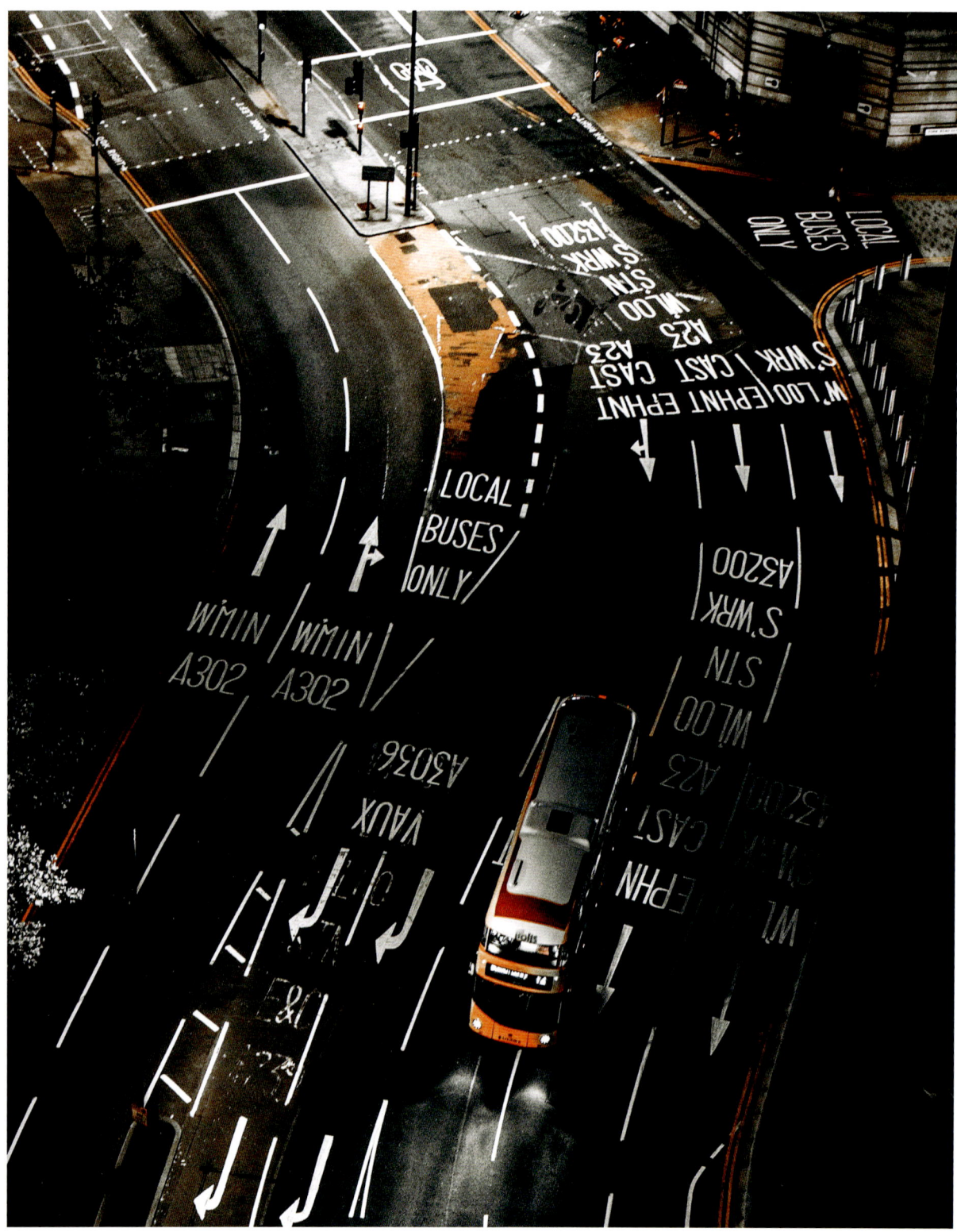

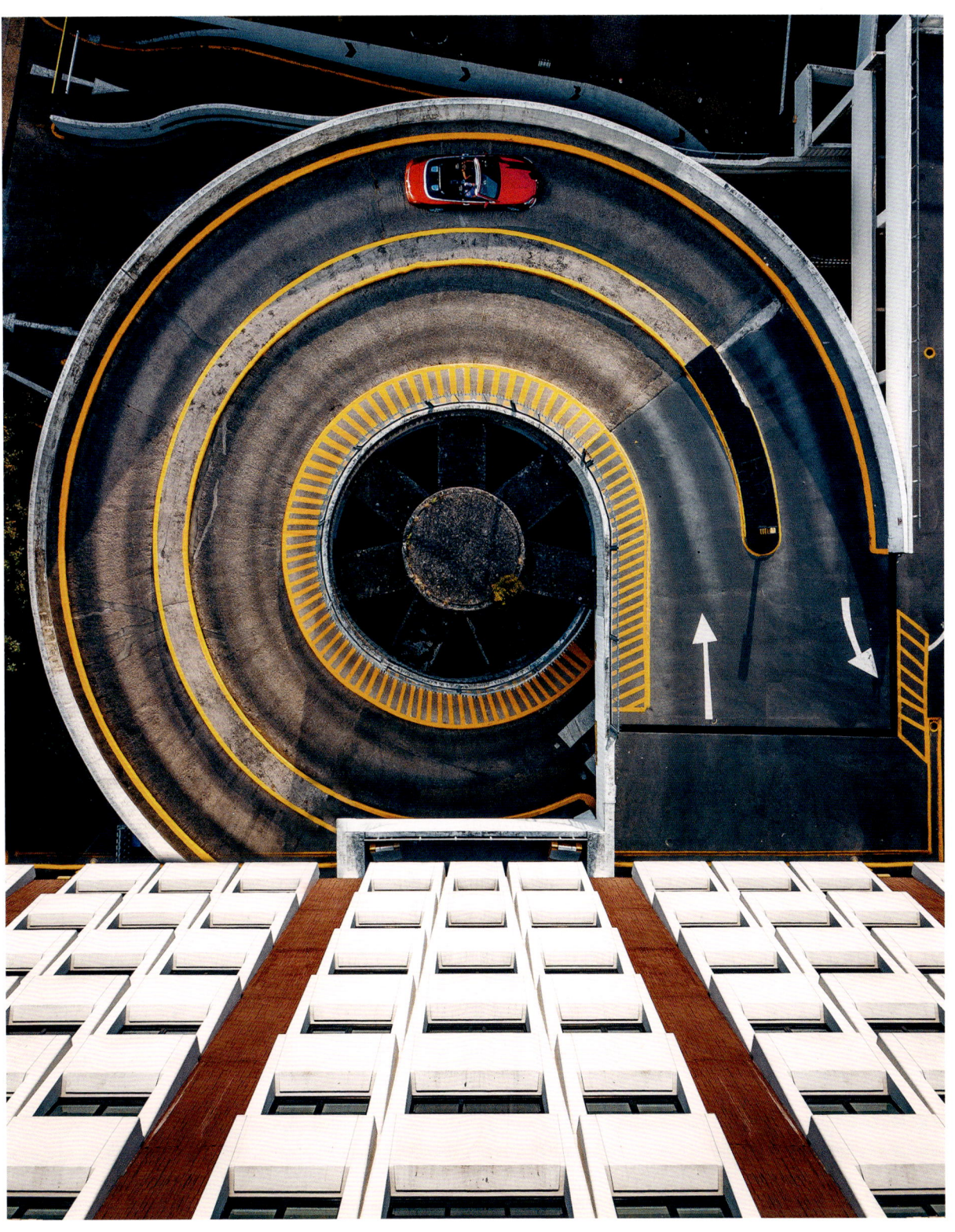

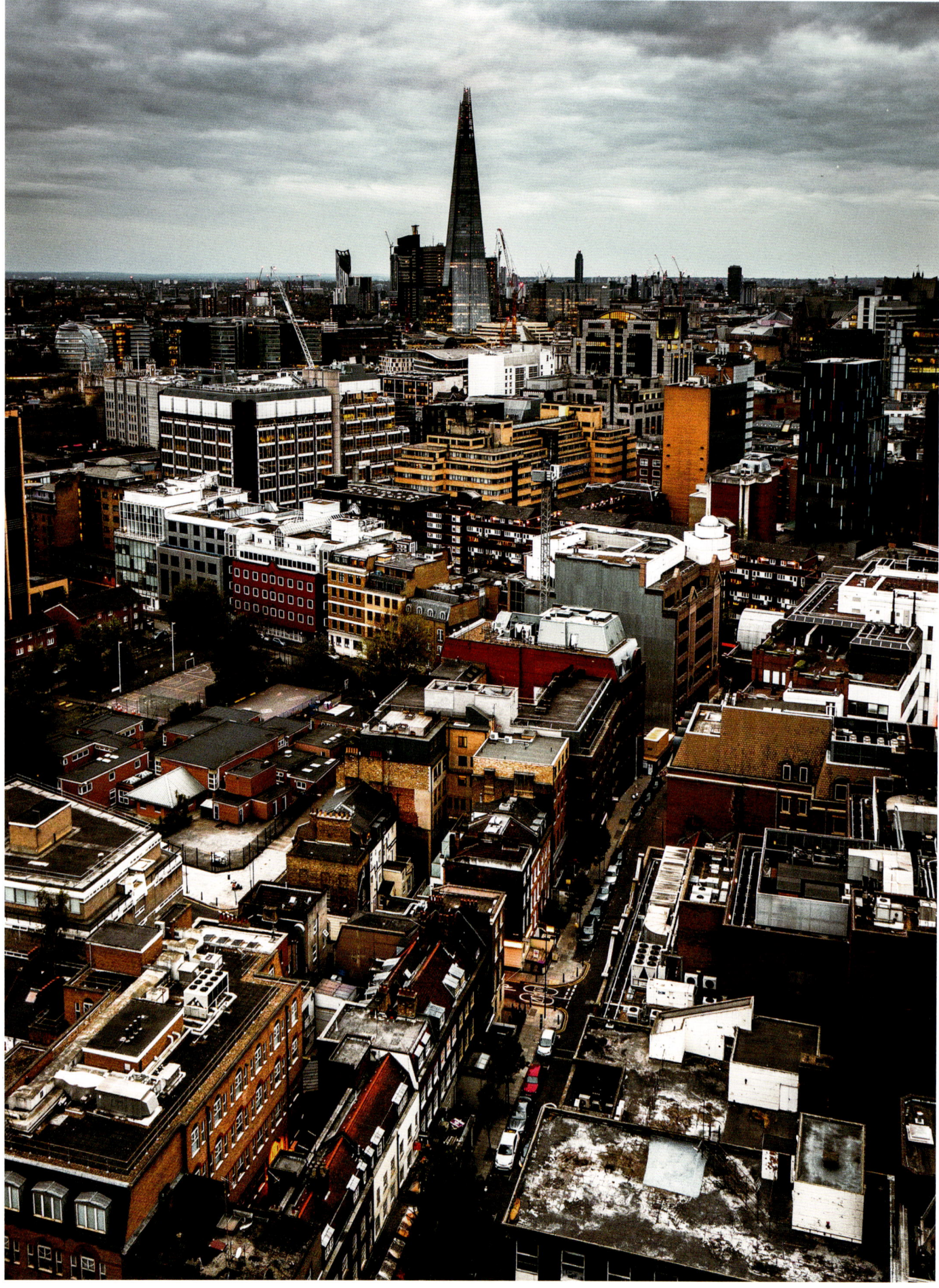

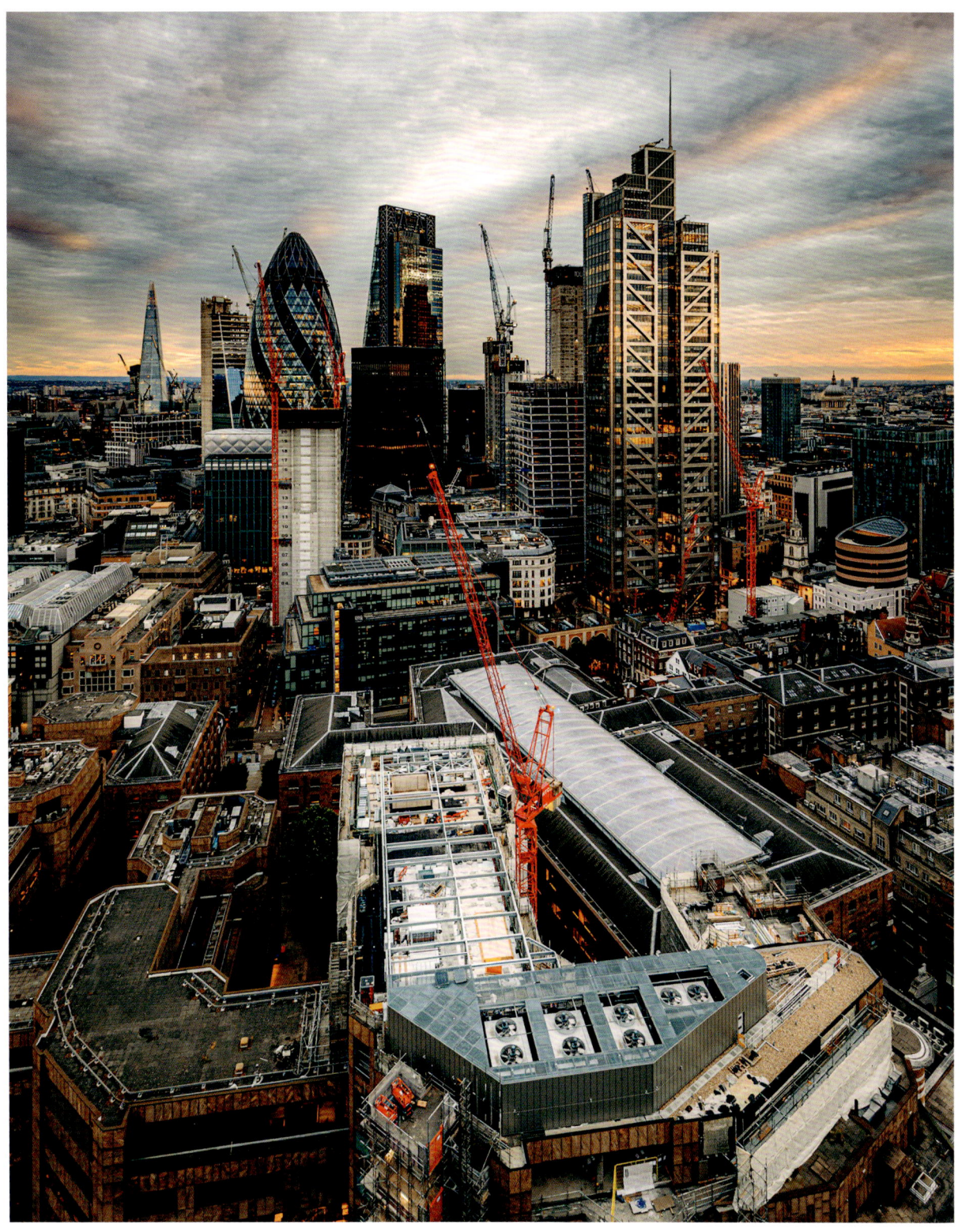

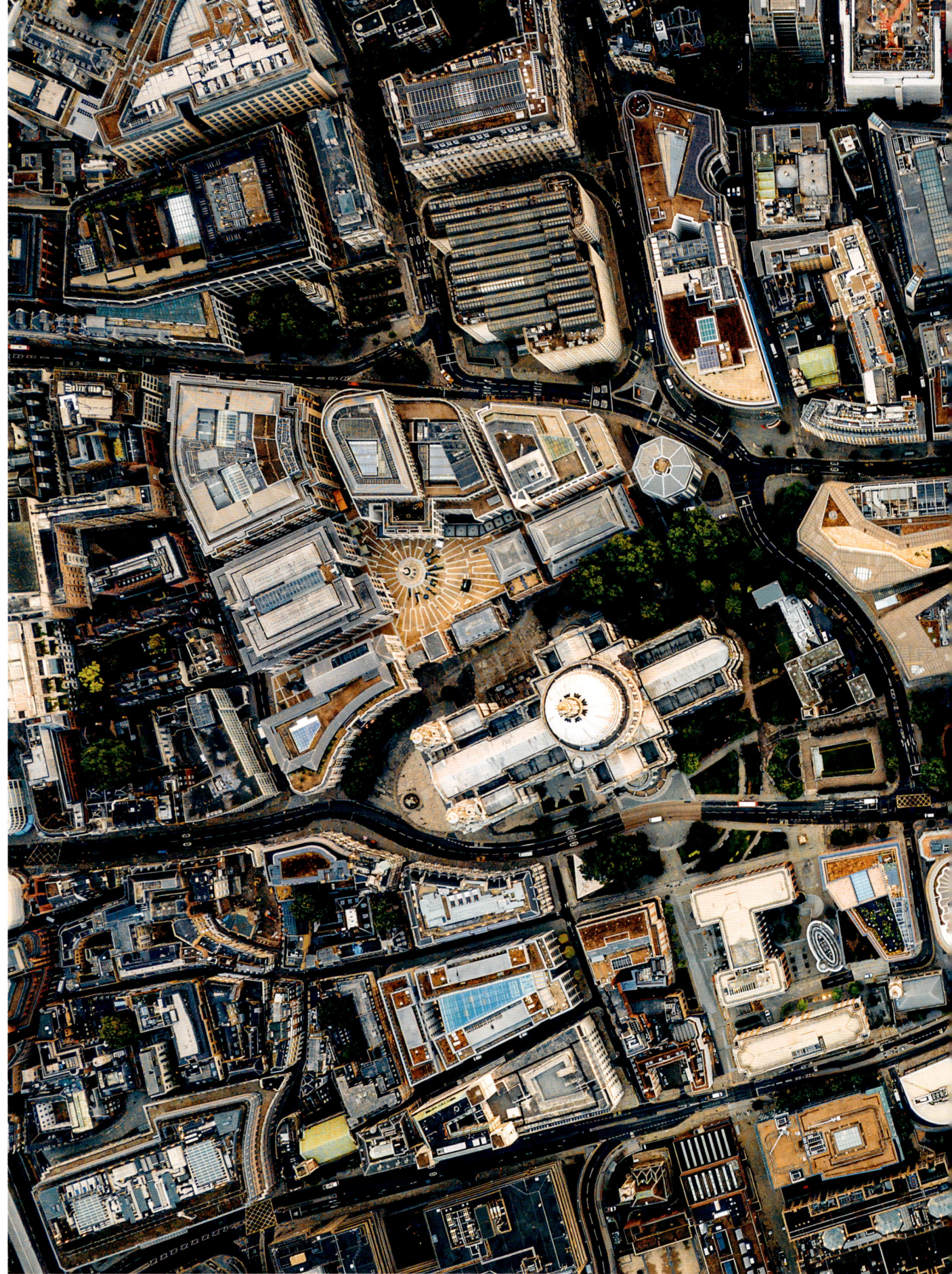

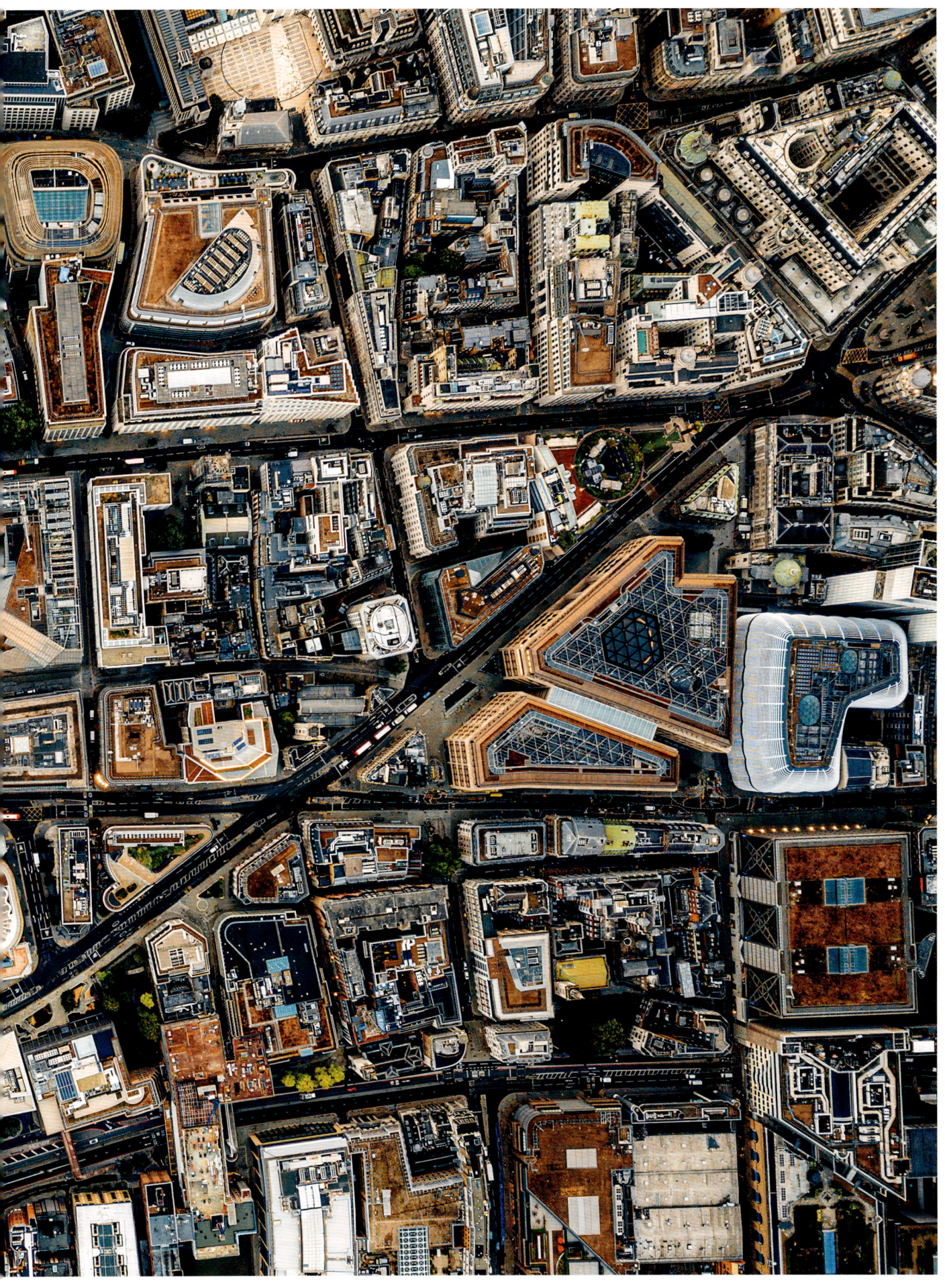

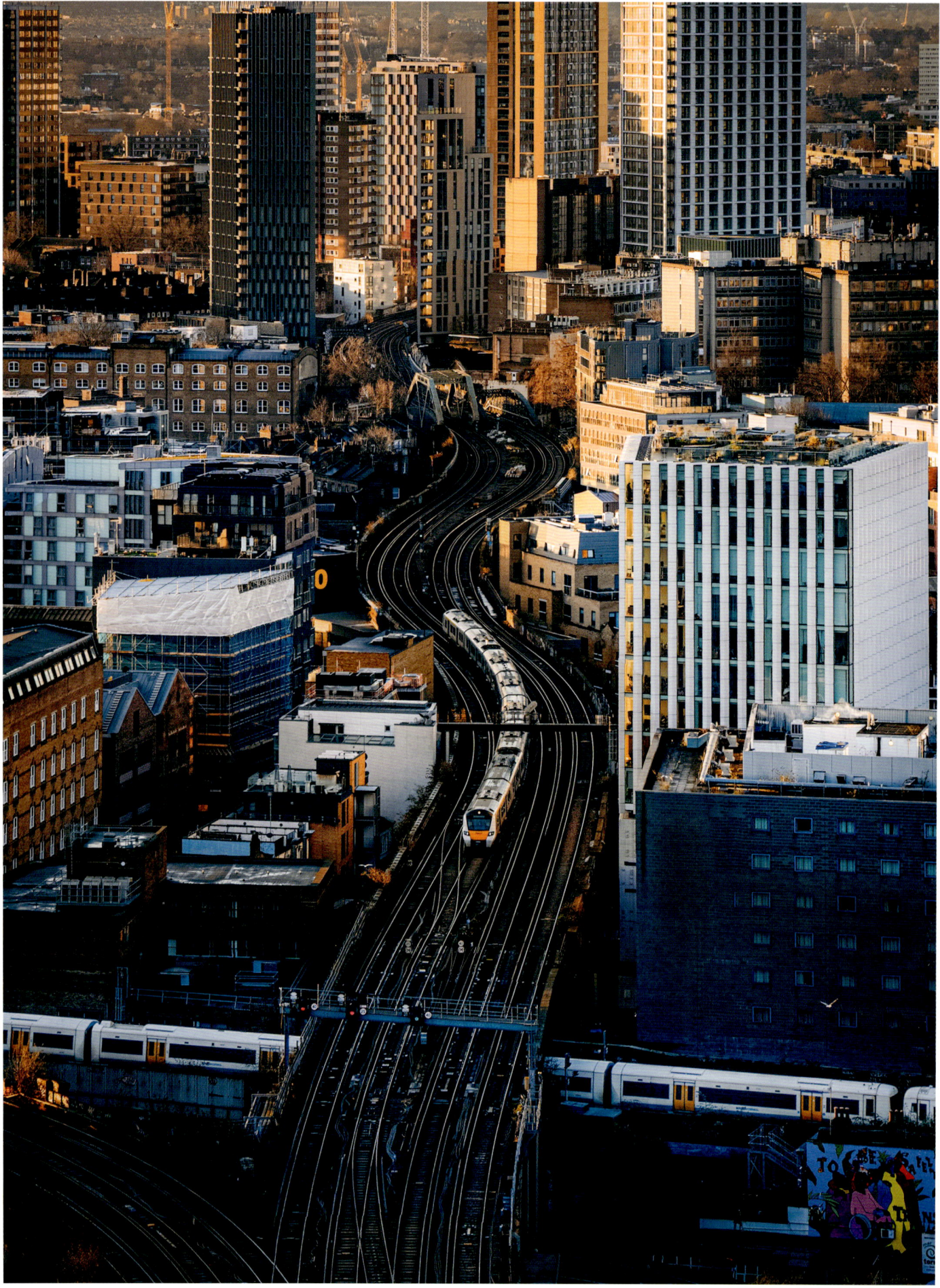

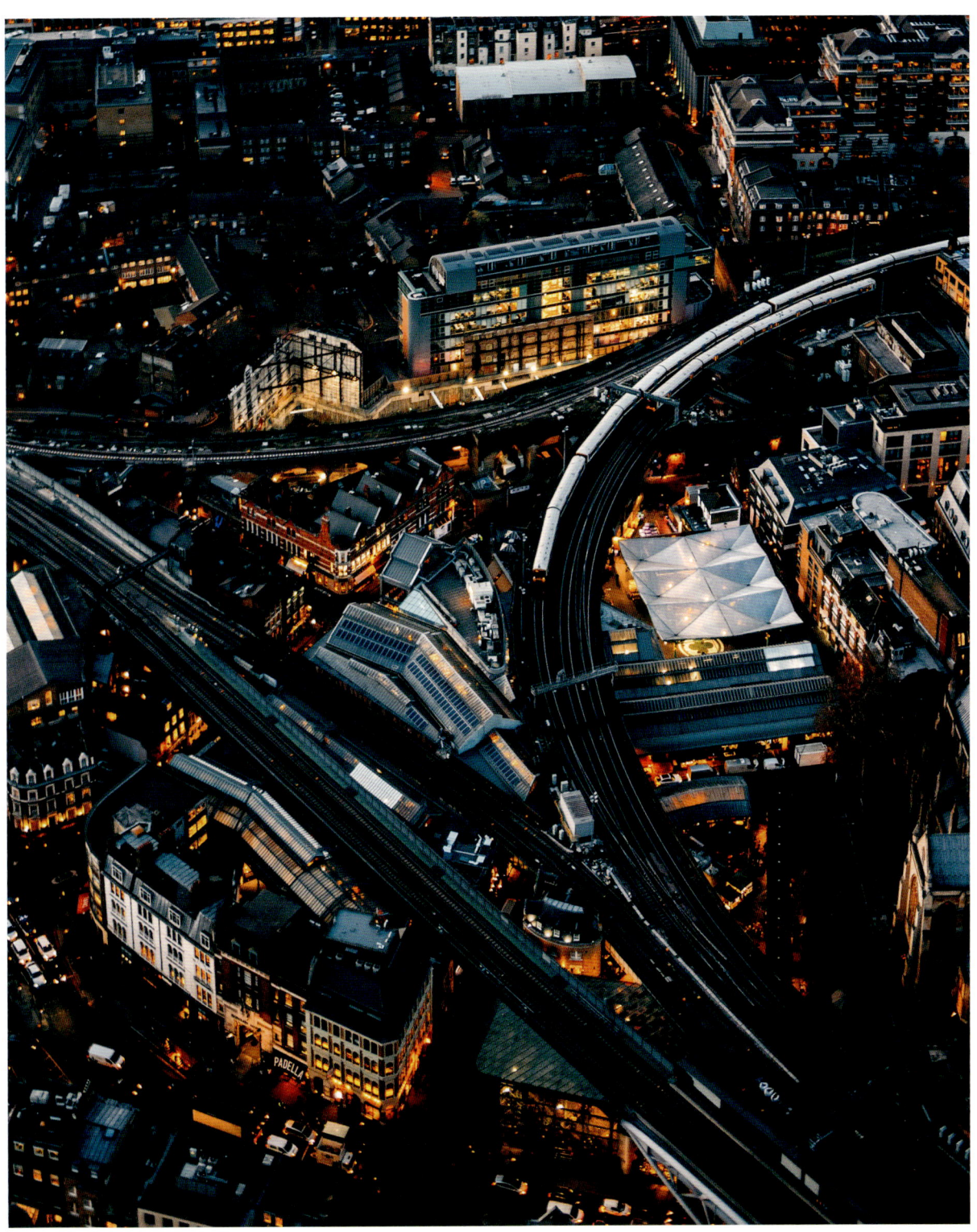

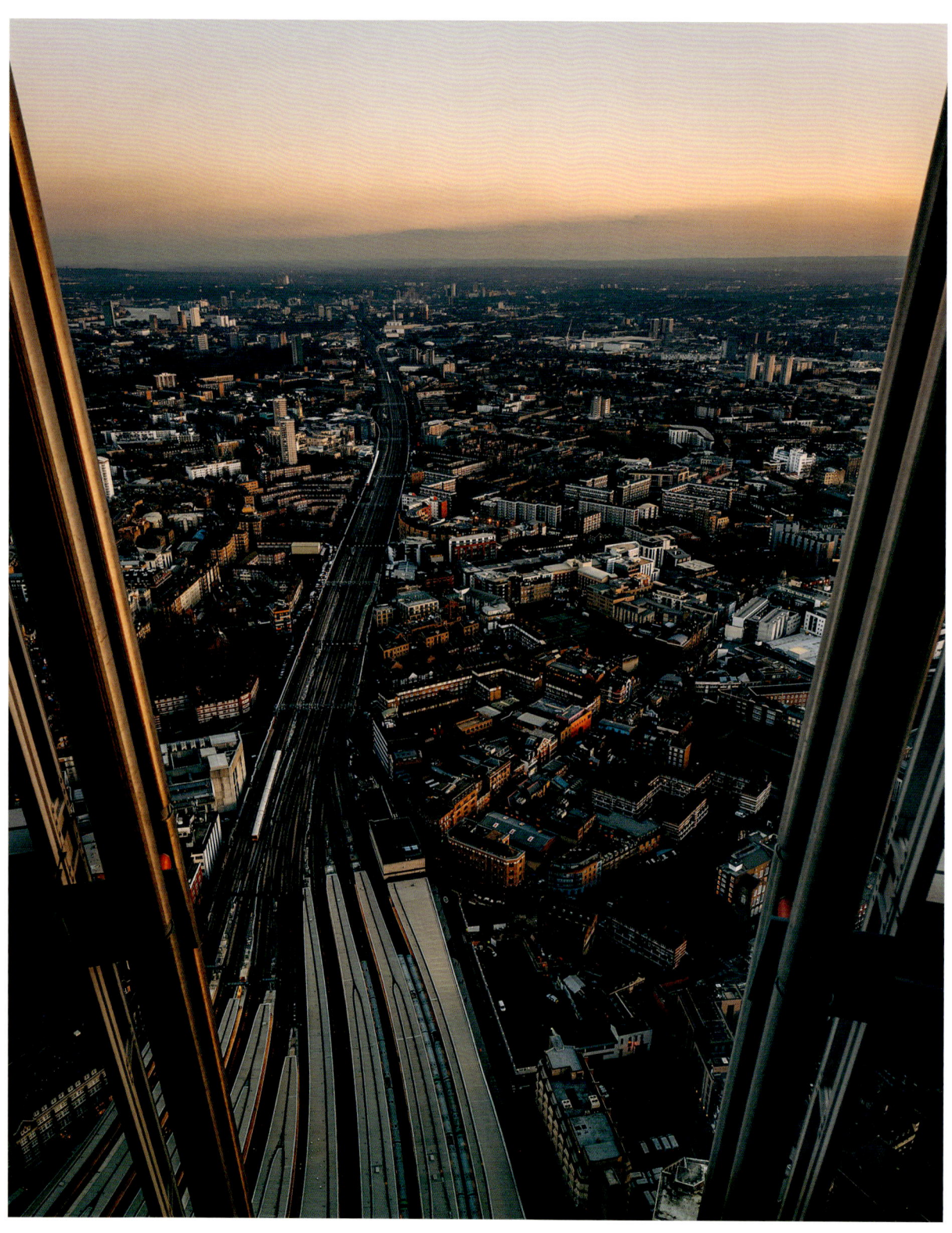

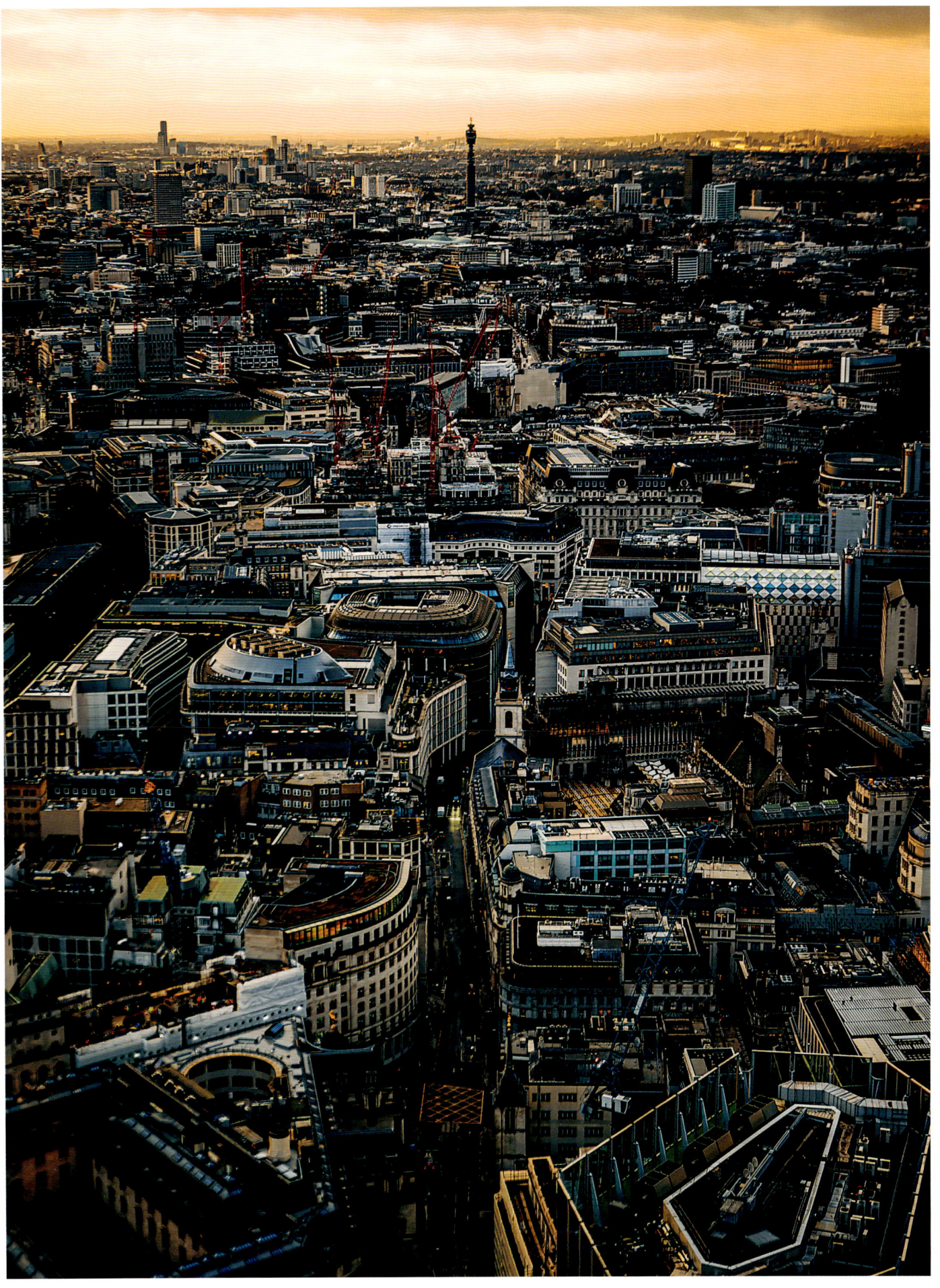

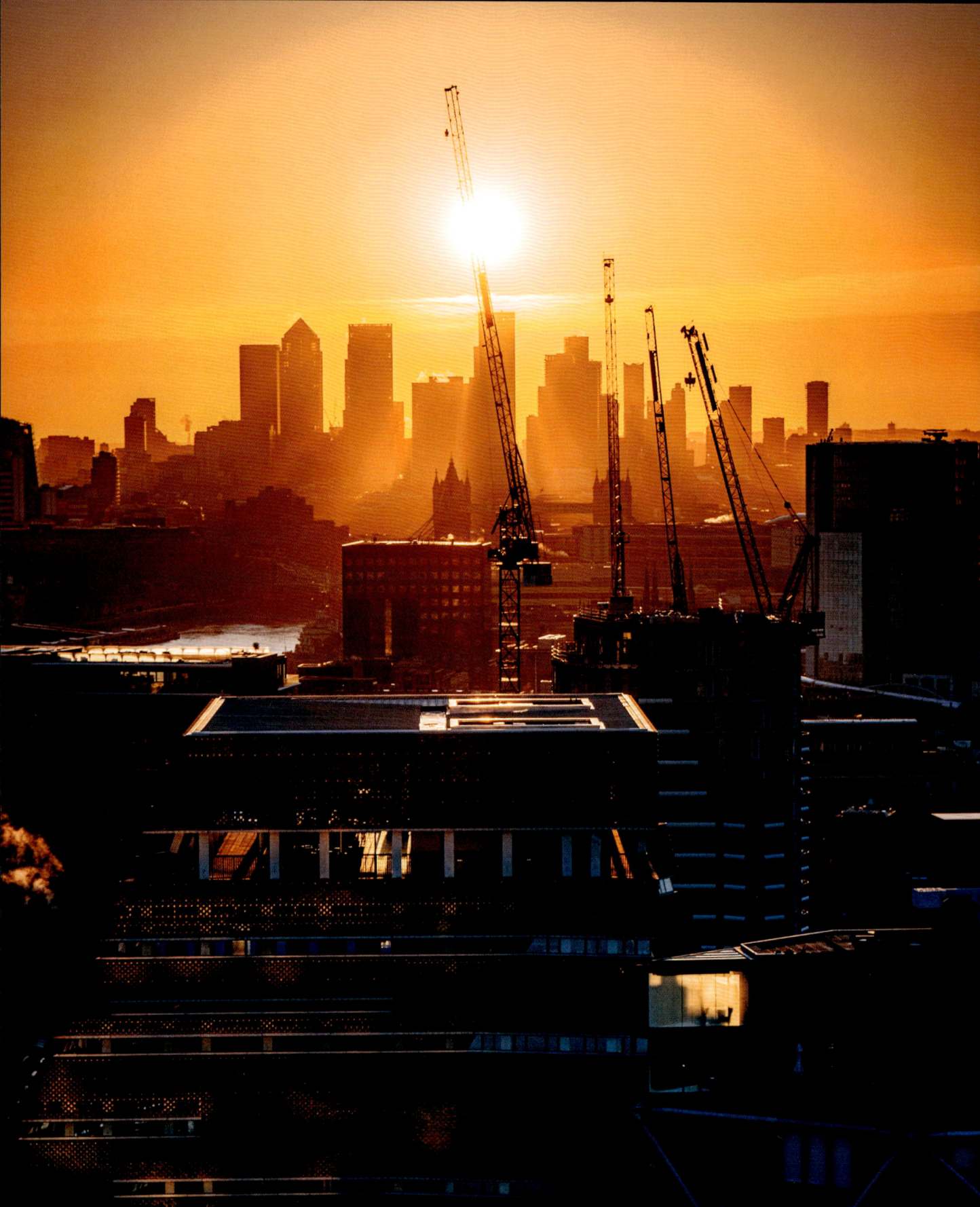

ABOVE & ACROSS
LONDON

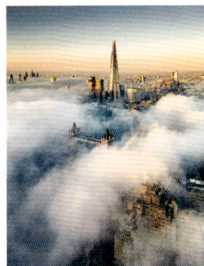

Front Cover View of The Shard and Tower Bridge

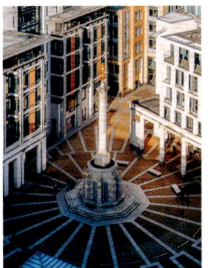

2 View of Paternoster Square

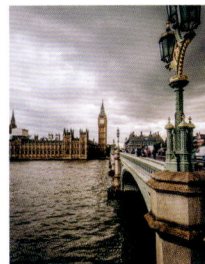

4 View of Westminster Bridge and Elizabeth Tower from Fountain of St Thomas Gardens

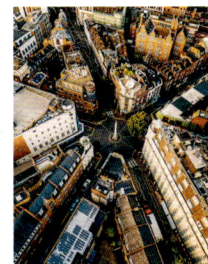

7 View of Seven Dials

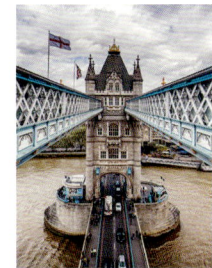

8 View of Tower Bridge

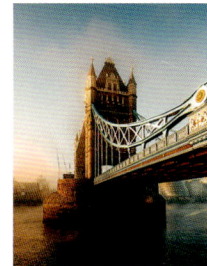

10 View of Tower Bridge

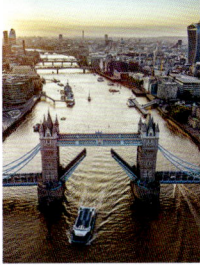

11 Above Tower Bridge

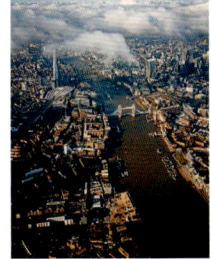

12 Above River Thames and City of London

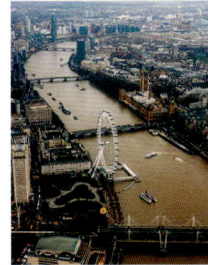

13 View of the London Eye and Westminster

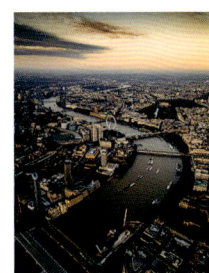

14 View of River Thames and Westminster

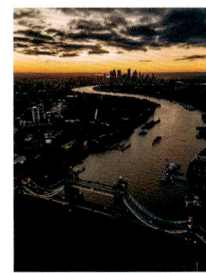

15 View of Tower Bridge and River Thames

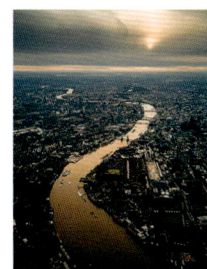

16 View of River Thames

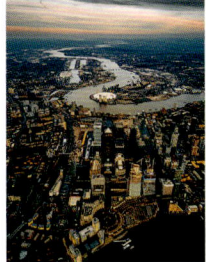

17 View of Canary Wharf and Millennium Dome

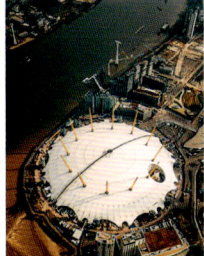

18 View of Millennium Dome

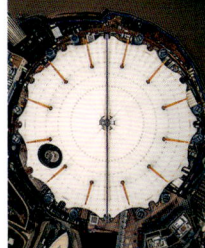

19 Above Millennium Dome

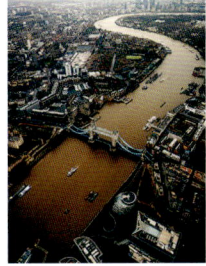

20 View of Tower Bridge and River Thames

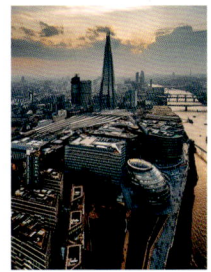

21 View of The Shard

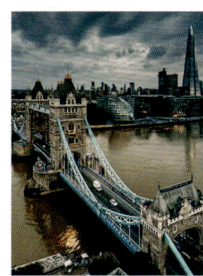

22 View of Tower Bridge

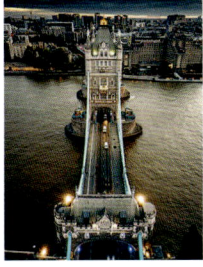

23 View of Tower Bridge

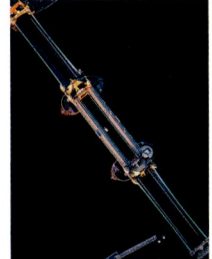

24 Above Tower Bridge

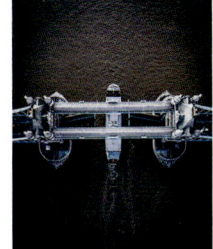

25 Above Tower Bridge

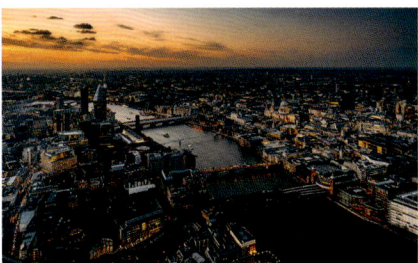

26-27 View of City of London

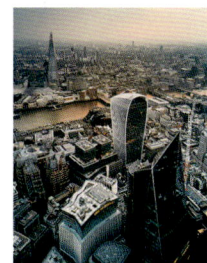

28 View of The Shard, Sky Garden, and The Scalpel

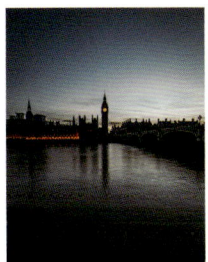

29 View of House of Parliament and Elizabeth Tower

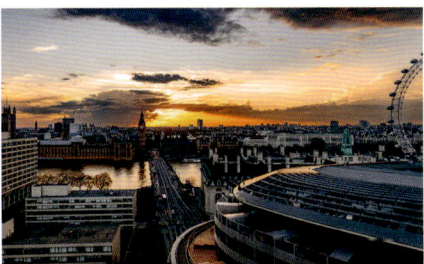

30-31 View of Westminster Bridge

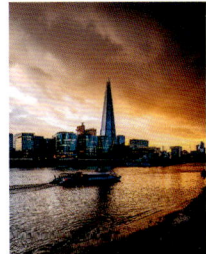

32 View of The Shard

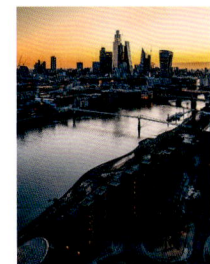

33 View of River Thames and Central London

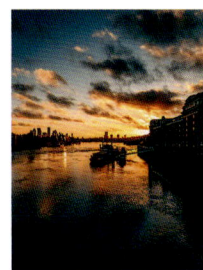

34 View of River Thames and Shad Thames

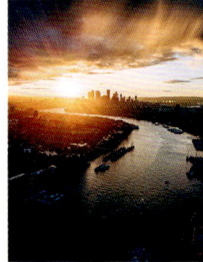
35 View of River Thames towards Canary Wharf

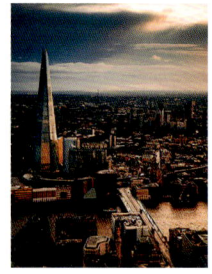
36 View of The Shard and London Bridge

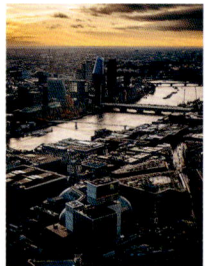
37 View of City of London

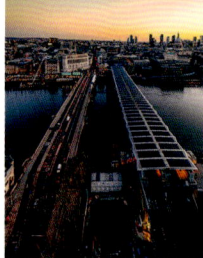
38 View of Blackfriars Bridge

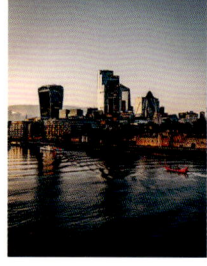
39 View of River Thames and London skyline

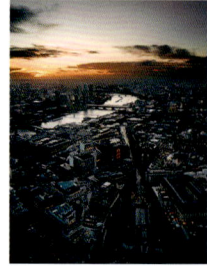
40 View of City of London

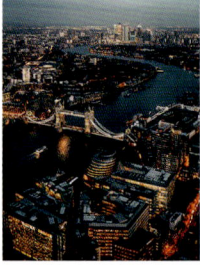
41 View of Tower Bridge, River Thames, and Canary Wharf

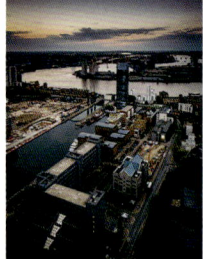
42 View of Millennium Dome

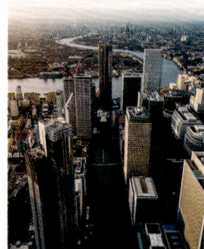
43 Above Canary Wharf

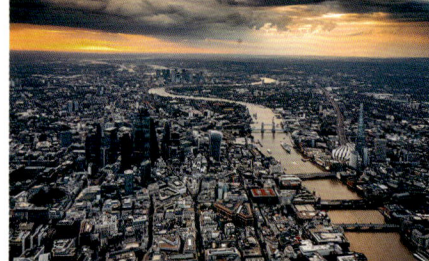
44-45 View of City of London

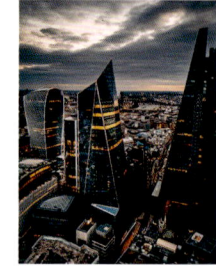
46 View of The Fenchurch Buidling, The Scalpel, and the Leadenhall Buildings

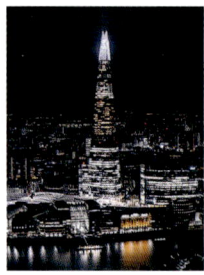
48 Night view of The Shard

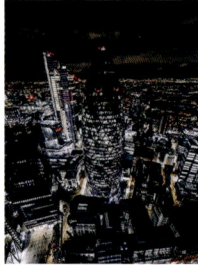
49 Night view of the Gherkin

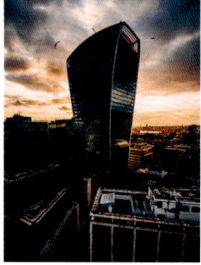
50 View of The Fenchurch Building

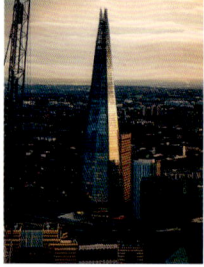
51 View of The Shard

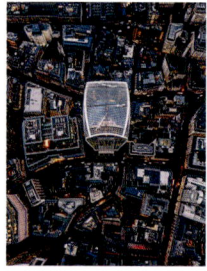
52 Above The Fenchurch Building

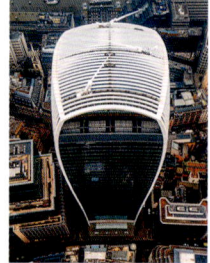
53 View of The Fenchurch Building

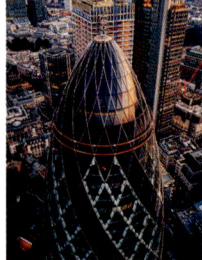
54 View of the Gherkin

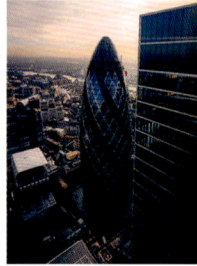
55 View of the Gherkin

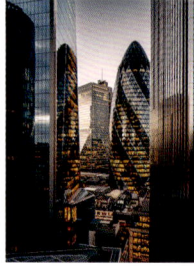
56 View of the Gherkin and Leadenhall Buildings

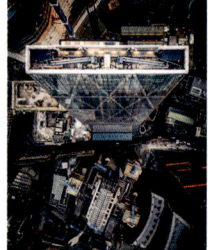
57 Above Leadenhall Building

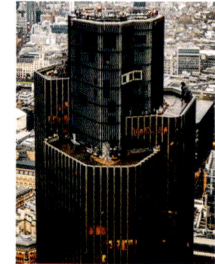
58 View of Tower 42

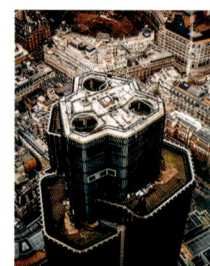
59 Above Tower 42

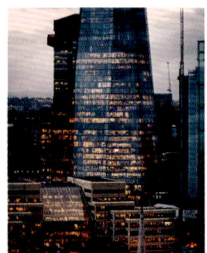
60 Detail view of The Shard

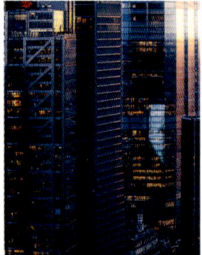
61 Detail view of London skyscrapers

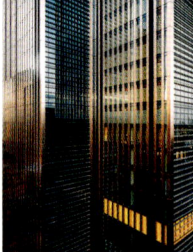
62 Detail view of London skyscrapers

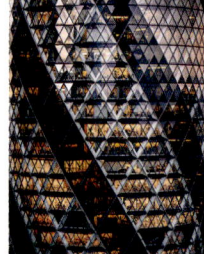
63 Detail view of the Gherkin

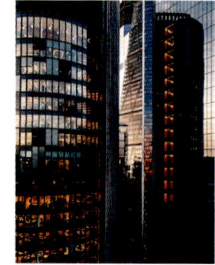
64 Detail view of London skyscrapers

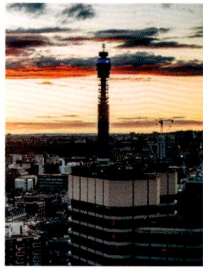
65 View of BT Tower

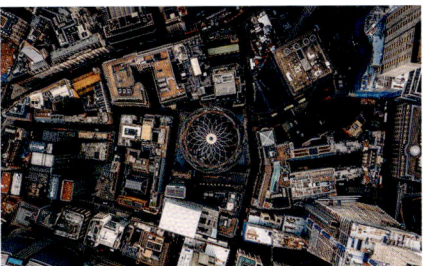
66-67 Above the Gherkin

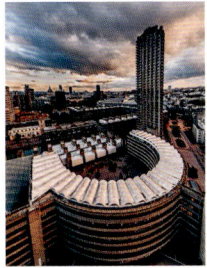
68 Above the Barbican

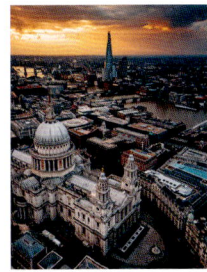
69 View of the Cliff House

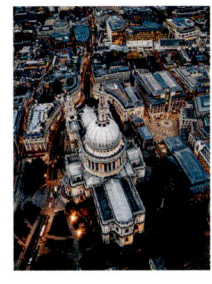
70 Above St Paul's Cathedral

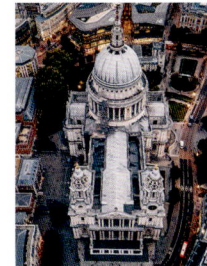
71 Above St Paul's Cathedral

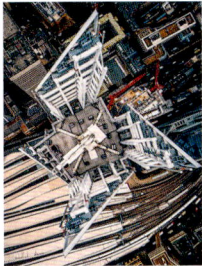
72 Above The Shard

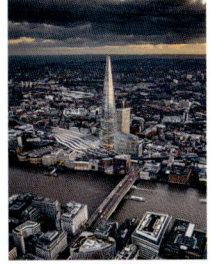
73 View of London Bridge and The Shard

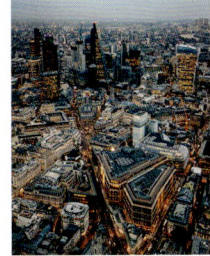
74 Above City of London

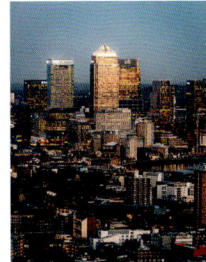
75 Above Canary Wharf

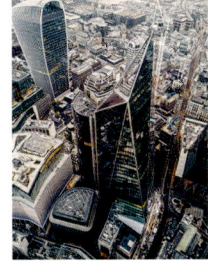
76 Above Canary Wharf

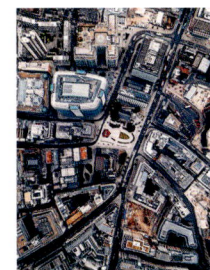
77 Above City of London

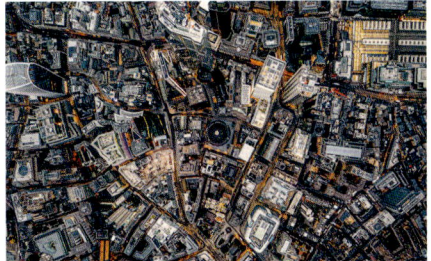
78-79 Above City of London

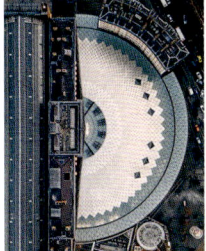
80 Above King's Cross Station

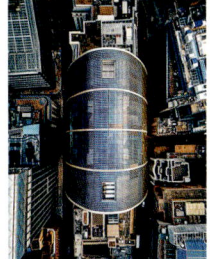
81 Above 1 Rebel St Mary Axe

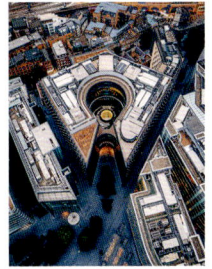
82 Above More London Place

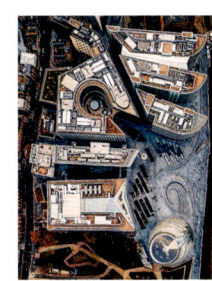
83 Above More London Place

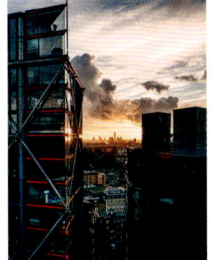
84 View of Holland Street

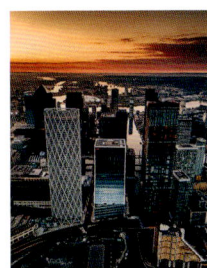
85 Above Canary Wharf

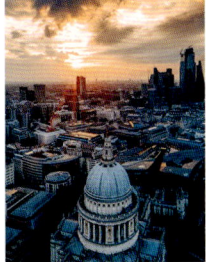
86 Above St Paul's Cathedral

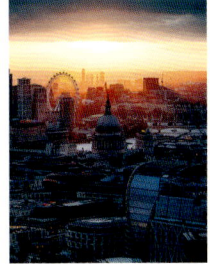
87 View of St Paul's Cathedral and Central London

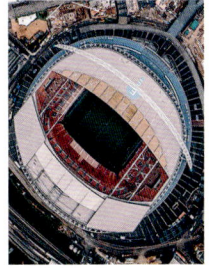
88 Above Wembley Stadium

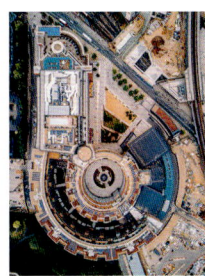
89 Above BBC Studios

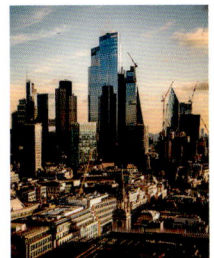
90 View of London skyline

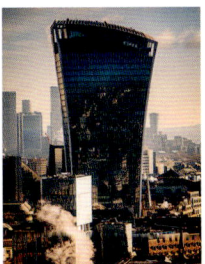
91 View of The Fenchurch Building

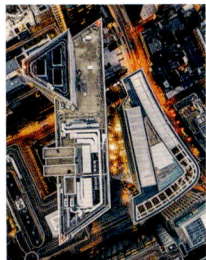
92 Above Broadgate Tower

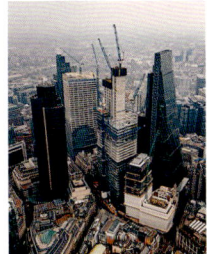
93 Above City of London

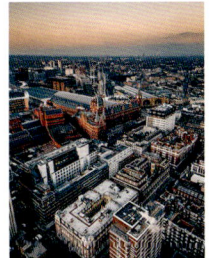
94 View of King's Cross

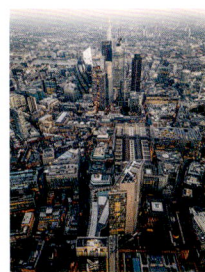
95 Above City of London

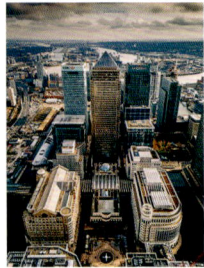

96 View of Canary Wharf

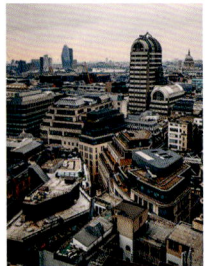

97 View of 20 Gracechurch

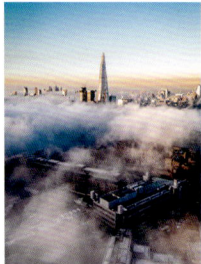

98 View of The Shard

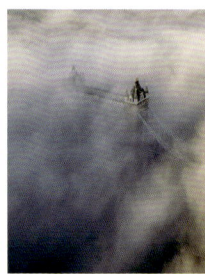

100 Above Tower Bridge

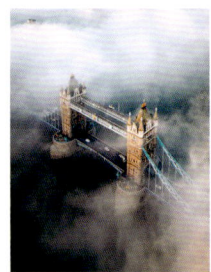

101 Above Tower Bridge

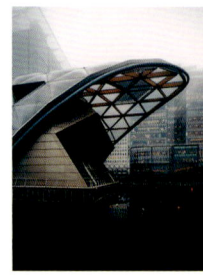

102 View of Big Easy Canary Wharf

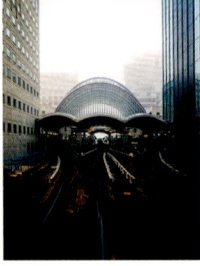

103 Canary DLR Station

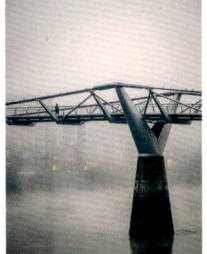

104 View of Millennium Bridge

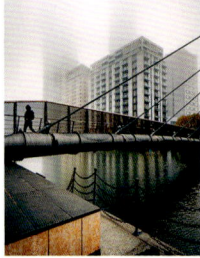

105 View of SouthQuay Footbridge

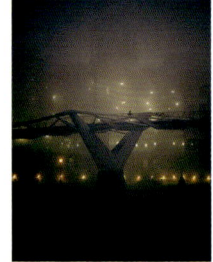

106 View of Millennium Bridge

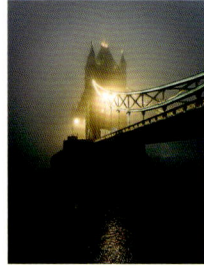

107 View of Tower Bridge

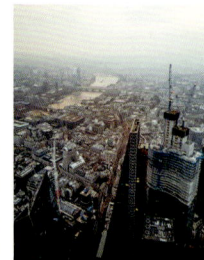

108 View of Leadenhall and Central London

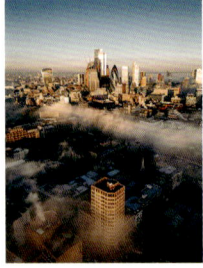

109 View of The Shard

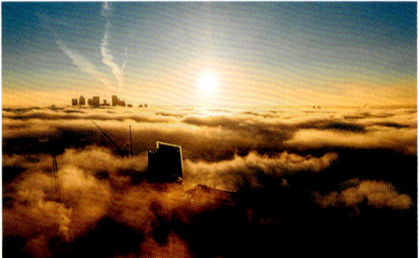

110-111 View of Canary Wharf

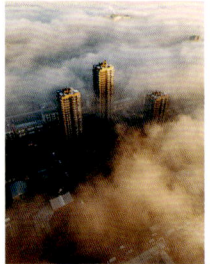

112 View of Stockholm House, Shearsmith House, and Hatton House

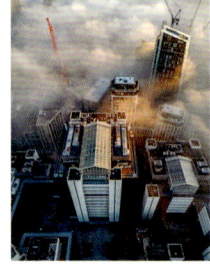

113 Above Thomas More Square

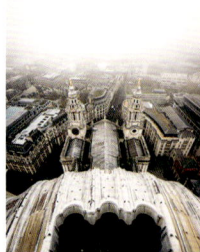

114 View from the top of St Paul's Cathedral

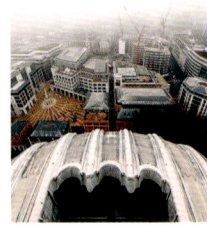

115 View from the top of St Paul's Cathedral

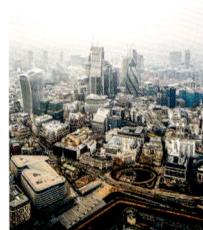

116 View of City of London

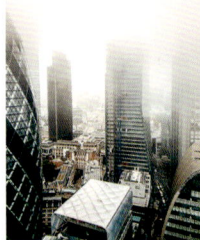

117 Detail view of London skyscrapers

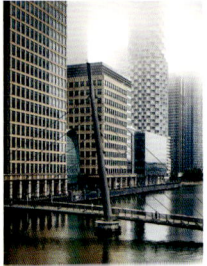

118 View of Canary Wharf

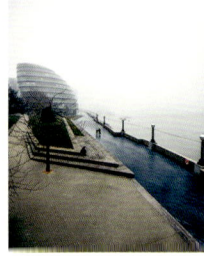

119 View of More London

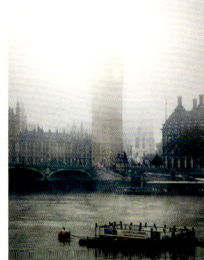

120 View of Elizabeth Tower

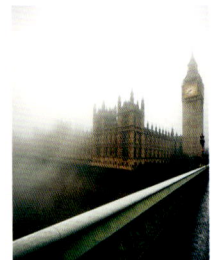

121 View of Westminster Bridge and Elizabeth Tower

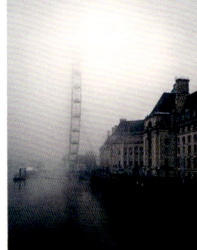

122 View of London Eye

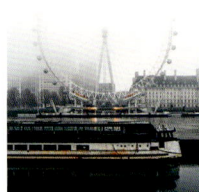

123 View of London Eye

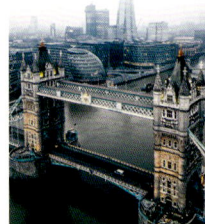

124 View of Tower Bridge and More London

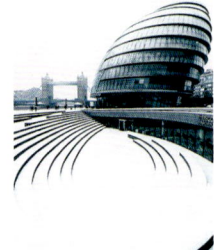

125 View of The Scoop at More London

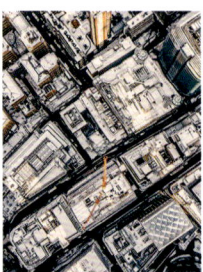

126 Above City of London

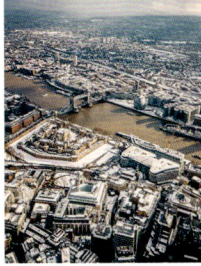

127 Above City of London

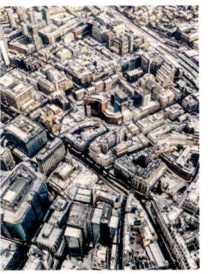

128 Above City of London

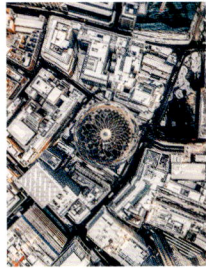

129 Above the Gherkin

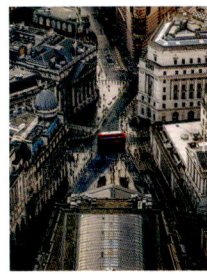

130 View of Bank Junction

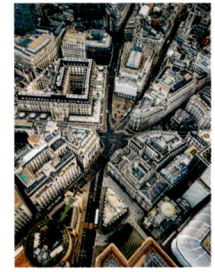

132 View of Bank Junction

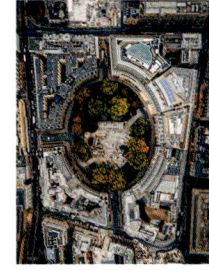

133 Above Finsbury Circus

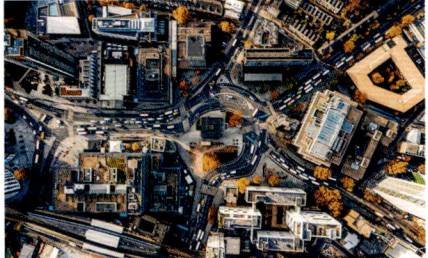

134-135 Above Elephant and Castle

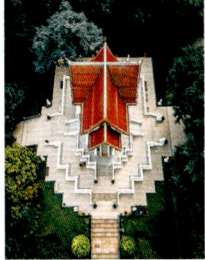

136 Above Buddhapadipa

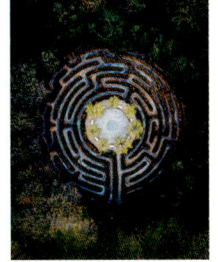

137 Above The Maze,
Crystal Palace Park

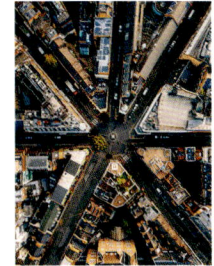

138 Above Seven Dials

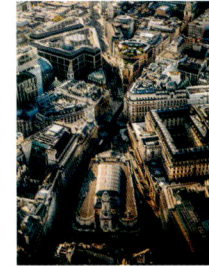

139 View of Bank Junction

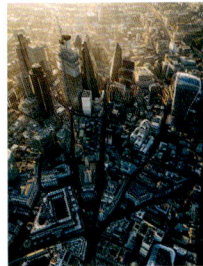

140 Above City of London

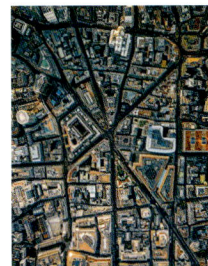

141 Above Bank Junction

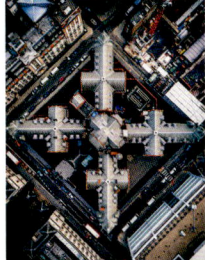

142 Above UCL Cruciform
Building

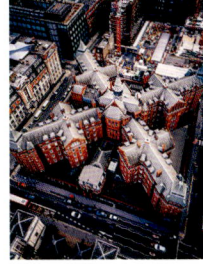

143 Above UCL Cruciform
Building

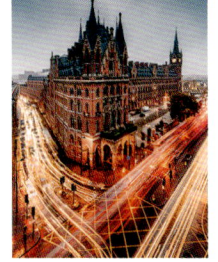

144 View of St Pancras Station

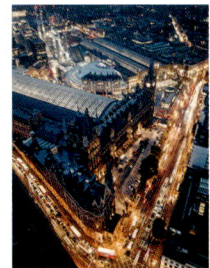

145 View of St Pancras Station

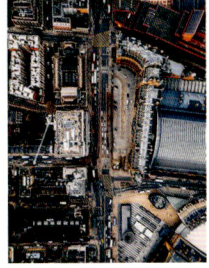

146 Above King's Cross

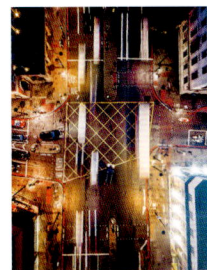

147 Above King's Cross

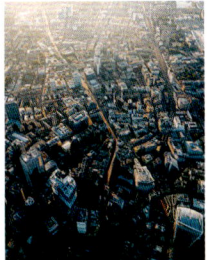

148 View of Central London

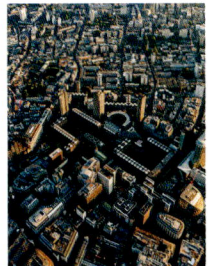

149 Above the Barbican

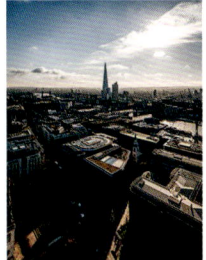

150 View of The Shard

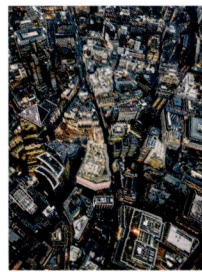

151 Above City of London

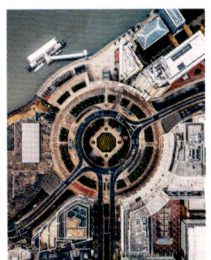

152 Above West Ferry Circus

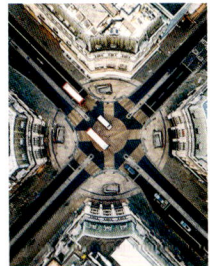

153 Above Oxford Circus

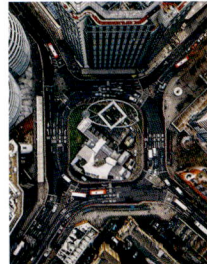

154 Above Old Street

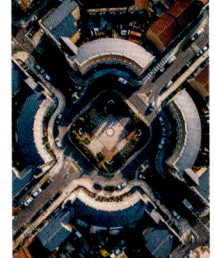

155 Above Carr Street

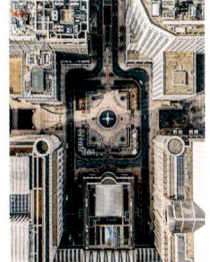

156 Above Cabot Square

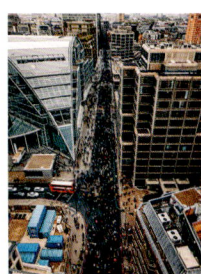

157 View of Victoria Street

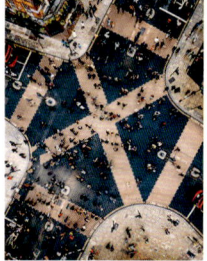
158 Above Victoria Street

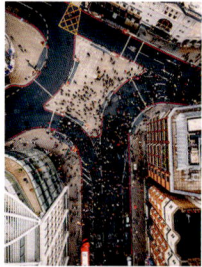
159 Above Vauxhall Bridge Road and Victoria Street

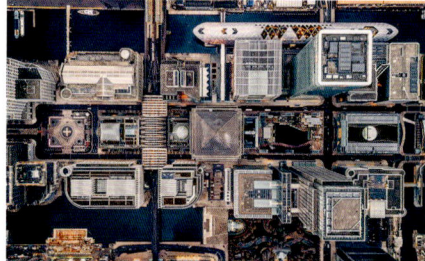
160-161 Above Canary Wharf

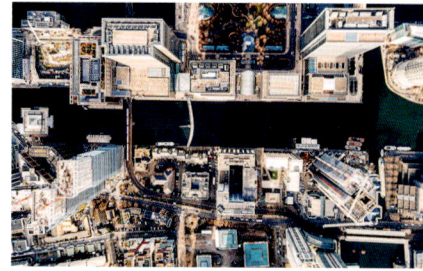
162-163 Above Canary Wharf

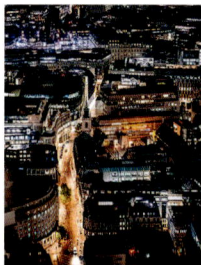
164 Above Gresham Street

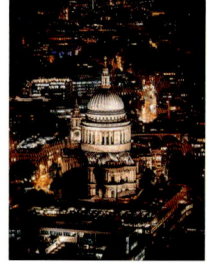
165 View of St Paul's Cathedral

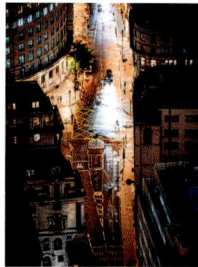
166 View of Loftbury

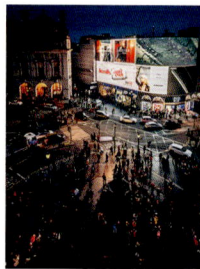
167 View of Piccadilly Circus

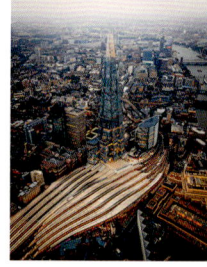
168 View of London Bridge Station and The Shard

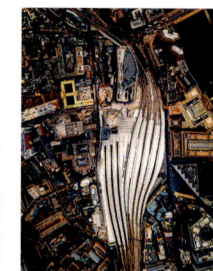
169 Above London Bridge Station and The Shard

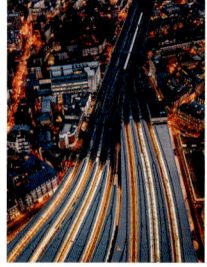
170 Above London Bridge Station

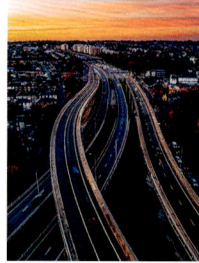
171 View above A406 Southend Road

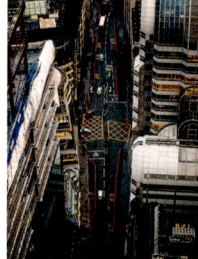
172 View of A10

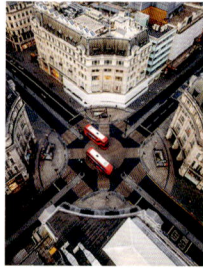
173 Above Oxford Circus

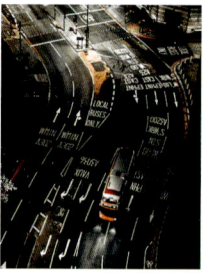
174 Above Westminster Bridge Road

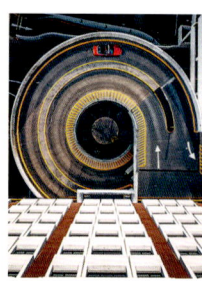
175 Above Q-Park Eden Walk

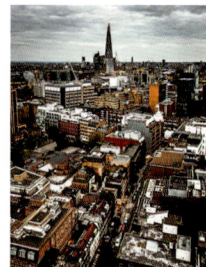
176 View of City of London and The Shard

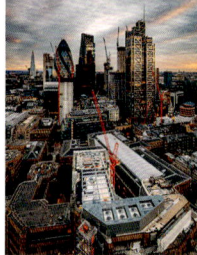
177 View of London skyline

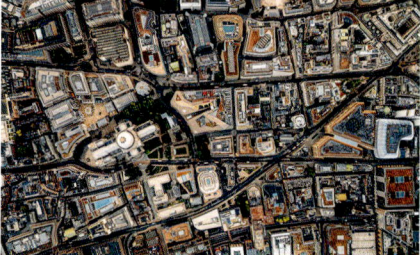
178-179 Above St Paul's Cathedral

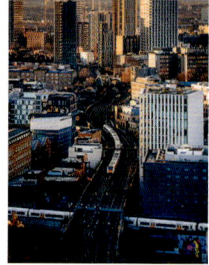
180 View of Bankside and Blackfriars Station

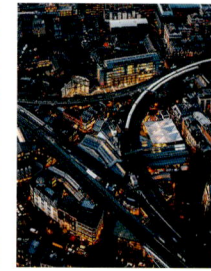
181 Above Borough Market

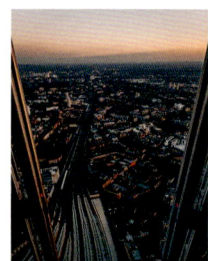
182 View of London Bridge station

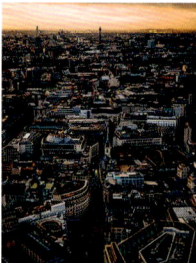
183 View of City of London

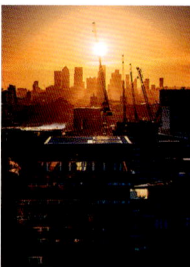
184 View of London skyline

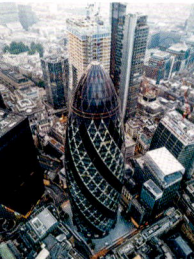
194 View of the Gherkin

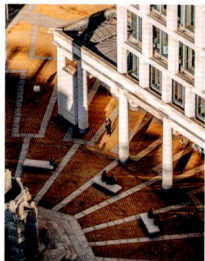
196 View of Paternoster Square

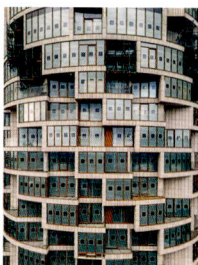
198 Detail of One Park Drive

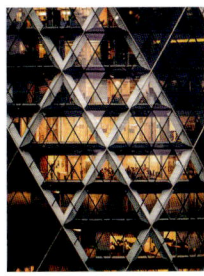

200 Detail view of the Gherkin

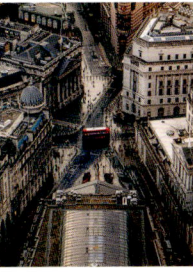

Back Cover View of
Bank Junction

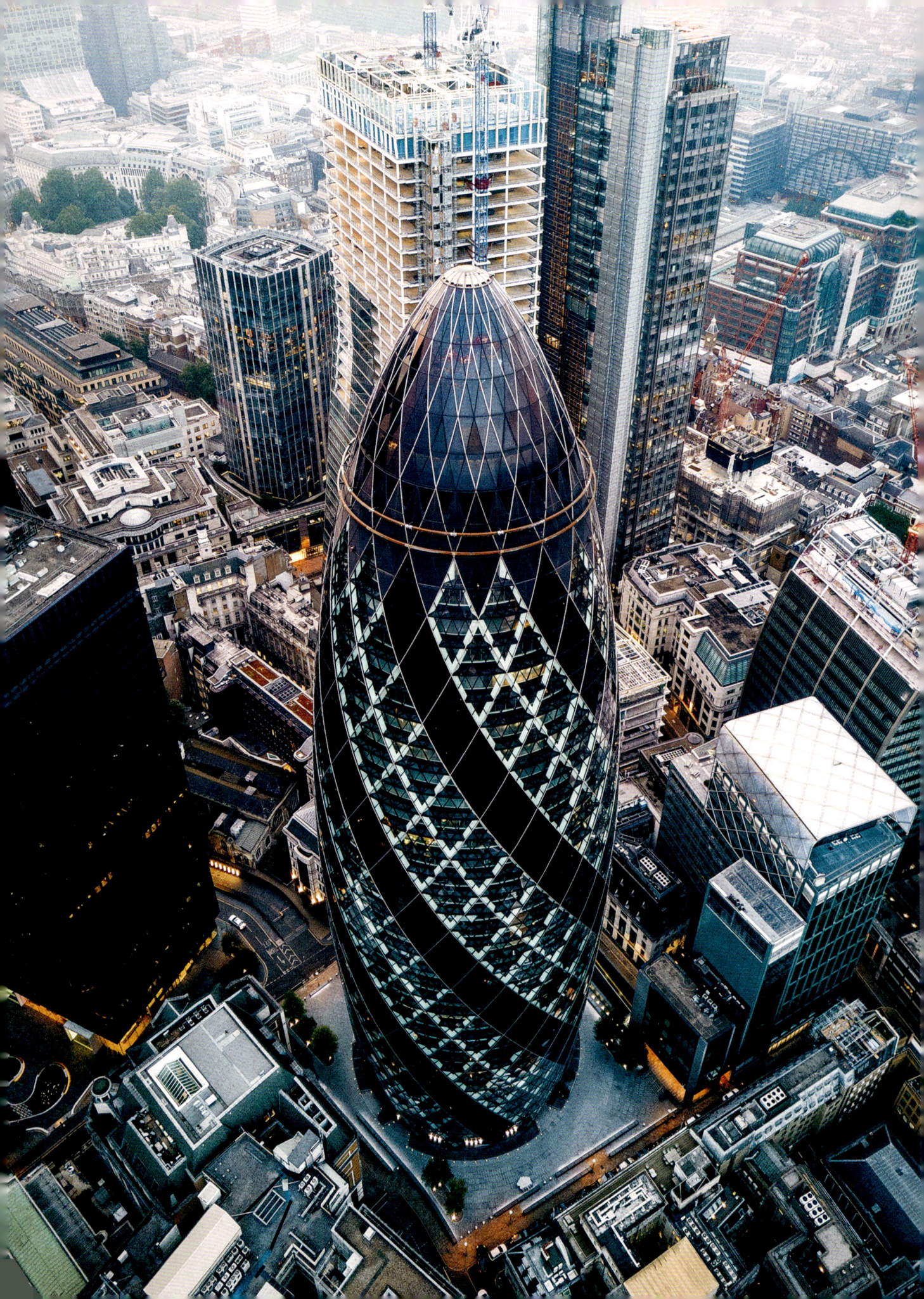

ACKNOWLEDGMENTS

First and foremost, I want to thank God most of all because all great things are done with his blessing.

My parents, Curnel Rodgers and Godfrun Moore, for allowing me to follow my creative passions and supporting me every step of the way.

My two amazing children, Donell Moore and Keira Moore, for supporting me and being proud of my creative talents.

To all my family and friends who have motivated and encouraged me over the years including my good friends Darren Boyd, Chima Amaluzor, and Maris Rätsep, for their endless encouragement and motivation.

To Ope Odueyungbo, a great photographer and friend who has supported my journey and inspired me.

My photography inspirations: Joel Grimes, Ryan Millier, and many more.

All the brands and creative agencies I've worked with over the years.

To everyone who came out and shot with me and put up with me or helped me get the photos that are in this book.

Last but not least, Michelle Fitzgerald and everybody at Trope Publishing for giving me this amazing opportunity.

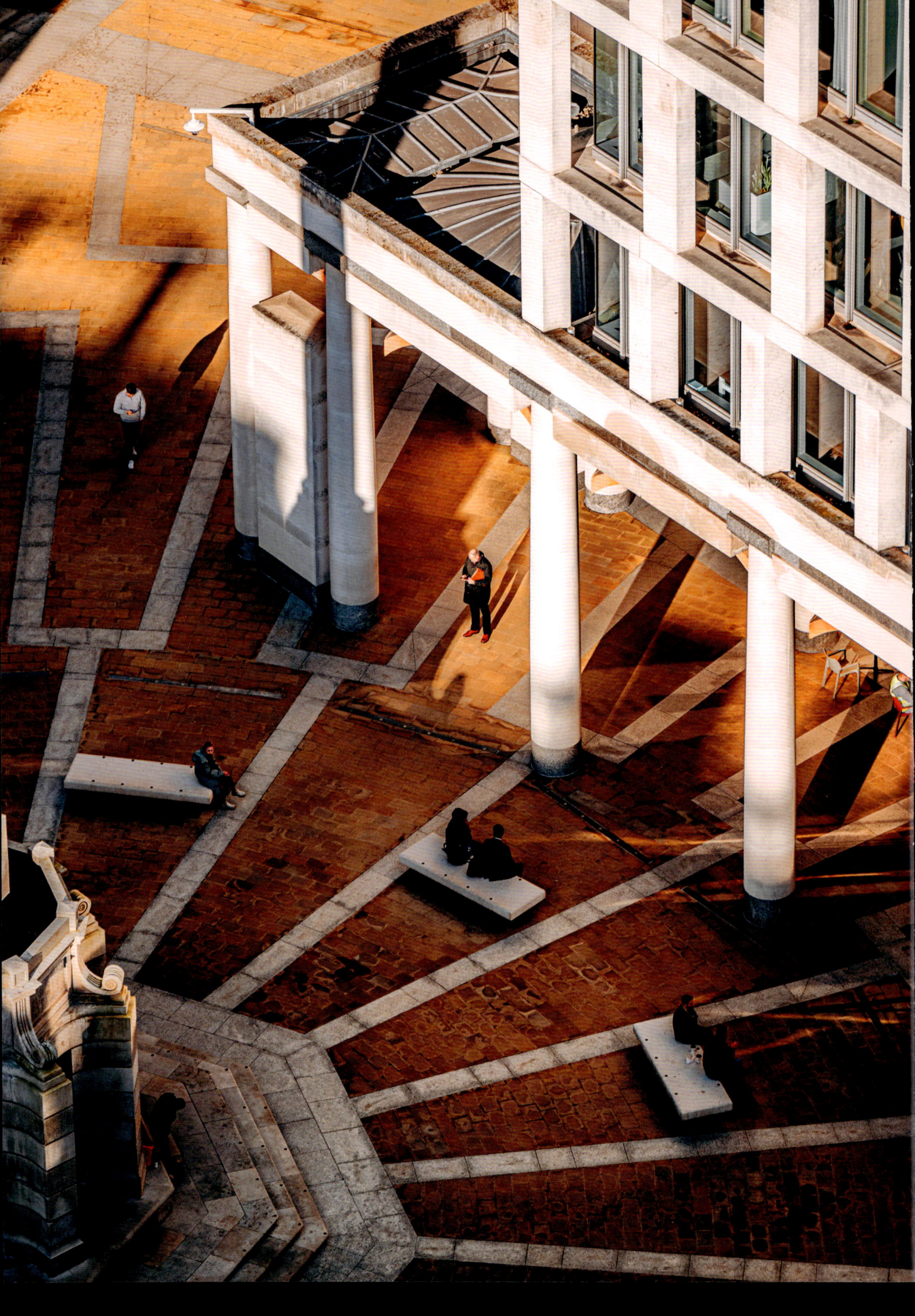

ABOUT THE ARTIST

Ben Moore, an award-winning freelance photographer based in London, defied conventional wisdom by embracing his passion for photography at the age of 30. Undeterred by the perceived late start, his relentless pursuit of excellence propelled him to become a highly sought-after self-taught commercial photographer specializing in aerial, architectural, and urban photography. He has built an impressive portfolio, collaborating with industry giants like Adobe, Nikon, and Samsung. His work, characterized by a captivating blend of moody and clean aesthetics with a touch of earthy warmth, has garnered millions of likes and features across major social media platforms. As a Nikon Ambassador/ Creator and a former judge for the "Environmental Photographer of the Year" competition, Ben has established himself as a respected figure in the photography world. His work has been extensively featured in numerous media publications. A distinctive element of his style is his masterful use of lines, creating a visual rhythm that resonates throughout his portfolio.

@bemorephotos

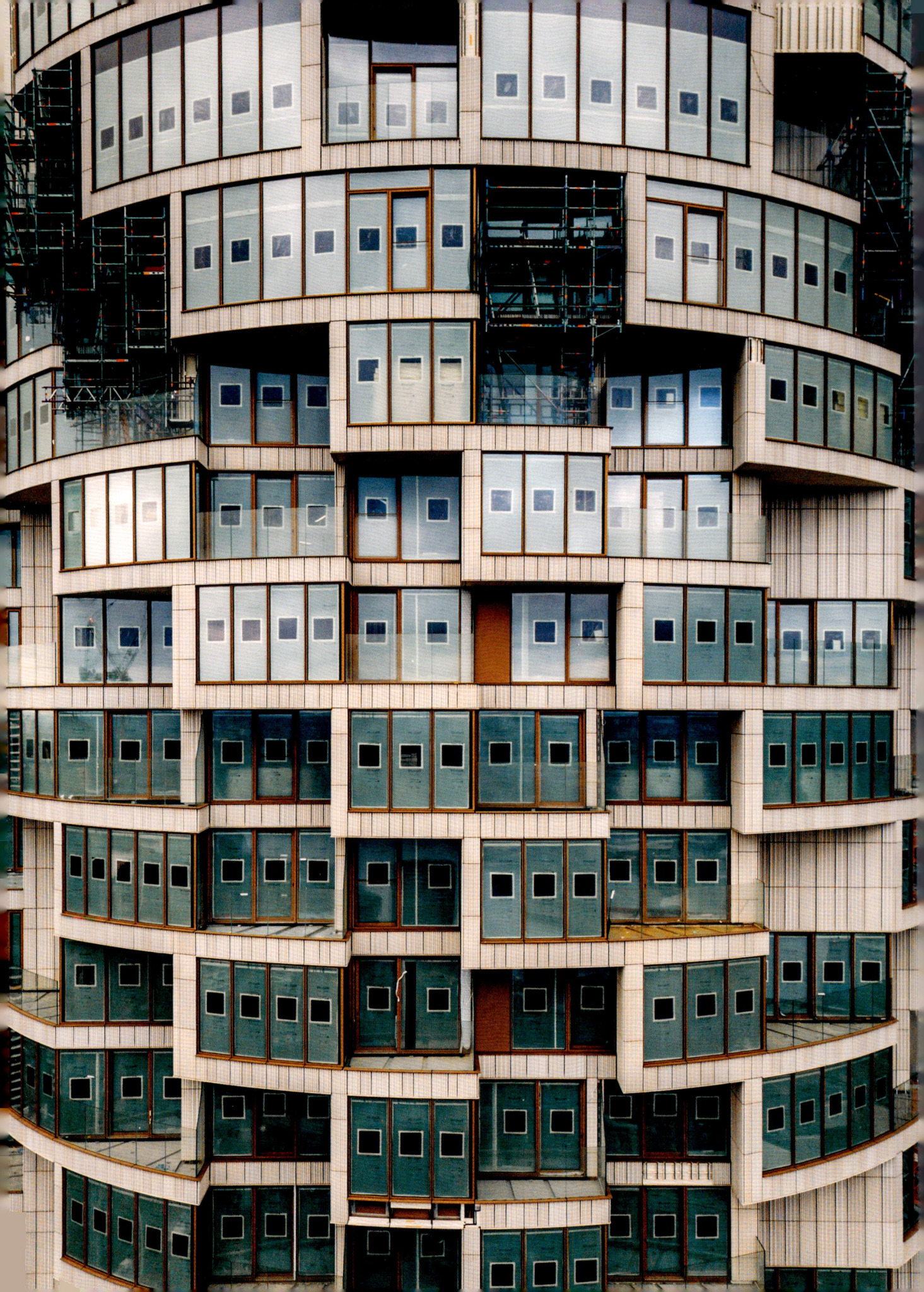

ABOUT THE EDITOR

+ MICHELLE FITZGERALD
Michelle Fitzgerald is the Associate Publisher at Trope Publishing Co. and served as editor for *New York*, *Paris*, *Los Angeles*, and *Rome*, part of Trope's City Edition series, as well as *Above & Across Chicago*, *Above & Across Atlanta*, and *Above & Across San Francisco*. A veteran of the book publishing industry, Michelle is a fierce advocate for books and is passionate about sharing them with the widest audience possible.

LCCN: 2025935446
ISBN: 978-1-951963-49-1

Printed and bound in China
First printing, 2025

+ INFORMATION:
For additional information on our books and prints, visit WWW.TROPE.COM

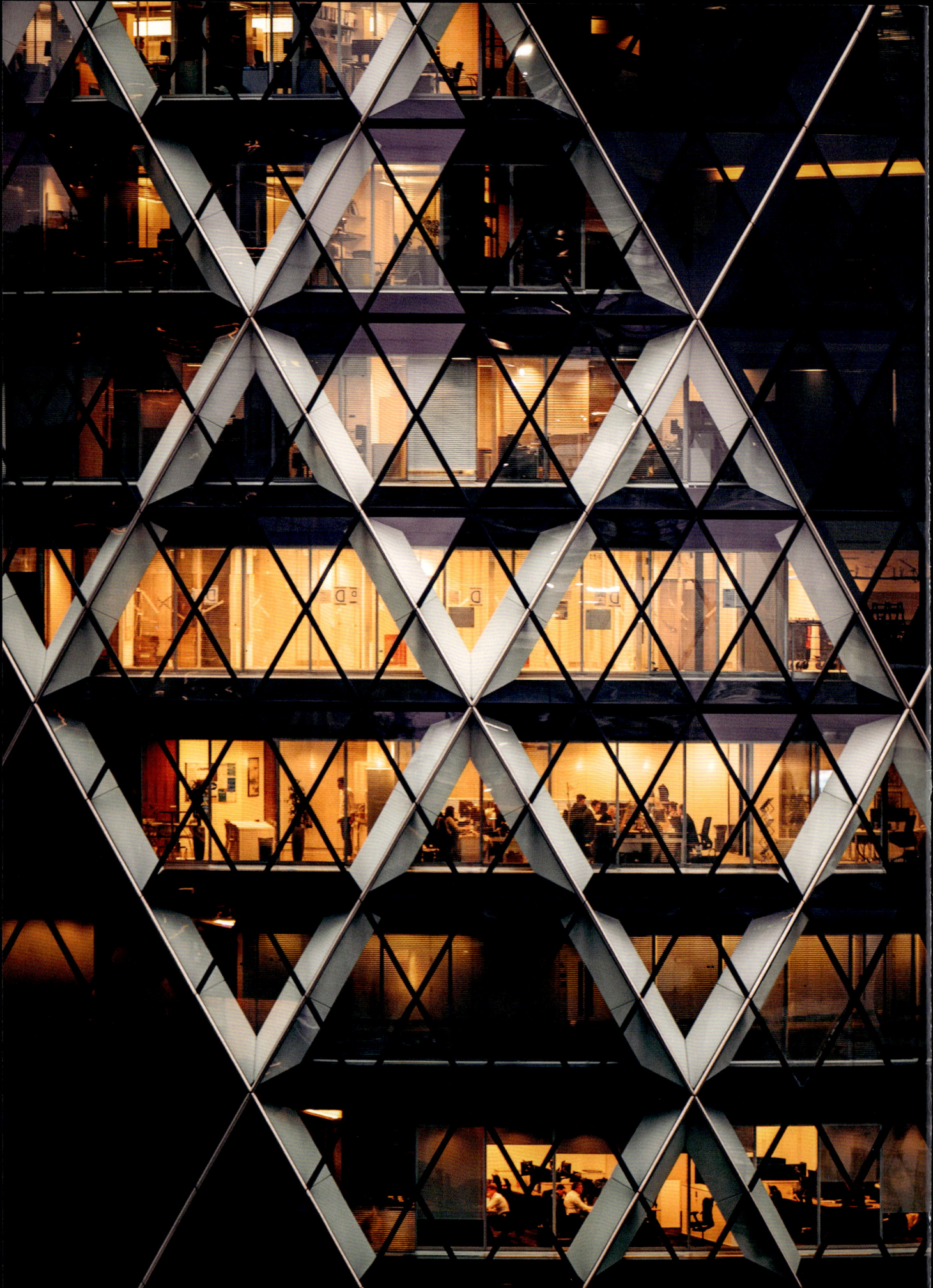